SAFETY PRACTICES IN THE ORGANIC LABORATORY[1]

GENERAL: Never work in the laboratory alone. Perform no unauthorized experiments. Do not use mouth suction to fill pipettes. Confine long hair and loose clothes while working in the laboratory. Wear shoes. Learn the location of and correct use of the nearest fire extinguisher. Learn the location of the safety shower and first aid kit, and be prepared to give help to others.

SAFETY GLASSES: Safety glasses should be worn **at all times** while in the laboratory, whether you actively engage in experimental work or not.

FIRE: Avoid unnecessary flames. Check the area near you for volatile solvents before lighting a burner. Check the area near you for flames if you are about to begin working with a volatile solvent. Be particularly careful of the volatile solvents diethyl ether, petroleum ether, ligroin, benzene, methanol, ethanol, and acetone.

CHEMICALS: Handle every chemical with care. Avoid contact with skin and clothing. Wipe up spills immediately, especially near the balances and reagent shelf. Replace caps on bottles as soon as possible. Do not use an organic solvent to wash a chemical from the skin as this may actually *increase* the rate of absorption of the chemical through the skin. Avoid the inhalation of organic vapors, particularly aromatic solvents and chlorinated solvents. Use care in smelling chemicals, and do not taste them unless instructed to do so. Drinking, eating, or smoking in the laboratory is forbidden.

DISPOSAL OF CHEMICALS: Dispose of chemicals as directed in each experiment's "Cleaning Up" section. In general, small quantities of nonhazardous water-soluble substances can be flushed down the drain with a large quantity of water. Hazardous waste, nonhazardous solid waste, organic solvents, and halogenated organic waste should be placed in the four containers provided.

CAUTION: It has been determined that several chemicals that are widely used in the organic laboratory (e.g., benzene and chloroform) cause cancer in test animals when administered in large doses. Where possible, the use of these chemicals is avoided in this book. In the few cases where suspected carcinogens are used, the precautions noted should be followed carefully. A case in point is chromium in the +6 oxidation stage. The *dust* of solid Cr^{+6} salts is carcinogenic. The hazards have been pointed out, and safe handling procedures are given.

---

[1] Adapted from *Safety in Academic Chemistry Laboratories*, prepared by the American Chemical Society Committee on Chemical Safety, March 1974.

IN CASE OF ACCIDENT[1]

*In case of accident notify the laboratory instructor **immediately**.*

FIRE

Burning Clothing. Prevent the person from running and fanning the flames. Rolling the person on the floor will help extinguish the flames and prevent inhalation of the flames. If a safety shower is nearby hold the person under the shower until flames are extinguished and chemicals washed away. Do not use a fire blanket if a shower is nearby. The blanket does not cool and smoldering continues. Remove contaminated clothing. Wrap the person in a blanket to avoid shock. Get prompt medical attention.

Do not, under any circumstances, use a carbon tetrachloride (toxic) fire extinguisher and be very careful using a CO_2 extinguisher (the person may smother).

Burning Reagents. Extinguish all nearby burners and remove combustible material and solvents. Small fires in flasks and beakers can be extinguished by covering the container with a fiberglass-wire gauze square, a big beaker, or a watch glass. Use a dry chemical or carbon dioxide fire extinguisher directed at the base of the flames. **Do not use water.**

Burns, Either Thermal or Chemical. Flush the burned area with cold water for at least 15 min. Resume if pain returns. Wash off chemicals with a mild detergent and water. Current practice recommends that no neutralizing chemicals, unguents, creams, lotions, or salves be applied. If chemicals are spilled on a person over a large area quickly remove the contaminated clothing while under the safety shower. Seconds count, and time should not be wasted because of modesty. Get prompt medical attention.

CHEMICALS IN THE EYE: Flush the eye with copious amounts of water for 15 min using an eyewash fountain or bottle or by placing the injured person face up on the floor and pouring water in the open eye. Hold the eye open to wash behind the eyelids. After 15 min of washing obtain prompt medical attention, regardless of the severity of the injury.

CUTS: Minor Cuts. This type of cut is most common in the organic laboratory and usually arises from broken glass. Wash the cut, remove any pieces of glass, and apply pressure to stop the bleeding. Get medical attention.

Major Cuts. If blood is spurting place a pad directly on the wound, apply firm pressure, wrap the injured to avoid shock, and get **immediate** medical attention. Never use a tourniquet.

POISONS: Call 800 information (1-800-555-1212) for the telephone number of the nearest Poison Control Center, which is usually also an 800 number.

---

[1] Adapted from *Safety in Academic Chemistry Laboratories*, prepared by the American Chemical Society Committee on Chemical Safety, March 1974.

ABBREVIATED THIRD EDITION

MACROSCALE & MICROSCALE

ORGANIC EXPERIMENTS

KENNETH L. WILLIAMSON
MOUNT HOLYOKE COLLEGE

SPECIAL EDITION FOR UNIVERSITY OF MICHIGAN

HOUGHTON MIFFLIN COMPANY   BOSTON   NEW YORK

Editor-in-Chief: Kathi Prancan
Senior Sponsoring Editor: Richard Stratton
Associate Editor: Marianne Stepanian
Packaging Services Supervisor: Charline Lake
Manufacturing Manager: Florence Cadran
Marketing Manager: Penelope Hoblyn

Custom Publishing Editor: Gina Montoya
Custom Publishing Production Manager: Kathleen McCourt
Custom Publishing Project Coordinator: Harmony Flewelling

Cover Designer: Joel Gendron
Cover Photograph: Photodisc, Inc.

Printed in the United States of America.

ISBN: 0-618-23342-3
N00729

1 2 3 4 5 6 7 8 9 – PP – 04 03 02 01

 Houghton Mifflin
Custom Publishing

222 Berkeley Street • Boston, MA 02116

Address all correspondence and order information to the above address.

Contents

Natural Product Chemistry and Biochemsitry

Preface

Innovation and exploration characterize this Third Edition of *Macroscale and Microscale Organic Experiments*. Building on the strength and success of prior editions, the Third Edition boasts a reorganization that more closely follows organic chemistry textbooks as well as innovative new techniques, features, and experiments. Additionally, throughout this edition one will find experiments and references that tie this course to biochemical and biomedical applications of organic chemistry.

New to This Edition

Techniques

A method has been devised, using the 105° adapter in every Williamson microscale kit, for each student to construct a gas phase IR cell at no cost. Now they can add the third state of matter to traditional solid and liquid phase samples and explore for the first time the gases that are produced in these experiments. In addition, they can explore the myriad gases found in aerosol cans, inhalants, refrigerants, and the like, as well as those from biological sources such as marsh gas and odors ranging from perfumes to putrefaction.

Another innovation, the Wilfilter, is a simple polypropylene adapter that converts every reaction tube into a superior Craig tube. This conversion allows the isolation of minute quantities of crystals without transfer losses, free of solvent and almost dry. We are now using this in many experiments; it is a fast and efficient technique.

Features

The opportunities for students to explore organic chemistry in a variety of ways is presented in the new feature entitled "For Further Investigation." These sections require running reactions and then deducing the nature of the products, usually by IR and NMR spectroscopy. Open-ended investigations include exploring the nature of the gases found in commercial products.

Exploration of another nature is included at the end of many experiments: "Surfing the Web." I have tried to locate a few relevant sites that add new dimensions to the topic at hand as the unwary student can be overwhelmed by the riches of the Web. "Surfing the Web" leads students to, for example, infrared spectra correlated to vibrations of specific atoms and groups of atoms in a molecule, very clear pictures of melting crystals for the melting point experiment, animations of reactions, and full-color, close-up photographs of many of the experiments presented in this text.

New and Updated Experiments

The "NMR Spectroscopy" chapter has been rewritten to guide students in the use of this powerful technique for structure identification based on the assumption they will be using high-field Fourier transform spectrometers. Most of the NMR spectra have been revised and expanded, and the elements of two-dimensional NMR spectra are also presented.

Similarly, the "Infrared Spectroscopy" chapter has been rewritten so that students can carry out a logical step-by-step analysis of their spectra. Fourier transform IR spectrometers are rapidly coming into general use, because not only do they allow spectra to be obtained in less time, but they also give peak frequencies in digital form. In this edition FTIR spectra have replaced the analog versions of the previous edition. Also new to this chapter is a section on "Gas Phase IR Spectroscopy"; six more gas phase spectra can be found in the *Instructor's Guide*.

New to this edition is an experiment that allows students to prove the stereochemistry of reduction of a diketone to a diol: In Chapter 57, "Synthesis of 2,2-Dimethyl-1,5-dioxolane," the acetonide derivative of hydrobenzoin is prepared and its NMR spectrum analyzed to prove whether the hydrobenzoin is the meso or d,l-compound. Chapter 67, "Isolation of Lycopene and β-Carotene," has been placed in a more appropriate place in the organization of the manual, giving emphasis to the biochemical nature of the experiment. Chapter 34, "1,2,3,4-Tetraphenylnaphthalene via Benzyne," is an experiment that has been reinstated from a previous edition.

Throughout the text the scale of the macroscale experiments has been reduced, in most cases to half the former size. This has been done because of the widespread use of 14/20 standard-taper apparatus, the savings in the cost of waste disposal and purchase of chemicals, and for safety reasons. In a few cases microscale experiments have been scaled up, simply to make it easier to isolate products.

The "Searching the Chemical Literature" chapter has been rewritten to reflect not only changes in the references but also the availability of computer databases of this material.

Innovative Techniques from Previous Editions

Innovations from the last edition of this text have proved to be just as valuable as when first introduced. Among the two most important are the use of *t*-butyl methyl ether in place of diethyl ether and the use of anhydrous calcium chloride pellets as a drying agent. *t*-Butyl methyl ether is one of the most common and cheapest solvents being produced because it has replaced tetraethyl lead as an antiknock additive and as an oxygenate, added to reduce pollution, in gasoline. Not only is it cheaper than diethyl ether, it does not easily form peroxides and therefore can be stored more than 30 days after the container is opened; it has a higher boiling point (55°C) than diethyl ether and is therefore somewhat less flammable; and it forms a 4% azeotrope with water, so as it is removed it also removes the last traces of water from a solution. All in all it should become the solvent of choice, replacing diethyl ether in all applications except the Grignard reaction.

We continue to be very enthusiastic about the use of anhydrous calcium chloride pellets as a drying agent, an innovation introduced in the last edition. These pellets do not fracture and powder and so are ideally suited to drying microscale quantities of solutions where the solvent can simply be drawn off with a Pasteur pipette, making conventional filtration unnecessary.

The unique chapter on computational chemistry and molecular mechanics is an introduction to a tool that, like spectroscopy, can give new insight into the structure of organic molecules. Procedures for the application of this tool are given to no fewer than 20 experiments.

Our students are very enthusiastic about the synthesis of a fluorescer using the Wittig reaction and the synthesis of a Cyalume in order to make their own light sticks. Transfer hydrogenation using cyclohexene as the source of hydrogen is another experiment unique to *Macroscale and Microscale Organic Experiments*. Olive oil is thus hydrogenated to a fat that can be converted to soap. The use of Multifiber Fabric in the experiment on dyes and dyeing, Norit decolorizing charcoal in the form of pellets, the microscale cracking of dicyclopentadiene, and the multistep syntheses starting with the benzoin condensation of benzaldehyde, benzyne experiments, and tetraphenylcyclopentadienone are among the innovative experiments that have appeared in previous editions of this text, which dates to 1935 when Louis Fieser was the author. Remember, you saw it first in Williamson.

The "Biomimetic Synthesis of Pseudopellitierene" following the classic work of Robert Robinson is a relatively new experiment, as is the "Conversion of Camphene to Camphor."

Waste Disposal and Safety

The section at the end of every experiment entitled "Cleaning Up" has been written with the intent of focusing students' attention on not just the desired product from a reaction but also on all of the other substances produced in a typical organic reaction.

As one of the coauthors of the first edition of *Prudent Practices for the Disposal of Chemicals from Laboratories,* I have continued to follow closely the rapidly evolving regulatory climate and changes in laboratory safety rules and regulations. The safety information in this text is about as current as possible, but this is a rapidly changing area of chemistry; local rules and regulations must be known and adhered to.

Supplements

Instructor's Guide

The *Instructor's Guide* is an important adjunct to this text. It contains discussions about the time needed to carry out each experiment and assessment of the relative difficulty of each experiment, problems that might be encountered, answers to end-of-chapter questions, a list of chemical and apparatus required for each experiment—both per student and per 24-student laboratory—sources of supply for unusual items, and a discussion of hardware and software needed for running calculational chemistry and molecular mechanics experiments.

Desk copies of this *Instructor's Guide* are available by contacting your local Houghton Mifflin sales representative or by contacting:

Houghton Mifflin Co.
222 Berkeley St.
Boston, MA 02116-3764
(800) 733-1717

Web Site

Please visit our Web sites at *http://www.mtholyoke.edu/courses/kwilliam/ microscale.shtml* and *www.hmco.com* for resource information intended to support users of this lab manual.

The Chemistry Tutor Version 2.0 CD-ROM

This CD, authored by Adam Drury of the University of Liverpool, is an interactive introduction to topics in organic chemistry, with a review of topics in general chemistry. It includes a tutorial with text, animations, and interactive problems. It contains 18 content modules of computer-assisted learning material plus four tools, including a periodic table database and chemical calculator.

Acknowledgments

I would like to acknowledge the help of many classes of Chemistry 302 at Mount Holyoke College in developing and refining the experiments in this text, as well as the contributions sent to me by students and faculty at many other institutions. I am also indebted to Rick Danheiser and Scott Virgil at MIT, where I taught in 1996 and 1997.

I also wish to express my thanks to my editor at Houghton Mifflin, Marianne Stepanian, as well as the reviewers of this text, Edward Alexander (San Diego Mesa College), Roger Murray (University of Delaware), George Thyvelikakath (Oral Roberts University), Grace B. Borowitz (Ramapo College of New Jersey), Janet E. Nelson (Middlebury College), Linda A. Jacob (Yale University), Ray Lutgring (University of Evansville), Tracy A. Oriskovich (The Pennsylvania State University), Robert D. Minard (The Pennsylvania State University), J. W. Sam Stevenson (Northeast State Technical Community College), Mark Arant (Northeast Louisiana University), William L. "Hank" Mancini (Paradise Valley Community College), Robert A. Braga (Georgia Institute of Technology), Leslie Gunatilaka (Virginia Polytechnic Institute and State University), and, in particular, Alan Shusterman (Reed) who reviewed the material on computational chemistry.

And finally I note with sadness the passing of Mary Fieser in 1997. While never a coauthor of Louis Fieser's laboratory manuals, this great chemist and author was a perceptive critic and constant inspiration.

ORGANIC EXPERIMENTS AND WASTE DISPOSAL

An unusual feature of this book is the advice at the end of each experiment on how to dispose of its chemical waste. Waste disposal thus becomes part of the experiment, which is not considered finished until the waste products are appropriately taken care of. This is a valuable addition to the book for several reasons.

Although chemical waste from laboratories is less than 0.1% of that generated in the United States, its disposal is nevertheless subject to many of the same federal, state, and local regulations as is chemical waste from industry. Accordingly, there are both strong ethical and legal reasons for proper disposal of laboratory wastes. These reasons are backed up by a financial concern, because the cost of waste disposal can become a significant part of the cost of operating a laboratory.

There is yet another reason to include instructions for waste disposal in a teaching laboratory. Students will someday be among those conducting and regulating waste disposal operations and voting on appropriations for them. Learning the principles and methods of sound waste disposal early in their careers will benefit them and society later.

The basics of waste disposal are easy to grasp. Some innocuous water-soluble wastes are flushed down the drain with a large proportion of water. Common inorganic acids and bases are neutralized and flushed down the drain. Containers are provided for several classes of solvents, for example, combustible solvents and halogenated solvents. (The containers are subsequently removed for suitable disposal by licensed waste handlers.) Some toxic substances can be oxidized or reduced to innocuous substances that can then be flushed down the drain; for example, hydrazines, mercaptans, and inorganic cyanides can be thus oxidized by sodium hypochlorite solution, widely available as household bleach. Dilute solutions of highly toxic cations are expensive to dispose of because of their bulk; precipitation of the cation by a suitable reagent followed by its separation greatly reduces its bulk and cost. These and many other procedures can be found throughout this book.

One other principle of waste control lies at the heart of this book. Microscale experimentation, by minimizing the scale of chemical operations, also minimizes the volume of waste. Chromatography procedures to separate and purify products, spectroscopy methods to identify and characterize products, and well-designed small-scale equipment enable one to conduct experiments today on a tenth to a thousandth the scale commonly in use a generation ago.

Chemists often provide great detail in their directions for preparing chemicals so that the synthesis can be repeated, but they seldom say much about how to dispose of the hazardous byproducts. Yet the proper disposal of a chemical's byproducts is as important as its proper preparation. Dr. Williamson sets a good example by providing explicit directions for such disposal.

Blaine C. McKusick

CHAPTER

1

Introduction

Prelab Exercise: Study the glassware diagrams and be prepared to identify the reaction tube, fractionating column, distilling head, addition port, and Hirsch funnel.

Welcome to the organic chemistry laboratory! This laboratory manual presents a unique approach for carrying out organic experiments—they can be conducted on either a microscale or a macroscale. The latter is the traditional way of teaching the principles of experimental organic chemistry and is the basis for all the experiments in this book, a book that traces its history to 1934 when Louis Fieser was its author. Most teaching institutions are equipped to carry out macroscale experiments. Instructors are familiar with these techniques and experiments, and much research in industry and academe is carried out on this scale. These experiments typically involve the use of about 10 g of *starting material,* the chief reagent used in the reaction.

For reasons primarily of safety and cost, there is a growing trend toward carrying out work in the laboratory on a microscale, a scale one-tenth to one-thousandth of that previously used. Using smaller quantities of chemicals exposes the laboratory worker to smaller amounts of toxic, flammable, explosive, carcinogenic, and teratogenic material. Microscale experiments can be carried out much more rapidly than macroscale experiments because of rapid heat transfer, rapid filtration, and rapid drying. Since the apparatus advocated by the author is inexpensive, more than one reaction can be set up at once. The cost of chemicals is, of course, greatly reduced. A principal advantage of microscale experimentation is that the quantity of waste is reduced by one-tenth to one-thousandth of that formerly produced.

To allow maximum flexibility in the conduct of organic experiments, this book presents procedures for the vast majority of the experiments on both the microscale and the macroscale. As will be seen, some of the equipment and techniques are different. A careful reading of the two procedures will indicate what changes and precautions must be employed in going from one scale to the other.

Synthesis and structure determination

Synthesis and structure determination are two major concerns of the organic chemist, and both are dealt with in this book. The rational synthesis of an organic compound, whether it involves the transformation of one functional group into another or a carbon–carbon bond-forming reaction, starts with a *reaction.*

Organic reactions usually take place in the liquid phase and are *homogeneous,* in that the reactants are all in one phase. The reactants can be solids and/or liquids dissolved in an appropriate solvent to mediate the reaction. Some reactions are *heterogeneous*—that is, one of the reactants is in the solid phase—and thus require stirring or shaking to bring the reactants in contact with one another. A few heterogeneous reactions involve the reaction of a gas, such as oxygen, carbon dioxide, or hydrogen, with material in solution. Examples of all of these are found among the experiments in this book.

An *exothermic* organic reaction evolves heat. If it is highly exothermic with a low activation energy, one reactant is added slowly to the other and heat is removed by external cooling. Most organic reactions are, however, mildly *endothermic*, which means the reaction mixture must be heated to overcome the activation barrier and to increase the rate of the reaction. A very useful rule of thumb is that *the rate of an organic reaction doubles with a 10°C rise of temperature.* The late Louis Fieser, an outstanding organic chemist and professor at Harvard University, introduced the idea of changing the traditional solvents of many reactions to high-boiling solvents in order to reduce reaction times. Throughout this book we will use solvents such as triethylene glycol, with a boiling point (bp) of 290°C, to replace ethanol (bp 78°C) and triethylene glycol dimethyl ether (bp 222°C) to replace dimethoxyethane (bp 85°C). The use of these high-boiling solvents can greatly increase the rates of many reactions.

Effect of temperature

Running an organic reaction is usually the easiest part of a synthesis. The challenge lies in isolating and purifying the product from the reaction because organic reactions seldom give quantitative yields of one pure substance.

In some cases the solvent and concentrations of reactants are chosen so that, after the reaction mixture has been cooled, the product will *crystallize.* It is then collected by *filtration,* and the crystals are washed with an appropriate solvent. If sufficiently pure at that point, the product is dried and collected; otherwise, it is purified by the process of recrystallization or, less commonly, by *sublimation.*

"Working up the reaction"
Chapter 3: Crystallization
Chapter 7: Vacuum Distillation and Sublimation

If the product of reaction does not crystallize from the reaction mixture, it is often isolated by the process of *extraction.* This involves adding a solvent to the reaction mixture that dissolves the product and is immiscible with the solvent used in the reaction. Shaking the mixture causes the product to dissolve in the extracting solvent, after which the two layers of liquid are separated and the product isolated from the extraction solvent.

Chapter 8: Extraction of Acids and Bases

If the product is a liquid, it is isolated by *distillation,* usually after extraction. Occasionally the product can be isolated by the process of *steam distillation* from the reaction mixture.

Chapter 5: Distillation
Chapter 6: Steam Distillation

Organic reactions are usually carried out by dissolving the reactants in a solvent and then heating the mixture to boiling. To keep the solvent from boiling away, the vapor is condensed to a liquid, which is allowed to run back into the boiling solvent.

On a microscale, reactions are carried out in a *reaction tube* (Fig. 1.1a). The mass of the reaction tube is so small that a milliliter of nitrobenzene (bp 210°C) will boil in 10 s and a milliliter of benzene (mp 5°C) will crystallize in the same period of time. Cooling is effected by simply shaking the tube in a small beaker of ice water and heating by immersing the reaction tube to the appropriate depth in an electrically heated sand bath. On a larger scale, heat transfer is not so fast because of the smaller ratio of surface area to volume in a round-bottomed flask.

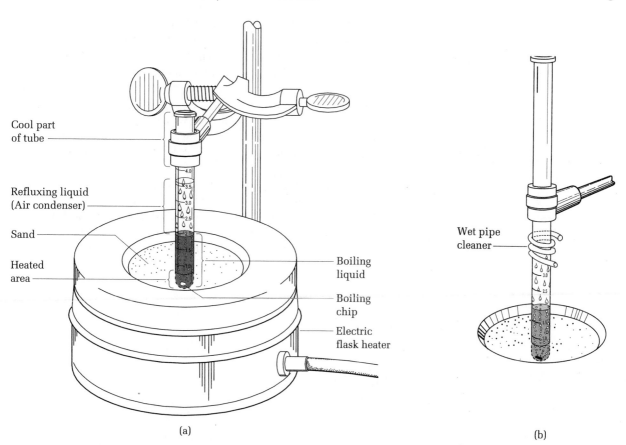

Cool part
of tube

Refluxing liquid
(Air condenser)

Sand

Heated
area

Boiling
liquid

Boiling
chip

Electric
flask heater

Wet pipe
cleaner

(a)

(b)

FIG. 1.1: (a) Reaction tube being heated on a hot sand bath in a flask heater. The area of the tube exposed to heat is small. The liquid boils and condenses on the cool upper portion of the tube, which functions as an air condenser. (b) The condensing area can be increased by adding the distilling column as an air condenser.

Cooling is again conducted using an ice bath, but heating is sometimes done on a steam bath for low-boiling liquids. Higher temperatures require electric *heating mantles* or *flask heaters*.

For microscale heating, a *sand bath* in an electric 100-mL flask heater filled with sand is a versatile heat source (Fig. 1.1a). The relatively poor heat conduction of sand results in a very large temperature difference between the top of the sand and the bottom. Thus, depending on the immersion depth in the sand, a similarly wide temperature range will be found in the reaction tube. Because the area of the tube exposed to heat is fairly small, it is difficult to transfer enough heat to the contents of the tube to cause solvents to boil away. The reaction tube is 100 mm long so that the upper part of the tube can function as an efficient *air condenser* (Fig. 1.1a), since the area of glass is large and the volume of vapor is comparatively small. The air condenser can be made even longer by attaching the empty *distilling column* to the reaction tube using the *connector with support rod*

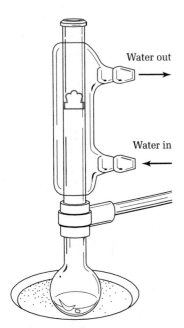

FIG. 1.2: Refluxing solvent in a 5-mL round-bottomed flask fitted with a water-cooled condenser.

(Fig. 1.1b). The black connector is made of Viton, which is resistant to high-boiling aromatic solvents. The cream-colored connector is made of Santoprene, which is resistant to all but high-boiling aromatic solvents. Solvents such as water and ethanol are boiled, and as the hot vapor ascends to the upper part of the tube, they condense and run back down the tube. This process is called *refluxing* and is the most common method for conducting a reaction at a constant temperature, the boiling point of the solvent. For very low-boiling solvents such as diethyl ether (bp 35°C), a pipe cleaner dampened with water makes an efficient cooling device. A water-cooled condenser is also available (Fig. 1.2) but is seldom needed.

On a larger scale, the same electric flask heater or a sand bath on a hot plate can be used to heat a flask that is connected via a *standard-taper ground glass joint* to a water-cooled *reflux condenser,* where the water flows in a jacket around the central tube. The high heat capacity of water makes it possible to remove the large amount of heat put into the larger volume of refluxing vapor (Fig. 1.3).

It is worth noting that the reaction tube (Fig. 1.1a) functions as both flask

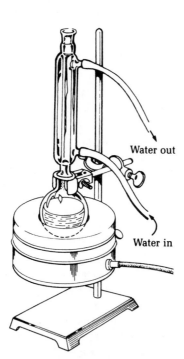

FIG. 1.3: Reflux apparatus for larger reactions. Liquid boils in the flask and condenses on the cold inner surface of the water-cooled condenser.

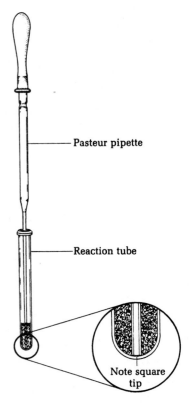

FIG. 1.4: Filtration using the Pasteur pipette and reaction tube.

Filter paper,
12 mm dia. ——

Polyethylene
filter disk (frit),
10 mm dia. ——

Hirsch
funnel——

To aspirator

25-mL Filter
flask ——

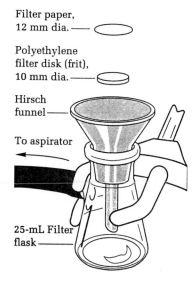

FIG. 1.5: Hirsch funnel with an integral adapter, polyethylene frit, and 25-mL filter flask.

and reflux condenser and is completely equivalent in function to the macroscale standard-taper flask and reflux condenser of Fig. 1.3 but costs about 1/40th as much.

The progress of a reaction can be followed by withdrawing tiny samples at intervals and analyzing them by *thin-layer chromatography*. If the product of a reaction crystallizes from the reaction mixture on cooling, it is isolated by *filtration*. On a microscale, this can be done in several ways. If the crystals are large enough and in the reaction tube, this is accomplished by inserting a *Pasteur pipette* to the bottom of the tube while expelling the air and withdrawing the solvent (Fig. 1.4). Very effective filtration occurs between the square tip of the pipette and the bottom of the tube. This method of filtration has several advantages over the alternatives. The mixture of crystals and solvent can be kept on ice during the entire process. This minimizes the solubility of the crystals in the solvent. There are no transfer losses of material because an external filtration device is not used. This technique allows several recrystallizations to be carried out in the same tube with final drying of the product under vacuum. Knowing the *tare* of the tube (the weight of the empty tube) allows the weight of the product to be determined without removing it from the tube. In this manner a compound can be synthesized, purified by crystallization, and dried without ever leaving the reaction tube. After removal of material for analysis, the compound in the tube can then be used for the next reaction. This technique is used in many of the microscale experiments in this book. When the crystals are dry, they are easily removed from the reaction tube. When they are wet, it is difficult to scrape them out. If the crystals are in more than about 2 mL of solvent, they can be isolated by filtration on the *Hirsch funnel*. The one that is in the microscale kit of apparatus is particularly easy to use because the funnel fits into the *filter flask* with no adapter, and it is equipped with a *polyethylene frit* for removal of the crystals (Fig. 1.5). The Wilfilter is especially good for collecting small quantities of crystals (Fig. 1.6).

Macroscale quantities of material are crystallized in *Erlenmeyer flasks;* the crystals are collected in porcelain or plastic *Büchner funnels* fitted with pieces of filter paper in the bottom of the funnel. A *filter adapter* (*Filtervac*) is used to form a vacuum-tight seal between the flask and funnel (Fig. 1.7).

Many solids can be purified by the process of *sublimation*. The solid is heated, and the vapor of the solid condenses on a cold surface to form crystals in an apparatus constructed from a *centrifuge tube* fitted with a rubber adapter (a *Pluro stopper*) and pushed into a *filter flask* (Fig. 1.8). Caffeine can be purified in this manner. This is primarily a microscale technique, although sublimers holding several grams of solid are available.

Mixtures of solids and, occasionally, of liquids can be separated and purified by *column chromatography*. The *chromatography column* for both microscale and macroscale work is very similar (Fig. 1.9).

Often the product of a reaction will not crystallize. It may be a liquid, it may be a mixture of compounds, or it may be too soluble in the solvent being used. In this case, an immiscible solvent is added, the two layers are shaken to effect *extraction,* and after the layers separate, one layer is removed. On a microscale, this can be done with a Pasteur pipette, and the process is repeated if necessary.

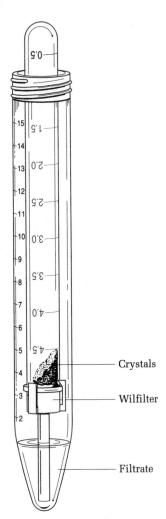

FIG. 1.6: Wilfilter filtration apparatus.

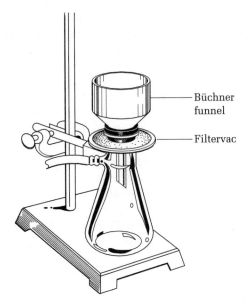

FIG. 1.7: Suction filter assembly.

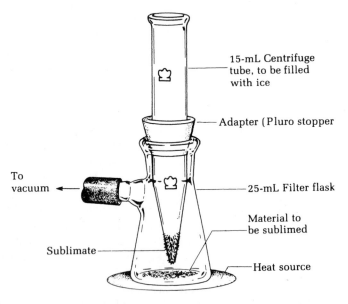

FIG. 1.8: Small-scale sublimation apparatus.

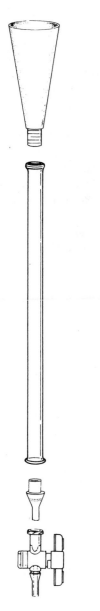

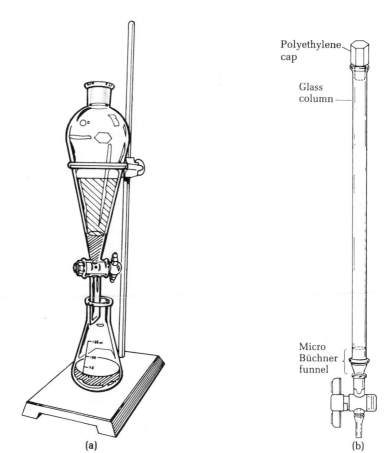

Polyethylene
cap

Glass
column

Micro
Büchner
funnel

(a)

(b)

FIG. 1.10:   (a) Separatory funnel with Teflon stopcock. (b) Microscale separatory funnel. Remove the polyethylene frit from the micro Büchner funnel before using.

A tall, thin column of liquid such as that produced in the reaction tube makes it easy to remove one layer selectively. This is much more difficult to do in the usual test tube because the height/diameter ratio is too small.

The chromatography column in the apparatus kit is also a *micro separatory funnel* (Fig. 1.10b). Remember to remove the frit at the column base of the micro Büchner funnel and to close the valve before adding liquid.

On a larger scale, a *separatory funnel* is used for extraction (Fig. 1.10a). The mixture can be shaken in the funnel and then the lower layer removed through the stopcock after the stopper is removed. These funnels are available in sizes from 10 to 5000 mL. The microscale version is seen in Fig. 1.10(b).

Some of the compounds to be synthesized in these experiments are liquids. On a very small scale, the best way to separate and purify a mixture of liquids is by *gas chromatography,* but this technique is limited to less than 100 mg of material on the usual gas chromatograph. For larger quantities of material, *distillation*

FIG. 1.9:   Chromatography column consisting of funnel, tube, base fitted with a polyethylene frit, and Leur valve.

Chapter 5: Distillation

is used. For this purpose, small distilling flasks are used. These flasks have a large surface area to allow sufficient heat input to cause the liquid to vaporize rapidly so that it can be distilled and then condensed for collection in a *receiver.* The apparatus (Fig. 1.11) consists of a *distilling flask, distilling adapter* (which also functions as an air condenser on a microscale), a *thermometer adapter, thermometer,* and on a macroscale a water-cooled *condenser* and *distilling adapter* (Fig. 1.12). *Fractional distillation* is carried out using a small packed *fractionating column* (Fig. 1.13). The apparatus is very similar on both a microscale and macroscale. On a microscale, 2 to 4 mL of a liquid can be fractionally distilled, and 1 mL or more can be simply distilled. The usual scale in these experiments for macroscale distillation is about 25 mL. The individual components for microscale experimentation are shown in Fig. 1.14 and for macroscale work in Fig. 1.15.

Chapter 6: Steam Distillation

Some liquids with a relatively high vapor pressure can be isolated and purified by *steam distillation,* a process in which the organic compound codistills

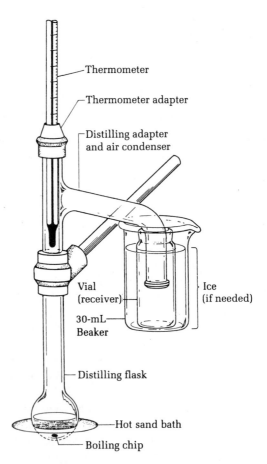

FIG. 1.11: Small-scale simple distillation apparatus.

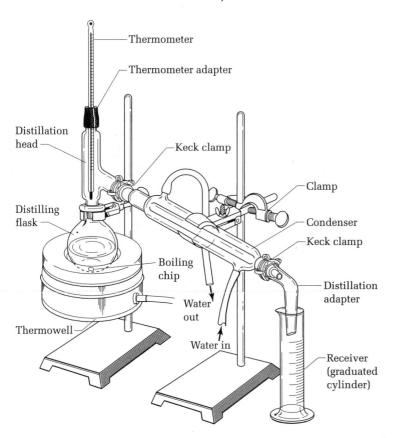

FIG. 1.12. Apparatus for simple distillation.

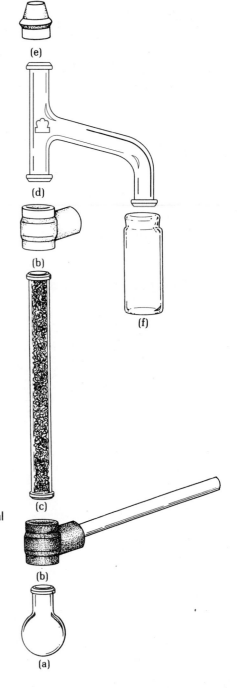

FIG. 1.13.   Microscale fractional distillation apparatus. (a) 5-mL round-bottomed flask. (b) Elastomeric connector [Santoprene (white) or Viton (black)]. (c) Fractionating column packed with copper sponge. (d) Distilling head and air condenser. (e) Thermometer adapter (Santoprene). (f) Receiver (1-dram vial).

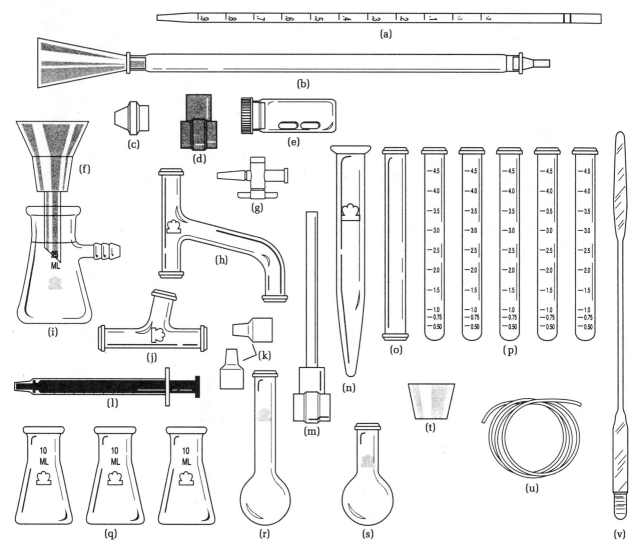

Fig. 1.14 Microscale apparatus kit.

(a) Pipette (1 mL), graduated in 1/100ths.

(b) Chromatography column (glass) with polypropylene funnel and 20-μm polyethylene frit in base, which doubles as a micro Büchner funnel. The column, base, and stopcock are also used as a separatory funnel.

(c) Thermometer adapter (Santoprene).

(d) Connector only (Viton).

(e) Magnetic stirring bars (4 × 12 mm) in distillation receiver vial.

(f) Hirsch funnel (polypropylene) with 20-μm fritted polyethylene disk.

(g) Stopcock for chromatography column and separatory funnel.

(h) Claisen adapter/distillation head with air condenser.

(i) Filter flask, 25 mL.

(j) Distillation head, 105° connecting adapter.

(k) Rubber septa/sleeve stoppers, 8 mm.

(l) Syringe (polypropylene).

(m) Connector (Santoprene) with support rod.

(n) Centrifuge tube (15 mL)/ sublimation receiver, with cap.

(o) Distillation column/air condenser.

(p) Reaction tube, calibrated, 10 × 100 mm.

(q) Erlenmeyer flasks, 10 mL.

(r) Long-necked flask, 5 mL.

(s) Short-necked flask, 5 mL.

(t) Filter adapter (Santoprene) for sublimation apparatus.

(u) Tubing (polyethylene), 1/16-in. diameter.

(v) Spatula (stainless steel) with scoop end.

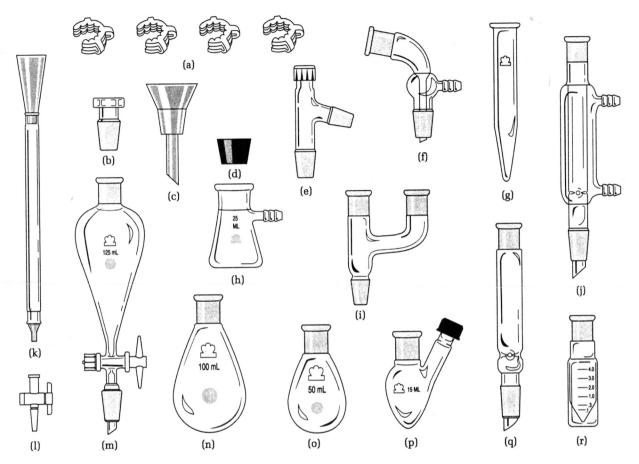

FIG. 1.15 Macroscale apparatus kit with 14/20 standard-taper ground-glass joints.

(a) Polyacetal Keck clamps, size 14.

(b) Hex-head glass stopper, 14/20 standard taper.

(c) Hirsch funnel (polypropylene) with 20-μm fritted polyethylene disk.

(d) Filter adapter (Santoprene) for sublimation apparatus.

(e) Distilling head with O-ring thermometer adapter.

(f) Vacuum adapter.

(g) Centrifuge tube (15 mL)/ sublimation receiver.

(h) Filter flask, 25 mL.

(i) Claisen adapter.

(j) Water-jacketed condenser.

(k) Chromatography column (glass) with polypropylene funnel and 20-μm polyethylene frit in base, which doubles as a micro Büchner funnel.

(l) Stopcock for chromatography column.

(m) Separatory funnel, 125 mL.

(n) Pear-shaped flask, 100 mL.

(o) Pear-shaped flask, 50 mL.

(p) Conical flask (15 mL) with side arm for inlet tube.

(q) Distilling column/air condenser.

(r) Conical reaction vial (5 mL)/distillation receiver.

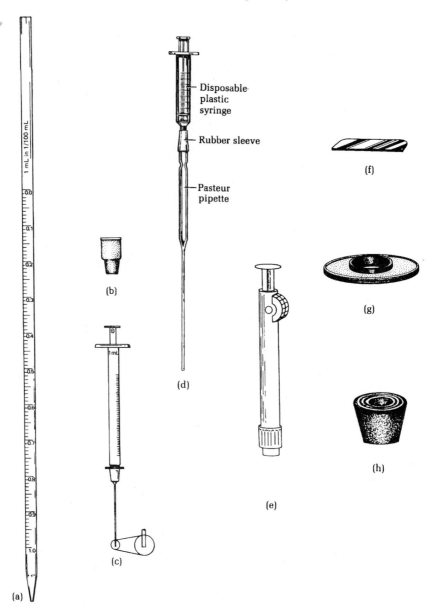

FIG. 1.16 Miscellaneous apparatus. (a) 1.0 ± 0.01 mL graduated pipette. (b) Septum. (c) 1.0-mL syringe with blunt needle. (d) Calibrated Pasteur pipette. (e) Pipette pump. (f) Glass scorer. (g) Filtervac. (h) Set of neoprene adapters.

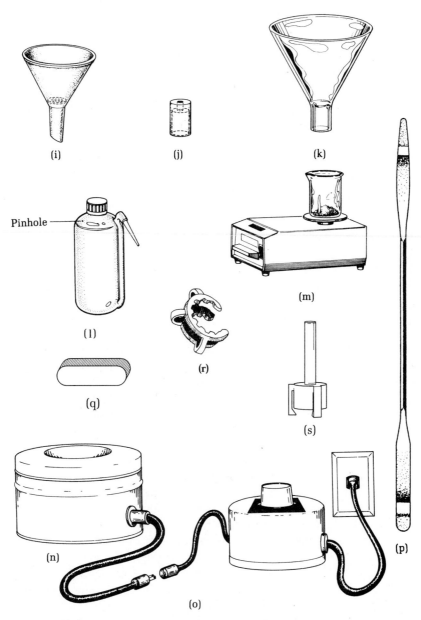

(i) Hirsch funnel with perforated plate in place. (j) Thermometer adapter. (k) Powder funnel. (l) Polyethylene wash bottle. (m) Single-pan electronic balance with automatic zeroing and digital readout, 100 g ± 0.001 g capacity. (n) Electric flask heater. (o) Solid-state control for electric flask heater. (p) Stainless steel spatula. (q) Stirring bar. (r) Keck clamp. (s) Wilfilter.

with water at a temperature below the boiling point of water. The microscale and macroscale apparatus for this process are shown in the chapter on steam distillation.

Other apparatus commonly used in the organic laboratory are shown in Fig. 1.16 on pages 12–13.

Check In

Your first duty will be to check in to your assigned desk. The identity of much of the apparatus should already be apparent from the preceding outline of the experimental processes used in the organic laboratory.

CAUTION: Notify your instructor immediately if you break a thermometer. Mercury is very toxic.

Check to see that your thermometer reads about 22–25°C (20°C = 68°F), normal room temperature. Examine the mercury column to see if the thread is broken—i.e., that the mercury column is continuous from the bulb up. Replace any flasks that have star-shaped cracks. Remember that apparatus with graduations and porcelain apparatus are expensive. Erlenmeyer flasks, beakers, and test tubes are, by comparison, fairly cheap.

Washing and Drying Laboratory Equipment

Clean apparatus immediately.

Considerable time can be saved by cleaning each piece of equipment soon after use, for you will know at that point what contaminant is present and be able to select the proper method for removal. A residue is easier to remove before it has dried and hardened. A small amount of organic residue usually can be dissolved with a few milliliters of an appropriate organic solvent. Acetone (bp 56.1°C) has great solvent power and is often effective, but it is extremely flammable and somewhat expensive. Because it is miscible with water and vaporizes readily, it is easy to remove from the vessel. Cleaning after an operation often can be carried out while another experiment is in process.

More experiments are ruined by damp or wet apparatus than for any other reason. Water is your enemy in the organic laboratory.

A *polyethylene bottle* [Fig. 1.16(l)] is a convenient wash bottle for acetone. The name, symbol, or formula of a solvent can be written on a bottle with a Magic Marker or wax pencil. For crystallizations, extractions, and quick cleaning of apparatus, it is convenient to have a bottle for each frequently used solvent—95% ethanol, ligroin, dichloromethane, and *t*-butyl methyl ether. A pinhole opposite the spout, which is covered with the finger when in use, will prevent the spout from dribbling the solvent. For microscale work, these solvents are best dispensed from 25- or 50-mL bottles with an attached test tube containing a graduated (1-mL) polypropylene pipette (Fig. 1.17).

Both ethanol and acetone are very flammable.

Pasteur pipettes (Fig. 1.18) are very useful for transferring small quantities of liquid, adding reagents dropwise, and carrying out crystallizations. Surprisingly, the acetone used to wash out a dirty Pasteur pipette usually costs more than the pipette itself. Discard used Pasteur pipettes in the special container for waste glass.

Sometimes a flask will not be clean after a washing with detergent and acetone. At that point try an abrasive household cleaner.

To dry a piece of apparatus rapidly, rinse with a few millimeters of acetone and invert over a beaker to drain. **Do not use compressed air,** which contains droplets of oil, water, and particles of rust. Instead draw a slow stream of air through the apparatus using the suction of your water aspirator.

Insertion of a glass tube into a rubber connector or adapter or hose is easy if the glass is lubricated with a very small drop of glycerol. Grasp the tube very close to the end to be inserted; if it is grasped at a distance, especially at the bend, the pressure applied for insertion may break the tube and result in a serious cut.

If a glass tube or thermometer should become stuck to a rubber connector, it can be removed by painting on glycerol and forcing the pointed tip of an 18-cm spatula between the rubber and glass. Another method is to select a cork borer that fits snugly over the glass tube, moisten it with glycerol, and slowly work it through the connector. When the stuck object is valuable, such as a thermometer, the best policy is to cut the rubber with a sharp knife.

Heat Source

A 10°C rise in temperature will approximately double the rate of an organic reaction. The processes of distillation, sublimation, and crystallization all require heat, which is most conveniently and safely applied from an electrically heated sand bath. A flask heater (see Fig. 1.16n, o) is two-thirds filled with sand, the temperature of which depends on the setting of the controller. This heater is small in diameter, giving good access to small apparatus, and the air above the heater is not hot. It is possible to hold a reaction tube containing refluxing solvents in the fingers of the hand. Because sand is a fairly poor conductor of heat, there is a very large variation in temperature in the sand bath depending on its depth. The temperature of a flask can be regulated by piling up or removing sand from near the flask with a spatula. The heater is easily capable of producing temperatures in excess of 300°C; therefore, never leave the controller at its maximum setting. Ordinarily, it is set at 20% of maximum. Because the flask heater can provide high temperatures, microscale equipment need not include a Bunsen burner, but on a macroscale, this has been a common way to heat reaction mixtures in the teaching laboratory. If at all possible, for safety reasons, use an electric flask heater. When the solvent boils below 90°C, the most common method for heating macroscale flasks is the *steam bath.*

A Petri dish containing sand and heated on a hot plate is not recommended for microscale experiments. It is too easy to burn oneself on the hot plate; too much heat wells up from the sand, so air condensers do not function well; the glass dishes break from thermal shock; and the ceramic coating on some hot plates chips and comes off.

Transfer of a Solid

A plastic funnel that fits the top of the reaction tube is most convenient for the transfer of solids to a reaction tube or to small Erlenmeyer flasks for microscale experiments (Fig. 1.19). It is also the top of the chromatography column (see Fig. 1.9). A special spatula with a scoop end is used to remove solid material from the

Wash acetone goes in the organic solvents waste container.

FIG. 1.17: Recrystallization solvent bottle and dispenser.

Turn on the Thermowell about 20 minutes before you intend to use it. The sand heats slowly.

CAUTION: Never put a mercury thermometer in a sand bath! It will break, releasing highly toxic mercury vapor.

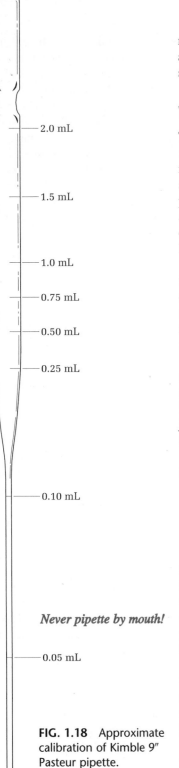

2.0 mL

1.5 mL

1.0 mL

0.75 mL

0.50 mL

0.25 mL

0.10 mL

Never pipette by mouth!

0.05 mL

FIG. 1.18 Approximate calibration of Kimble 9″ Pasteur pipette.

reaction tube (see Fig. 1.16p). On a large scale, a powder funnel is useful for adding solids to a flask (see Fig. 1.16k). A funnel also can be fashioned from a sheet of weighing paper.

Weighing and Measuring

The single-pan electronic balance (see Fig. 1.16m) capable of weighing to ±0.001 g and having a capacity of 100 g is the single most important instrument making small-scale organic experiments possible. Most of the quantitative measurements made in microscale experiments will use this balance. Weighing is a pleasure with these balances. For larger-scale experiments, a balance of such high accuracy is not necessary. Although the top-loading digital balances are the easiest to use, a triple-beam balance will work just as well. There should be one top-loading scale for every 12 students.

A container such as a reaction tube standing in a beaker or flask is placed on the pan. At the touch of a bar, the digital readout registers zero, and the desired quantity of the reagent can be added to the reaction tube as the weight is measured periodically to the nearest milligram. Even liquids are weighed when accuracy is needed. It is much easier to weigh a liquid to ±0.001 g than it is to measure it volumetrically to ±0.001 mL.

It is often convenient to weigh reagents on glossy weighing paper and then transfer the chemical to the reaction container. The success of an experiment often depends on using just the right amount of starting materials and reagents. Inexperienced workers might think that if one milliliter of a reagent will do the job, then two milliliters will do the job twice as well. Such assumptions are usually erroneous.

Liquids can be measured by either volume or weight according to the relationship

$$\text{Volume (mL)} = \frac{\text{weight (g)}}{\text{density (g/mL)}}$$

Modern Erlenmeyer flasks and beakers have approximate volume calibrations fused into the glass, but these are *very* approximate. Better graduations are found on the microscale *reaction tube*. Somewhat more accurate volumetric measurements are made in the 10-mL graduated cylinders. For volumes less than 4 mL, use a graduated pipette. **Never** apply suction to a pipette by mouth. The pipette can be fitted with a small rubber bulb. A Pasteur pipette can be converted into a calibrated pipette with the addition of a plastic syringe body (see Fig. 1.16d). Also see the calibration marks for a 9-in. Pasteur pipette in Fig. 1.18. You will find among your equipment a 1-mL pipette, calibrated in hundredths of a milliliter (see Fig. 1.16a). Determine whether it is designed to *deliver* 1 mL or *contain* 1 mL between the top and bottom calibration marks. For our purposes, the latter is the better pipette.

Because the viscosity, surface tension, vapor pressure, and wetting characteristics of organic liquids are different from those of water, the so-called automatic pipette (designed for aqueous solutions) gives poor accuracy in measuring organic liquids. *Syringes* (see Fig. 1.16c) and *pipette pumps* (Fig. 1.20), on the other hand, are quite useful, and frequent use will be made of them. Do not use a syringe that is equipped with a metal needle to measure corrosive reagents. Several reactions that require especially dry or oxygen-free atmospheres will be run in sealed systems. Reagents can be added to the system via syringe through a rubber *septum* (see Fig. 1.16b).

Careful measurements of weights and volumes take more time than less accurate measurements. Think carefully about which measurements need to be made with accuracy and which do not.

Tares

The tare of a container is its weight when empty. Throughout this laboratory course it will be necessary to know the tares of containers so that the weights of the compounds within can be calculated. If identifying marks can be placed on the containers (e.g., with a diamond stylus) you may want to record tares for fre-

Tare = weight of empty container

in your laboratory notebook.

rect we should use the word *mass* instead of *weight*, celeration is not constant at all places on earth. But elec- weights, unlike two-pan or triple-beam balances, which

otebook

cord is an essential part of laboratory work. Failure to s laboratory labor lost. An adequate record includes the ne), observations (what happened), and conclusions

The labor
What y
How yo
What y
Your co

ng on scraps of paper. Use a lined, $8\frac{1}{2}$- × 11-in. paper- rd all data in ink. Allow space at the front for a table of es throughout, and date each day's work. Reserve the tions and numerical data, and use the right-hand page **nything** on scraps of paper to be recorded later in the emove, or obliterate notes; simply draw a single line

contain a statement or title for each experiment and its nced equations for all principal and side reactions, and, ns of the reactions. Consult your textbook for supple- he class of compounds or type of reaction involved. cedure used; do not copy verbatim the procedure in the articular note of safety precautions and the procedures f the experiment.

lab to do preparative experiments, prepare a table (in to be used and the products expected, with their phys- able, use the molar ratios of reactants to determine the alculate the theoretical yield (in grams) of the desired nent on a new page.

(overlaid slip, handwritten)

(make sure this slip is returned to you when equipment is returned)

STUDENT'S NAME (write legibly)
Kristina Mariquita

needle

18 gauge

___ I have misplaced
___ I have broken
_X_ I am borrowing

DATE 4/10   DESK# 6(?)

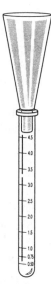

FIG. 1.19: Funnel for addition of solids and liquids to a reaction tube.

Include an outline of the procedure and the method of purification of the product in a flow sheet if this is the best way to organize the experiment (for example, an extraction; see Chapter 8). The flow sheet should list all possible products, byproducts, unused reagents, solvents, and so on that are expected to appear in the crude reaction mixture. On the flow sheet diagram indicate how each of these is removed, for example, by extraction, various washing procedures, distillation, or crystallization. With this information entered in the notebook before coming to the laboratory, you will be ready to carry out the experiments with the utmost efficiency. Plan your time before the laboratory period. Often two or three experiments can be run simultaneously.

When working in the laboratory, record everything you do and everything you observe **as it happens.** The recorded observations constitute the most important part of the laboratory record, since they form the basis for the conclusions you will draw at the end of each experiment. One way to do this is in a narrative form. Alternatively, the procedure can be written in outline form on the left-hand side of the page and the observations recorded on the right-hand side.

In some colleges and universities, you will be expected to have all the relevant information about the running of an experiment entered in your notebook *before coming to the laboratory* so that your textbook will not be needed when you are conducting experiments. In industrial laboratories, your notebook may be designed so that carbon copies of all entries are kept. These are signed and dated by your supervisor and removed from your notebook each day. Your notebook becomes a legal document in case you make a discovery worth hundreds of millions of dollars!

Record the physical properties of the product from your experiment, the yield in grams, and the percent yield. Analyze your results. When things do not turn out as expected, explain why. When your record of an experiment is complete, another chemist should be able to understand your account and determine what you did, how you did it, and what conclusions you reached. That is, from the information in your notebook, a chemist should be able to repeat your work.

Preparing a Laboratory Record

Use the following steps to prepare your laboratory record. The letters correspond to the completed laboratory records that appear at the end of this chapter. Because your laboratory notebook is so important, two examples, written in alternative forms, are presented.

A. Number each page. Allow space at the front of the notebook for a table of contents. Use a hardbound, lined notebook, and keep all notes in ink.
B. Date each entry.
C. Give a short title to the experiment, and enter it in the table of contents.
D. State the purpose of the experiment.
E. Write balanced equation(s) for the reaction(s).
F. Give a reference to the source of the experimental procedure.
G. Prepare a table of quantities and physical constants. Look up the needed data in the *Handbook of Chemistry and Physics.*

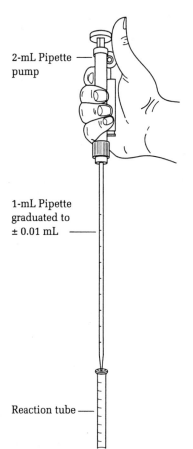

2-mL Pipette pump

1-mL Pipette graduated to ± 0.01 mL

Reaction tube

FIG. 1.20 Use of a pipette pump to measure liquids to ±0.01 mL.

H. Write equation(s) for the principal side reaction(s).

I. Write out the procedure with just enough information so that you can follow it easily. Do not simply copy the procedure from the text. Note any hazards and safety precautions. A very experienced chemist might write a procedure in a formal report as follows: "Dibenzalacetone was prepared by condensing at room temperature 1 mmol acetone with 2 mmol benzaldehyde in 1.6 mL of 95% ethanol to which was added 2 mL of aqueous 3 *M* sodium hydroxide solution. After 30 min the product was collected and crystallized from 70% ethanol to give 0.17 g (73%) of flat yellow plates of dibenzalacetone, mp 110.5–111.5°C." Note that in this formal report, no jargon (for example, EtOH for 95% ethanol, ΦCHO for benzaldehyde) is used and that the names of reagents are written out (sodium hydroxide, not NaOH). In this report the details of measuring, washing, drying, crystallizing, collecting the product, and so on are assumed to be understood by the reader.

J. Don't forget to note how to dispose of the byproducts from the experiment using the "Cleaning Up" section of the experimental procedure.

K. Record what you do as you do it. These observations are the most important part of the experiment. Note that conclusions do not appear among these observations.

L. Calculate the theoretical yield in grams. The experiment calls for exactly 2 mmol fluorobenzaldehyde and 1 mmol acetone, which will produce 1 mmol of product. The equation for the experiment also indicates that the product will be formed from exactly a 2:1 ratio of the reactants. Often, experiments are designed to have one reactant in great excess. In this experiment, a very slight excess of fluorobenzaldehyde was used inadvertently, so acetone becomes the limiting reagent.

M. Once the product is obtained, dried, and weighed, calculate the ratio of product actually isolated to the amount theoretically possible. Express this ratio as the percent yield.

N. Write out the mechanism of the reaction. If it is not given in the text of the experiment, look it up in your lecture text.

O. Draw conclusions from the observations. Write this part of the report in narrative form in complete English sentences. This part of the report can, of course, be written after leaving the laboratory.

P. Analyze TLC, IR, and NMR spectra if they are a part of the experiments. Rationalize observed versus reported melting points.

Q. Answer assigned questions from the end of the experiment.

R. This page presents an alternative method for entering the experimental procedure and observations in the notebook. Before coming to the laboratory, enter the procedure in outline form on the left side of the page. Then enter observations in brief form on the right side of the page as the experiment is carried out. Draw a single line through any words incorrectly entered. Do not erase or obliterate entries in the notebook, and never remove pages from the notebook.

Two samples of completed laboratory records follow. An alternative method for recording procedure, cleaning up, and observations is given on p. 24. The other parts of the report are the same.

Ⓐ p. 35
Ⓑ Sept. 23, 2001

Ⓒ **DIFLUORODIBENZALACETONE**

Ⓓ *Purpose:* To observe and carry out an aldol condensation reaction.

Ⓔ

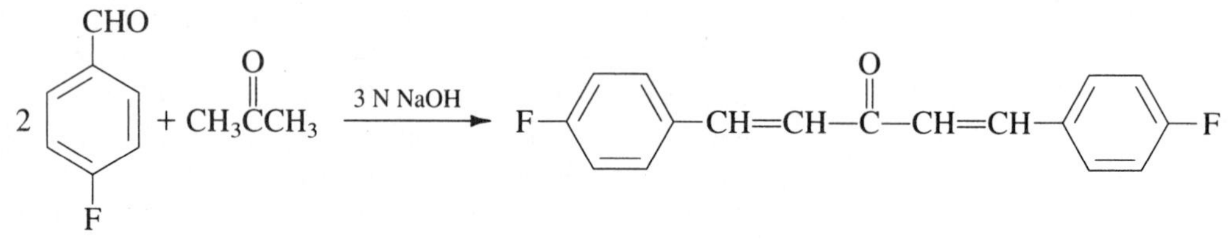

$$2 \text{ } \underset{\text{F}}{\underset{|}{\bigcirc}}\text{CHO} + CH_3\overset{O}{\overset{\|}{C}}CH_3 \xrightarrow{3 \text{ N NaOH}} F\text{—}\bigcirc\text{—CH=CH—}\overset{O}{\overset{\|}{C}}\text{—CH=CH—}\bigcirc\text{—F}$$

4-Fluorobenzaldehyde Acetone   **4,4′-Difluorodibenzalacetone**

Ⓕ *Reference:* Williamson, *Macroscale and Microscale Organic Experiments,* p. 792.

Table of Quantities and Physical Constants   Ⓖ

Substance	Mol wt	G/mol Used or Produced	Mol Needed (from eq.)	Density	mp	bp	Solubility
4-Fluorobenzaldehyde	124.11	0.248/0.002	0.002	1.157		181°C	Slightly soluble in H_2O; soluble in ethanol, diethyl ether, acetone
Acetone	58.08	0.058/0.001	0.001	0.790		56°C	Soluble in H_2O, ethanol, diethyl ether, acetone
4,4′-Difluoro-dibenzalacetone	270.34	0.273/0.001			167°C		Insoluble in H_2O; slightly soluble in ethanol, diethyl ether, acetone
4-Fluoro-benzalacetone	164.19					54°C	Insoluble in H_2O; slightly soluble in ethanol, diethyl ether, acetone
Sodium hydroxide	40.01						Soluble in H_2O; insoluble in ethanol, diethyl ether, acetone

Ⓗ *Side Reactions:* No important side reactions, but if excess acetone is used, product will be contaminated with 4-fluorobenzalacetone.

p. 36

(I)   *Procedure:* To a reaction tube, add 0.248 g (0.002 mole) of benzaldehyde and then 16 g of an ethanol solution that contains 0.58 mg of acetone. Mix the solution and observe it for 1 min. Remove sample for TLC. Then add 2 mL of 3 *M* NaOH(*aq*). Cap the tube with a septum and shake it at intervals over a 30-min period. Collect product on Hirsch funnel, wash crystals thoroughly with water, press as dry as possible, determine crude weight, and save sample for mp. Recrystallize product from 70% ethanol in a 10-mL Erlenmeyer flask. Cool solution slowly, scratch or add seed crystal, cool in ice, and collect product on Hirsch. Wash crystals with a few drops of ice-cold ethanol. Run TLC on silica gel plates using hexane to elute, develop in iodine chamber. Run NMR spectrum in deuterochloroform and IR spectrum as a mull.

(J)   *Cleaning Up:* Neutralize filtrate with HCl and flush solution down the drain. Put recrystallization filtrate in organic solvents container.

(K)   *Observations:* Into a reaction tube, 0.250 g of 4-fluorobenzaldehyde was weighed (0.248 called for). Using the 1.00-mL graduated pipette and pipette pump, 1.61 mL of the stock ethanol solution containing 0.58 mg of acetone was added (16 mL called for). The contents of the tube were mixed by flicking the tube, and then a drop of the reaction mixture was removed and diluted with 1 mL of hexane for later TLC. The water-clear solution did not change in appearance during 1 min.

Then about 2 mL of 3 *M* NaOH(*aq*) was added using graduations on side of reaction tube. The tube was capped with a septum and shaken. The clear solution changed to a light yellow color immediately and got slightly warm. Then after about 50 sec, the entire solution became opaque. Then yellow oily drops collected on sides and bottom of tube. Shaken every 5 min for ½ hr. The oily drops crystallized, and more crystals formed. At the end of 30 min, the opaque solution became clear, and yellow crystals had formed. Tube filled with crystals.

Product was collected on 12-mm filter paper on a Hirsch funnel; transfer of material to funnel was completed using the filtrate to wash out the tube. Crystals were washed with about 15 mL of water. The filtrate was slightly cloudy and yellow. It was poured into a beaker for later disposal. The crude product was pressed as dry as possible with a cork. Wt (damp) 270 mg. Sample saved for mp.

Recrystallized from about 50 mL of 70% ethanol on sand bath. Almost forgot to add boiling stick! Clear, yellow solution cooled slowly by wrapping tube in cotton. A seed crystal from Julie added to start crystallization. After about 25 min, flask was placed in ice bath for 15 min, then product was collected on Hirsch funnel (filter paper), washed with a few drops of ice-cold solvent, pressed dry and then spread out on paper to dry. Wt 0.19 mg. Very nice flat, yellow crystals, mp 179.5–180.5°C. The crude material before recrystallization had mp 177.5–179°C.

TLC on silica gel using hexane to elute gave only one spot, R_f 0.23, for the starting material and only one spot for the product, R_f 0.66. See attached plate.

The NMR spectrum that was run on the Bruker in deuterochloroform containing TMS showed a complex group of peaks centered at about 7 ppm with an integrated value of 17.19 and a sharp, clear quartet of peaks centered at 6.5 ppm with an integral of 8.62. The coupling constant of the AB quartet was 7.2 Hz. See attached spectrum.

The IR spectrum, run as a Nujol mull on the Mattson FT IR, showed intense peaks at 1590 and 1655 cm^{-1}, as well as small peaks at 3050, 3060, and 3072 cm^{-1}. See attached spectrum.

Cleaning Up: Recrystallization filtrate put in organic solvents container. First filtrate neutralized with HCl and poured down the drain.

(L) *Theoretical yield calculations:*

$$0.250 \text{ g fluorobenzaldehyde used } \frac{0.250 \text{ g}}{124.11 \text{ g/mole}} = 0.00201 \text{ mole}$$

$$0.058 \text{ g of acetone used } \frac{0.058 \text{ g}}{58.08 \text{ g/mole}} = 0.001 \text{ mole}$$

The moles needed (from equation) are 2 mmol of the benzaldehyde and 1 mmol of acetone. Therefore, acetone is the limiting reagent, and 1.00 mmol of product should result. The MW of the product is 270.34 g/mol.

$$0.001 \text{ mol} \times 270.34 \text{ g/mol}$$
$$= 0.270 \text{ g, theoretical yield of difluorodibenzalacetone}$$

(M) *Percent Yield of Product:*

$$\frac{0.19 \text{ g}}{0.270 \text{ g}} \times 100 = 70\%$$

(N) *The Mechanism of the Reaction:*

p. 38

CH₃C—C—C—⟨benzene ring⟩—F ⟶ CH₃C—C=C—⟨benzene ring⟩—F + H₂O + OH⁻

(The structure shows the aldol intermediate with OH attacking, converting to the α,β-unsaturated ketone with fluorophenyl group.)

(O) *Discussion and Conclusions:* Mixing the fluorobenzaldehyde, acetone, and ethanol gave no apparent reaction because the solution did not change in appearance, but less than a minute after adding the NaOH, a yellow oil appeared and the reaction mixture got slightly warm, indicating that a reaction was taking place. The mechanism given in the text (above) indicates that hydroxide ion is a catalyst for the reaction, confirmed by this observation. The reaction takes place spontaneously at room temperature. The reaction was judged to be complete when the liquid surrounding the crystals became clear (it was opaque) and the amount of crystals in the tube did not appear to change. This took 30 min. The crude product was collected and washed with water. Forgot to cool it in ice before filtering it off. The crude product weighed more than the theoretical because it must still have been damp. However, this amount of crude material indicates that the reaction probably went pretty well to completion. The crude product was recrystallized from 5 mL of 70% ethanol. This was probably too much, since it dissolved very rapidly in that amount. This and the fact that the reaction mixture was not cooled in ice probably accounts for the relatively low 70% yield. Probably could have obtained second crop of crystals by concentrating filtrate. It turned very cloudy when water was added to it.

    Theoretically, it is possible for this reaction to give three different products (*cis, cis-; cis, trans-;* and *trans, trans*-isomers). Because the mp of the crude and recrystallized products were close to each other and rather sharp, and because the TLC of the product gave only one spot, it is presumed that the product is just one of these three possible isomers. The NMR spectrum shows a sharp quartet of peaks from the vinyl protons, which also indicates only one isomer. Since the coupling constant observed is 7.2 Hz, the protons must be *cis* to each other. Therefore, the product is the *cis, cis*-isomer.

(P)   The infrared spectrum shows two strong peaks at 1590 and 1655 cm⁻¹, indicative of an α-β-unsaturated ketone. The small peaks at 3050, 3060, and 3072 cm⁻¹ are consistent with aromatic and vinyl protons. The yellow color indicates that the molecule must have a long conjugated system.

    The fact that the TLC of the starting material showed only one peak is probably due to the evaporation of the acetone from the TLC plate. The spot with R_f 0.23 must be from the 4-fluorobenzaldehyde.

(Q)   Answers to assigned questions are written at the end of the report.

An alternative method for recording procedures, cleaning up, and observations:

p. 36

Ⓡ

Sept. 23, 2001 Procedure	Sept. 24, 2001 Observations
Weigh 0.248 g of 4-fluorobenz-aldehyde into reaction tube.	Actually used 0.250 g.
Add 1.6 mL of ethanol stock soln that contains 0.58 g of acetone.	Actually used 1.61 mL.
Mix, observe for 1 min.	Nothing seems to happen. Water clear soln.
Add 2 mL of 3 M NaOH(aq).	Clear, then faintly yellow but clear, then after about 50 sec, the entire soln very suddenly turned opaque. Got slightly warm. Light yellow color.
Cap tube with septum; shake at 5-min intervals for 30 min.	Oily drops separate on sides and bottom of tube. These crystallized; more crystals formed. Tube became filled with crystals. Liquid around crystals became clear.
Filter on Hirsch funnel.	Filtered (filter paper) on Hirsch.
Wash crystals with much water.	Washed with about 150 mL of H_2O. Transfer of crystals done using filtrate.
Press dry.	Crystals pressed dry with cork.
Weigh crude.	Crude (damp) wt 0.27 g.
Save sample for mp.	Crude mp 177.5–179°C.
Recrystallize from 70% ethanol; wash with a few drops of ice-cold solvent.	Used about 50 mL of 70% EtOH. Too much. Dissolved very rapidly.
Dry product.	Dried on paper for 30 min.
Weigh.	Wt 0.19 g.
Take mp.	Mp 179.5–180.5°C.
Run IR as mull.	Done.
Run NMR in CDCl$_3$.	Done.
Neutralize first filtrate with HCl, pour down drain.	Done.
Org. filtrate in waste organic bottle.	Done.

2

Laboratory Safety and Waste Disposal

Prelab Exercise: Read this chapter carefully. Locate the emergency eyewash station, safety shower, and fire extinguisher in your laboratory. Check your safety glasses or goggles for size and transparency. Learn which reactions must be carried out in the hood. Learn to use your laboratory fire extinguisher; learn how to summon help and how to put out a clothing fire. Learn first aid procedures for acid and alkali spills on the skin. Learn how to tell if your laboratory hood is working properly. Learn which operations under reduced pressure require special precautions. Check to see that compressed gas cylinders in your lab are firmly fastened to benches or walls. Learn the procedures for properly disposing of solid and liquid waste in your laboratory.

Small-scale organic experiments are much safer to conduct than their counterparts run on a scale 10 to 100 times larger. However, on either a microscale or a macroscale, the organic chemistry laboratory is an excellent place to learn and practice safety. Commonsense procedures practiced here also apply to other laboratories as well as the shop, kitchen, and studio.

General laboratory safety information particularly applicable to this organic chemistry laboratory course is presented in this chapter. It is not comprehensive. Throughout this text you will find specific cautions and safety information presented as margin notes printed in red. For a brief and thorough discussion of the topics in this chapter you should read the first 35 pages of *Safety in Academic Chemistry Laboratories,* American Chemical Society, Washington, DC, 1990, except for the admonition regarding contact lenses (see below).

Important General Rules

Know the safety rules of your particular laboratory. Know the locations of emergency eyewashes and safety showers. Never eat, drink, or smoke in the laboratory. Don't work alone. Perform no unauthorized experiments, and don't distract your fellow workers; horseplay has no place in the laboratory.

Eye protection

Eye protection is extremely important. Safety glasses of some type must be worn at all times. It has recently been determined "that contact lenses can be worn in most work environments provided the same approved eye protection is worn as required of other workers in the area" (*Chemical and Engineering News,* June 1, 1998, p. 6).

Ordinary prescription eyeglasses don't offer adequate protection. Laboratory safety glasses should be of plastic or tempered glass. If you do not have such glasses, wear goggles that afford protection from splashes and objects coming

FIG. 2.1 Safety goggles and safety glasses.

Dress sensibly.

from the side as well as the front. If plastic safety glasses are permitted in your laboratory, they should have side shields (see Fig. 2.1).

Dress sensibly in the laboratory. Wear shoes, not sandals or cloth-top sneakers. Confine long hair and loose clothes. Don't wear shorts. Don't use mouth suction to fill a pipette, and wash your hands before leaving the laboratory. Don't use a solvent to remove chemicals from skin. This will only hasten the absorption of the chemical through the skin.

Working with Flammable Substances

Relative flammability of organic solvents

FIG. 2.2 Solvent safety can.

Flammable vapors travel along bench tops.

Flammable substances are the most common hazard of the organic laboratory; two factors can make this laboratory much safer than its predecessor: making the scale of the experiments as small as possible and not using burners. Diethyl ether (bp 35°C), the most flammable substance you will usually work with in this course, has an ignition temperature of 160°C, which means that a hot plate at that temperature will cause it to burn. For comparison, *n*-hexane (bp 69°C), a constituent of gasoline, has an ignition temperature of 225°C. The flash points of these organic liquids—that is, the temperatures at which they will catch fire if exposed to a flame or spark—are below −20°C. These are very flammable liquids; however, if you are careful, they are not difficult to work with. Except for water, almost all of the liquids you will use in the laboratory will be flammable.

Bulk solvents should be stored in and dispensed from *safety cans* (see Fig. 2.2). These and other liquids will burn in the presence of the proper amount of their flammable vapors, oxygen, and a source of ignition (most commonly a flame or spark). It is usually difficult to remove oxygen from a fire, although it is possible to put out a fire in a beaker or a flask by simply covering the vessel with a flat object, thus cutting off the supply of air. Your lab notebook might do in an emergency. The best solution is to pay close attention to sources of ignition— open flames, sparks, and hot surfaces. Remember the vapors of flammable liquids are **always** heavier than air and thus will travel along bench tops and down drain troughs and will remain in sinks. For this reason all flames within the vicinity of a flammable liquid must be extinguished. Adequate ventilation is one of the best ways to prevent flammable vapors from accumulating. Work in an exhaust hood when manipulating large quantities of flammable liquids.

Should a person's clothing catch fire with a safety shower close at hand, shove the person under it. Otherwise, shove the person down and roll him or her over to extinguish the flames. It is extremely important to prevent the victim from running or standing because the greatest harm comes from breathing the hot vapors that rise past the mouth. The safety shower might then be used to extinguish glowing cloth that is no longer aflame. A so-called fire blanket should not

FIG. 2.3 Carbon dioxide fire extinguisher.

be used—it tends to funnel flames past the victim's mouth, and clothing continues to char beneath it. However, it is useful for retaining warmth to ward off shock after the flames are out.

An organic chemistry laboratory should be equipped with a carbon dioxide or dry chemical (monoammonium phosphate) *fire extinguisher* (see Fig. 2.3). To use this type of extinguisher, lift it from its support, pull the ring to break the seal, raise the horn, aim it at the base of the fire, and squeeze the handle. Do not hold onto the horn because it will become extremely cold. Do not replace the extinguisher; report the incident so the extinguisher can be refilled.

When disposing of certain chemicals, be alert for the possibility of *spontaneous combustion*. This may occur in oily rags; organic materials exposed to strong oxidizing agents such as nitric acid, permanganate ion, and peroxides; alkali metals such as sodium; or very finely divided metals such as zinc dust and platinum catalysts. Fires sometimes start when these chemicals are left in contact with filter paper.

Working with Hazardous Chemicals

If you do not know the properties of a chemical you will be working with, it is wise to regard the chemical as hazardous. The *flammability* of organic substances poses the most serious hazard in the organic laboratory. There is the possibility that storage containers in the laboratory may contribute to a fire. Large quantities of organic solvents should not be stored in glass bottles. Use safety cans. Do not store chemicals on the floor.

Flammable vapors plus air in a confined space are explosive.

A flammable liquid can often be vaporized to form, with air, a mixture that is *explosive* in a confined space. The beginning chemist is sometimes surprised to learn that diethyl ether is more likely to cause a laboratory fire or explosion than a worker's accidental anesthesia. The chances of being confined in a laboratory with a high enough concentration of ether to cause loss of consciousness are extremely small, but a spark in such a room would probably eradicate the building.

The probability of forming an explosive mixture of volatile organic liquids with air is much greater than that of producing an explosive solid or liquid. The chief functional groups that render compounds explosive are the *peroxide, acetylide, azide, diazonium, nitroso, nitro,* and *ozonide* groups (see Fig. 2.4). Not all

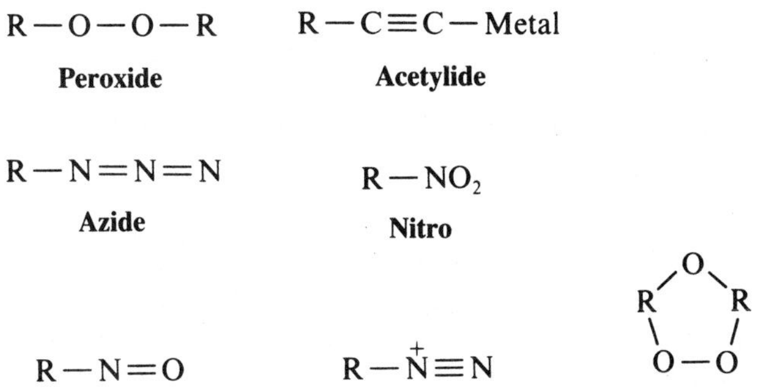

$$R-O-O-R \qquad R-C\equiv C-Metal$$

Peroxide   **Acetylide**

$$R-N=N=N \qquad R-NO_2$$

Azide   **Nitro**

FIG. 2.4 Functional groups that can be explosive in some compounds.

$$R-N=O \qquad R-\overset{+}{N}\equiv N$$

members of these groups are equally sensitive to shock or heat. You would find it difficult to detonate trinitrotoluene (TNT) in the laboratory, but nitroglycerine is treacherously explosive. Peroxides present special problems that are dealt with below.

Safety glasses must be worn at all times.

You will need to contend with the corrosiveness of many of the reagents you will handle. The danger here is principally to the eyes. Proper eye protection is *mandatory,* and even small-scale experiments can be hazardous to the eyes. It takes only a single drop of a corrosive reagent to do lasting damage. Handling concentrated acids and alkalis, dehydrating agents, and oxidizing agents calls for commonsense care to avoid spills and splashes and to avoid breathing the often corrosive vapors.

Certain organic chemicals present problems with acute toxicity from short-duration exposure and chronic toxicity from long-term or repeated exposure. Exposure can come about through ingestion, contact with the skin, or, most commonly, inhalation. Currently, great attention is being focused on chemicals that are teratogens (chemicals that often have no effect on a pregnant woman but cause abnormalities in a fetus), mutagens (chemicals causing changes in the structure of the DNA, which can lead to mutations in offspring), and carcinogens (cancer-causing chemicals). Small-scale experiments reduce these hazards greatly but do not eliminate them.

Peroxides

Ethers form explosive peroxides.

Certain functional groups can make an organic molecule become sensitive to heat and shock, such that it will explode. Chemists work with these functional groups only when there are no good alternatives. One of these functional groups, the *peroxide* group, is particularly insidious because it can form spontaneously when oxygen and light are present (see Fig. 2.5). Ethers, especially *cyclic ethers* and those made from primary or secondary alcohols (such as tetrahydrofuran, diethyl ether, and diisopropyl ether), form peroxides. Other compounds that form peroxides are *aldehydes, alkenes* that have allylic hydrogen atoms (such as cyclohexene), compounds having benzylic hydrogens on a tertiary carbon atom (such as

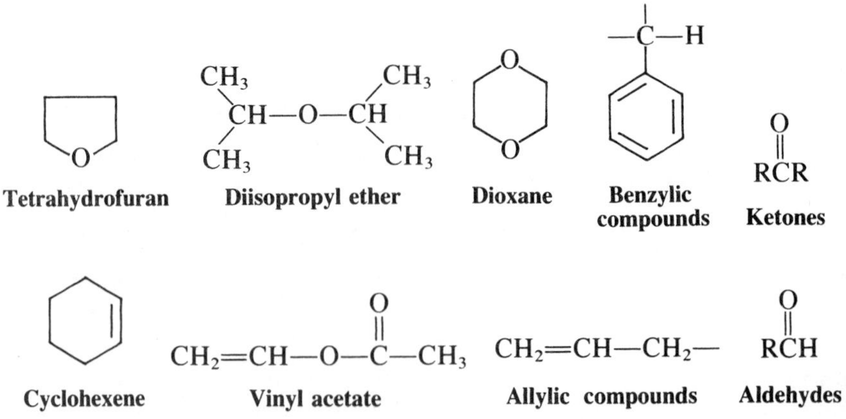

FIG. 2.5 Some compounds that form peroxides.

Tetrahydrofuran   Diisopropyl ether   Dioxane   Benzylic compounds   Ketones

Cyclohexene   Vinyl acetate   Allylic compounds   Aldehydes isopropyl benzene), and vinyl compounds (such as vinyl acetate). Peroxides are low-power explosives but are extremely sensitive to shock, sparks, light, heat, friction, and impact. The biggest danger from peroxide impurities comes when the peroxide-forming compound is distilled. The peroxide has a higher boiling point than the parent compound and remains in the distilling flask as a residue that can become overheated and explode. This is one reason why it is very poor practice to distill anything to dryness.

Don't distill to dryness.

Detection of Peroxides	Removal of Peroxides
To a solution of 0.01 g of sodium iodide in 0.1 mL of glacial acetic acid, add 0.1 mL of the liquid suspected of containing a peroxide. If the mixture turns brown, a high concentration of peroxide is present; if it turns yellow, a low concentration of peroxide is present.	Pouring the solvent through a column of activated alumina will simultaneously remove peroxides and dry the solvent. Do not allow the column to dry out while in use. When the alumina column is no longer effective, wash the column with 5% aqueous ferrous sulfate, and discard it as nonhazardous waste.

Problems with peroxide formation are especially critical for ethers. Ethers form peroxides readily, and, because they are frequently used as solvents, they are often used in quantity and then removed to leave reaction products. Cans of diethyl ether should be dated when opened and if not used within one month should be treated for peroxides or disposed of.

tert-Butyl methyl ether with a primary carbon on one side of the oxygen and a tertiary carbon on the other does not form peroxides easily. It should be used in place of diethyl ether for extraction. See sidebar in Chapter 8.

You may have occasion to use *30% hydrogen peroxide*. This material causes severe burns if it contacts the skin, and it decomposes violently if contaminated with metals or their salts. Be particularly careful not to contaminate the reagent bottle.

Working with Corrosive Substances

Handle strong acids, alkalis, dehydrating agents, and oxidizing agents carefully so as to avoid contact with the skin and eyes and to avoid breathing the corrosive vapors that attack the respiratory tract. All strong concentrated acids attack the skin and eyes. *Concentrated sulfuric acid* is both a dehydrating agent and a strong acid and will cause very severe burns. *Nitric acid* and *chromic acid* (used in cleaning solutions) also cause bad burns. *Hydrofluoric acid* is especially harmful, causing deep, painful, and slow-healing wounds. It should be used only after thorough instruction.

Sodium, potassium, and *ammonium hydroxides* are common bases you will encounter. The first two are extremely damaging to the eye, and ammonium

Add H_2SO_4, P_2O_5, CaO, and NaOH to water, not the reverse.

hydroxide is a severe bronchial irritant. Like sulfuric acid, *sodium hydroxide, phosphorous pentoxide,* and *calcium oxide* are powerful dehydrating agents. Their great affinity for water will cause burns to the skin. Because they release a great deal of heat when they react with water, to avoid spattering they should always be added to water rather than water being added to them. That is, the heavier substance should always be added to the lighter one so that rapid mixing results as a consequence of the law of gravity.

You will receive special instruction when it comes time to handle *metallic sodium, lithium aluminum hydride,* and *sodium hydride,* substances that can react explosively with water.

$HClO_4$ perchloric acid

Among the strong oxidizing agents, *perchloric acid* is probably the most hazardous. It can form heavy metal and organic *perchlorates* that are *explosive,* and it can react explosively if it comes in contact with organic compounds.

Should one of these substances get on the skin or in the eyes, wash the affected area with very large quantities of water, using the safety shower and/or eyewash foundation (Fig. 2.6). Do not attempt to neutralize the reagent chemically. Remove contaminated clothing so that thorough washing can take place. Take care to wash the reagent from under the fingernails.

When you are using very small quantities of these reagents, no particular safety equipment is needed except for *safety glasses.* Take care not to let the reagents, such as sulfuric acid, run down the outside of a bottle or flask and come in contact with the fingers. Wipe up spills immediately with a very damp sponge, especially in the area around the balances. Pellets of sodium and potassium hydroxide are very hygroscopic and will dissolve in the water they pick up from the air; therefore, they should be wiped up very quickly. When working with larger quantities of these corrosive chemicals, wear protective gloves; with still larger quantities, use a face mask, gloves, and a neoprene apron. The corrosive vapors can be avoided by carrying out work in a good exhaust hood.

Wipe up spilled hydroxide pellets rapidly.

Do not use the plastic syringe with the metal needle to dispense corrosive inorganic reagents, such as concentrated acids or bases.

Working with Toxic Substances

Many chemicals have very specific toxic effects. They interfere with the body's metabolism in a known way. For example, the cyanide ion combines irreversibly with hemoglobin to form cyanometmyoglobin, which can no longer carry oxygen. Aniline acts in the same way. Carbon tetrachloride and some other halogenated compounds cause liver and kidney failure. Carcinogenic and mutagenic substances deserve special attention because of their long-term insidious effects. The ability of certain carcinogens to cause cancer is very great; for example, special precautions are needed in handling aflatoxin B_1. In other cases, such as with dioxane, the hazard is so low that no special precautions are needed beyond reasonable normal care in the laboratory.

Women of childbearing age should be careful when handling any substance of unknown properties. Certain substances are highly suspect teratogens and will cause abnormalities in an embryo or fetus. Among these are benzene, toluene, xylene, aniline, nitrobenzene, phenol, formaldehyde, dimethylformamide (DMF),

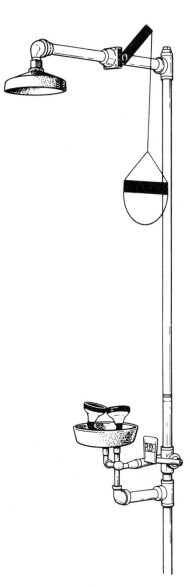

FIG. 2.6 Emergency shower and eyewash station.

dimethyl sulfoxide (DMSO), polychlorinated biphenyls (PCBs), estradiol, hydrogen sulfide, carbon disulfide, carbon monoxide, nitrites, nitrous oxide, organolead and mercury compounds, and the notorious sedative thalidomide. Some of these substances will be used in subsequent experiments. Use care. Of course, the leading known cause of embryotoxic effects is ethyl alcohol in the form of maternal alcoholism. The amount of ethanol vapor inhaled in the laboratory or absorbed through the skin is so small it is unlikely to have these morbid effects.

It is impossible to avoid handling every known or suspected toxic substance, so it is wise to know what measures should be taken. Because the eating of food or the consumption of beverages in the laboratory is strictly forbidden and because one should never taste material in the laboratory, the possibility of poisoning by mouth is remote. Be more careful than your predecessors—the hallucinogenic properties of LSD and **all** artificial sweeteners were discovered by accident. The two most important measures to be taken, then, are avoiding skin contact by wearing the *proper* type of protective gloves (see next section) and avoiding inhalation by working in a good exhaust hood.

Many of the chemicals used in this course will be unfamiliar to you. Their properties can be looked up in reference books, a very useful one being the *Aldrich Catalog Handbook of Fine Chemicals*. Note that 1,4-dichlorobenzene is listed as a "toxic irritant" and naphthalene is listed as an "irritant." Both are used as moth balls. Camphor, used in vaporizers, is classified as a "flammable solid irritant." Salicylic acid, which we will use to synthesize aspirin (Chapter 41) is listed as "moisture-sensitive toxic." Aspirin (acetylsalicylic acid) is classified as an "irritant." Caffeine, which we will isolate from tea or cola syrup (Chapter 8), is classified as "toxic." Substances not so familiar to you—1-naphthol and benzoic acid—are classified respectively as "toxic irritants" and "irritant." To put things in some perspective, nicotine is classified as "highly toxic." Pay attention to these health warnings. In laboratory quantities, common chemicals can be hazardous. Wash your hands carefully after coming in contact with laboratory chemicals. Consult Margaret-Ann Armour, *Hazardous Laboratory Chemicals Disposal Guide,* Lewis Publishers, Inc., 1996, for information on truly hazardous chemicals.

Because you have not had previous experience working with organic chemicals, most of the experiments you will carry out in this course will not involve the use of known carcinogens, although you will work routinely with flammable, corrosive, and toxic substances. A few experiments involve the use of substances that are suspected of being carcinogenic, such as hydrazine. If you pay proper attention to the rules of safety, you should find working with these substances no more hazardous than working with ammonia or nitric acid. The single, short-duration exposure you might receive from a suspected carcinogen, should an accident occur, would probably have no long-term consequences. The reason for taking the precautions noted in each experiment is to learn, from the beginning, good safety habits.

Gloves

Be aware that "protective gloves" in the organic laboratory may not offer much protection. Polyethylene and latex rubber gloves are very permeable to many organic liquids. An undetected pinhole can mean long-term contact with reagents. Disposable polyvinyl chloride (PVC) gloves offer reasonable protection from contact with aqueous solution of acids, bases, and dyes, but no one type of glove is useful as protection against all reagents. It is for this reason that no less than 25 different types of chemically resistant gloves are available from laboratory supply houses.

It is probably safer not to wear gloves and immediately wash your hands with soap and water after accidental contact with any harmful reagent or solvent than to wear inappropriate or defective gloves.

Using the Laboratory Hood

Modern practice dictates that in laboratories where workers spend most of their time working with chemicals, there should be one exhaust hood for every two people. This precaution is often not possible in the beginning organic chemistry laboratory, however. In this course you will find that for some experiments the hood must be used and for others it is adivsable; in these instances, it may be necessary to schedule experimental work around access to the hoods. However, many experiments formerly carried out in the hood can now be carried out at the desk because the concentration of vapors will be minimal when working at a microscale.

The hood offers a number of advantages for work with toxic and flammable substances. Not only does it draw off the toxic and flammable fumes, it also affords an excellent physical barrier on all four sides of a reacting system when the sash is pulled down. And should a chemical spill occur, it is nicely contained within the hood.

Keep the hood sash closed.

It is your responsibility each time you use a hood to see that it is working properly. You should find some type of indicating device that will give you this information on the hood itself. A simple propeller on a cork works well (Fig. 2.7). The hood is a backup device. Don't use it alone to dispose of chemicals by evaporation; use an aspirator tube or carry out a distillation. Toxic and flammable fumes should be trapped or condensed in some way and disposed of in the prescribed manner. Except when you are actually carrying out manipulations on the experimental apparatus, the sash should be pulled down. The water, gas, and elec-

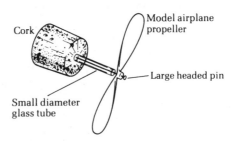

FIG. 2.7 Air flow indicator for hoods. The indicator should be permanently mounted in the hood and should be spinning whenever the hood is in operation.

trical controls should be on the outside of the hood so it is not necessary to open the hood to adjust them. The ability of the hood to remove vapors is greatly enhanced if the apparatus is kept as close to the back of the hood as possible. Everything should be at least 15 cm back from the hood sash. Chemicals should not be stored permanently in the hood but should be removed to ventilated storage areas. If the hood is cluttered with chemicals, you will not have good, smooth air flow or adequate room for experiments.

Working at Reduced Pressure

Implosion

Whenever a vessel or system is evacuated, an implosion could result from atmospheric pressure on the empty vessel. It makes little difference whether the vacuum is perfect or just 10 mm Hg; the pressure difference is almost the same (760 versus 750 mm Hg). An implosion may occur if there is a star crack in the flask or if the flask is scratched or etched. Only with heavy-walled flasks specifically designed for vacuum filtration is the use of a safety shield (Fig. 2.8) ordinarily unnecessary. The chances of implosion of the apparatus used for microscale experiments are very small.

Dewar flasks (thermos bottles) are often found in the laboratory without shielding. They should be wrapped with friction tape or covered with plastic net to prevent the glass from flying about in case of an implosion (Fig. 2.9). Similarly, vacuum desiccators should be wrapped with tape before being evacuated.

FIG. 2.8 Safety shield.

Working with Compressed Gas Cylinders

Many reactions are carried out under an inert atmosphere so that the reactants and/or products will not react with oxygen or moisture in the air. Nitrogen and argon are the inert gases most frequently used. Oxygen is widely used both as a reactant and to provide a hot flame for glassblowing and welding. It is used in the oxidative coupling of alkynes (Chapter 24). Helium is the carrier gas used in gas chromatography. Some other gases commonly used in the laboratory are ammonia, often used as a solvent; chlorine, used for chlorination reactions; acetylene, used in combination with oxygen for welding; and hydrogen used for high- and low-pressure hydrogenation reactions.

Always clamp gas cylinders.

The following rule applies to all compressed gases: Compressed gas cylinders should be firmly secured at all times. For temporary use, a clamp that attaches to the laboratory bench top and has a belt for the cylinder will suffice (Fig. 2.10). Eyebolts and chains should be used to secure cylinders in permanent installations.

A variety of outlet threads are used on gas cylinders to prevent incompatible gases from becoming mixed because of an interchange of connections. Both right- and left-handed external and internal threads are used. Left-handed nuts are notched to differentiate them from right-handed nuts. Right-handed threads are used on nonfuel and oxidizing gases, and left-handed threads are used on fuel gases, such as hydrogen.

FIG. 2.9 Dewar flask with safety net in place.

Cylinders come equipped with caps that should be left in place during storage and transportation. These caps can be removed by hand. Under these caps is

FIG. 2.10   Gas cylinder clamp.

a hand wheel valve. It can be opened by turning the wheel counterclockwise; however, because most compressed gases in full cylinders are under very high pressure (commonly up to 3000 lb/in.^{2}), a pressure regulator must be attached to the cylinder. This pressure regulator is almost always of the diaphragm type and has two gauges, one indicating the pressure in the cylinder, the other the outlet pressure (Fig. 2.11). On the outlet, low-pressure side of the regulator is located a

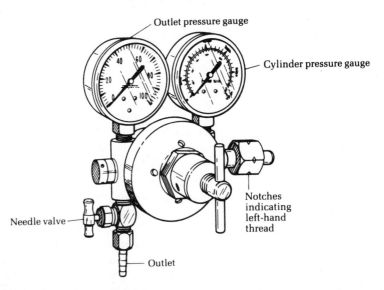

FIG. 2.11   Gas pressure regulator. Turn two-flanged diaphragm valve *clockwise* to increase outlet pressure.

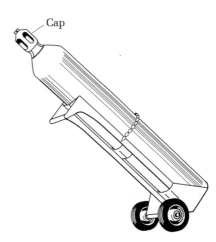

FIG. 2.12 Gas cylinder cart.

small needle valve and then the outlet connector. After connecting the regulator to the cylinder, unscrew the diaphragm valve (turn it counterclockwise) before opening the hand wheel valve on the top of the cylinder. This valve should be opened only as far as necessary. For most gas flow rates in the laboratory, this will be a very small amount. The gas flow and/or pressure is increased by turning the two-flanged diaphragm valve **clockwise**. When the apparatus is not being used, turn off the hand wheel valve (clockwise) on the top of the cylinder (Fig. 2.10). Before removing the regulator from the cylinder, reduce the flow or pressure to zero. Cylinders should never be emptied to zero pressure and left with the valve open because the residual contents will become contaminated with air. Empty cylinders should be labeled "empty," and their valves should be closed, capped, and returned to the storage area, separated from full cylinders. Gas cylinders should never be dragged or rolled from place to place but should be fastened into and moved in a cart designed for the purpose (Fig. 2.12).

Clockwise movement of diaphragm valve handle increases pressure.

Waste Disposal—Cleaning Up

Spilled solids should simply be swept up and placed in the appropriate solid waste container. This should be done promptly, because many solids are hygroscopic and become difficult if not impossible to sweep up in a short time. This is particularly true of sodium hydroxide and potassium hydroxide.

Spilled acids should be neutralized. Use sodium carbonate or, for larger spills, cement or limestone. For bases use sodium bisulfate. If the spilled material is very volatile, clear the area and let it evaporate, provided there is no chance of igniting flammable vapors. Other liquids can be taken up into such absorbents as vermiculite, diatomaceous earth, dry sand, kitty litter, or paper towels. Be particularly careful in wiping up spills with paper towels. If a strong oxidizer is present, the towels can later ignite. Bits of sodium metal will also cause paper towels to ignite. Sodium metal is best destroyed with *n*-butyl alcohol. Unless you are sure

Clean up spills rapidly.

Mercury requires special measures—see instructor.

the spilled liquid is not toxic, wear gloves when using paper towels or a sponge to remove the liquid.

Cleaning Up.

Waste containers:
  Nonhazardous solid waste
  Organic solvents
  Halogenated organic solvents
  Hazardous waste (various types)

Cleaning Up.   In the not-too-distant past it was common practice to wash all unwanted liquids from the organic laboratory down the drain and to place all solid waste in the trash basket. This was never a wise practice, and now, for environmental reasons, this is no longer allowed by law.

Organic reactions usually employ a solvent and often involve the use of a strong acid, a strong base, an oxidant, a reductant, or a catalyst. None of these should be washed down the drain or placed in the wastebasket. We will place the material we finally classify as waste in containers labeled for nonhazardous solid waste, organic solvents, halogenated organic solvents, and hazardous wastes of various types.

Nonhazardous waste encompasses such solids as paper, corks, sand, alumina, and sodium sulfate. These ultimately will end up in a sanitary landfill (the local dump). Any chemicals that are leached by rainwater from this landfill must not be harmful to the environment. In the *organic solvents* container are placed the solvents that are used for recrystallization and for running reactions, cleaning apparatus, etc. These solvents can contain dissolved, solid, nonhazardous organic solids. This solution will go to an incinerator where it will be burned. If the solvent is a halogenated one (e.g., dichloromethane) or contains halogenated material, it must go in the *halogenated organic solvents* container. Ultimately this will go to a special incinerator equipped with a scrubber to remove HCl from the combustion gases. The final container is for various *hazardous wastes*. Because hazardous wastes are often incompatible (oxidants with reductants, cyanides with acids, etc.), several different containers may be provided in the laboratory for these, e.g., for phosphorus compounds, heavy metal hydroxides, mercury salts, etc.

Waste disposal is very expensive.

Some hazardous wastes are concentrated nitric acid, platinum catalysts, sodium hydrosulfite (a reducing agent), and Cr^{6+} (an oxidizing agent). To dispose of small quantities of a hazardous waste, e.g., concentrated sulfuric acid, the material must be carefully packed in bottles and placed in a 55-gal drum called a lab pack, to which is added an inert packing material. The lab pack is carefully documented and then hauled off by a bonded, licensed, and heavily regulated waste disposal company to a site where such waste is disposed of. Formerly, many hazardous wastes were disposed of by burial in a "secure landfill." The kinds of hazardous waste that can be thus disposed of have become extremely limited in recent years, and much of the waste undergoes various kinds of treatment at the disposal site (e.g., neutralization, incineration, reduction) to put it in a form that can be safely buried in a secure landfill or flushed to a sewer. There are relatively few places for approved disposal of hazardous waste. For example, there are none in New England, so most hazardous waste from this area is trucked to South Carolina! The charge to small generators of waste is usually based on the volume of waste. So, 1000 mL of a 2% cyanide solution would cost much more to dispose of than 20 g of solid cyanide, even though the total amount of this poisonous substance is the same. It now costs much more to dispose of most hazardous chemicals than it does to purchase them new.

The law: A waste is not a waste until the laboratory worker declares it a waste.

Cleaning up: reducing the volume of hazardous waste or converting hazardous waste to less hazardous or nonhazardous waste

American law states that a material is not a waste until the laboratory worker declares it a waste. So for pedagogical and practical reasons, we would like you to regard the chemical treatment of the byproducts of each reaction in this text as a part of the experiment.

In the section entitled "Cleaning Up" at the end of each experiment, the goal is to reduce the volume of hazardous waste, to convert hazardous waste to less hazardous waste, or to convert it to nonhazardous waste. The simplest example is concentrated sulfuric acid. As a byproduct from a reaction, it is obviously hazardous. But after careful dilution with water and neutralization with sodium carbonate, the sulfuric acid becomes a dilute solution of sodium sulfate, which in almost every locale can be flushed down the drain with a large excess of water. Anything flushed down the drain must be accompanied by a large excess of water. Similarly, concentrated base can be neutralized, oxidants such as Cr^{6+} can be reduced, and reductants such as hydrosulfite can be oxidized (by hypochlorite—household bleach). Dilute solutions of heavy metal ions can be precipitated as their insoluble sulfides or hydroxides. The precipitate may still be a hazardous waste, but it will have a much smaller volume.

Disposing of solids wet with organic solvents: alumina and anhydrous calcium chloride pellets

One type of hazardous waste is unique: a harmless solid that is damp with an organic solvent. Alumina from a chromatography column and calcium chloride used to dry an ether solution are examples. Being solids, they obviously can't go in the organic solvents container, and being flammable they can't go in the nonhazardous waste container. A solution to this problem is to spread the solid out in the hood to let the solvent evaporate. You can then place the solid in the nonhazardous waste container. The saving in waste disposal costs by this operation is enormous.

Our goal in "Cleaning Up" is to make you more aware of *all* aspects of an experiment. Waste disposal is now an extremely important aspect. Check to be sure the procedure you use is legal in your location. Three sources of information have been used as the basis of the procedures at the end of each experiment: the *Aldrich Catalog Handbook of Fine Chemicals,* which gives brief disposal procedures for every chemical in their catalog; *Prudent Practices in the Laboratory: Handling and Disposal of Chemicals,* National Academy Press, Washington, DC, 1995; and *Hazardous Laboratory Chemicals Disposal Guide,* M.-A. Armour, Lewis Publishers, Inc., 1996. The last title should be on the bookshelf of every laboratory. This 464-page book gives detailed information about several hundred hazardous substances, including physical properties, hazardous reactions, physiological properties and health hazards, spillage disposal, and waste disposal. Many of the treatment procedures in "Cleaning Up" are adaptations of these procedures. *Destruction of Hazardous Chemicals in the Laboratory*, G. Lunn and E. B. Sansone, Wiley, New York, NY, 1994, complements this book.

The area of waste disposal is changing rapidly. Many different laws apply—local, state, and federal. What may be permissible to wash down the drain or evaporate in the hood in one jurisdiction may be illegal in another, so before carrying out this part of the experiment check with your college or university waste disposal officer.

Questions

1. Write a balanced equation for the reaction between iodide ion, a peroxide, and hydrogen ion. What causes the orange or brown color?

2. Why does the horn of the carbon dioxide fire extinguisher become cold when the extinguisher is used?

3. Why is water not used to put out most fires in the organic laboratory?

3

Crystallization

Prelab Exercise: Write an expanded outline for the seven-step process of crystallization.

Crystallization: the most important purification method for solids, especially for small-scale experiments

On both a large and small scale, *crystallization* is the most important method for the purification of solid organic compounds. A crystalline organic substance is made up of a three-dimensional array of molecules held together primarily by van der Waals forces. These intramolecular attractions are fairly weak; most organic solids melt in the range of room temperature to 250°C.

Crystals can be grown from the molten state just as water is frozen into ice, but it is not easy to remove impurities from crystals made in this way. Thus most purifications in the laboratory involve dissolving the material to be purified in the appropriate hot solvent. As the solvent cools, the solution becomes saturated with respect to the substance, which then crystallizes. As the perfectly regular array of a crystal is formed, foreign molecules are excluded, and thus the crystal is one pure substance. Soluble impurities stay in solution because they are not concentrated enough to saturate the solution. The crystals are collected by *filtration,* the surface of the crystals is washed with cold solvent to remove the adhering impurities, and then the crystals are dried. This process is carried out on an enormous scale in the commercial purification of sugar.

In the organic laboratory, crystallization is usually the most rapid and convenient method for purifying the products of a reaction. Initially you will be told which solvent to use to crystallize a given substance and how much of it to use; later on you will judge how much solvent is needed; and finally the choice of both the solvent and its volume will be left to you. It takes both experience and knowledge to pick the correct solvent for a given purification.

The Seven Steps of Crystallization

The process of crystallization can be broken into seven discrete steps: choosing the solvent, dissolving the *solute, decolorizing* the solution, removing suspended solids, crystallizing the solute, collecting and washing the crystals, and drying the product. The process involves dissolving the impure substance in an appropriate hot solvent, removing some impurities by decolorizing and/or filtering the hot solution, allowing the substance to crystallize as the temperature of the solution falls, removing the crystallization solvent, and drying the resulting purified crystals.

How crystallization starts

Crystallization is initiated at a point of nucleation—a seed crystal, a speck of dust, or a scratch on the wall of the test tube if the solution is supersaturated

TABLE 3.1   Crystallization Solvents

Solvent	Boiling Point (°C)	Remarks
Water (H_2O)	100	The solvent of choice because it is cheap, nonflammable, and nontoxic and will dissolve a large variety of polar organic molecules. Its high boiling point and high heat of vaporization make it difficult to remove from crystals.
Acetic acid (CH_3COOH)	118	Will react with alcohols and amines. Difficult to remove from crystals. Not a common solvent for recrystallizations, although used as a solvent when carrying out oxidation reactions.
Dimethyl sulfoxide (DMSO), methyl sulfoxide (CH_3SOCH_3)	189	Also not a commonly used solvent for crystallization, but used for reactions.
Methanol (CH_3OH)	64	A very good solvent, used often for crystallization. Will dissolve molecules of higher polarity than will the other alcohols.
95% Ethanol (CH_3CH_2OH)	78	One of the most commonly used crystallization solvents. Its high boiling point makes it a better solvent for the less polar molecules than methanol. Evaporates readily from the crystals. Esters may undergo interchange of alcohol groups on recrystallization.
Acetone (CH_3COCH_3)	56	An excellent solvent, but its low boiling point means there is not much difference in solubility of a compound at its boiling point and at room temperature.
2-Butanone, methyl ethyl ketone, MEK ($CH_3COCH_2CH_3$)	80	An excellent solvent with many of the most desirable properties of a good crystallization solvent.
Ethyl acetate ($CH_3COOC_2H_5$)	78	Another excellent solvent that has about the right combination of moderately high boiling point and yet the volatility needed to remove it from crystals.
Dichloromethane, methylene chloride (CH_2Cl_2)	40	Although a common extraction solvent, dichloromethane boils too low to make it a good crystallization solvent. It is useful in a solvent pair with ligroin.

(continued)

Note: The solvents in this table are listed in decreasing order of polarity. Adjacent solvents in the list will in general be miscible with each other.

with respect to the substance being crystallized (the solute). Supersaturation will occur if a hot, saturated solution cools and crystals do not form. Large crystals, which are easy to isolate, are formed by nucleation and then slow cooling of the hot solution.

1. Choosing the Solvent and Solvent Pairs

Similia similibus solvuntur

In choosing the solvent the chemist is guided by the dictum "like dissolves like." Even the nonchemist knows that oil and water do not mix and that sugar and salt dissolve in water but not in oil. Hydrocarbon solvents such as hexane will dissolve hydrocarbons and other nonpolar compounds, and hydroxylic solvents such as water and ethanol will dissolve polar compounds. Often it is difficult to decide, simply by looking at the structure of a molecule, just how polar or nonpolar it is

TABLE 3.1   *continued*

Solvent	Boiling Point (°C)	Remarks
Diethyl ether, ether ($CH_3CH_2OCH_2CH_3$)	35	Its boiling point is too low for crystallization, although it is an extremely good solvent and fairly inert. Used in solvent pair with ligroin.
Methyl *t*-butyl ether ($CH_3OC(CH_3)_3$)	52	A relatively new solvent that is very inexpensive because of its large-scale use as an antiknock agent and oxygenate in gasoline. Does not easily form peroxides, and is less volatile than diethyl ether, but has the same solvent characteristics. See sidebar in Chapter 8.
Dioxane ($C_4H_8O_2$)	101	A very good solvent, not too difficult to remove from crystals; a mild carcinogen, forms peroxides.
Toluene ($C_6H_5CH_3$)	111	An excellent solvent that has replaced the formerly widely used benzene (a weak carcinogen) for crystallization of aryl compounds. Because of its boiling point it is not easily removed from crystals.
Pentane (C_5H_{12})	36	A widely used solvent for nonpolar substances. Not often used alone for crystallization, but good in combination with a number of other solvents as part of a solvent pair.
Hexane (C_6H_{14})	69	Frequently used to crystallize nonpolar substances. It is inert and has the correct balance between boiling point and volatility. Often used as part of a solvent pair. See ligroin.
Cyclohexane (C_6H_{12})	81	Similar in all respects to hexane. See ligroin.
Petroleum ether	30–60	A mixture of hydrocarbons of which pentane is a chief component. Used interchangeably with pentane because it is cheap. Unlike diethyl ether or *t*-butyl methyl ether, it is not an ether in the modern chemical sense.
Ligroin	60–90	A mixture of hydrocarbons with the properties of hexane and cyclohexane. A very commonly used crystallization solvent. Also sold as "hexanes."

The ideal solvent

Miscible: capable of being mixed

and therefore which solvent would be best. Therefore, the solvent is often chosen by experimentation.

The best crystallization solvent (and none is ideal) will dissolve the solute when the solution is hot but not when the solution is cold; it will either not dissolve the impurities at all or it will dissolve them very well (so they won't crystallize out along with the solute); it will not react with the solute; and it will be nonflammable, nontoxic, inexpensive, and very volatile (so it can be removed from the crystals).

Some common solvents and their properties are presented in Table 3.1 in order of decreasing polarity of the solvent. Solvents adjacent to each other in the list will dissolve in each other, i.e., they are miscible with each other, and each solvent will, in general, dissolve substances that are similar to it in chemical structure. These solvents are used both for crystallization and as solvents in which reactions are carried out.

Procedure

Picking a Solvent.

To pick a solvent for crystallization, put a few crystals of the impure solute in a small test tube or centrifuge tube, and add a very small drop of the solvent. Allow it to flow down the side of the tube and onto the crystals. If the crystals dissolve instantly at room temperature, that solvent cannot be used for crystallization because too much of the solute will remain in solution at low temperatures. If the crystals do not dissolve at room temperature, warm the tube on the hot sand bath, and observe the crystals. If they do not go into solution, add a drop more solvent. If the crystals go into solution at the boiling point of the solvent and then crystallize when the tube is cooled, you have found a good crystallization solvent. If not, remove the solvent by evaporation, and try another solvent. In this trial-and-error process it is easiest to try low-boiling solvents first, because they can be removed most easily. Occasionally no single satisfactory solvent can be found, so mixed solvents, or *solvent pairs,* are used.

Solvent Pairs. To use a mixed solvent, dissolve the crystals in the better solvent, and add the poorer solvent to the hot solution until it becomes cloudy and the solution is saturated with the solute. The two solvents must, of course, be miscible with each other. Some useful solvent pairs are given in Table 3.2.

2. Dissolving the Solute

Microscale Procedure

Once a crystallization solvent has been found, the impure crystals are placed in a reaction tube, solvent is added dropwise, the crystals are stirred with a microspatula or a small glass rod, and the tube is warmed on a steam bath or sand bath with the addition of more solvent until the crystals dissolve. A solution of this type can become *superheated,* that is, heated above its boiling point without actually boiling. When boiling does suddenly occur, it can happen with almost explosive violence. To prevent this from happening, a *wood applicator stick* can be added to the solution (Fig. 3.1). Air trapped in the wood comes out of the stick and forms the nuclei on which even boiling can occur. Porous porcelain *boiling chips* work in the same way. Never add a boiling chip or boiling stick to a hot solution, since it may be superheated and boil over.

Prevention of bumping

Do not use wood boiling sticks in place of boiling chips in a reaction. Use them only for crystallization.

    To remove solid impurities (insoluble byproducts of reaction, lint, dust, etc.), it is necessary to dilute the solution with excess solvent (the better solvent if a solvent mixture is being used), carry out the filtration near room temperature, and then evaporate the solvent to a point at which the hot solution is once more

TABLE 3.2 Solvent Pairs

Acetic acid–water	Ethyl acetate–cyclohexane
Ethanol–water	Acetone–ligroin
Acetone–water	Ethyl acetate–ligroin
Dioxane–water	*t*-Butyl methyl ether–ligroin
Acetone–ethanol	Dichloromethane–ligroin
Ethanol–*t*-butyl methyl ether	Toluene–ligroin

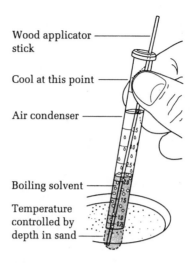

Wood applicator stick

Cool at this point

Air condenser

Boiling solvent

Temperature controlled by depth in sand

FIG. 3.1   The reaction tube being used for crystallization. The wood applicator stick ("boiling stick") promotes even boiling and is easier to remove than a boiling chip. The Thermowell sand is cool on top and hotter down deeper, so it provides a range of temperatures. The reaction tube is long and narrow; it can be held in the hand while the solvent refluxes. Do not use a boiling stick in place of a boiling chip in a reaction.

saturated with respect to the solute so that crystallization can take place in the usual way. This is described in Step 4.

Care must be exercised to use the correct amount of solvent. Observe the mixture carefully as solvent is being added. Allow sufficient time for the boiling solvent to dissolve the solute, and note the rate at which most of the material dissolves. When you believe most of the material has been dissolved, stop adding solvent. There is the possibility that your sample is contaminated with a small quantity of an insoluble impurity that never will dissolve. To hasten the solution process, crush large crystals with a stirring rod, taking care not to break the tube.

Don't use too much solvent.

On a microscale, there is a tendency to use too much solvent so that on cooling the hot solution little or no material crystallizes. This is not a hopeless situation. The remedy is to evaporate some of the solvent and repeat the cooling process. Inspect the hot solution. If it contains no undissolved impurities and is not colored from impurities, you can simply let it cool, allowing the solute to crystallize (Step 5), and then collect the crystals (Step 6). On the other hand, if the solution is colored, it must be treated with activated (decolorizing) charcoal and then filtered before crystallization (Step 3). If it contains solid impurities, it must be filtered before crystallization takes place (Step 4).

 ## Macroscale Procedure

Place the substance to be crystallized in an Erlenmeyer flask (never use a beaker), add enough solvent to cover the crystals, and then heat the flask on a steam bath (if the solvent boils below 90°C) or a hot plate until the solvent boils. Stir the

FIG. 3.2 Swirling of a solution to mix contents and help dissolve material to be crystallized.

MICROSCALE
AND MACROSCALE

Activated charcoal = decolorizing carbon = Norit

Pelletized Norit (also called active carbon, activated charcoal, decolorizing carbon)

mixture or, better, swirl it (Fig. 3.2) to promote dissolution. Add solvent gradually, keeping it at the boil, until all of the solute dissolves. Addition of a boiling stick or a boiling chip to the solution once most of the solid is gone will promote even boiling. It is not difficult to superheat the solution, i.e., heat it above the boiling point with no boiling taking place. Once the solution does boil it does so with explosive violence. Never add a boiling chip or boiling stick to a hot solution. A glass rod with a flattened end can sometimes be of use in crushing large particles of solute to speed up the dissolving process. Be sure no flames are nearby when working with flammable solvents.

Be careful not to add too much solvent. Note how rapidly most of the material dissolves, and then stop adding solvent when you suspect that almost all of the desired material has dissolved. It is best to err on the side of too little solvent rather than too much. Undissolved material noted at this point could be an insoluble impurity that never will dissolve. Allow the solvent to boil, and if no further material dissolves, proceed to Step 4 to remove suspended solids from the solution by filtration, or if the solution is colored, go to Step 3 to carry out the decolorization process. If the solution is clear, proceed to Step 5, Crystallizing the Solute.

3. Decolorizing the Solution; Use of Pelletized Norit

The vast majority of pure organic chemicals are colorless or a light shade of yellow. Occasionally a chemical reaction will produce high molecular weight byproducts that are highly colored. The impurities can be adsorbed onto the surface of activated charcoal by simply boiling the solution with charcoal. Activated charcoal has an extremely large surface area per gram (several hundred square meters) and can bind a large number of molecules to this surface. On a commercial scale, the impurities in brown sugar are adsorbed onto charcoal in the process of refining sugar.

In the past, laboratory manuals have advocated the use of finely powdered activated charcoal for removal of colored impurities. This has two drawbacks. Because the charcoal is so finely divided it can only be separated from the solution by filtration through paper, and even then some of the finer particles pass through the filter paper. And the presence of the charcoal completely obscures the color of the solution, so that adding the correct amount of charcoal is mostly a matter of luck. If too little charcoal is added, the solution will still be colored after filtration, making repetition necessary; if too much is added, it will absorb some of the product in addition to the impurities. We have found that charcoal extruded as short cylindrical pieces measuring about 0.8 × 3 mm made by the Norit Company solves both of these problems. It works just as well as the finely divided powder, and it does not obscure the color of the solution. It can be added in small portions until the solution is decolorized and the size of the pieces makes it easy to remove from the solution.[1]

---

1. Available from Aldrich Chemical Co., 940 West St. Paul Ave., Milwaukee, WI 53233. Catalog number 32942-8 as Norit RO 0.8. This form of Norit is an extrudate 0.8 mm dia. It has a surface area of 1000 m^2/g, a total pore volume of 1.1 mL/g.

Add a small amount (0.1% of the solute weight is sufficient) of pelletized Norit to the colored solution, and then boil the solution for a few minutes. Be careful not to add the charcoal pieces to a superheated solution; the charcoal functions like hundreds of boiling chips and will cause the solution to boil over. Remove the Norit by filtration as described in Step 4.

4. Filtering Suspended Solids

The filtration of a hot, saturated solution to remove solid impurities or charcoal can be done in a number of ways. Processes include gravity filtration, pressure filtration, decantation, or removal of the solvent using a Pasteur pipette. Vacuum filtration is not used because the hot solvent will cool during the process and the product will crystallize in the filter.

Microscale Procedure

(A) Removal of Solution with a Pasteur Pipette. If the solid impurities are large in size, they can be removed by filtration of the liquid through the small space between the square end of a Pasteur pipette and the bottom of a reaction tube (Fig. 3.3). Expel air from the pipette as it is being pushed to the bottom of the tube. Use a small additional quantity of solvent to rinse the tube and pipette. Anhydrous calcium chloride, a drying agent, is removed easily in this way. Removal of very fine material, such as traces of charcoal, is facilitated by filtration of the solution through a small piece of filter paper (3 mm^2) placed in the reaction tube. This process is even easier if the filter paper is the thick variety, such as that from which Soxhlet extraction thimbles are made.[2]

(B) Filtration in a Pasteur Pipette. To filter 0.1 to 2 mL of a solution, dilute the solution with enough solvent that the solute will not crystallize out at room temperature. Prepare a filter pipette by pushing a tiny bit of cotton into a Pasteur pipette, put the solution to be filtered into this filter pipette using another Pasteur pipette, and then force the liquid through the filter using air pressure from a pipette bulb (Fig. 3.4). Fresh solvent should be added to rinse the pipette and cotton. The filtered solution is then concentrated by evaporation. One problem encountered with this method is using too much cotton packed too tightly in the pipette so that the solution cannot be forced through it. To remove very fine impurities, such as traces of decolorizing charcoal, a 3- to 4-mm layer of Celite filter aid can be added to the top of the cotton.

(C) Removal of Fine Impurities by Centrifugation. To remove fine solid impurities from up to 4 mL of solution, dilute the solution with enough solvent that the solute will not crystallize out at room temperature. Counterbalance the reaction tube, and centrifuge for about two min at high speed in a laboratory

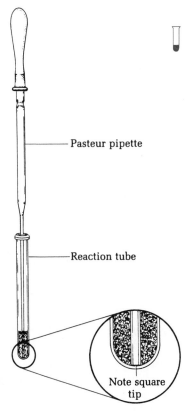

Pasteur pipette

Reaction tube

Note square tip

FIG. 3.3 Filtration using the Pasteur pipette and reaction.

---

2. J. L. Belletire and N. O. Mahmoodi, *J. Chem. Ed.* **66**:964, 1989.

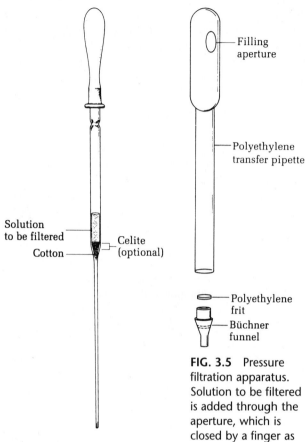

Solution
to be filtered

Celite
(optional)

Cotton

FIG. 3.4 Filtration of a
solution in a Pasteur
pipette.

Filling
aperture

Polyethylene
transfer pipette

Polyethylene
frit

Büchner
funnel

FIG. 3.5 Pressure
filtration apparatus.
Solution to be filtered
is added through the
aperture, which is
closed by a finger as
pressure is applied.

FIG. 3.6 Gravity filtration of
hot solution through fluted filter
paper.

centrifuge. The clear supernatant can be decanted (poured off) from the solid on
the bottom of the tube. Alternatively, with care, the solution can be removed with
a Pasteur pipette, leaving the solid behind.

(D) Pressure Filtration with Micro Büchner Funnel.

The technique
applicable to volumes from 0.1 to 5 mL is the use of the *micro Büchner funnel.* It
is made of polyethylene and is fitted with a porous *polyethylene frit* 6 mm in
diameter. This funnel fits in the bottom of an inexpensive disposable polyethylene pipette in which a hole is cut (Fig. 3.5). The solution to be filtered is placed
in the pipette using a Pasteur pipette. The thumb covers the hole in the plastic
pipette, and pressure is applied to filter the solution. It is good practice to place a
6-mm-diameter piece of filter paper over the frit, which can otherwise become
clogged with insoluble material.

Use filter paper on top of frit.

*Using the chromatography
column for pressure filtration*

The glass chromatography column can be used in the same way. A piece of
filter paper is placed over the frit. The solution to be filtered is placed in the chromatography column, and pressure is applied to the solution using a pipette bulb.
In both procedures, dilute the solution to be filtered so that it does not crystallize

out in the apparatus, and use a small amount of clean solvent to rinse the apparatus. The filtered solution is then concentrated by evaporation.

Macroscale Procedure

Decant: to pour off. A fast, easy separation procedure

(A) Decantation. On a large scale, it is often possible to pour off (decant) the hot solution leaving the insoluble material behind. This is especially easy if the solid is granular like sodium sulfate. The solid remaining in the flask and the inside of the flask should be rinsed with a few milliliters of the solvent in order to recover as much of the product as possible.

(B) Gravity Filtration. The most common method for the removal of insoluble solid material is gravity filtration through a fluted filter paper (Fig. 3.6). This is the method of choice for the removal of finely divided charcoal, dust, lint, etc. The following equipment is needed for this process: three Erlenmeyer flasks on a steam bath or hot plate—one to contain the solution to be filtered, one to contain a few milliliters of solvent and a stemless funnel, and the third to contain several milliliters of the crystallizing solvent to be used for rinsing purposes—a fluted piece of filter paper, a towel for holding the hot flask and drying out the stemless funnel, and boiling chips for all solutions.

A piece of filter paper is fluted as shown in Fig. 3.7 and is then placed in a stemless funnel. Appropriate sizes of Erlenmeyer flasks, stemless funnels, and filter paper are shown in Fig. 3.8. The funnel is stemless so that the saturated solution being filtered will not have a chance to cool and clog the stem with crystals. The filter paper should fit entirely inside the rim of the funnel; it is fluted to allow rapid filtration. Test to see that the funnel is stable in the neck of the Erlenmeyer flask. If it is not, support it with a ring attached to a ring stand. A few milliliters of solvent and a boiling chip should be placed in the flask into which the solution is to be filtered. This solvent is brought to a boil on the steam bath or hot plate along with the solution to be filtered.

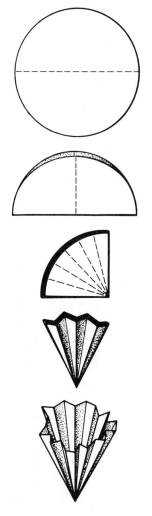

FIG. 3.7 Fluting a filter paper.

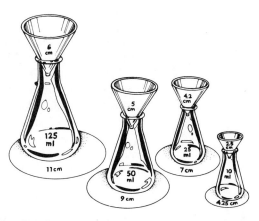

FIG. 3.8 Assemblies for gravity filtration. Stemless funnels have diameters of 2.5, 4.2, 5.0, and 6.0 cm.

The solution to be filtered should be saturated with the solute at the boiling point. Note the volume, and then add 10% more solvent. The resulting slightly dilute solution is not as likely to crystallize out in the funnel in the process of filtration. Bring the solution to be filtered to a boil, grasp the flask in a towel, and pour the solution into the filter paper in the stemless funnel (Fig. 3.6).

The funnel should be warm in order to prevent crystallization from occurring in the funnel. This can be accomplished in two ways: (1) Invert the funnel over a steam bath for a few seconds, then pick up the funnel with a towel, wipe it perfectly dry, place it on top of the Erlenmeyer flask, and add the fluted filter paper, or (2) place the stemless funnel in the neck of the Erlenmeyer flask and allow the solvent to reflux into the funnel, thereby warming it.

Pour the solution to be filtered at a steady rate into the fluted filter paper. Check to see whether crystallization is occurring in the filter. If it does, add boiling solvent (from the third Erlenmeyer flask heated on the steam bath or hot plate) until the crystals dissolve, dilute the solution being filtered, and carry on. Rinse the flask that contained the solution to be filtered with a few milliliters of boiling solvent, and rinse the fluted filter paper with this same solvent.

Be aware that the vapors of low-boiling solvents can ignite on an electric hot plate.

Because the filtrate has been diluted in order to prevent it from crystallizing during the filtration process, the excess solvent must now be removed by boiling the solution. The process can be speeded up somewhat by blowing a slow current of air into the flask in the hood or using an aspirator tube to pull vapors into the aspirator (Figs. 3.9 and 3.10). However, the fastest method is to heat the solvent in the filter flask on the sand bath while the flask is connected to the water aspirator. The vacuum is controlled with the thumb (Fig. 3.11).[3] If your thumb is not large enough, put a one-holed rubber stopper into the Hirsch funnel or the filter flask and again control the vacuum with the thumb. If the vacuum is not controlled, the solution may boil over and go out the vacuum hose.

5. Crystallizing the Solute

On both a macroscale and a microscale, the crystallization process should normally start from a solution that is saturated with the solute at the boiling point. If it has been necessary to remove impurities or charcoal by filtration, the solution has been diluted. To concentrate the solution, simply boil off the solvent under an aspirator tube as shown in Fig. 3.9 (macroscale) or blow off solvent using a gentle stream of air or, better, nitrogen in the hood as shown in Fig. 3.10 (microscale). Be sure to have a boiling chip (macroscale) or a boiling stick (microscale) in the solution during this process, and then do not forget to remove it before initiating crystallization.

A saturated solution

Once it has been ascertained that the hot solution is saturated with the compound just below the boiling point of the solvent, it is allowed to cool slowly to room temperature. Crystallization should begin immediately. If it does not, add a

---

3. D. W. Mayo, R. M. Pike, and S. M. Butcher, *Microscale Organic Laboratory* (New York, Wiley, 1986), p. 97.

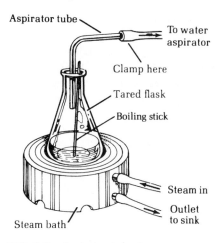

FIG. 3.9 Aspirator tube in use. A boiling stick may be necessary to promote even boiling.

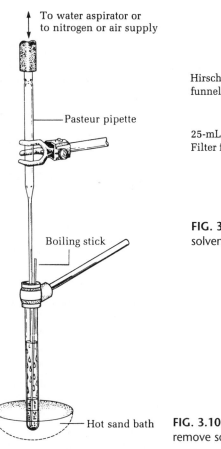

FIG. 3.10 Tube being used to remove solvent vapors.

FIG. 3.11 Evaporation of a solvent under a vacuum.

Add a seed crystal.

seed crystal or scratch the inside of the tube with a glass rod at the liquid–air interface. Crystallization must start on some nucleation center. A minute crystal of the desired compound saved from the crude material will suffice. If a seed crystal is not available, crystallization can be started on the rough surface of a fresh scratch on the inside of the container.

Slow cooling is important.

Once it is ascertained that crystallization has started, the solution must be cooled slowly without disturbing the container in order that large crystals can form. On a microscale, it is best to allow the reaction tube to cool in a beaker filled with cotton or paper towels, which act as insulation so cooling takes place slowly. Even insulated in this manner, the small reaction tube will cool to room temperature within a few minutes. Slow cooling will guarantee the formation of large crystals, which are easily separated by filtration and easily washed free of adhering impure solvent. On a small scale, it is difficult to obtain crystals that are too large and occlude impurities. Once the tube has cooled to room temperature without disturbance, it can be cooled in ice to maximize the amount of product that comes out of solution. The crystals are then separated from the *mother liquor* (the *filtrate*) by filtration.

On a macroscale, the Erlenmeyer flask is set atop a cork ring or other insulator and allowed to cool spontaneously to room temperature. If the flask is moved during crystallization, many nuclei will form and the crystals will be small and will have a large surface area. They will not be so easy to filter and wash clean of mother liquor. Once crystallization ceases at room temperature, the flask should be placed in ice to cool further. Take care to clamp the flask in the ice bath so that it does not tip over.

6. Collecting and Washing the Crystals

Once crystallization is complete, the crystals must be separated from the ice-cold mother liquor, washed with ice-cold solvent, and dried.

Microscale Procedure

(A) Filtration Using the Pasteur Pipette.
The most important filtration technique to be used in microscale organic experiments employs the Pasteur pipette (Fig. 3.12). About 70% of the crystalline products from the experiments in this text can be isolated in this way. The others will be isolated by filtration on the Hirsch funnel.

The ice-cold crystalline mixture is stirred with the Pasteur pipette, and while air is being expelled from the pipette, it is forced to the bottom of the reaction tube. The bulb is released, and the solvent is drawn into the pipette through the very small space between the square tip of the pipette and the curved bottom of the reaction tube. When all the solvent has been withdrawn, it is expelled into another reaction tube containing the crystals. It is sometimes useful to rap the tube containing the wet crystals against a hard surface to pack them so that more solvent can be removed. The tube is returned to the ice bath, and a few drops of cold solvent are added to the crystals. The mixture is stirred to wash the crystals, and the solvent is again removed. This process can be repeated as many times as necessary. Volatile solvents can be removed from the damp crystals under vacuum (Fig. 3.13). Alternatively, the last traces of solvent can be removed by centrifugation using the Wilfilter (C), (Fig. 3.15.)

(B) Filtration Using the Hirsch Funnel.
When the volume of material to be filtered is larger than about 1.5 mL, then the material is collected on the Hirsch funnel.

The Hirsch funnel in the Williamson/Kontes kit is unique. It is made of polypropylene and has an integral molded stopper that fits the 25-mL filter flask. It comes fitted with a 20-μm polyethylene fritted disk, which is not meant to be disposable, although it costs only about twice as much as an 11-cm piece of filter paper (Fig. 3.14). While products can be collected directly on this disk, it is good practice to place an 11- or 12-mm-diameter piece of no. 1 filter paper on the disk. In this way the frit will not become clogged with insoluble impurities. The disk of filter paper can be cut with a cork borer or leather punch. A piece of filter paper *must* be used on the old-style porcelain Hirsch funnels.

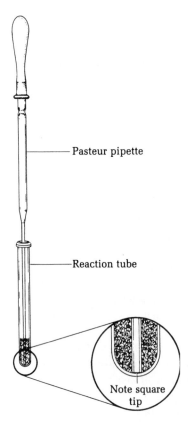

Pasteur pipette

Reaction tube

Note square tip

FIG. 3.12 Filtration using the Pasteur pipette and reaction tube.

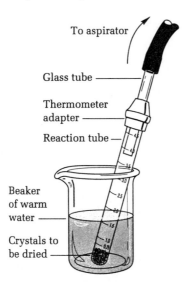

FIG. 3.13 Drying crystals under reduced pressure in a reaction tube.

To aspirator

Glass tube

Thermometer adapter

Reaction tube

Beaker of warm water

Crystals to be dried

Clamp the clean, dry 25-mL filter flask in an ice bath to prevent it from falling over, and place the Hirsch funnel with filter paper in the flask. Wet the filter paper with the solvent used in the crystallization, turn on the water aspirator (see below), and ascertain that the filter paper is pulled down onto the frit. Pour and scrape the crystals and mother liquor onto the Hirsch funnel, and as soon as the liquid is gone from the crystals, break the vacuum at the filter flask by removing the rubber hose. The filtrate can be used to rinse out the container that contained the crystals. Again, break the vacuum as soon as all the liquid has disappeared from the crystals; this prevents impurities from drying on the crystals. The

Break the vacuum, add a very small quantity of ice-cold wash solvent, reapply vacuum.

Filter paper, 12 mm dia.

Polyethylene filter disk (frit), 10 mm dia.

Hirsch funnel

To aspirator

25-mL Filter flask

FIG. 3.14 Hirsch funnel used for vacuum filtration. This unique design has a removable and replaceable 20-μm polyethylene frit. No adapter is needed because there is a vacuum-tight fit to the filter flask. Always clamp the flask. Always use a piece of filter paper.

reason for cooling the filter flask is to keep the mother liquor cold so that it will not dissolve the crystals on the Hirsch funnel when the filtrate is used to wash crystals from the container onto the funnel. With a very few drops of ice-cold solvent, rinse the crystallization flask. This container should still be ice cold. Place the ice-cold solvent on the crystals, and then reapply the vacuum. As soon as the liquid is pulled from the crystals, break the vacuum. Repeat this washing process as many times as necessary to remove colored material or other impurities from the crystals. In some cases, only one very small wash will be needed. After the crystals have been washed with ice-cold solvent, the vacuum can be left on to dry the crystals. Sometimes it is useful to press solvent from the crystals using a cork.

(C) Filtration with the Wilfilter (Replacing the Craig Tube).

The isolation of less than 100 mg of recrystallized material from a reaction tube (or any other container) is not easy. If the amount of solvent is large enough (a milliliter or more) the material can be recovered by filtration on the Hirsch funnel (B). But when the volume of liquid is less than a milliliter, much product is left in the tube during the transfer to the Hirsch filter. The solvent can be removed with a Pasteur pipette pressed against the bottom of the tube, a very effective filtration technique, but scraping the damp crystals from the reaction tube results in major losses. If the solvent is relatively low-boiling, it can be evaporated by connecting the tube to a water aspirator (Fig. 3.13). Once the crystals are dry they are easily scraped from the tube with little or no loss. But some solvents, and water is the principal culprit, are not easily removed by evaporation. And even when removal of the solvent under vacuum is not terribly difficult, it takes time.

We have invented a filtration device that circumvents these problems, the Wilfilter. After crystallization has ceased most of the solvent is removed from the crystals using a Pasteur pipette in the usual way (Fig. 3.12). Then the polypropylene Wilfilter is placed on the top of the reaction tube followed by a 15 mL polypropylene centrifuge tube (Fig. 3.15). The assembly is inverted and placed in a centrifuge such as the International Clinical Centrifuge that holds 12 15-mL tubes. The assembly, properly counterbalanced, is centrifuged for about a minute at top speed. The centrifuge tube is removed from the centrifuge, and the reaction tube is then removed from the centrifuge tube. The three fingers on the Wilfilter keep it attached to the reaction tube. The filtrate is left in the centrifuge tube.

Filtration with the Wilfilter occurs between the top surface of the reaction tube and the flat surface of the Wilfilter. Liquid will pass through that space during centrifugation; crystals will not. The crystals will be found on the top of the Wilfilter and inside the reaction tube. The very large centrifugal forces remove all the liquid, so the crystals will be virtually dry and thus easily removed from the reaction tube by shaking or scraping with the metal spatula.

The Wilfilter replaces an older device known as the Craig tube (Fig. 3.16), which consists of an outer tube of 1-, 2-, or 3-mL capacity with an inner plunger made of Teflon (expensive) or glass (fragile). The material to be crystallized is transferred to the outer tube and crystallized in the usual way. The inner plunger is added, and a wire hanger is fashioned so that the assembly can be removed from the centrifuge tube without the plunger falling off. Filtration in this device

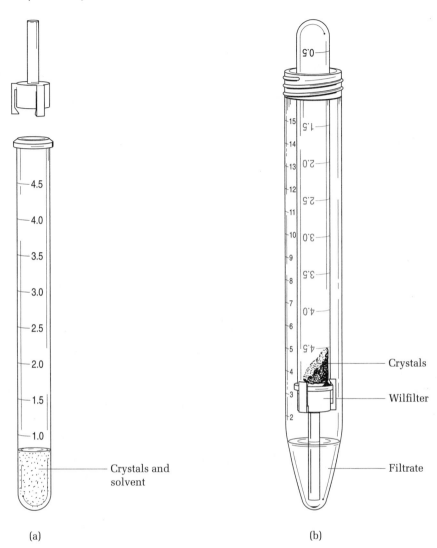

(a)   (b)

FIG. 3.15 The Wilfilter filtration apparatus. Filtration occurs between the flat face of the polypropylene Wilfilter and the top of the reaction tube.

occurs through the rough surface that has been ground into the shoulder of the outer tube.

The Wilfilter has the advantages that a special recrystallization device is not needed, no transfers of material are needed, it is not as limited in capacity (which is 4.5 mL), and its cost is one-fifth that of the Craig tube assembly.

(D) Filtration into a Reaction Tube on the Hirsch Funnel. If it is
desired to have the filtrate in a reaction tube instead of spread all over the bottom of the 25-mL filter flask, then the process described above can be carried out in

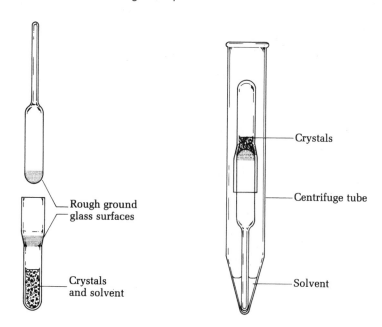

FIG. 3.16   Craig tube filtration apparatus. Filtration occurs between the rough ground glass surfaces when the apparatus is centrifuged.

the apparatus shown in Fig. 3.17. The vacuum hose is connected to the side arm using the thermometer adapter and a short length of glass tubing. Evaporate the filtrate in the reaction tube to collect a second crop of crystals.

(E) Filtration into a Reaction Tube on the Micro Büchner Funnel.
If the quantity of material being collected is very small, the bottom of the chromatography column is a micro Büchner funnel, which can be fitted into the top of the thermometer adapter as shown in Fig. 3.18. Again, it is good practice to cover the frit with a piece of 6-mm filter paper (cut with a cork borer).

(F) The Micro Büchner Funnel in an Enclosed Filtration Apparatus.
In the apparatus shown in Fig. 3.19, crystallization is carried out in the upper reaction tube in the normal way. The apparatus is then turned upside down, the crystals shaken down onto the micro Büchner funnel, and a vacuum applied through the side arm. In this apparatus, crystals can be collected in an oxygen-free atmosphere. This resembles a Schlenk tube.

Macroscale Apparatus

Filtration on the Hirsch Funnel and the Büchner Funnel.   If the quantity of material is small (<2 g), the Hirsch funnel can be used in exactly the way described above. For larger quantities, the Büchner funnel is used. Properly

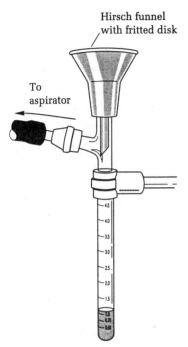

Hirsch funnel
with fritted disk

To
aspirator

FIG. 3.17   Microscale Hirsch
filtration assembly. The Hirsch
funnel gives a vacuum-tight seal
to the 105° adapter.

Clamp the filter flask.

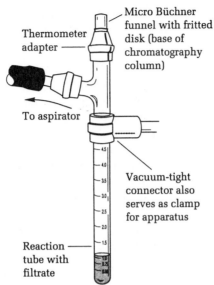

Micro Büchner
funnel with fritted
disk (base of
chromatography
column)

Thermometer
adapter

To aspirator

Vacuum-tight
connector also
serves as clamp
for apparatus

Reaction
tube with
filtrate

FIG. 3.18   Filtration using the
microscale Büchner funnel.

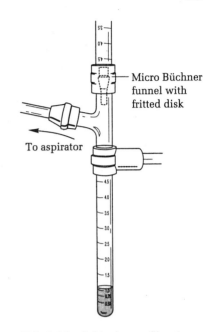

Micro Büchner
funnel with
fritted disk

To aspirator

FIG. 3.19   Schlenk-type filtration
apparatus. The apparatus is
inverted to carry out the filtration.

matched Büchner funnels, filter paper, and flasks are shown in Fig. 3.20. The
Hirsch funnel shown in the figure has a 5-cm bottom plate to accept 3.3-cm paper.

Place a piece of filter paper in the bottom of the Büchner funnel. Wet it with
solvent, and be sure it lies flat so that crystals cannot escape around the edge and
under the filter paper. Then with the vacuum off, pour the cold slurry of crystals
into the center of the filter paper. Apply the vacuum; as soon as the liquid disappears from the crystals break the vacuum to the flask by disconnecting the
hose. Rinse the Erlenmeyer flask with cold solvent. Add this to the crystals, and

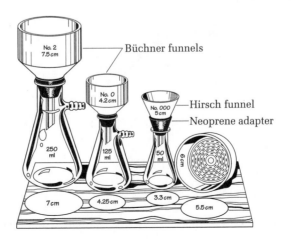

Büchner funnels

Hirsch funnel

Neoprene adapter

FIG. 3.20   Matching filter
assemblies. The 6.0-cm
polypropylene Büchner funnel
(*right*) resists breakage and can
be disassembled for cleaning.

reapply the vacuum just until the liquid disappears from the crystals. Repeat this process as many times as necessary, and then leave the vacuum on to dry the crystals.

The Water Aspirator and Trap.

The most common way to produce a vacuum in the organic laboratory for filtration purposes is by employing a *water aspirator.* Air is efficiently entrained in the water rushing through the aspirator so that it will produce a vacuum roughly equal to the vapor pressure of the water going through it (17 torr at 20°C, 5 torr at 4°C). A check valve is built into the aspirator, but even so when the water is turned off it may back into the evacuated system. For this reason a *trap* is always installed in the line (Fig. 3.21). *The water passing through the aspirator should always be turned on full force.* The system can be opened to the atmosphere by removing the hose from the small filter flask or by opening the screw clamp on the trap. Open the system, then turn off the water to avoid having water sucked back into the filter trap. Thin rubber tubing on the top of the trap will collapse and bend over when a good vacuum is established. You will, in time, learn to hear the difference in the sound of an aspirator when it is pulling a vacuum and when it is working on an open system.

Use a trap.

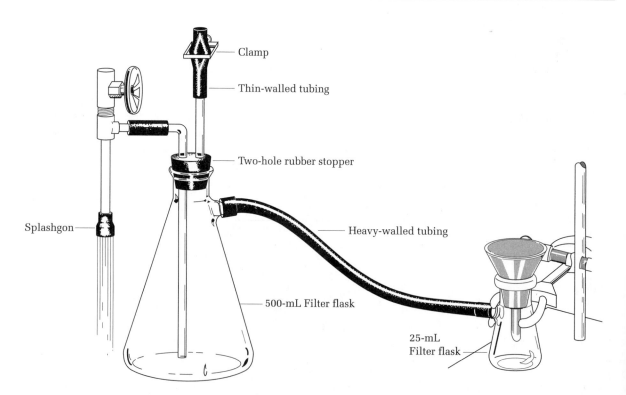

Clamp

Thin-walled tubing

Two-hole rubber stopper

Heavy-walled tubing

Splashgon

500-mL Filter flask

25-mL Filter flask

FIG. 3.21   Aspirator, filter trap, and Hirsch funnel. Clamp small filter flask to prevent its turning over.

Collecting a Second Crop of Crystals. Regardless of the method used to collect the crystals on either a macroscale or a microscale, the filtrate and washings can be combined and evaporated to the point of saturation to obtain a second crop of crystals—hence the necessity for having a clean receptacle for the filtrate. This second crop will increase the overall yield, but the crystals will not usually be as pure as the first crop.

7. Drying the Product

Microscale Procedure

If possible, dry the product in the reaction tube after removal of the solvent using a Pasteur pipette. This can be done simply by connecting the tube to the water aspirator. If the tube is clamped in a beaker of hot water, the solvent will evaporate more rapidly under vacuum, but take care not to melt the product (Fig. 3.13). Water, which has a high heat of vaporization, is difficult to remove this way. Scrape the product out onto a watch glass, and allow it to dry to constant weight, which will indicate that all the solvent is gone. If the product is collected on the Hirsch funnel or the Wilfilter, the last bit of solvent can be removed by squeezing the crystals between sheets of filter paper before drying them on the watch glass.

Macroscale Procedure

Once the crystals have been washed on the Hirsch funnel or the Büchner funnel, press them down with a clean cork or other flat object and allow air to pass through them until they are substantially dry. Final drying can be done under reduced pressure (Fig. 3.22). The crystals can then be turned out of the funnel and squeezed between sheets of filter paper to remove the last bit of solvent before final drying on a watch glass.

FIG. 3.22 Drying a solid by reduced air pressure.

Test Compounds:

OH
OH
Resorcinol

Experiments

1. Solubility Tests

To test the solubility of a solid, transfer an amount roughly estimated to be about 10 mg (the amount that forms a symmetrical mound on the end of a stainless steel spatula) into a reaction tube and add about 0.25 mL of solvent from a calibrated dropper or pipette. Stir with a fire-polished stirring rod (4-mm), break up any lumps, and determine if the solid is readily soluble at room temperature. If the substance is readily soluble in methanol, ethanol, acetone, or acetic acid at room temperature, add a few drops of water from a wash bottle to see if a solid precipitates. If it does, heat the mixture, adjust the composition of the solvent pair to produce a hot solution saturated at the boiling point, let the solution stand undisturbed, and note the character of the crystals that form. If the substance fails to dissolve in a given solvent at room temperature, heat the suspension and see if

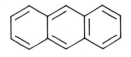

Anthracene

O OH
C

Benzoic acid

$SO_3^- Na^+$

NH_2

4-Amino-1-naphthalenesulfonic acid, sodium salt

solution occurs. If the solvent is flammable, heat the test tube on the steam bath or in a small beaker of water kept warm on the steam bath or a hot plate. If the solid completely dissolves, it can be declared readily soluble in the hot solvent; if some but not all dissolves, it is said to be moderately soluble, and further small amounts of solvent should then be added until solution is complete. When a substance has been dissolved in hot solvent, cool the solution by holding the flask under the tap and, if necessary, induce crystallization by rubbing the walls of the tube with a stirring rod to make sure that the concentration permits crystallization. Then reheat to dissolve the solid, let the solution stand undisturbed, and inspect the character of the ultimate crystals.

Make solubility tests on the test compounds shown to the left in each of the solvents listed below. Note the degree of solubility in the solvents, cold and hot, and suggest suitable solvents, solvent pairs, or other expedients for crystallization of each substance. Record the crystal form, at least to the extent of distinguishing between needles (pointed crystals), plates (flat and thin), and prisms. How do your observations conform to the generalization that like dissolves like?

Solvents:

Water—hydroxylic, ionic
Toluene—an aromatic hydrocarbon
Ligroin—a mixture of aliphatic hydrocarbons

Cleaning Up[4] Place organic solvents and solutions of the compounds in the organic solvents container. Dilute the aqueous solutions with water, and flush down the drain.

MICROSCALE AND MACROSCALE

2. Crystallization of Pure Phthalic Acid, Naphthalene, and Anthracene

Phthalic acid   **Naphthalene**   **Anthracene**

The process of crystallization can be observed readily using phthalic acid. In the reference book *The Handbook of Chemistry and Physics,* in the table "Physical Constants of Organic Compounds," the entry for phthalic acid gives the following solubility data (in grams of solute per 100 mL of solvent). The superscripts refer to temperature in °C:

---

4. For this and all other "Cleaning Up" sections, see Chapter 2 for a complete discussion of waste disposal procedures.

Water	Alcohol	Ether, etc.
0.54^{14}	11.71^{18}	0.69^{15} eth., i. chl.
18^{99}		

The large difference in solubility in water as a function of temperature suggests this as the solvent of choice. The solubility in alcohol is high at room temperature. Ether is difficult to use because it is so volatile; the compound is insoluble in chloroform (i. chl.).

Microscale Procedure, Phthalic Acid

Set the heater control to about 20% of the maximum.

Crystallize 60 mg (0.060 g) of phthalic acid from the minimum volume of water, using the above data to calculate the required volume. First, turn on the electrically heated sand bath. Add the solid to a 10×100 mm reaction tube, and then, using a Pasteur pipette, add water dropwise. Use the calibration marks found in Fig. 1.18 to measure the volume of water in the pipette and the reaction tube. Add a boiling stick (a wooden applicator stick) to facilitate even boiling and prevent bumping. After a portion of the water has been added, gently heat the solution to boiling on a hot *sand bath* in the electric heater. The deeper the tube is placed in the sand, the hotter it will be. As soon as boiling begins, continue to add water dropwise until all the solid just dissolves. Cork the tube and clamp it as it cools, and observe the phenomenon of crystallization.

Alternate procedure: Dry the crystals under vacuum in a steam bath in the reaction tube.

After the tube reaches room temperature, cool it in ice, stir the crystals with a Pasteur pipette, and expel the air from the pipette as the tip is pushed to the bottom of the tube. When the tip is firmly and squarely seated in the bottom of the tube, release the bulb and withdraw the water. Rap the tube sharply on a wood surface to compress the crystals and remove as much of the water as possible with the pipette. Then cool the tube in ice and add a few drops of ice-cold ethanol to the tube in order to remove water from the crystals. Connect the tube to a water aspirator, and warm it in a beaker of hot water (see Fig. 3.13). Once all the solvent is removed, using the stainless steel spatula, scrape the crystals onto a piece of filter paper, fold the paper over the crystals, and squeeze out excess water before allowing the crystals to dry to constant weight. Weigh the dry crystals, and calculate the percent recovery of product.

Microscale Procedure, Naphthalene and Anthracene

These compounds can also be isolated using the Wilfilter.

Following the procedure outlined above, crystallize 40 mg of naphthalene from 80% aqueous methanol or 10 mg of anthracene from ethanol. These are more typical of compounds to be crystallized in later experiments in that they are soluble in organic solvents. It will be much easier to remove these solvents from the crystals under vacuum than it is to remove water from phthalic acid. You will seldom have occasion to crystallize less than 30 mg of a solid in these experiments.

Cleaning Up   Dilute the aqueous filtrate with water, and flush the solution down the drain. Phthalic acid is not considered toxic to the environment. Methanol and ethanol filtrates go in the organic solvents container.

Macroscale Procedure

Crystallize 1.0 g of phthalic acid from the minimum volume of water, using the above data to calculate the required volume. Add the solid to the smallest practical Erlenmeyer flask, and then, using a Pasteur pipette, add water dropwise from a full 10-mL graduated cylinder. A boiling stick (a stick of wood) facilitates even boiling and will prevent bumping. After a portion of the water has been added, gently heat the solution to boiling on a hot plate. As soon as boiling begins, continue to add water dropwise until all the solid just dissolves. Place the flask on a cork ring or other insulator, and allow it to cool undisturbed to room temperature, during which time the crystallization process can be observed. Slow cooling favors large crystals. Then cool the flask in an ice bath, decant (pour off) the mother liquor (the liquid remaining with the crystals), and remove the last traces of liquid with a Pasteur pipette. Scrape the crystals onto a filter paper using a stainless steel spatula, squeeze the crystals between sheets of filter paper to remove traces of moisture, and allow the crystals to dry. Alternatively, the crystals can be collected on a Hirsch funnel. Compare the calculated volume of water with the volume of water actually used to dissolve the acid. Calculate the percent recovery of dry, recrystallized phthalic acid.

Cleaning Up   Dilute the filtrate with water, and flush the solution down the drain. Phthalic acid is not considered toxic to the environment.

 MICROSCALE

3. Decolorizing a Solution with Decolorizing Charcoal

Into a reaction tube place 1.0 mL of a solution of methylene blue dye that has been made up at a concentration of 10 mg per 100 mL of water. Add to the tube a few pieces (10 or 12) of decolorizing charcoal, shake, and observe the color over a period of a minute or two. Heat the contents of the tube to boiling (reflux), and observe the color by holding the tube in front of a piece of white paper from time to time. How rapidly is the color removed? If the color is not removed in a minute or so, add more charcoal pellets.

Decolorizing using pelletized Norit

Cleaning Up   Place the Norit in the nonhazardous solid waste container.

 MACROSCALE

4. Decolorization of Brown Sugar (Sucrose, $C_{12}H_{22}O_{11}$)

Raw sugar is refined commercially with the aid of decolorizing charcoal. The clarified solution is seeded generously with small sugar crystals and excess water removed under vacuum to facilitate crystallization. The pure white crystalline product is collected by centrifugation. Brown sugar is partially refined sugar and can be decolorized easily using charcoal.

Dissolve 15 g of dark brown sugar in 30 mL of water in a 50-mL Erlenmeyer flask by heating and stirring. Pour half the solution into another 50-mL flask. Heat one of the solutions nearly to the boiling point, allow it to cool slightly, and add to it 250 mg (0.25 g) of decolorizing charcoal (Norit pellets). Bring the solution back to near the boiling point for 2 minutes; then filter the hot solution into an Erlenmeyer flask through a fluted filter paper held in a previously heated funnel. Treat the other half of the sugar solution in exactly the same way, but use only 50 mg of decolorizing charcoal. In collaboration with a fellow student, try heating the solutions for only 15 s after addition of the charcoal. Compare your results.

Cleaning Up   Decant (pour off) the aqueous layer. Place the Norit in the non-hazardous solid waste container. The sugar solution can be flushed down the drain.

MICROSCALE

COOH

Benzoic acid

5. Crystallization of Benzoic Acid from Water and a Solvent Pair

Crystallize 50 mg of benzoic acid from water in the same way phthalic acid was crystallized. Then in a dry reaction tube dissolve another 50-mg sample of benzoic acid in the minimum volume of hot toluene, and add cyclohexane to the hot solution dropwise. When the hot solution becomes cloudy and crystallization has started, allow the tube to cool slowly to room temperature; then cool it in ice and collect the crystals. Compare crystallization in water to that in the solvent pair.

Cleaning Up   The aqueous solution, after dilution with water, can be flushed down the drain. The toluene and cyclohexane filtrates should be placed in the organic solvents container.

MACROSCALE

Naphthalene

Do not try to grasp Erlenmeyer flasks with a test tube holder.

Support the funnel in a ring stand.

6. Recrystallization of Naphthalene from a Mixed Solvent

Add 2.0 g of impure naphthalene[5] to a 50-mL Erlenmeyer flask along with 3 mL of methanol and a boiling stick to promote even boiling. Heat the mixture to boiling over a steam bath or hot plate, and then add methanol dropwise until the naphthalene just dissolves when the solvent is boiling. The total volume of methanol should be 4 mL. Remove the flask from the heat, and cool it rapidly in an ice bath. Note that the contents of the flask set to a solid mass, which would be impossible to handle. Add enough methanol to bring the total volume to 25 mL, heat the solution to the boiling point, remove the flask from the heat, allow it to cool slightly, and add 30 mg of decolorizing charcoal pellets to remove the colored impurity in the solution. Heat the solution to the boiling point for 2 min; if the color is not gone, add more Norit and boil again, then filter through a fluted filter paper in a previously warmed stemless funnel into a 50-mL Erlenmeyer flask. Sometimes

5. A mixture of 100 g of naphthalene, 0.3 g of a dye such as congo red, and perhaps sand, magnesium sulfate, dust, etc.

filtration is slow because the funnel fits so snugly into the mouth of the flask that a back pressure develops. If you note that raising the funnel increases the flow of filtrate, fold a small strip of paper two or three times and insert it between the funnel and flask. Wash the used flask with 2 mL of hot methanol, and use this liquid to wash the filter paper, transferring the solvent with a Pasteur pipette in a succession of drops around the upper rim of the filter paper. When the filtration is complete, the volume of methanol should be 15 mL. If it is not, evaporate excess methanol.

Because the filtrate is far from being saturated with naphthalene at this point, it will not yield crystals on cooling; however, the solubility of naphthalene in methanol can be greatly reduced by addition of water. Heat the solution to the boiling point, and add water dropwise from a 10-mL graduated cylinder, using a Pasteur pipette (or use a precalibrated pipette). After each addition of water the solution will turn cloudy for an instant. Swirl the contents of the flask, and heat to redissolve any precipitated naphthalene. After the addition of 3.5 mL of water the solution will be almost saturated with naphthalene at the boiling point of the solvent. Remove the flask from the heat, and place it on a cork ring or other insulating surface to cool, without being disturbed, to room temperature.

Immerse the flask in an ice bath along with another flask containing methanol and water in the ratio of 30 : 7. This cold solvent will be used for washing the crystals. The cold crystallization mixture is collected by vacuum filtration on a small Büchner funnel (50-mm) (Fig. 3.23). The water flowing through the aspirator should always be turned on full force. In collecting the product by suction filtration, use a spatula to dislodge crystals and ease them out of the flask. If crystals still remain in the flask, some filtrate can be poured back into the crystallization flask as a rinse for washing as often as desired, because it is saturated with solute. To free the crystals from contaminating mother liquor, break the suction, pour a few milliliters of the fresh cold solvent mixture into the Büchner funnel, and immediately reapply suction. Repeat this process until the crystals and the filtrate are free of color. Press the crystals with a clean cork to eliminate excess solvent, pull air through the filter cake for a few minutes, and then put the large flat platelike crystals out on a filter paper to dry. The yield of pure white crystalline naphthalene should be about 1.6 g. The mother liquor contains about 0.25 g, and about 0.15 g is retained in the charcoal and on the filter paper.

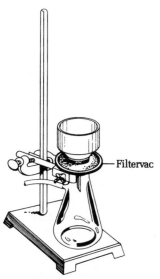

FIG. 3.23 Suction filter assembly clamped to provide firm support. The funnel must be pressed down on the Filtervac to establish reduced pressure in the flask.

Cleaning Up   Place the Norit in the nonhazardous solid waste container. The methanol filtrate and washings are placed in the organic solvents container.

7. Purification of an Unknown

Bear in mind the seven-step crystallization procedure:

1. Choose the solvent.
2. Dissolve the solute.
3. Decolorize the solution (if necessary).
4. Filter suspended solids (if necessary).

5. Crystallize the solute.
6. Collect and wash the crystals.
7. Dry the product.

You are to purify 2.0 g of an unknown provided by the instructor. Conduct tests for solubility and ability to crystallize in several organic solvents, solvent pairs, and water. Conserve your unknown by using very small quantities for solubility tests. If only a drop or two of solvent is used, the solvent can be evaporated by heating the test tube on the steam bath or sand bath, and the residue can be used for another test. Submit as much pure product as possible with evidence of its purity (i.e., the melting point). From the posted list identify the unknown.

Cleaning Up   Place decolorizing charcoal, if used, and filter paper in the non-hazardous solid waste container. Put organic solvents in the organic solvents container, and flush aqueous solutions down the drain.

Crystallization Problems and Their Solutions

Induction of Crystallization

Seeding

Occasionally a sample will not crystallize from solution on cooling, even though the solution is saturated with the solute at elevated temperature. The easiest method for inducing crystallization is to add to the supersaturated solution a seed crystal that has been saved from the crude material (if it was crystalline before recrystallization was attempted). In a probably apocryphal tale, the great sugar chemist Emil Fischer merely had to wave his beard over a recalcitrant solution and the appropriate seed crystals would drop out, causing crystallization to occur. In the absence of seed crystals, crystallization can often be induced by scratching the inside of the flask with a stirring rod at the air/liquid interface. One theory holds that part of the freshly scratched glass surface has angles and planes corresponding to the crystal structure, and crystals start growing on these spots. Often crystallization is very slow to begin, and placing the sample in a refrigerator overnight will bring success. Other expedients are to change the solvent (usually to a poorer one) and to place the sample in an open container where slow evaporation and dust from the air may help induce crystallization.

Scratching

Oils and "Oiling Out"

Crystallize at a lower temperature

Some saturated solutions, especially those containing water, when they cool deposit not crystals but small droplets referred to as oils. Should these droplets subsequently crystallize and be collected, they will be found to be rather impure. Should the temperature of the saturated solution be above the melting point of the solute when it starts to come out of solution, the solute will, of necessity, be deposited as an oil. Similarly, the melting point of the desired compound may be depressed to a point such that a low-melting eutectic mixture of the solute and the solvent comes out of solution. The simplest remedy for this latter problem is to lower the temperature at which the solution becomes saturated with the solute by simply adding more solvent. In extreme cases it may be necessary to lower this temperature well below room temperature by cooling the solution with dry ice.

Crystallization Summary

1. **Choosing the solvent.** "Like dissolves like." Some common solvents are water, methanol, ethanol, ligroin, and toluene. When you use a solvent pair, dissolve the solute in the better solvent, and add the poorer solvent to the hot solution until saturation occurs. Some common solvent pairs are ethanol–water, *t*-butyl methyl ether–ligroin, and toluene–ligroin.

2. **Dissolving the solute.** To the crushed or ground solute in an Erlenmeyer flask or reaction tube add solvent; heat the mixture to boiling. Add more solvent as necessary to obtain a hot, saturated solution.

3. **Decolorizing the solution.** If it is necessary to remove colored impurities, cool the solution to near room temperature, and add more solvent to prevent crystallization from occurring. Add decolorizing charcoal in the form of pelletized Norit to the cooled solution, and then heat it to boiling for a few minutes, taking care to swirl the solution to prevent bumping. Remove the Norit by filtration, then concentrate the filtrate.

4. **Filtering suspended solids.** If it is necessary to remove suspended solids, dilute the hot solution slightly to prevent crystallization from occurring during filtration. Filter the hot solution. Add solvent if crystallization begins in the funnel. Concentrate the filtrate to obtain a saturated solution.

5. **Crystallizing the solute.** Let the hot saturated solution cool spontaneously to room temperature. Do not disturb the solution. Then cool it in ice. If crystallization does not occur, scratch the inside of the container or add seed crystals.

6. **Collecting and washing the crystals.** Collect the crystals using the Pasteur pipette method, the Wilfilter, or by vacuum filtration on a Hirsch funnel or a Büchner funnel. If the latter technique is employed, wet the filter paper with solvent, apply vacuum, break vacuum, add crystals and liquid, apply vacuum until solvent just disappears, break vacuum, add cold wash solvent, apply vacuum, and repeat until crystals are clean and filtrate comes through clear.

7. **Drying the product.** Press the product on the filter to remove solvent. Then remove it from the filter, squeeze it between sheets of filter paper to remove more solvent, and spread it on a watch glass to dry.

Questions

1. A sample of naphthalene, which should be pure white, was found to have a grayish color after the usual purification procedure. The melting point was correct and the melting point range small. Explain the gray color.

2. How many milliliters of boiling water are required to dissolve 25 g of phthalic acid? If the solution were cooled to 14°C, how many grams of phthalic acid would crystallize out?

3. What is the reason for using activated carbon during a crystallization?

4. If a little activated charcoal does a good job removing impurities in a crystallization, why not use a lot?

5. Under what circumstances is it wise to use a mixture of solvents to carry out a crystallization?

6. Why is gravity filtration and not suction filtration used to remove suspended impurities and charcoal from a hot solution?

7. Why is a fluted filter paper used in gravity filtration?

8. Why are stemless funnels used instead of long-stem funnels to filter hot solutions through fluted filter paper?

9. Why is the final product from the crystallization process isolated by vacuum filtration and not by gravity filtration?

4

Melting Points, Boiling Points, and Refractive Indices

Prelab Exercise: Predict what the melting points of the three urea–cinnamic acid mixtures will be.

Part 1. Melting Points

Melting points—a micro technique

The melting point of a pure solid organic compound is one of its characteristic physical properties, along with molecular weight, boiling point, refractive index, and density. A pure solid will melt reproducibly over a narrow range of temperatures, typically less than 1°C. The process of determining this melting "point" is done on a truly micro scale using less than 1 mg of material. The apparatus is very simple, consisting of a thermometer, a capillary tube to hold the sample, and a heating bath.

Characterization

Melting points are determined for three reasons. If the compound is a known one, the melting point will help to characterize the sample in hand. If the compound is new, then the melting point is recorded in order to allow future characterization by others. And finally the range of the melting point is indicative of the purity of the compound; an impure compound will melt over a wide range of temperatures. Recrystallization of the compound will purify it, and the melting point range will decrease. In addition, the entire range will be displaced upward. For example, an impure sample might melt from 120–124°C and after recrystallization melt at 125–125.5°C. A solid is considered pure if the melting point does not rise after recrystallization.

An indication of purity

A crystal is an orderly arrangement of molecules in a solid. As heat is added to the solid, the molecules will vibrate and perhaps rotate but still remain a solid. At a characteristic temperature it will suddenly acquire the necessary energy to overcome the forces that attract one molecule to another, and it will undergo translational motion—in other words, it will become a liquid.

The forces by which one molecule is attracted to another include ionic attraction, van der Waals forces, hydrogen bonds, and dipole–dipole attraction. Most, but by no means all, organic molecules are covalent in nature and melt at temperatures below 300°C. Typical inorganic compounds are ionic and have much higher melting points; e.g., sodium chloride melts at 800°C. Ionic organic molecules often decompose before melting, as do compounds having strong hydrogen bonds such as sucrose.

Melting point generalizations

Other factors being equal, larger molecules melt at higher temperatures than

FIG. 4.1 Melting point–composition diagram for mixtures of the solids X and Y.

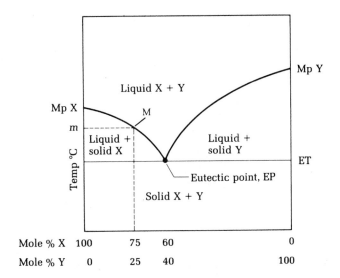

| Mole % X | 100 | 75 | 60 | | 0 |
| Mole % Y | 0 | 25 | 40 | | 100 |

A phase diagram

smaller ones. Among structural isomers the more symmetrical will have the higher melting point. Among optical isomers the R and S enantiomers will have the same melting points; but the racemate, the mixture of equal parts of R and S, will usually have a different melting point. Molecules that can form hydrogen bonds will usually have higher melting points than their counterparts of similar molecular weight.

The melting point behavior of impure compounds is best understood by consideration of a simple binary mixture of compounds X and Y (Fig. 4.1). This melting point–composition diagram shows the melting point behavior as a function of composition. The melting point of a pure compound is the temperature at which the vapor pressures of the solid and liquid are equal. But in dealing with a mixture the situation is different. Consider the case of a mixture of 75% X and 25% Y. At a temperature below ET, the eutectic temperature, the mixture is solid Y and solid X. At the eutectic temperature the solid begins to melt. The melt is a solution of Y dissolved in liquid X. The vapor pressure of the solution of X and

Melting point depression

Y together is less than that of pure X at the melting point; therefore, the temperature at which X will melt is lower when mixed with Y. This is an application of Raoult's law (Chapter 5). As the temperature is raised, more and more of solid X melts until it is all gone at point *M* (temperature *m*). The melting point range is thus from ET to *m*. In practice it is very difficult to detect point ET when a melting point is determined in a capillary because it represents the point at which an infinitesimal amount of the liquid solution has started to melt.

In this hypothetical example the liquid solution becomes saturated with Y at point EP. This is the point at which X and Y and their liquid solutions are in equilibrium. A mixture of X and Y containing 60% X will appear to have a sharp melting point at temperature ET. This point, EP, is the eutectic point.

The eutectic point

In general the melting point range of a mixture of compounds is broad, and the breadth of the range is an indication of purity. The chances of accidentally coming on the eutectic composition are small. Recrystallization will enrich the predominant compound while excluding the impurity, and therefore the melting point range will decrease.

It should be apparent that the impurity must be soluble in the compound, so an insoluble impurity such as sand or charcoal will not depress the melting point. The impurity does not need to be a solid. It can be a liquid such as water (if it is soluble) or an organic solvent, such as the one used to recrystallize the compound; hence the necessity for drying the compound before determining the melting point.

Mixed melting points

Advantage is taken of the depression of melting points of mixtures to prove whether two compounds having the same melting points are identical. If X and Y are identical, then a mixture of the two will have the same melting point; but if X and Y are not identical, then a small amount of X in Y or of Y in X will cause the melting point to be lowered.

Apparatus

The apparatus needed for determining an accurate melting point need not be elaborate; the same results are obtained on the simplest as on the most complex devices.

Thomas–Hoover Uni-Melt

The Thomas–Hoover Uni-Melt apparatus (Fig. 4.2) will accommodate seven capillaries in a small, magnified, lighted beaker of high-boiling silicone oil that is stirred and heated electrically. The heating rate is controlled with a variable transformer that is part of the apparatus. The rising mercury column of the thermometer can be observed with an optional traveling periscope device so the eye need not move away from the capillary. For industrial analytical and control work there is even an apparatus (Mettler) that automatically determines the melting point and displays the result in digital form.

Mel-Temp

The Mel-Temp apparatus (Fig. 4.3) consists of an electrically heated aluminum block that accommodates three capillaries. The sample is illuminated through the lower port and observed with a six-power lens through the upper port. The heating rate can be controlled, and with a special thermometer the apparatus can be used up to 500°C, far above the useful limit of silicone oil (about 350°C).

In this melting point apparatus (Fig. 4.3) it is advisable to use a digital thermometer (Fig. 4.4) in place of the mercury-in-glass thermometer. The digital thermometer has a small heat capacity and fast response time. It is more robust than a glass thermometer and does not, of course, contain mercury, which is very toxic.

Capillaries can be obtained commercially or can be made by drawing out 12-mm soft-glass tubing. The tubing is rotated in the hottest part of the Bunsen burner flame until it is very soft and begins to sag. It should not be drawn out during heating, but is removed from the flame and after a moment's hesitation drawn steadily and not too rapidly to arm's length. With some practice it is possible to produce 10 to 15 good tubes in a single drawing. The long capillary tube can be

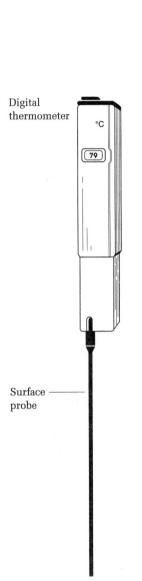

Digital
thermometer

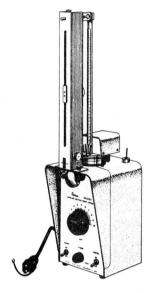

FIG. 4.2   Thomas–
Hoover Uni-Melt melting
point apparatus.

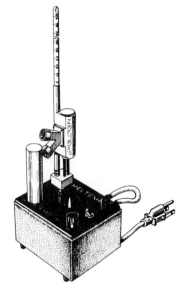

FIG. 4.3   Mel-Temp melting
point apparatus.

cut into 100-mm lengths with a glass scorer. Each tube is sealed by rotating the
end in the edge of a small flame, as seen in Fig. 4.5.

Filling Melting Point Capillaries

The dry sample is ground to a fine powder on a watch glass or a piece of glassine
paper on a hard surface using the flat portion of a spatula. It is formed into a small
pile and the melting point capillary forced down into the pile. The sample is
shaken into the closed end of the capillary by rapping sharply on a hard surface
or by dropping it down a 2-ft length of glass tubing onto a hard surface. The
height of the sample should be no more than 2–3 mm.

Surface
probe

FIG. 4.4   Digital thermometer.   **FIG. 4.5**   Sealing a melting point capillary tube.

Sealed Capillaries

Samples that sublime

Some samples sublime (go from the solid directly to the vapor phase without appearing to melt) or undergo rapid air oxidation and decompose at the melting point. These samples should be sealed under vacuum. This can be accomplished by forcing a capillary through a hole previously made in a rubber septum and evacuating the capillary using the water aspirator or a mechanical vacuum pump (Fig. 4.6). Using the flame from a small micro burner, the tube is gently heated about 15 mm above the tightly packed sample. This will cause any material in this region to sublime away. It is then heated more strongly in the same place to collapse the tube, taking care that the tube is straight when it cools. It is also possible to seal the end of a Pasteur pipette, add the sample, pack it down, and seal off a sample under vacuum in the same way.

Handle flame with great care in the organic laboratory.

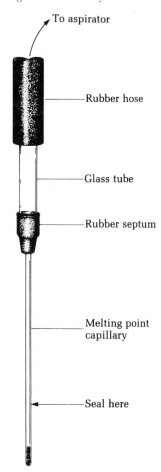

FIG. 4.6   Evacuation of a melting point capillary prior to sealing.

 MICROSCALE

Determining the Melting Point

The accuracy of the melting point depends on the accuracy of the thermometer, so the first exercise in this experiment will be to calibrate the thermometer. Melting points of pure, known compounds will be determined and deviations recorded so that a correction can be applied to future melting points. Be forewarned, however, that thermometers are usually fairly accurate.

The most critical factor in determining an accurate melting point is the rate of heating. At the melting point the temperature rise should not be greater than 1°C per minute. This may seem extraordinarily slow, but it is necessary in order for heat from the bath to be transferred equally to the sample and to the glass and mercury of the thermometer.

From experience you know the rate at which ice melts. Consider doing a melting point experiment on an ice cube. Because water melts at 0°C, you would need to have a melting point bath a few degrees below zero. To observe the true melting point of the ice cube, you would need to raise the temperature extraordinarily slowly. The ice cube would appear to begin to melt at 0°C and, if you waited for temperature equilibrium to be established, it would all be melted at 0.5°C. If you were impatient and raised the temperature too rapidly, the ice might appear to melt over the range 0 to 20°C. Similarly, melting points determined in capillaries will not be accurate if the rate of heating is too fast.

The rate of heating is the most important factor in obtaining accurate melting points. Heat no faster than 1°C per minute.

Experiments

1. Calibration of the Thermometer

Determine the melting point of standard substances (Table 4.1) over the temperature range of interest. The difference between the values found and those expected constitutes the correction that must be applied to future temperature readings. If the thermometer has been calibrated previously, then determine one or more melting points of known substances to familiarize yourself with the technique. If the determinations do not agree within 1°C, then repeat the process. Both mercury-in-glass and digital thermometers will need to be calibrated.

MICROSCALE

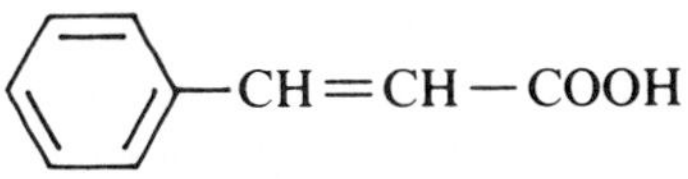

Cinnamic acid

2. Melting Points of Pure Urea and Cinnamic Acid

Using a metal spatula, crush the sample to a fine powder on a hard surface such as a watch glass. Push a melting point capillary into the powder, and force the powder down in the capillary by tapping the capillary or by dropping it through a long glass tube held vertically and resting on a hard surface. The column of solid should be no more than 2–3 mm in height and should be tightly packed.

TABLE 4.1   Melting Point Standards

Compound	Structure	Melting Point (°C)
Naphthalene	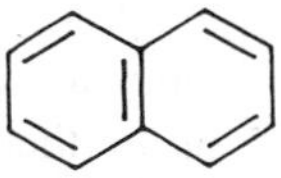	80–82
Urea	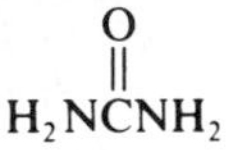	132.5–133
Sulfanilamide	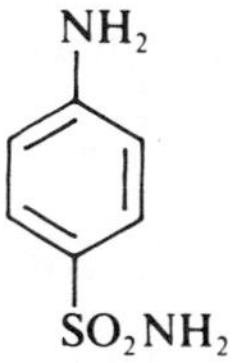	164–165
4-Toluic acid	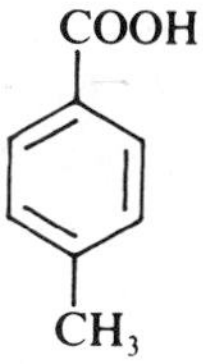	180–182
Anthracene	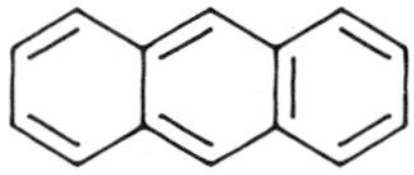	214–217
Caffeine (evacuated capillary)	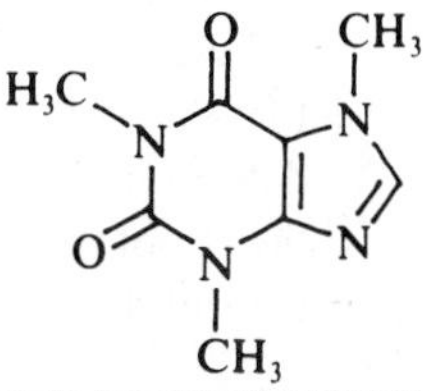	234–236.5

Heat rapidly to within 20°C of the melting point.

Except for the Thomas–Hoover and Mel-Temp apparatus, the capillary is held to the thermometer with a rubber band made by cutting a slice off the end of a piece of ³⁄₁₆-in. (5 mm) rubber tubing. This rubber band must be above the level of the oil bath; otherwise, it will break in the hot oil. Insertion of a fresh tube under the rubber band is facilitated by leaving the used tube in place. The sample should be close to and on a level with the center of the thermometer bulb.

If the approximate melting temperature is known, the bath can be heated rapidly until the temperature is about 20°C below this point, but the heating during the last 15–20°C should slow down considerably so that the rate of heating at the melting point is no more than 1°C per minute while the sample is melting. As the melting point is approached the sample may shrink because of crystal structure changes. However, the melting process begins when the first drops of liquid are seen in the capillary and ends when the last trace of solid disappears. For a pure compound this whole process may occur over a range of only 0.5°C; hence the necessity of having the temperature rise slowly during the determination.

Two or three melting points at once

If determinations are to be done on two or three samples that differ in melting point by as much as 10°C, two or three capillaries can be secured to the thermometer together and the melting points observed in succession without removal of the thermometer from the bath. As a precaution against interchange of tubes while they are being attached, use some system of identification, such as one, two, and three dots made with a marking pencil.

Determine the melting point of either urea (mp 132.5–133°C) or cinnamic acid (mp 132.5–133°C). Repeat the determination, and if the two determinations do not check within 1°C, do a third one.

MICROSCALE

3. Melting Points of Urea–Cinnamic Acid Mixtures

Make mixtures of urea and cinnamic acid in the approximate proportions 1:4, 1:1, and 4:1 by putting side by side the correct number of equal-sized small piles of the two substances and then mixing them. Grind the mixture thoroughly for at least a minute on a watch glass using a metal spatula. Note the ranges of melting of the three mixtures, and use the temperatures of complete liquefaction to construct a rough diagram of mp versus composition.

MICROSCALE

4. Unknowns

Determine the melting point of one or more of the following unknowns to be selected by the instructor (Table 4.2), and on the basis of the melting point identify the substance. Prepare two capillaries of each unknown. Run a very fast determination on the first sample to ascertain the approximate melting point, and then cool the melting point bath to just below the melting point and make a slow, careful determination using the other capillary.

TABLE 4.2   Melting Point Unknowns

Compound	Melting Point (°C)
Benzophenone	49–51
Maleic anhydride	52–54
4-Nitrotoluene	54–56
Naphthalene	80–82
Acetanilide	113.5–114
Benzoic acid	121.5–122
Urea	132.5–133
Salicylic acid	158.5–159
Sulfanilamide	165–166
Succinic acid	184.5–185
3,5-Dinitrobenzoic acid	205–207
p-Terphenyl	210–211

Part 2. Boiling Points

The boiling point of a pure organic liquid is one of its characteristic physical properties, just like its density, molecular weight, and refractive index, and the melting point of a solid. The boiling point is used to characterize a new organic liquid, and knowledge of the boiling point helps to compare one organic liquid with another, as in the process of identifying an unknown organic substance.

Comparison of boiling points with melting points is instructive. The process of determining the boiling point is more complex than that for the melting point: It requires more material, and because it is affected less by impurities, it is not as good an indication of purity. Boiling points can be determined on a few microliters of a liquid, but on a small scale it is difficult to determine the boiling point *range*. This requires enough material to distill—about 1 to 2 mL. Like the melting point, the boiling point of a liquid is affected by the forces that attract one molecule to another—ionic attraction, van der Waals forces, dipole–dipole interactions, and hydrogen bonding.

Structure and Boiling Point

In a homologous series of molecules the boiling point increases in a perfectly regular manner. The normal saturated hydrocarbons have boiling points ranging from $-162°C$ for methane to $330°C$ for $n\text{-}C_{19}H_{40}$, an increase of about $27°C$ for each CH_2 group. It is convenient to remember that n-heptane with a molecular weight of 100 has a boiling point near $100°C$ ($98.4°C$). A spherical molecule such as 2,2-dimethylpropane has a lower boiling point than n-pentane because it cannot have as many points of attraction to adjacent molecules. For molecules of the same molecular weight, those with dipoles, such as carbonyl groups, will have higher boiling points than those without, and molecules that can form hydrogen bonds will boil even higher. The boiling point of such molecules depends on the number of hydrogen bonds that can be formed, so that an alcohol with one hydroxyl group will boil lower than one with two if they both have the same molecular weight. A number of other generalizations can be made about boiling point behavior as a function of structure; you will learn about these throughout your study of organic chemistry.

Boiling Point as a Function of Pressure

Since the boiling point of a pure liquid is defined as the temperature at which the vapor pressure of the liquid exactly equals the pressure exerted on it, the boiling point will be a function of atmospheric pressure. At an altitude of 14,000 ft the boiling point of water is $81°C$. At pressures near that of the atmosphere at sea level (760 mm), the boiling point of most liquids decreases about $0.5°C$ for each 10-mm decrease in atmospheric pressure. This generalization does not hold for greatly reduced pressures because the boiling point decreases as a nonlinear function of pressure (see Fig. 5.1). Under these conditions a nomograph relating observed boiling point, boiling point at 760 mm, and pressure in millimeters should be consulted (see Fig. 7.10). This nomograph is not highly accurate; the change in boiling point as a function of pressure also depends on the type of compound (polar, nonpolar, hydrogen bonding, etc.). Consult the *Handbook of Chemistry and Physics* for the correction of boiling points to standard pressure.

The Laboratory Thermometer

CAUTION: Mercury is toxic. Report broken thermometers to your instructor.

Most mercury-in-glass laboratory thermometers have a mark around the stem that is three inches (76 mm) from the bottom of the bulb. This is the immersion line; the thermometer will record accurate temperatures if immersed to this line. Should you break a mercury thermometer, immediately inform your instructor, who will use special apparatus to clean up the mercury. Mercury vapor is very toxic.

Prevention of Superheating—Boiling Sticks and Boiling Stones

A very clean liquid in a very clean vessel will superheat and not boil when subjected to a temperature above its boiling point. This means that a thermometer placed in the liquid will register a temperature higher than the boiling point of the liquid. If boiling does occur under these conditions, it occurs with explosive violence. To avoid this problem, boiling stones are always added to liquids before heating them to boiling—whether to determine a boiling point or to carry out a reaction or distillation. The stones provide the nuclei on which the bubble of vapor indicative of a boiling liquid can form. Some boiling stones, also called boiling chips, are porous unglazed porcelain. This material is filled with air in numerous fine capillaries. Upon heating, this air expands to form the fine bubbles on which even boiling can take place. Once the liquid cools it will fill these capillaries and the boiling chip will become ineffective, so another must be added each time the liquid is heated to boiling. Sticks of wood—so-called applicator sticks about 1.5 mm in diameter—also promote even boiling and, unlike stones, are easy to remove from the solution. None of these work well for vacuum distillation.

Apparatus and Technique

By Distillation.   When enough material is available, the best method for determining the boiling point of a liquid is to distill it (Chapter 5). Distillation allows the boiling range to be determined and thus gives an indication of purity. Bear in mind, however, that a constant boiling point is not a guarantee of homogeneity and thus purity. Constant-boiling azeotropes such as 95% ethanol abound.

Using a Digital Thermometer and a Reaction Tube.   Boiling points can be measured rapidly and accurately using an electronic digital thermometer as depicted in Fig. 4.7. While digital thermometers are too expensive at present for each student to have one, two or three of these in the laboratory can greatly

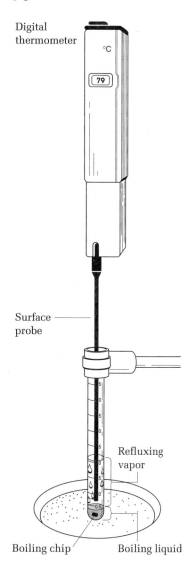

Digital
thermometer

Surface
probe

Refluxing
vapor

Boiling chip   Boiling liquid

FIG. 4.7 Use of a digital thermometer for determining boiling points.

Smaller-scale boiling point apparatus

speed up the determination of boiling points, and they are much safer to use because there is no danger from toxic mercury vapor if the thermometer is accidentally dropped.

A surface probe is the active element. Unlike the bulb of mercury at the end of a thermometer, this element has a very low heat capacity and a very fast response time, so boiling points can be determined very quickly in this apparatus. About 0.2–0.3 mL of the liquid and a boiling chip are heated on a sand bath until the liquid refluxes about 3 cm up the tube. The boiling point is the highest temperature recorded by the thermometer and maintained for about 1 min. Application of heat will drive tiny bubbles of air from the boiling chip. Do not mistake these tiny bubbles for real boiling. This can happen if the unknown has a very high boiling point. The probe should not touch the side of the reaction tube and should be about 5 mm above the liquid.

In a Reaction Tube.

If a digital thermometer is not available, use the apparatus shown in Fig. 4.8. Use of the distilling adapter on the top of the reaction tube allows access to the atmosphere. Place 0.3 mL of the liquid along with a boiling stone in a 10 × 100 mm reaction tube, clamp a thermometer so that the bulb is just above the level of the liquid, and then heat the liquid with a sand bath. It is *very important* that no part of the thermometer touch the reaction tube. Heating is regulated so that the boiling liquid refluxes (condenses the drips down) about 3 cm up the thermometer but does not boil out of the apparatus. If you cannot see the refluxing liquid, carefully run your finger down the side of the reaction tube until you feel heat. This indicates where the liquid is refluxing. Droplets of liquid must drip from the thermometer bulb in order to heat the mercury thoroughly. The boiling point is the highest temperature recorded by the thermometer and maintained over about a 1-min time interval.

Application of heat will drive tiny bubbles of air from the boiling chip. Do not mistake these tiny bubbles for real boiling. This can happen if the unknown has a very high boiling point. It may take several minutes to heat up the mercury in the thermometer bulb. True boiling is indicated by drops dripping from the thermometer and a constant temperature recorded on the thermometer. If the temperature is not constant, then you are probably not observing true boiling.

Using a 3- to 5-mm Tube.

For smaller quantities, the tube is attached to the side of the thermometer (Fig. 4.9) and heated with a liquid bath. The tube, which can be made from tubing 3 to 5 mm in diameter, contains a small inverted capillary. This is made by cutting a 6-mm piece from the sealed end of a melting point capillary, inverting it, and sealing it again to the capillary. A centimeter/millimeter ruler is printed on the inside cover of this book.

When the sample is heated in this device, the air in the inverted capillary will expand and an occasional bubble will escape. At the boiling point a continuous and rapid stream of bubbles will emerge from the inverted capillary. At this point the heating is stopped and the bath allowed to cool. A time will come when bubbling ceases and the liquid just begins to rise in the inverted capillary. The temperature at which this happens is recorded. The liquid is allowed to partially fill

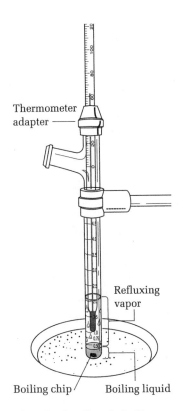

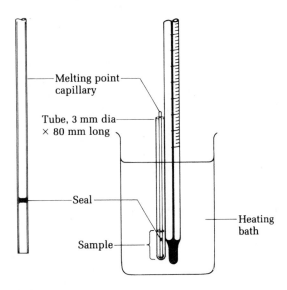

FIG. 4.9   Smaller-scale boiling point apparatus.

Thermometer adapter

Refluxing vapor

Boiling chip

Boiling liquid

FIG. 4.8   Small-scale boiling-point apparatus. Be sure the thermometer does not touch the tube.

the small capillary, and the heat is applied carefully until the first bubble comes from the capillary. The temperature is recorded at that point. The two temperatures approximate the boiling point range for the liquid. The explanation: As the liquid was being heated, the air expanded in the inverted capillary and was replaced by vapor of the liquid. The liquid was actually slightly superheated when rapid bubbles emerged from the capillary, but on cooling the point was reached at which the pressure on the inside of the capillary matched the outside (atmospheric) pressure. This is, by definition, the boiling point.

Cleaning Up   Place the boiling point sample in either the halogenated or nonhalogenated waste container. Do not pour it down the sink.

Part 3. Refractive Indices

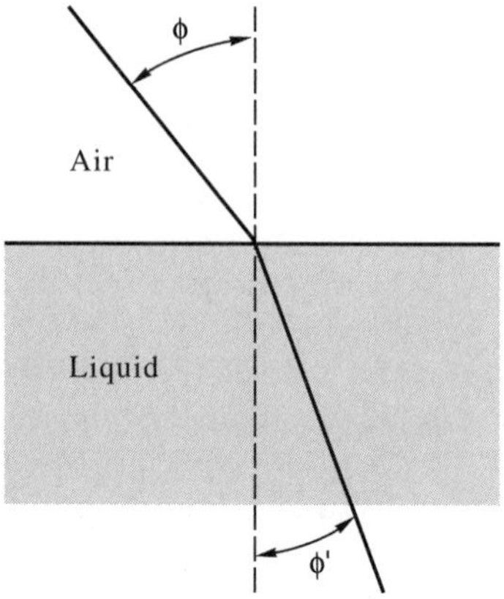

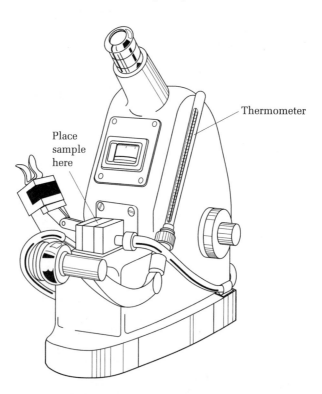

FIG. 4.10 Refraction of light.

The refractive index n is a physical constant that, like the boiling point, can be used to characterize liquids. It is the ratio of the velocity of light in air to the velocity of light in the liquid (Fig. 4.10). It is also equal to the ratio of the sine of the angle of incidence ϕ to the sine of the angle of refraction ϕ':

$$n = \frac{\text{Velocity in air}}{\text{Velocity in liquid}} = \frac{\sin \phi}{\sin \phi'}$$

The angle of refraction is also a function of temperature and the wavelength of light (consider the dispersion of white light by a prism). Because the velocity of light in air (strictly speaking, a vacuum) is always greater than that through a liquid, the refractive index is a number greater than 1; for example, hexane n_D^{20} 1.3751; diiodobenzene, n_D^{20} 1.7179. The superscript 20 indicates that the refractive index was measured at 20°C, and the subscript D refers to the yellow D-line from a sodium vapor lamp, light with a wavelength of 589 nm.

The measurement is made on a refractometer using a few drops of liquid. Compensation is made within the instrument for the fact that white light and not sodium vapor light is used, but a temperature correction must be applied to the observed reading by adding 0.00045 for each degree above 20°C:

$$n_D^{20} = n_D^t + 0.00045(t - 20°C)$$

Thermometer

Place
sample
here

FIG. 4.11 Abbé refractometer.
Sample block can be
thermostatted.

 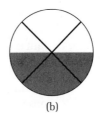 

(a)   (b)   (c)

FIG. 4.12 (a) View into refractometer when index knob is out of adjustment. (b) View into refractometer when properly adjusted. (c) View when chromatic adjustment is incorrect.

The refractive index can be determined to 1 part in 10,000, but because the value is quite sensitive to impurities, there is not always very good agreement in the literature with regard to the last figure. For this reason, the refractive indices in this book have been rounded to the nearest part per thousand, as have the refractive indices reported in the Aldrich catalog of chemicals. To master the technique of using the refractometer, measure the refractive indices of several known, pure liquids before measuring an unknown.

Procedure

Refractometers come in many designs. In the most common, the Abbé design (Fig. 4.11), two or three drops of the sample are placed on the open prism using a polyethylene Beral pipette (to avoid scratching the prism face). The prism is closed, and the light is turned on and positioned for maximum brightness as seen through the eyepiece. If the refractometer is set to a nearly correct value, then a partially gray image will be seen, as in Fig. 4.12(a). Turn the knob so that the line separating the dark and light areas is at the crosshairs, as in Fig. 4.12(b). Sometimes the line separating the dark and light areas is fuzzy and colored. Turn the chromatic adjustment until the demarcation line is sharp and colorless. Then read the refractive index. On a newer instrument, press a button to light up the scale in the field of vision. On older models, read the refractive index through a separate eyepiece. Read the temperature on the thermometer attached to the refractometer, and make the appropriate temperature correction to the observed index of refraction.

Cleaning Up   When the measurement is completed, open the prism and wipe off the sample with lens paper using ethanol, acetone, or hexane as necessary.

Questions ————————————————————

1. What effect would poor circulation of the melting point bath liquid have on the observed melting point?

2. What is the effect of an insoluble impurity, such as sodium sulfate, on the observed melting point of a compound?

3. Three test tubes, labeled A, B, and C, contain substances with approximately the same melting points. How could you prove the test tubes contain three different chemical compounds?

4. One of the most common causes of inaccurate melting points is too rapid heating of the melting point bath. Under these circumstances, how will the observed melting point compare with the true melting point?

5. Strictly speaking, why is it incorrect to speak of a melting *point*?

6. What effect would the incomplete drying of a sample (for example, the incomplete removal of a recrystallization solvent) have on the melting point?

7. Why should the melting point sample be finely powdered?

8. You suspect that an unknown is acetanilide (mp 113.5–114°C). Give a qualitative estimation of the melting point when the acetanilide is mixed with 10% by weight of naphthalene.

9. You have an unknown with an observed melting point of 90–93°C. Is your unknown compound A with a reported melting point of 95.5–96°C or compound B with a reported melting point of 90.5–91°C? Explain.

10. Why is it important to heat the melting point bath or block slowly and steadily when the temperature gets close to the mp?

11. Why is it important to pack the sample tightly in the melting point capillary?

12. An unknown compound is suspected to be acetanilide (mp 113.5–114°C). What would happen to the mp if this unknown were mixed with (a) an equal quantity of pure acetanilide? (b) an equal quantity of benzoic acid?

13. Which would be expected to have the higher boiling point, *t*-butyl alcohol (2-methyl-2-propanol) or *n*-butyl alcohol (1-butanol)? Explain.

14. When borosilicate glass (Kimax, Pyrex), n^{20} 1.474, is immersed in a solution having the same refractive index, it is almost invisible. Soft glass with n^{20} 1.52 is quite visible. This is an easy way to distinguish between the two types of glass. Calculate the mole percents of toluene and heptane that will have a refractive index of 1.474 assuming a linear relationship between the refractive indices of the two.

Reference

A. Weissberger and B. W. Rossiter (eds.). *Physical Methods of Chemistry*, Vol. 1, Part V, Wiley-Interscience, New York, 1971.

Surfing the Web

http://ull.chemistry.uakron.edu/organic_lab/melting_point/

The melting points of pure urea and cinnamic acids and mixtures of the two, as well as the melting points of unknowns (Experiments 2, 3, and 4), are carried out on a Thomas–Hoover apparatus and illustrated with 12 extraordinarily clear color photos in this University of Akron site.

For updated information visit:

www.mtholyoke.edu/courses/kwilliam/microscale.shtml

or

www.hmco.com/amco/college/chemistry/Home.html

5

Distillation

Prelab Exercise: Predict what a plot of temperature vs. volume of distillate will look like for the simple distillation and the fractional distillation of (a) a cyclohexane–toluene mixture and (b) an ethanol–water mixture.

The origins of distillation are lost in antiquity as humans in their thirst for more potent beverages found that dilute solutions of alcohol from fermentation could be separated into alcohol-rich and water-rich portions by heating the solution to boiling and condensing the vapors above the boiling liquid—the process of distillation. Since ethyl alcohol, ethanol, boils at 78°C and water boils at 100°C, one might naively assume that heating a 50:50 mixture of ethanol and water to 78°C would cause the ethanol molecules to leave the solution as a vapor that could be condensed to give pure ethanol. Such is not the case. A mixture of 50:50 ethanol:water boils near 87°C, and the vapor above it is not 100% ethanol.

Consider a better-behaved mixture, cyclohexane and toluene. The vapor pressures as a function of temperature are plotted in Fig. 5.1. When the vapor pressure of the liquid equals the applied pressure the liquid boils, so this diagram shows that at 760 mm pressure, standard atmospheric pressure, these pure liquids boil at 78 and 111°C, respectively. If one of these pure liquids were to be distilled,

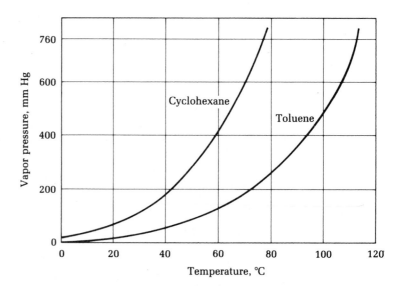

FIG. 5.1 Vapor pressure vs. temperature for cyclohexane and toluene.

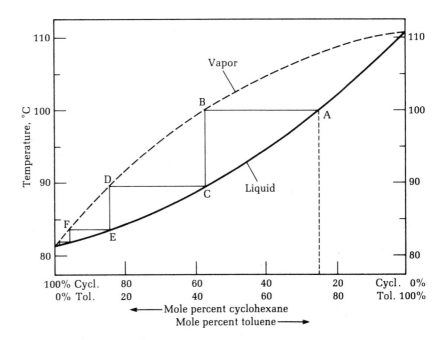

FIG. 5.2 Boiling point–composition curves for cyclohexane–toluene mixtures.

we would find that the boiling point of the liquid would equal the temperature of the vapor and that the temperature of the vapor would remain constant throughout the distillation.

Figure 5.2 is a boiling point–composition diagram for the cyclohexane–toluene system. If a mixture of 75 mole percent toluene and 25 mole percent cyclohexane is heated, we find from Fig. 5.2 that it boils at 100°C, or point A. Above a binary mixture of cyclohexane and toluene the vapor pressure has contributions from each component. Raoult's law states that the vapor pressure of the cyclohexane is equal to the product of the vapor pressure of pure cyclohexane and the mole fraction of cyclohexane in the liquid mixture:

$$P_c = P_c^\circ N_c$$

where P_c is the partial pressure of cyclohexane, P_c° is the vapor pressure of pure cyclohexane at the given temperature, and N_c is the mole fraction of cyclohexane in the mixture. Similarly for toluene:

$$P_t = P_t^\circ N_t$$

and the total vapor pressure above the solution, P_{Tot}, is given by the sum of the partial pressures due to cyclohexane and toluene:

$$P_{Tot} = P_c + P_t$$

Dalton's law states that the mole fraction of cyclohexane in the vapor at a given temperature is equal to the partial pressure of the cyclohexane at that temperature divided by the total pressure:

$$X_c = \frac{P_c}{\text{total vapor pressure}}$$

At 100°C cyclohexane has a partial pressure of 433 mm and toluene a partial pressure of 327 mm; the sum of the partial pressures is 760 mm, and so the liquid boils. If some of the liquid in equilibrium with this boiling mixture were condensed and analyzed, it would be found to be 433/760 or 57 mole percent cyclohexane (point B, Fig. 5.2). This is the best separation that can be achieved on simple distillation of this mixture. As the simple distillation proceeds, the boiling point of the mixture moves toward 110°C along the line from A, and the vapor composition becomes richer in toluene as it moves from B to 110°C. To obtain pure cyclohexane, it would be necessary to condense the liquid at B and redistill it. When this is done it is found that the liquid boils at 90°C (point C) and the vapor equilibrium with this liquid is about 85 mole percent cyclohexane (point D). So to separate a mixture of cyclohexane and toluene, a series of fractions would be collected and each of these partially redistilled. If this fractional distillation were done enough times the two components could be separated.

This series of redistillations can be done "automatically" in a fractionating column. Perhaps the easiest to understand is the bubble cap column used to distill crude oil fractionally. These columns dominate the skyline of oil refineries, some being 150 ft high and capable of distilling 200,000 barrels of crude oil per day. The crude oil enters the column as a hot vapor (Fig. 5.3). Some of this vapor with high-boiling components condenses on one of the plates. The more volatile substances travel through the bubble cap to the next higher plate where some of the less-volatile components condense. As high-boiling liquid material accumulates on a plate it descends through the overflow pipe to the next lower plate, and vapor rises through the bubble cap to the next higher plate. The temperature of the vapor that is rising through a cap is above the boiling point of the liquid on that plate. As bubbling takes place, heat is exchanged, and the less volatile components on that plate vaporize and go on to the next plate. The composition of the liquid on a plate is the same as that of the vapor coming from the plate below. So on each plate a simple distillation takes place. At equilibrium, vapor containing low-boiling material is ascending, and high-boiling liquid is descending through the column.

Figure 5.2 shows that the condensations and redistillations in a bubble cap column consisting of three plates correspond to moving on the boiling point–composition diagram from point A to point E.

In the laboratory the successive condensations and distillations that occur in the bubble cap column take place in a distilling column. The column is packed with some material on which heat exchange between ascending vapor and descending liquid can take place. A large surface area for this packing is desirable, but the packing cannot be so dense that pressure changes take place within

Fractional distillation

Overflow pipe

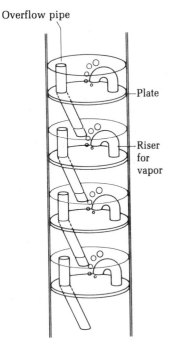

Plate

Riser for vapor

FIG. 5.3 Bubble plate distilling column.

Heat exchange between ascending vapor and descending liquid

Holdup: unrecoverable distillate that wets the column packing

Column packing

Height equivalent to a theoretical plate (HETP)

Equilibration is slow.

Good fractional distillation takes a long time.

the column causing nonequilibrium conditions. Also, if the column packing has a very large surface area, it will absorb (hold up) much of the material being distilled. A number of different packings for distilling columns have been tried—glass beads, glass helices, carborundum chips, etc. We find one of the best packings is a copper or steel sponge (Chore Boy). It is easy to put into the column, does not come out of the column as beads do, and has a large surface area, good heat transfer characteristics, and low holdup. It can be used in both microscale and macroscale apparatus.

The ability of different column packings to separate two materials of differing boiling points is evaluated by calculating the number of theoretical plates, each theoretical plate corresponding to one distillation and condensation as discussed above. Other things being equal, the number of theoretical plates is proportional to the height of the column, so various packings are evaluated according to the height equivalent to a theoretical plate (HETP); the smaller the HETP, the more plates the column will have and the more efficient it will be. The calculation is made by analyzing the proportion of lower- to higher-boiling material at the top of the column and in the distillation pot.[1]

Although not obvious, the most important variable contributing to a good fractional distillation is the rate at which the distillation is carried out. A series of simple distillations takes place within a fractionating column, and it is important that complete equilibrium be attained between the ascending vapors and the descending liquid. This process is not instantaneous. It should be an adiabatic process; that is, heat should be transferred from the ascending vapor to the descending liquid with no net loss or gain of heat. In larger, more complex distilling columns, a means is provided for adjusting the ratio between the amount of material that boils up and condenses (refluxes) and is returned to the column (thus allowing equilibrium to take place) and the amount that is removed as distillate. A reflux ratio of 30:1 or 50:1 would not be uncommon for a 40-plate column; distillation would take several hours.

Carrying out a fractional distillation on the truly microscale (<1 mg) is impossible, and it is even impossible on a small scale (10–400 mg). It can be carried out on a 4-mL scale. As seen in later chapters, various types of chromatography are employed for the separation of micro and semimicro quantities of material, while distillation is the best method for separating more than a few grams of material.

Azeotropes

Not all liquids form ideal solutions and conform to Raoult's law. Ethanol and water are such liquids. Because of molecular interaction, a mixture of 95.5% (by weight) of ethanol and 4.5% of water boils *below* (78.15°C) the boiling point of pure ethanol (78.3°C). Thus, no matter how efficient the distilling apparatus,

---

1. See A. Weissberger (ed.), *Technique of Organic Chemistry,* Vol. IV, "Distillation," Wiley-Interscience, New York, 1951.

The ethanol–water azeotrope

100% ethanol cannot be obtained by distillation of a mixture of, say, 75% water and 25% ethanol. A mixture of liquids of a certain definite composition that distills at a constant temperature without change in composition is called an *azeotrope;* 95% ethanol is such an azeotrope. The boiling point–composition curve for the ethanol–water mixture is seen in Fig. 5.4. To prepare 100% ethanol the water can be removed chemically (reaction with calcium oxide) or by removal of the water as an azeotrope (with still another liquid). An azeotropic mixture of 32.4% ethanol and 67.6% benzene (bp 80.1°C) boils at 68.2°C. A ternary azeotrope (bp 64.9°C) contains 74.1% benzene, 18.5% ethanol, and 7.4% water. Absolute alcohol (100% ethanol) is made by addition of benzene to 95% alcohol and removal of the water in the volatile benzene–water–alcohol azeotrope.

Ethanol and water form a minimum boiling azeotrope. Other substances, such as formic acid (bp 100.7°C) and water (bp 100°C), form maximum boiling azeotropes. For these two compounds the azeotrope boils at 107.3°C.

A pure liquid has a constant boiling point. A change in boiling point during distillation is an indication of impurity. The converse proposition, however, is not always true, and constancy of a boiling point does not necessarily mean that the liquid consists of only one compound. For instance, two miscible liquids of similar chemical structure that boil at the same temperature individually will have nearly the same boiling point as a mixture. And, as noted previously,

A constant bp on distillation does not guarantee that the distillate is one pure compound.

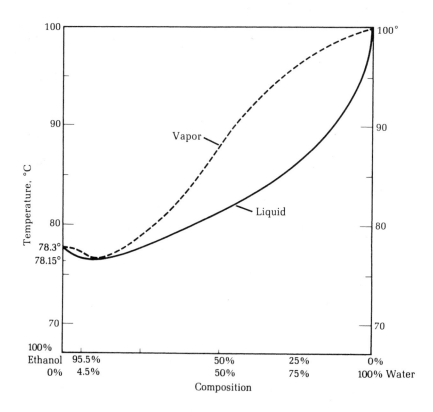

FIG. 5.4 Boiling point–composition curves for ethanol–water mixtures.

TABLE 5.1   Variation in Boiling Point with Pressure

Pressure (mm)	Water (°C)	Benzene (°C)
780	100.7	81.2
770	100.4	80.8
760	100.0	80.3
750	99.6	79.9
740	99.2	79.5
584*	92.8	71.2

*Instituto de Quimica, Mexico City, altitude 7,700 ft (2,310 m).

Distilling a mixture of sugar and water

azeotropes have constant boiling points that can be either above or below the boiling points of the individual components.

When a solution of sugar in water is distilled, the boiling point recorded on a thermometer located in the vapor phase is 100°C (at 760 torr) throughout the distillation, whereas the temperature of the boiling sugar solution itself is initially somewhat above 100°C and continues to rise as the concentration of sugar in the remaining solution increases. The vapor pressure of the solution is dependent on the number of water molecules present in a given volume; and hence with increasing concentration of nonvolatile sugar molecules and decreasing concentration of water, the vapor pressure at a given temperature decreases and a higher temperature is required for boiling. However, sugar molecules do not leave the solution, and the drop clinging to the thermometer is pure water in equilibrium with pure water vapor.

Bp changes with pressure.

When a distillation is carried out in a system open to the air and the boiling point is thus dependent on existing air pressure, the prevailing barometric pressure should be noted and allowance made for appreciable deviations from the accepted boiling point temperature (see Table 5.1). Distillation can also be done at the lower pressures that can be achieved by an oil pump or an aspirator with substantial reduction of boiling point.

Experiments

MICROSCALE

1. Calibration of Thermometer

If you have not previously carried out a calibration, test the 0°C point of your thermometer with a well-stirred mixture of crushed ice and distilled water. To check the 100°C point, put 2 mL of water in a test tube with a boiling chip to prevent bumping and boil the water gently over a hot sand bath with the thermometer in the vapor from the boiling water. Take care to see that the thermometer does not touch the side of the test tube. Then immerse the bulb of the thermometer in the liquid, and see if you can observe superheating. Check the atmospheric pressure to determine the true boiling point of the water.

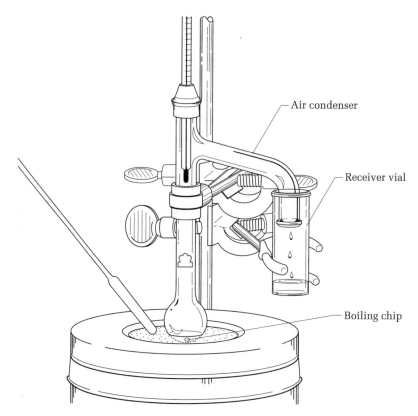

FIG. 5.5 Small-scale simple distillation apparatus. This apparatus can be adapted for fractional distillation by packing the long neck with a copper sponge. The temperature is regulated by either scraping sand away from or piling sand up around the flask.

MICROSCALE

Apparatus for simple distillation.

Apparatus

In this experiment, the two liquids to be separated are placed in a 5-mL round-bottomed long-necked flask that is fitted to a distilling head (Fig. 5.5). The flask has a larger surface area exposed to heat than the reaction tube, so the necessary thermal energy can be put into the system to cause the materials to distill. The hot vapor rises and completely envelops the bulb of the thermometer before passing over it and down toward the receiver. The downward-sloping portion of the distilling head functions as an air condenser.

The rate of distillation is determined by the heat input to the apparatus. This is most easily controlled by using a spatula to pile up or scrape away hot sand from around the flask. This works very well. The effect of a column packing on separation efficiency can be evaluated by carrying out a careful distillation of cyclohexane and toluene in this apparatus and then packing the long neck of the flask with a copper sponge and repeating the distillation. Fractional distillation is best carried out using the 10-cm packed column (Fig. 5.6).

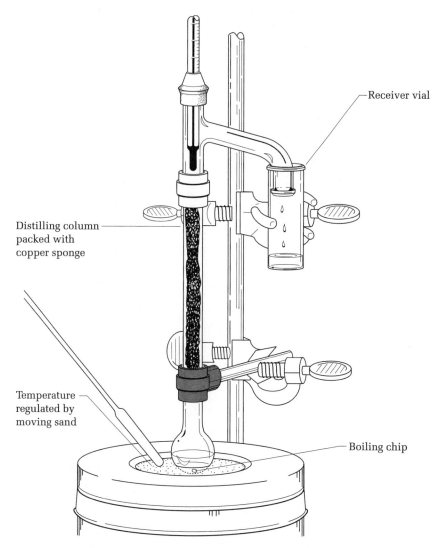

Receiver vial

Distilling column
packed with
copper sponge

Temperature
regulated by
moving sand

Boiling chip

FIG. 5.6   Small-scale fractional distillation apparatus. The 10-cm column is
packed with 1.5 g of copper sponge (Chore Boy).

Another simple distillation
apparatus.

Another design for a simple distillation apparatus is shown in Fig. 5.7. The
long air condenser will condense even low-boiling liquids, and the receiver is far
from the heat.

MICROSCALE

2. Instant Microscale Distillation

Frequently, a very small quantity of freshly distilled material is needed in an
experiment. For example, two compounds that need to be distilled freshly are aniline, which turns black because of the formation of oxidation products, and
benzaldehyde, a liquid that easily oxides to solid benzoic acid. The impurities in

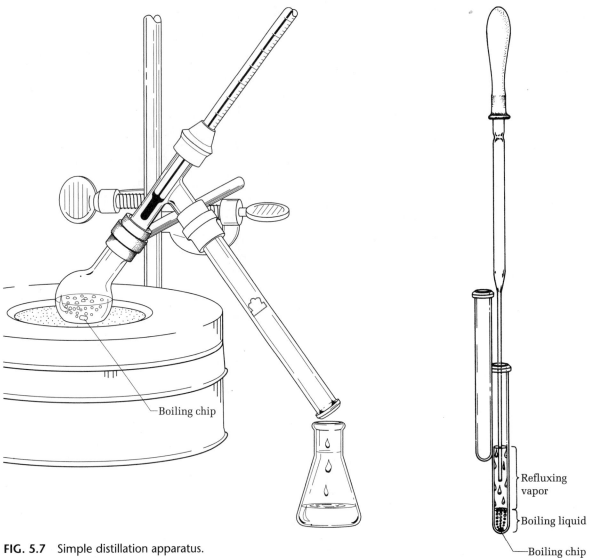

FIG. 5.7 Simple distillation apparatus.

Refluxing vapor

Boiling liquid

Boiling chip

FIG. 5.8 Apparatus for instant microscale distillation.

both these compounds have much higher boiling points than the parent substance, so a very simple distillation suffices to separate them. This is accomplished as follows.

Place a few drops of the impure liquid in a reaction tube along with a boiling chip. Clamp the tube in a hot sand bath, and adjust the heat so that the liquid refluxes about halfway up the tube. Expel the air from a Pasteur pipette, thrust it down in the hot vapor, and then pull the hot vapor into the cold upper portion of the pipette. The vapor will immediately condense, and it can then be expelled into another reaction tube held adjacent to the hot one (Fig. 5.8). In this way enough pure material can be distilled to determine a boiling point, run a spectrum, make a derivative, or carry out a reaction. Sometimes the first drop or two will be cloudy, indicating the presence of water. This fraction should be discarded in order to obtain pure dry material.

Experiments

🧪🍶 MICROSCALE AND MACROSCALE

1. Calibration of Thermometer

If you have not previously carried out a calibration, test the 0°C point of your thermometer with a well-stirred mixture of crushed ice and distilled water. To check the 100°C point, put 2 mL of water in a reaction tube with a boiling chip to prevent bumping, and boil the water gently over a hot sand bath with the thermometer in the vapor from the boiling water. Take care to see that the thermometer does not touch the side of the reaction tube. Then immerse the bulb of the thermometer in the liquid, and see if you can observe superheating. Check the atmospheric pressure to determine the true boiling point of the water.

🧪 MICROSCALE

2. Simple Distillation

(A) Simple Distillation of a Cyclohexane–Toluene Mixture. To a 5-mL long-necked round-bottomed flask is added 2.0 mL of dry cyclohexane, 2.0 mL of dry toluene, and a boiling chip (see Fig. 5.5). This flask is joined by means of a Viton (black) connector to a distilling head fitted with a thermometer using a rubber connector. The thermometer bulb should be completely below the side arm of the Claisen head so that the mercury reaches the same temperature as the vapor that distills. The end of the distilling head dips well down into a vial, which rests on the bottom of a 30-mL beaker filled with ice. The distillation is started by piling up hot sand to heat the flask. As soon as boiling starts, the vapors can be seen to rise up the neck of the flask. Adjust the rate of heating by piling up or scraping away sand from the flask so that it takes *several minutes* for the vapor to rise to the thermometer: **The rate of distillation should be no faster than two drops per minute.**

Viton is resistant to hot aromatic vapors.

The thermometer bulb must be completely below the side arm.

Record the temperature versus the number of drops during the entire distillation. If the rate of distillation is as slow as it should be, there will be sufficient time between drops to read and record the temperature. Continue the distillation until only about 0.4 mL remains in the distilling flask. At the end of the distillation, measure as accurately as possible, perhaps using a syringe, the volume of the distillate and, after it cools, the volume left in the pot; the difference is the holdup of the column if none has been lost by evaporation. Note the barometric pressure, make any thermometer corrections necessary, and make a plot of milliliters (drop number) versus temperature for the distillation.

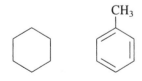

Cyclohexane
bp 81°C
MW 84.16
n_D^{20} 1.4260

Toluene
bp 111°C
MW 92.14
n_D^{20} 1.4960

There are 21 ± 3 drops per milliliter.

Cleaning Up The pot residue should be placed in the organic solvents container. The distillate can be placed there, or it can be recycled.

(B) Simple Distillation of an Ethanol–Water Mixture.   In a 5-mL round-bottomed long-necked flask place 4 mL of a 10% to 20% ethanol–water mixture. It could come from the fermentation of glucose (Chapter 59). Assemble the apparatus as described above, and carry out the distillation until you believe a representative sample of ethanol has collected in the receiver. In the hood place three drops of this sample on a watch glass, and try to ignite it with the blue cone of a microburner flame. Does it burn? Is any unburned residue observed? There was a time when alcohol–water mixtures were mixed with gunpowder and ignited to give proof that the alcohol had not been diluted. One hundred proof alcohol is 50% ethanol by volume.

Cleaning Up   The distillate and pot residue can be flushed down the drain.

MICROSCALE

3. Fractional Distillation

Apparatus

Assemble the apparatus shown in Fig. 5.6. The 10-cm column is packed with 1.5 g of copper sponge and connected to the 5-mL short-necked flask using the black (Viton) connector. The column should be vertical, and care should be taken to ensure that the bulb of the thermometer does not touch the side of the distilling head. The column, but not the distilling head, will be insulated with glass wool or cotton at the appropriate time to ensure that the process is adiabatic. Alternatively, the column can be insulated with a cut-off 15-mL polyethylene-centrifuge tube.

Adjust the heat input to the flask by piling up or scraping away sand around the flask.

Never distill in an airtight system.

Insulate the distilling column but not the head.

21 ± 3 drops = 1 mL

(A)   Fractional Distillation of a Cyclohexane–Toluene Mixture.   To the short-necked flask is added 2.0 mL of cyclohexane, 2.0 mL of toluene, and a boiling chip. The distilling column is packed with 1.5 g of copper sponge (Fig. 5.6). The mixture is brought to a boil over a hot sand bath. Observe the ring of condensate that should rise slowly through the column; if you cannot at first see this ring, locate it by touching the column with the fingers. Reduce the heat by scraping sand away from the flask, and wrap the column, but not the distilling head, with glass wool or cotton if it is not already insulated.

The distilling head and the thermometer function as a small reflux condenser. Again, apply the heat, and as soon as the vapor reaches the thermometer bulb, reduce the heat by scraping away sand. **Distill the mixture at a rate no faster than two drops per minute,** and record the temperature as a function of the number of drops. If the heat input has been *very* carefully adjusted, the distillation will cease and the temperature reading will drop after the cyclohexane has distilled. Increase the heat input by piling up the sand around the flask in order to cause the toluene to distill. Stop the distillation when only about 0.4 mL remains in the flask, and measure the volume of distillate and the pot residue as before. Make a plot of boiling point versus milliliters of distillate (drops), and compare it to the simple distillation carried out in the same apparatus. Compare your results with those of Fig. 5.9.

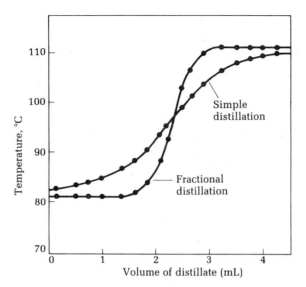

FIG. 5.9 Simple and fractional distillation curves for cyclohexane and toluene.

Cleaning Up The pot residue should be placed in the organic solvents container. The distillate can be placed there or recycled.

(B) Fractional Distillation of an Ethanol–Water Mixture.

Distill 4 mL of the same ethanol–water mixture used in the simple distillation experiment following the procedure used for cyclohexane–toluene with either the short or the long distilling column. Remove what you regard to be the ethanol fraction, and repeat the ignition test. Is any difference noted?

Cleaning Up The pot residue and distillate can be flushed down the drain.

(C) Fractional Distillation of an Unknown Mixture.

Distill 4 mL of a mixture of two of the compounds from Table 5.2 (at the end of the chapter). The two liquids will have boiling points at least 20°C apart. The composition of the mixture will be 20/80, 30/70, 40/60, 50/50, 60/40, 70/30, or 80/20 percents of the two components. Identify the two compounds, and determine the percent composition of each.

Once the mixture has been distilled and the volumes of the lower- and higher-boiling components determined, the mixture might be redistilled and separated into three fractions: the lower-boiling one, a small middle fraction, and the higher-boiling one. The composition and purity of the lower- and higher-boiling fractions can be determined by measuring the refractive indices of each.

Cleaning Up Place all fractions and the pot residue in the organic solvents waste container.

4. Simple Distillation

Apparatus

In any distillation, the flask should not be more than two-thirds full at the start. Great care should be taken not to distill to dryness because, in some cases, high-boiling explosive peroxides can become concentrated.

Assemble the apparatus for simple distillations shown in Fig. 5.10, starting with the support ring followed by the electric flask heater (Fig. 1.16n) and then the flask. One or two boiling stones are put in the flask to promote even boiling. Each ground joint is greased by putting three or four stripes of grease lengthwise around the male joint and pressing the joint firmly into the other without twisting. The air is thus eliminated, and the joint will appear almost transparent. (Do not use excess grease because it will contaminate the product.) Water enters the condenser at the tublature nearest the receiver. Because of the large heat capacity of water, only a very small stream (3 mm diameter) is needed; too much water pressure will cause the tubing to pop off. A heavy rubber band, or better, a Keck clamp, can be used to hold the condenser to the distillation head. Note that the bulb of the thermometer is below the opening into the side arm of the distillation head.

CAUTION: Cyclohexane and toluene are flammable; make sure distilling apparatus is tight.

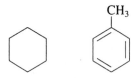

Cyclohexane
MW 84.16
bp 81.4°C
den 0.78
n_D^{20} 1.4260

Toluene
MW 92.14
bp 110.8°C
den 0.87
n_D^{20} 1.4960

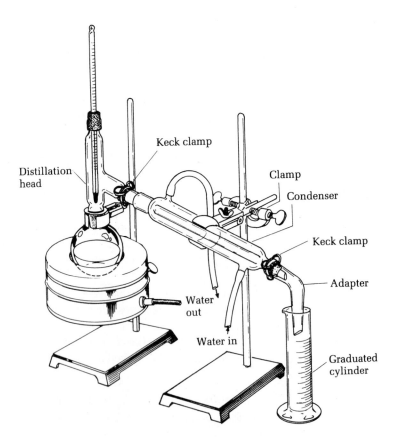

FIG. 5.10 Apparatus for simple distillation.

Do not add a boiling chip to a hot liquid. It may boil over.

Dispose of cyclohexane and toluene in the container provided. Do not pour them down the drain.

(A) Simple Distillation of a Cyclohexane–Toluene Mixture.   Place a mixture of 30 mL cyclohexane and 30 mL toluene and a boiling chip in a dry 100-mL round-bottomed flask, and assemble the apparatus for simple distillation. After making sure all connections are tight, heat the flask strongly until boiling starts. Then adjust the heat until the distillate drops at a regular rate of about one drop per second. Record both the temperature and the volume of distillate at regular intervals. After 50 mL of distillate is collected, discontinue the distillation. Record the barometric pressure, make any thermometer correction necessary, and plot boiling point versus volume of distillate. Save the distillate for fractional distillation.

Cleaning Up   The pot residue should be placed in the organic solvents container. The distillate also can be placed there or it can be recycled.

A 10% to 12% solution of ethanol in water is produced by fermentation. See Chapter 59.

(B) Simple Distillation of an Ethanol–Water Mixture.   In a 500-mL round-bottomed flask place 200 mL of a 20% aqueous solution of ethanol. Follow the procedure (above) for the distillation of a cyclohexane–toluene mixture. Discontinue the distillation after 50 mL of distillate has been collected. In the hood place three drops of distillate on a Pyrex watch glass, and try to ignite it with the blue cone of a microburner flame. Does it burn? Is any unburned residue observed?

Cleaning Up   The pot residue and distillate can be flushed down the drain.

 **MACROSCALE**

5. Fractional Distillation

Apparatus

Assemble the apparatus shown in Figs. 5.11 and 5.12. The fractionating column is packed with one-fourth to one-third of a metal sponge. The column should be perfectly vertical, and it should be insulated with glass wool covered with aluminum foil with the shiny side in. However, in order to observe what is taking place within the column, insulation is omitted for this experiment.

(A) Fractional Distillation of a Cyclohexane–Toluene Mixture.   After the flask from the simple distillation experiment has cooled, pour the 50 mL of distillate back into the distilling flask, add one or two new boiling chips, and assemble the apparatus for fractional distillation. The stillhead delivers into a short condenser fitted with a bent adapter leading into a 10-mL graduated cylinder. Gradually turn up the heat to the electric flask heater until the mixture of cyclohexane and toluene just begins to boil. As soon as boiling starts, turn down the power. Heat slowly at first. A ring of condensate will rise slowly through the column; if you cannot at first see this ring, locate it by cautiously touching the column with the fingers. The rise should be very gradual, in order that the column can acquire a uniform temperature gradient. Do not apply more heat until you are sure that the ring of condensate has stopped rising; then increase the heat gradu-

FIG. 5.11 Apparatus for fractional distillation. The position of the thermometer bulb is critical.

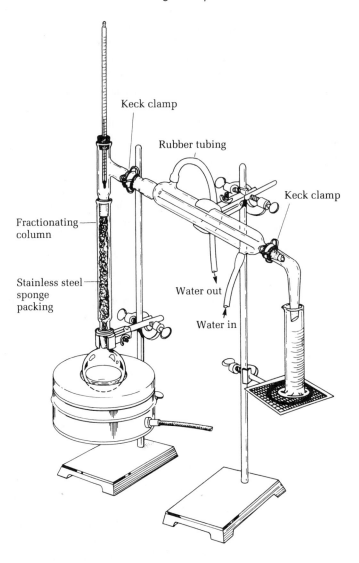

Keck clamp

Rubber tubing

Keck clamp

Fractionating column

Stainless steel sponge packing

Water out

Water in

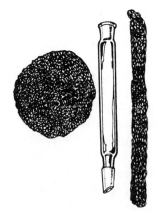

FIG. 5.12 Fractionating column and packing. Use one-third of sponge (Chore Boy).

ally. In a properly conducted operation, the vapor-condensate mixture reaches the top of the column only after several minutes. Once distillation has commenced, it should continue steadily without any drop in temperature at a rate not greater than 1 mL in 1.5–2 min. Observe the flow, and keep it steady by slight increases in heat as required. Protect the column from drafts by wrapping it with aluminum foil, glass wool, or even a towel. This insulation will help prevent flooding of the column, as will slow and steady distillation.

Record the temperature as each milliliter of distillate collects, and make more frequent readings when the temperature starts to rise abruptly. Each time the graduated cylinder fills, quickly empty it into a series of labeled 25-mL Erlenmeyer flasks. Stop the distillation when a second constant temperature is reached. Plot a distillation curve, and record what you observed inside the column in the course of the fractionation. Combine the fractions that you think are pure, and turn in the product in a bottle labeled with your name, desk number, the name of the product, the bp range, and the weight.

Cleaning Up   The pot residue should be placed in the organic solvents container. The cyclohexane and toluene fractions can be placed there also, or they can be recycled.

(B) Fractional Distillation of Ethanol–Water Mixtures. Place the 50 mL of distillate from the simple distillation experiment in a 100-mL round-bottomed flask, add one or two boiling chips, and assemble the apparatus for fractional distillation. Follow the procedure (above) for the fractional distillation of a cyclohexane–toluene mixture. Repeat the ignition test. Is any difference noted? Alternatively distill 60 mL of the 10–20% ethanol–water mixture that results from the fermentation of glucose (Chapter 65).

Cleaning Up   The pot residue and distillate can be flushed down the drain.

MICROSCALE AND MACROSCALE   **6. Unknowns**

You will be supplied with an unknown, prepared by the instructor, that is a mixture of two solvents from those listed in Table 5.2, only two of which form azeotropes. The solvents in the mixture will be mutually soluble and differ in boiling point by more than 20°C. Fractionate the unknown, and identify the components from the boiling points. Prepare a distillation curve. You may be directed to analyze your distillate by gas chromatography (Chapter 11) or refractive index (Chapter 4).

Cleaning Up   Organic material goes in the organic solvents container. Water and aqueous solutions can be flushed down the drain.

TABLE 5.2   Some Properties of Common Solvents

Solvent	Boiling Point (°C)
Acetone	56.5
Methanol	64.7
Hexane	68.8
1-Butanol	117.2
2-Methyl-2-propanol	82.2
Water	100.0
Toluene*	110.6

*Methanol and toluene form an azeotrope, bp 63.8°C (69% methanol).

Questions

1. In the simple distillation experiment (2), can you account for the boiling point of your product in terms of the known boiling points of the pure components of your mixture?

2. From the plot of boiling point versus volume of distillate in the simple distillation experiment, what can you conclude about the purity of your product?

3. From the boiling point versus volume of distillate plot in the fractional distillation of the cyclohexane–toluene mixture (3), what conclusion can you draw about the homogeneity of the distillate?

4. From the boiling point versus volume of distillate in the fractional distillation of the ethanol–water mixture (3), what conclusion can you draw about the homogeneity of the distillate? Does it have a constant boiling point? Is it a pure substance because it has a constant boiling point?

5. What is the effect on the boiling point of a solution (e.g., water) produced by a soluble nonvolatile substance (e.g., sodium chloride)? What is the effect of an insoluble substance such as sand or charcoal? What is the temperature of the vapor above these two boiling solutions?

6. In the distillation of a pure substance (e.g., water), why doesn't all the water vaporize at once when the boiling point is reached?

7. In fractional distillation, liquid can be seen running from the bottom of the distillation column back into the distilling flask. What effect does this returning condensate have on the fractional distillation?

8. Why is it extremely dangerous to attempt to carry out a distillation in a completely closed apparatus (one with no vent to the atmosphere)?

9. Why is better separation of two liquids achieved by slow rather than fast distillation?

10. Explain why a packed fractionating column is more efficient than an unpacked one.

11. In the distillation of the cyclohexane–toluene mixture, the first few drops of distillate may be cloudy. Explain.

12. What effect does the reduction of atmospheric pressure have on the boiling point? Can cyclohexane and toluene be separated if the external pressure is 350 mm Hg instead of 760 mm Hg?

13. When water-cooled condensers are used for distillation or for refluxing a liquid, the water enters the condenser at the lowest point and leaves at the highest. Why?

Extraction of Acids and Bases and the Isolation of Caffeine from Coffee, Tea, and Cola Syrup

Extraction is one of humankind's oldest chemical operations. The preparation of a cup of coffee or tea involves the extraction of flavor and odor components from dried vegetable matter with hot water. Aqueous extracts of bay leaves, stick cinnamon, peppercorns, and cloves are used as food flavorings, along with alcoholic extracts of vanilla and almond. For the last century and a half, organic chemists have been extracting, isolating, purifying, and then characterizing the myriad compounds produced by plants that have been used for centuries as drugs and perfumes—substances such as quinine from cinchona bark, morphine from the opium poppy, cocaine from coca leaves, and menthol from peppermint oil. In research a Soxhlet extractor is often used (Fig. 8.1). The organic chemist commonly employs, in addition to solid/liquid extraction, two other types of extraction: liquid/liquid extraction and acid/base extraction.

Part 1. Liquid/Liquid Extraction

After a chemical reaction has been carried out, the organic product is often separated from inorganic substances by liquid/liquid extraction. For example, in the synthesis of 1-bromobutane (Chapter 16)

$$2\ CH_3CH_2CH_2CH_2OH + 2\ NaBr + H_2SO_4 \rightarrow$$
$$2\ CH_3CH_2CH_2CH_2Br + 2\ H_2O + Na_2SO_4$$

1-butanol, also a liquid, is heated with an aqueous solution of sodium bromide and sulfuric acid to produce the product and sodium sulfate. The 1-bromobutane is isolated from the reaction mixture by extraction with *t*-butyl methyl ether, a solvent in which 1-bromobutane is soluble and in which water and sodium sulfate are insoluble. The extraction is accomplished by simply adding *t*-butyl methyl ether to the aqueous mixture and shaking it. The *t*-butyl methyl ether is

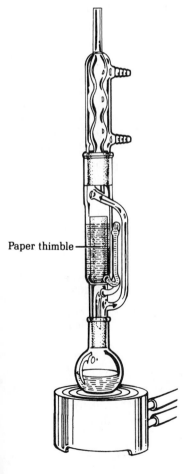

Paper thimble

FIG. 8.1 Soxhlet extractor; for extraction of solids, e.g. dried leaves or seeds. The solid is put in a filter paper thimble. Solvent vapor rises in the tube on the right, and condensate drops onto the solid in the thimble, leaches out soluble material, and, after initiating an automatic siphon, carries it to the flask where nonvolatile extracted material accumulates. Substances of very slight solubility can be extracted by prolonged operation.

less dense than water and floats on top; it is removed and evaporated to leave the bromo compound free of inorganic substances.

Properties of Extraction Solvents

The solvent used for extraction should have many properties of a satisfactory recrystallization solvent. It should readily dissolve the substance to be extracted; it should have a low boiling point so that it can readily be removed; it should not react with the solute or the other solvent; it should not be flammable or toxic; and it should be relatively inexpensive. In addition, it should not be miscible with water (the usual second phase). No solvent meets all the criteria, but several come close. Diethyl ether, usually referred to simply as ether, is probably the most common solvent used for extraction, but it is extremely flammable.

In the past, diethyl ether has been the most common solvent for extraction in the laboratory. It has high solvent power for hydrocarbons and for oxygen-containing compounds. It is highly volatile (bp 34.6°C) and therefore is easily removed from an extract. However, diethyl ether has two big disadvantages. It is highly flammable and so poses a great fire threat, and it easily forms peroxides. The reaction of diethyl ether with air is catalyzed by light. The resulting peroxides are higher boiling than the ether and are left as a residue when the ether evaporates. If the residue is heated, it will explode, since ether peroxides are treacherous high explosives. But in recent years, a new solvent has come on the scene.

$$CH_3CH_2-O-CH_2CH_3$$

Diethyl ether
"Ether"
MW 74.12, den. 0.708
bp 34.6°C, n_D^{20} 1.3530

$$H_3C-\underset{\underset{CH_3}{|}}{\overset{\overset{CH_3}{|}}{C}}-O-CH_3$$

tert-Butyl methyl ether
MW 88.14, den. 0.741
bp 55.2°C, n_D^{20} 1.369

***tert*-Butyl Methyl Ether, the Extraction Solvent of Choice.** *tert*-Butyl methyl ether, called methyl *tert*-butyl ether (MTBE) in industry, has many advantages over diethyl ether as an extraction solvent. Most important, it does not easily form peroxides, so it can be stored for much longer periods than diethyl ether. And, in the United States, it is less than one-half the price of diethyl ether. It is slightly less volatile (bp 55°C), so it does not pose the same fire threat as diethyl ether, although one must be as careful in handling this solvent as in handling any other highly volatile, flammable substance. The explosion limits for *tert*-butyl methyl ether mixed with air are much narrower than for diethyl ether, the toxicity is less, the solvent power is the same, and the ignition temperature is higher (224 versus 180°C).

The weigh percent solubility of diethyl ether dissolved in water is 7.2%, while that of the butyl ether is 4.8%. The solubility of water in diethyl ether is 1.2%, while in the butyl ether it is 1.5%. Unlike diethyl ether, *t*-butyl methyl ether forms an azeotrope with water (4% water) that boils at 52.6°C, which aids in the removal of the last traces of water from an extract.

The low price and ready availability of *tert*-butyl methyl ether come about because it has replaced tetraethyl lead as the antiknock additive for high-octane gasoline and as a fuel oxygenate, which helps reduce air pollution. In this text, *tert*-butyl methyl ether is suggested wherever diethyl ether formerly would have been used in an extraction. It will not, however, work as the only solvent in the Grignard reaction, probably because of steric hindrance.

Partition Coefficient

The extraction of a compound such as 1-butanol, which is slightly soluble in water as well as very soluble in ether, is an equilibrium process governed by the solubilities of the alcohol in the two solvents. The ratio of the solubilities is known as the *distribution coefficient,* also called the *partition coefficient, k,* and is an equilibrium constant with a certain value for a given substance, pair of solvents, and temperature.

To a good approximation the *concentration* of the solute in each solvent can be correlated with the *solubility* of the solute in the pure solvent, a figure that can be found readily in tables of solubility in reference books.

$$k = \frac{\text{Concentration of C in } t\text{-butyl methyl ether}}{\text{Concentration of C in water}}$$

$$\cong \frac{\text{Solubility of C in } t\text{-butyl methyl ether (g/100 mL)}}{\text{Solubility of C in water (g/100 mL)}}$$

Consider a compound, A, that dissolves in *t*-butyl methyl ether to the extent of 12 g/100 mL and dissolves in water to the extent of 6 g/100 mL.

$$k = \frac{12 \text{ g/100 mL } t\text{-butyl methyl ether}}{6 \text{ g/100 mL water}} = 2$$

If a solution of 6 g of A in 100 mL of water is shaken with 100 mL of *t*-butyl methyl ether, then

$$k = \frac{(x \text{ grams of A/100 mL } t\text{-butyl methyl ether})}{(6 - x \text{ grams of A/100 mL water})} = 2$$

from which

$$x = 4.0 \text{ g of A in the ether layer}$$

$$6 - x = 2.0 \text{ g left in the water layer}$$

It is, however, more efficient to extract the 100 mL of aqueous solution twice with 50-mL portions of *t*-butyl methyl ether rather than once with a 100-mL portion.

$$k = \frac{(x \text{ g of A/50 mL})}{(6 - x \text{ g of A/100 mL})} = 2$$

from which

$$x = 3.0 \text{ g in the } t\text{-butyl methyl ether layer}$$

$$6 - x = 3.0 \text{ g in the water layer}$$

If this 3.0 g/100 mL of water is extracted once more with 50 mL of *t*-butyl methyl ether, we can calculate that 1.5 g will be in the ether layer, leaving 1.5 g in the water layer. So two extractions with 50-mL portions of ether will extract 3.0 g + 1.5 g = 4.5 g of A, while one extraction with a 100-mL portion of *t*-butyl methyl ether removes only 4.0 g of A. Three extractions with $33\frac{1}{3}$-mL portions of *t*-butyl methyl ether would extract 4.7 g. Obviously there is a point at which the increased amount of A extracted does not repay the effort of multiple extractions, but keep in mind that several small-scale extractions are more effective than one large-scale extraction.

Technique of Liquid/Liquid Extraction

Place 1 to 2 mL of an aqueous solution of the compound to be extracted in a reaction tube. Add about 1 mL of dichloromethane. Note, as you add the dichloromethane, whether it is the top or bottom layer.

Mixing the Layers.
An effective way to do this is to flick the tube with a finger. Grasp the tube firmly at the very top between thumb and forefinger, and flick it vigorously at the bottom (Fig. 8.2). You will find that this violent motion mixes the contents well, but nothing comes out the top. Another good mixing technique is to pull the contents of the reaction tube into a Pasteur pipette and then expel the mixture back into the tube with force. Doing this several times will effect good mixing of the two layers. A stopper can be placed in the top of the tube and the contents mixed by shaking the tube, but the problem with this technique is that the high vapor pressure of the solvent often will force liquid out around the cork or stopper.

Separating the Layers.
After thorough mixing of the two layers, allow them to separate. Tap the tube if droplets of one layer are in the other layer or on the side of the tube. After the layers separate completely, draw up the lower dichloromethane layer into a Pasteur pipette. Leave behind any middle emulsion layer. The easiest way to do this is to attach the pipette to a pipette pump (Fig. 8.3). This allows very precise control of the liquid being removed. It takes more skill and practice to remove the lower layer cleanly with a 2-mL rubber bulb attached to the pipette, because the high vapor pressure of the solvent tends to make it dribble out of the pipette. To avoid losing any of the solution, it is best to grasp a clean, dry, empty tube in the same hand as the full tube to receive the organic layer (Fig. 8.4).

From the discussion of the distribution coefficient in the preceding section you know that several small extractions are better than one big one, so repeat the extraction process with two further 1-mL portions of dichloromethane. An experienced chemist might summarize all the preceding with the notebook entry, "Aqueous layer extracted 3 × 1-mL portions CH_2Cl_2," and in a formal report would write, "The aqueous layer was extracted three times with 1-mL portions of dichloromethane." If any water droplets have inadvertently been transferred, the easiest way to eliminate them is to again transfer the organic layer to a clean, dry reaction tube.

MICROSCALE

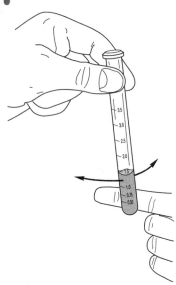

FIG. 8.2 Mixing the contents of a reaction tube by flicking it. Grasp the tube firmly at the very top, and flick it vigorously at the bottom. The contents will mix without coming out of the tube.

Always draw out the lower layer and place it in another container.

Larger Microscale Technique

A separatory funnel, regardless of size, should be filled only to about two-thirds of its capacity so the layers can be mixed by shaking. The microscale separatory

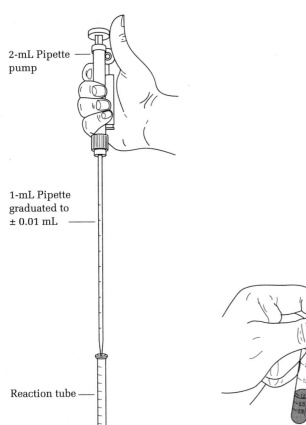

FIG. 8.3 Removal of a solvent from a reaction tube using a pipette and pipette pump.

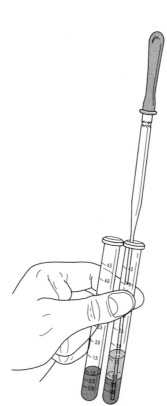

FIG. 8.4 Grasp both reaction tubes in one hand when transferring material from one tube to another using a Pasteur pipette.

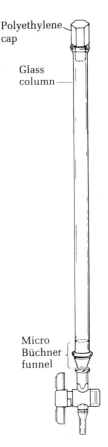

FIG. 8.5 Microscale separatory funnel. Remove the polyethylene frit from the micro Büchner funnel before using.

funnel (Fig. 8.5) has a capacity of 8.5 mL when full, so it is useful for an extraction with a total volume of about 6 mL.

Poke out the polyethylene frit from the bottom part of the separatory funnel using a wood boiling stick. Store it for later replacement. Close the valve, add up to about 5 mL of the solution to be extracted to the separatory funnel, then add the extraction solvent so that the total volume does not exceed 6 mL.

Cap the separatory funnel, and mix the contents by inverting the funnel several times. If the two layers separate fairly easily, then the contents can be shaken more thoroughly. If the layers do not separate easily, be careful not to shake the funnel too vigorously; intractable emulsions can form.

Remove the stopper from the funnel, clamp it, and then, grasping the valve with two hands, empty the bottom layer into an Erlenmeyer flask or other container. If the top layer is desired, pour it out through the top of the separatory funnel at this time—don't drain it through the valve, which may have a drop of the lower layer remaining in it.

↑ To water aspirator or
to nitrogen or air supply

—— Pasteur pipette

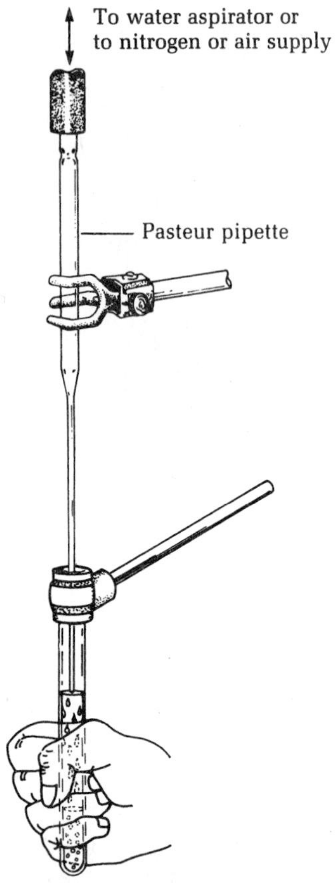

FIG. 8.6 Aspirator tube being used to remove solvent vapors.

Record the tare of the final container.

MICROSCALE

Drying the Solvent.

Dichloromethane dissolves a very small quantity of water, and microscopic droplets of water are suspended in the organic layer, often making it cloudy. To remove the water, a drying agent, anhydrous calcium chloride pellets, is added to the dichloromethane solution.

How Much Drying Agent Should Be Used?

When a small quantity of the drying agent is added, the crystals or pellets become sticky with water, clump together, and fall rapidly as a lump to the bottom of the reaction tube. There will come a point when a new small quantity of drying agent no longer clumps together, but the individual particles settle slowly throughout the solution. As they say in Scandinavia, "Add drying agent until it begins to snow." The drying process takes about 10 to 15 min, during which time the tube contents should be mixed occasionally by flicking the tube. The solution should no longer be cloudy, but clear (although it may be colored).

Once drying is judged complete, the solvent is removed by forcing a Pasteur pipette to the bottom of the reaction tube and pulling the solvent in. Air is expelled from the pipette as it is being pushed through the crystals or pellets so that no drying agent will enter the pipette. It is very important to wash the drying agent left in the reaction tube with several small quantities of pure solvent to transfer all the extract.

Removing the Solvent.

If the quantity of extract is relatively small, say three mL or less, then the easiest way to remove the solvent is to blow a stream of air (or nitrogen) onto the surface of the solution from a Pasteur pipette (Fig. 8.6). Be sure that the stream of air is very gentle before inserting it into the reaction tube. The heat of vaporization of the solvent will cause the tube to get rather cold during the evaporation and, of course, slow down the process. The easiest way to add heat is to hold the tube in your hand.

Another way to remove the solvent is to attach the Pasteur pipette to an aspirator and pull air over the surface of the liquid. This is not so fast as blowing air onto the surface of the liquid and runs the danger of sucking the liquid up into the aspirator.

If the volume of liquid is more than about three mL, then put it into the 25-mL filter flask, put the plastic Hirsch funnel in place, and attach the flask to the aspirator. By placing your thumb in the Hirsch funnel, the vacuum can be controlled, and heat can be applied by holding the flask in the other hand while swirling the contents (Fig. 8.7).

The reaction tube or filter flask in which the solvent is evaporated should be tared (weighed empty), and this weight recorded in the notebook. In this way, the weight of material extracted can be determined by again weighing the container.

Experiment

Partition Coefficient of Benzoic Acid

In a reaction tube, place about 100 mg of benzoic acid (weighed to the nearest milligram), and to this add exactly equal volumes of water followed by

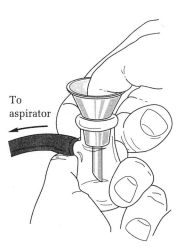

To
aspirator

FIG. 8.7 Apparatus for removal of a solvent under vacuum.

dichloromethane (about 1.6 mL each). While making this addition, note which layer is the organic layer and which the aqueous. Put a septum on the tube, and shake the contents vigorously for at least 2 min. Allow the tube to stand undisturbed until the layers separate, and then carefully draw off, using a Pasteur pipette, *all* the aqueous layer without removing any of the organic layer. It may be of help to draw out the tip of the pipette to a fine point in a flame and, using this, to tilt the reaction tube on its side to make this separation as clean as possible.

Add anhydrous calcium chloride pellets to the dichloromethane in very small quantities until it no longer clamps together. Mix the contents of the tube by flicking it, and allow it to stand for about 5 min to complete the drying process. Using a dry Pasteur pipette, transfer the dichloromethane to a tared (previously weighed) dry reaction tube or 10-mL Erlenmeyer flask containing a boiling chip. Complete the transfer by washing the drying agent with two more portions of solvent that are added to the original solution, and then evaporate the solvent. This can be done by boiling off the solvent while removing solvent vapors with an aspirator tube or by blowing a stream of air or nitrogen into the container while warming it in the hand (see Fig. 8.6). This operation should be performed in a hood.

From the weight of the benzoic acid in the dichloromethane layer, the weight in the water layer can be obtained by difference. The ratio of the weight in dichloromethane to the weight in water is the distribution coefficient, because the volumes of the two solvents were equal. Report the value of the distribution coefficient.

Cleaning Up   The aqueous layer can be flushed down the drain. Dichloromethane goes in the halogenated organic solvents container, and after allowing the solvent to evaporate from the sodium sulfate in the hood, place it in the nonhazardous solid waste container.

Part 2. Acid/Base Extraction

The third type of extraction, acid/base extraction, involves carrying out simple acid/base reactions in order to separate strong organic acids, weak organic acids, neutral organic compounds, and basic organic substances. The chemistry involved is given in the equations that follow, using benzoic acid, phenol, naphthalene, and aniline as examples of the four types of compounds. Chapter 44 is also an acid/base extraction experiment; the components of analgesic tablets are separated.

Here is the strategy: The four organic compounds are dissolved in *t*-butyl methyl ether. The ether solution is shaken with a saturated aqueous solution of sodium bicarbonate, a weak base. This will react only with the strong acid, benzoic acid (**1**) to form the ionic salt, sodium benzoate (**5**), which dissolves in the aqueous layer and is removed. The ether solution now contains just phenol (**2**), naphthalene (**4**), and aniline (**3**). A 3 *M* aqueous solution of sodium hydroxide is added and the mixture shaken. The hydroxide, a strong base, will react only with the phenol (**2**) a weak acid, to form sodium phenoxide (**6**), an ionic compound that dissolves in the aqueous layer and is removed. The ether now contains only naphthalene (**4**) and aniline (**3**). Shaking it with dilute hydrochloric acid removes the aniline, a base, as the ionic anilinium chloride (**7**). The aqueous layer is removed. Evaporation of the *t*-butyl methyl ether now leaves naphthalene (**4**), the neutral compound. The other three compounds are recovered by adding acid to the sodium benzoate (**5**) and sodium phenoxide (**6**) and base to the anilinium chloride (**7**) to regenerate the covalent compounds benzoic acid (**1**), phenol (**2**), and aniline (**3**). These operations are conveniently represented in a flow diagram (Fig. 8.8).

The ability to separate strong from weak acids depends on the acidity constants of the acids and the basicity constants of the bases as follows. In the first equation consider the ionization of benzoic acid, which has an equilibrium constant, K_a, of 6.8×10^{-5}. The conversion of benzoic acid to the benzoate anion in Eq. 4 is governed by the equilibrium constant, K (Eq. 5), obtained by combining the third and fourth equations.

The pK_a of carboric acid, H_2CO_3, is 6.35.

$$C_6H_5COOH + H_2O \rightleftharpoons C_6H_5COO^- + H_3O^+ \tag{1}$$

$$K_a = \frac{[C_6H_5COO^-][H_3O^+]}{[C_6H_5COOH]} = 6.8 \times 10^{-5}, pK_a = 4.17 \tag{2}$$

$$K_w = [H_3O^+][OH^-] = 10^{-14} \tag{3}$$

$$C_6H_5COOH + OH^- \rightleftharpoons C_6H_5COO^- + H_2O \tag{4}$$

$$K = \frac{[C_6H_5COO^-]}{[C_6H_5COOH][OH^-]} = \frac{K_a}{K_w} = \frac{6.8 \times 10^{-5}}{10^{-14}} = 3.2 \times 10^8 \tag{5}$$

For phenol with a K_a of 10^{-10}, the minimum hydroxide ion concentration that will produce the phenoxide anion in 99% conversion is 10^{-2} *M*. The concentration of hydroxide in 10% sodium hydroxide solution is 10^{-1} *M*, and so phenol in strong base is entirely converted to the water-soluble salt.

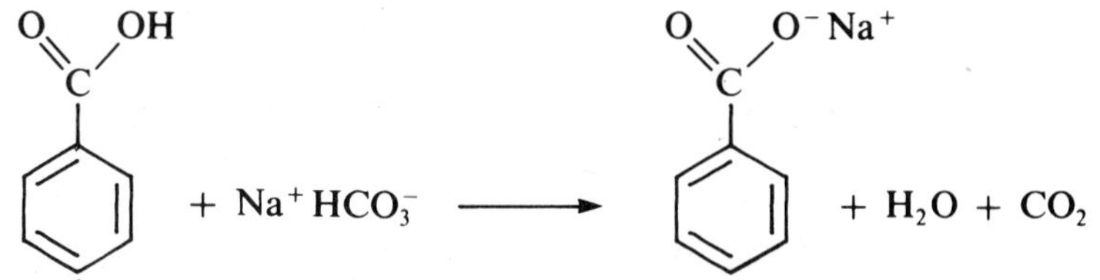

1
Benzoic acid
$pK_a = 4.17$
Covalent, sol. in org. solvents

$+ Na^+HCO_3^-$ ⟶

5
Sodium benzoate
Ionic, sol. in water

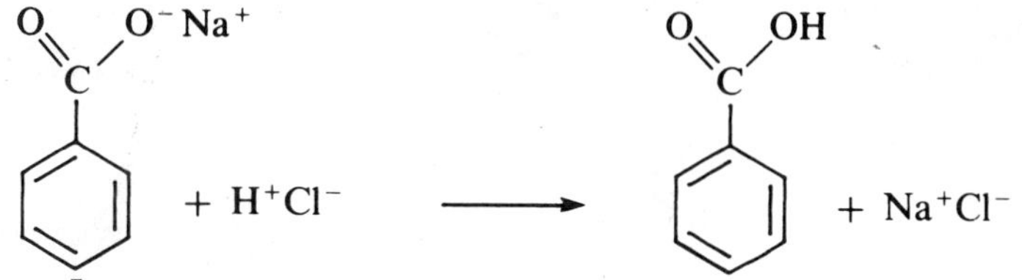

$+ H_2O + CO_2$

5

$+ H^+Cl^-$ ⟶

1

$+ Na^+Cl^-$

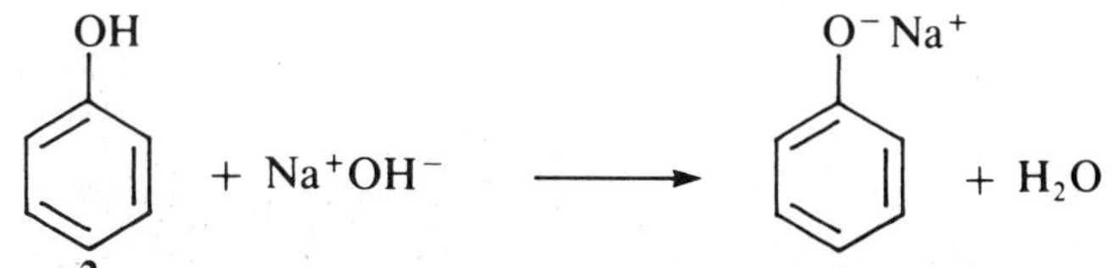

2
Phenol
$pK_a = 10$
Covalent, sol. in org. solvents

$+ Na^+OH^-$ ⟶

6
Sodium phenoxide
Ionic, sol. in water

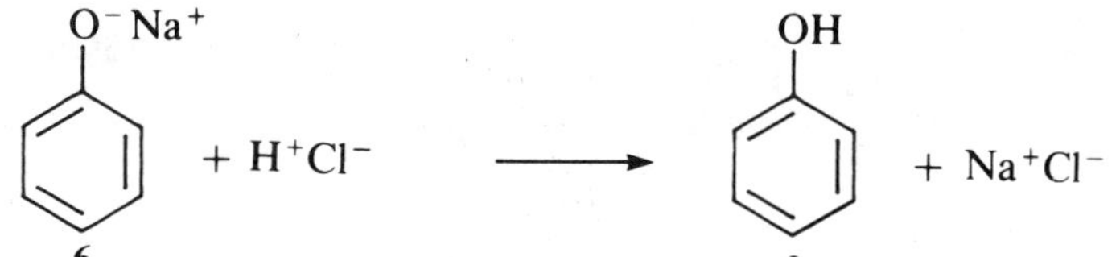

$+ H_2O$

6

$+ H^+Cl^-$ ⟶

2

$+ Na^+Cl^-$

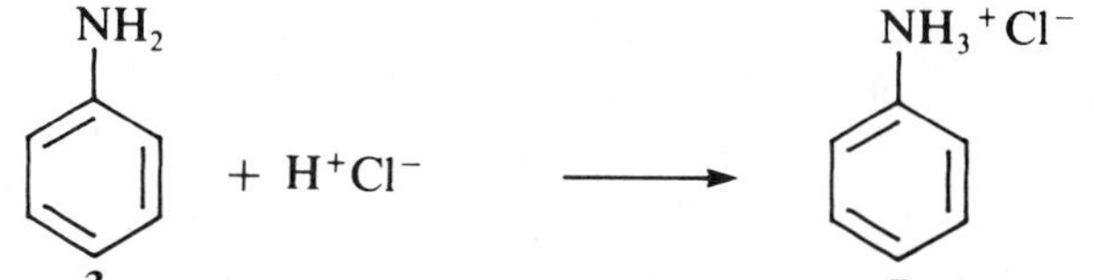

3
Aniline
$pK_b = 9.30$
Covalent, sol. in org. solvents

$+ H^+Cl^-$ ⟶

7
Anilinium chloride
Ionic, sol. in water

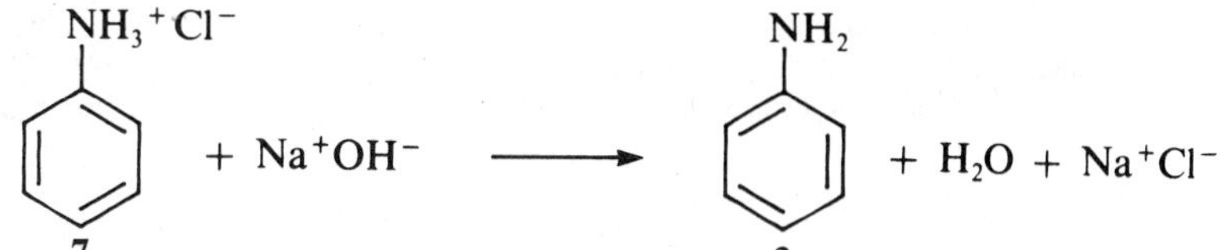

7

$+ Na^+OH^-$ ⟶

3

$+ H_2O + Na^+Cl^-$

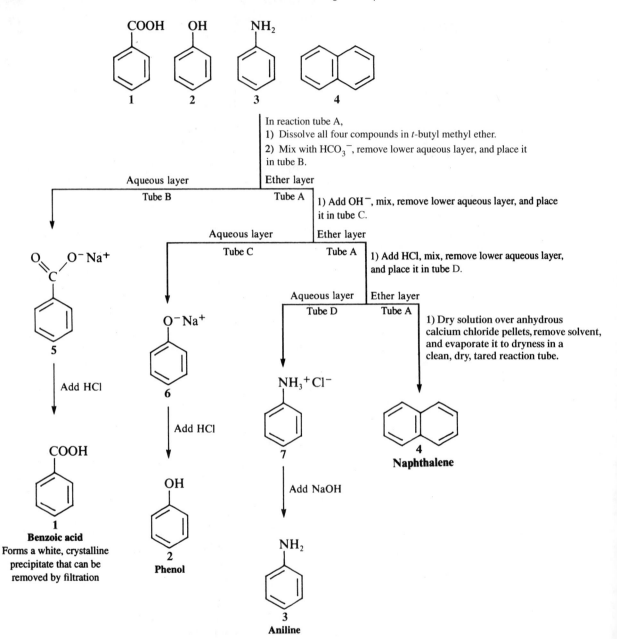

In reaction tube A,
1) Dissolve all four compounds in *t*-butyl methyl ether.
2) Mix with HCO_3^-, remove lower aqueous layer, and place it in tube B.

Aqueous layer — Tube B   Ether layer — Tube A

1) Add OH^-, mix, remove lower aqueous layer, and place it in tube C.

Aqueous layer — Tube C   Ether layer — Tube A

1) Add HCl, mix, remove lower aqueous layer, and place it in tube D.

Aqueous layer — Tube D   Ether layer — Tube A

1) Dry solution over anhydrous calcium chloride pellets, remove solvent, and evaporate it to dryness in a clean, dry, tared reaction tube.

5

Add HCl

1
Benzoic acid
Forms a white, crystalline precipitate that can be removed by filtration

6

Add HCl

2
Phenol

7

Add NaOH

3
Aniline

4
Naphthalene

Phenol and aniline each form oily layers on the top of the aqueous layer. Extract each with *t*-butyl methyl ether: Add ether to the tube, mix, separate layers, dry the ether layer over anhydrous calcium chloride pellets, remove solution from drying agent, and evaporate the solvent.

FIG. 8.8 Flow diagram for the separation of a strong acid, a weak acid, a neutral compound, and a base: benzoic acid, phenol, naphthalene, and aniline.

Liquid/liquid extraction and acid/base extraction are employed in the majority of organic reactions because it is unusual to have the product crystallize from the reaction mixture or to be able to distill the reaction product directly from the reaction mixture. In the research literature, one will often see the statement "the reaction mixture was worked up in the usual way," which implies an extraction process of the type described here. Good laboratory practice dictates, however, that the details of the process be written out.

Practical Considerations

Emulsions

Imagine trying to extract a soap solution, e.g., a nonfoaming dishwasher detergent, into an organic solvent. After a few shakes with an organic solvent, you would have an absolutely intractable emulsion. An emulsion is a suspension of one liquid as droplets in another. Detergents stabilize emulsions, and so any time a detergentlike molecule happens to be in the material being extracted there is the danger that emulsions will form. Substances of this type are commonly found in nature, so one must be particularly wary of emulsion formation when making organic extracts of aqueous plant material, such as caffeine from tea. Emulsions, once formed, can be quite stable. You would be quite surprised to open your refrigerator one morning and see a layer of clarified butter floating on the top of a perfectly clear aqueous solution that had once been milk, but that is the classic example of an emulsion.

Shake gently to avoid emulsions.

Prevention is the best cure for emulsions. This means shaking the solution to be extracted *very gently* until you see that the two layers will separate readily. If a bit of emulsion forms it may break simply on standing for a sufficient length of time. Making the aqueous layer highly ionic will help. Add as much sodium chloride as will dissolve, and shake the mixture gently. Vacuum filtration sometimes works and, when the organic layer is the lower layer, filtration through silicone-impregnated filter paper is an aid. Centrifugation works very well for breaking emulsions. This is easy on a small scale, but often the equipment is not available for large-scale centrifugation of organic liquids.

Pressure Buildup

The heat of the hand or heat from acid/base reactions will cause pressure buildup in an extraction mixture that contains a very volatile solvent such as dichloromethane. The extraction container, be it a test tube or a separatory funnel, must be opened carefully to vent this pressure.

Sodium bicarbonate solution is often used to neutralize acids when carrying out acid/base extractions. The result is the formation of carbon dioxide, which can cause foaming and high pressure buildup. Whenever bicarbonate is used, add it very gradually with thorough mixing and frequent venting of the extraction device. If a large amount of acid is to be neutralized with bicarbonate, the process should be carried out in a beaker.

Removal of Water from Extraction Solvents

The organic solvents used for extraction dissolve not only the compound being extracted but also water. Evaporation of the solvent then leaves the desired compound contaminated with water. At room temperature water dissolves 4.8% of *t*-butyl methyl ether by weight, and the ether dissolves 1.5% of water. But ether is virtually insoluble in water saturated with sodium chloride (36.7 g/100 mL). If ether that contains dissolved water is shaken with a saturated aqueous solution of sodium chloride, water will be transferred from the *t*-butyl methyl ether to the aqueous layer. So, strange as it may seem, ethereal extracts routinely are dried by shaking them with aqueous saturated sodium chloride solution.

Saturated aqueous sodium chloride solution removes water from ether.

Solvents such as dichloromethane do not dissolve nearly as much water and so are dried over a chemical drying agent. Many choices of chemical drying agents are available for this purpose, and the choice of which one to use is governed by four factors: the possibility of reaction with the substance being extracted, the speed with which it removes water from the solvent, the efficiency of the process, and the ease of recovery from the drying agent.

Some very good but specialized and reactive drying agents are potassium hydroxide, anhydrous potassium carbonate, sodium metal, calcium hydride, lithium aluminum hydride, and phosphorus pentoxide. Substances that are essentially neutral and unreactive and are widely used as drying agents include anhydrous calcium sulfate (Drierite), magnesium sulfate, molecular sieves, calcium chloride, and sodium sulfate.

Drierite, $CaSO_4$

Drierite, a specially prepared form of calcium sulfate, is a fast and effective drying agent. However, it is difficult to ascertain whether enough has been used. An indicating type of Drierite is impregnated with cobalt chloride, which turns from blue to red when it is saturated with water. This works well when gases are being dried, but it should not be used for liquid extractions because the cobalt chloride dissolves in many protic solvents.

Magnesium sulfate, $MgSO_4$

Magnesium sulfate is also a fast and fairly effective drying agent, but it is so finely powdered that it always requires careful filtration for removal.

Molecular sieves, zeolites

Molecular sieves are sodium alumino-silicates (zeolites) that have well-defined pore sizes. The 4A size adsorbs water to the exclusion of almost all organic substances and is a fast and effective drying agent, but like Drierite it is impossible to ascertain by appearance whether enough has been used. Molecular sieves in the form of 1/16-in. pellets are often used to dry solvents by simply adding them to the container.

Calcium chloride ($CaCl_2$) pellets, the drying agent of choice for small-scale experiments

Calcium Chloride Pellets, the Drying Agent of Choice   *Calcium chloride,* recently available in the form of pellets[1] (4 to 80 mesh), is a very fast and effective drying agent. It has the advantage that it clumps together when excess water is present so that it is possible, by observing its behavior, to know how much to add. Unlike the older granular form, the pellets do not disintegrate

---

1. Fisher, Cat. No. 614-3.

Add anhydrous drying agent until it begins to snow.

to give a fine powder. These pellets are admirably suited to microscale experiments where the solvent is removed from the drying agent with a Pasteur pipette. It is much faster and much more effective than anhydrous sodium sulfate; after much experimentation, we have decided that this is the agent of choice for microscale experiments in particular. These pellets are used for most of the drying operations in this text. But calcium chloride reacts with some alcohols, phenols, amides, and some carbonyl-containing compounds. Advantage is sometimes taken of this property to remove not only water from a solvent but also, for example, a contaminating alcohol (see the synthesis of 1-bromobutane from 1-butanol, Chapter 16).

Sodium sulfate, Na₂SO₄

Sodium sulfate is a very poor drying agent. It has a very high capacity for water but is slow and not very efficient in the removal of water. It, like calcium chloride pellets, clumps together when wet, and solutions are easily removed from it using a Pasteur pipette. It has been used extensively in the past and should still be used for compounds that react with calcium chloride.

⊓ MICROSCALE

Benzoic acid
mp 123°C, pK_a 4.17

1,4-Dimethoxybenzene
(Hydroquinone dimethyl ether)
mp 57°C

1. Separation of a Carboxylic Acid, a Phenol, and a Neutral Substance

A mixture of equal parts of a carboxylic acid, a phenol, and a neutral substance is to be separated by extraction from an ether solvent. Note carefully the procedure for this extraction. In the next experiment you are to work out your own extraction procedure. Your unknown will consist of either benzoic acid or 2-chlorobenzoic acid (the carboxylic acid), 4-*tert*-butyl phenol or 4-bromophenol and biphenyl or 1,4-dimethoxybenzene (the neutral substance). The object of this experiment is to identify the three substances in the mixture and to determine the percent recovery of each from the mixture.

Procedure

Dissolve about 0.18 g of the mixture (record the exact weight) in 2 mL of *tert*-butyl methyl ether or diethyl ether in a reaction tube. Then add 1 mL of a saturated aqueous solution of sodium bicarbonate to the tube. Use the graduations on the side of the tube to measure the amounts, because they do not need to be exact. Mix the contents of the tube thoroughly by pulling the two layers into a Pasteur pipette and expelling them forcefully into the reaction tube. Do this for about 3 min. Allow the layers to separate completely, and then draw off the lower layer into another reaction tube (tube 2). Add another 0.15 mL of sodium bicarbonate solution to the tube, mix the contents as before, and add the lower layer to tube 2. Exactly what chemical species is in tube 2? Add 0.2 mL of ether to tube 2, mix it thoroughly, remove the ether layer, and discard it. This is called *backwashing* and serves to remove any organic material that might contaminate the contents of tube 2.

OH

Br

4-Bromophenol
mp 66°C, pK_a 10.2

Add HCl with care. CO$_2$ is released.

Biphenyl
mp 71°C

OH

H$_3$C—C—CH$_3$
CH$_3$

4-*tert*- Butylphenol
mp 101°C, pK_a 10.17

Best way to remove the solvent: under a gentle stream of air or nitrogen.

Add 1.0 mL of 3 M aqueous sodium hydroxide to tube 1, shake the mixture thoroughly, allow the layers to separate, draw off the lower layer using a clean Pasteur pipette, and place it in tube 3. Extract tube 1 with two 0.15-mL portions of water, and add these to tube 3. Backwash the contents of tube 3 with 0.15 mL of ether, and discard the ether wash just as was done for tube 2. Exactly what chemical species is in tube 3?

To tube 1 add saturated sodium chloride solution, mix, remove the aqueous layer, and then add to the ether anhydrous calcium chloride pellets until the drying agent no longer clumps together. Wash it off with ether after the drying process is finished. Allow 5 to 10 min for drying of the ether solution.

Using the concentration information given in the inside back cover of this book, calculate exactly how much concentrated hydrochloric acid is needed to neutralize the contents of tube 2. Then, by dropwise addition of concentrated hydrochloric acid, carry out this neutralization while testing the solution with litmus paper. An excess of hydrochloric acid does no harm. This reaction must be carried out with *extreme care* because much carbon dioxide is released in the neutralization. Add a boiling stick to the tube, and very cautiously heat the tube to bring most of the solid carboxylic acid into solution. Allow the tube to cool slowly to room temperature, and then cool it in ice. Remove the solvent with a Pasteur pipette, and recrystallize the residue from boiling water. Again allow the tube to cool slowly to room temperature, and then cool it in ice. At the appropriate time stir the crystals, and collect them on the Hirsch funnel using the procedures detailed in Chapter 3. The crystals can be transferred and washed on the funnel using a small quantity of ice water. The solubility of benzoic acid in water is 1.9 g/L at 0°C and 68 g/L at 95°C. The solubility of chlorobenzoic acid is similar. Turn the crystals out onto a tared piece of paper, allow them to dry thoroughly, and determine the percent recovery of the acid. Assess the purity of the product by melting point.

In exactly the same way, neutralize the contents of tube 3 with concentrated hydrochloric acid. This time, of course, there will be no carbon dioxide evolution. Again, heat the tube to bring most of the material into solution, allow it to cool slowly, remove the solvent, and recrystallize the phenol from boiling water. At the appropriate time, after the product has cooled slowly to room temperature and then in ice, it is also collected on the Hirsch funnel, washed with a very small quantity of ice water, and allowed to dry. The percent recovery and melting point are determined.

The neutral compound is recovered using the Pasteur pipette to remove the ether from the drying agent and to transfer it to a tared reaction tube. The drying agent is washed two or three times with additional ether to ensure complete transfer of the product.

Evaporate the solvent by placing the tube in a warm water bath and directing a stream of nitrogen or air onto the surface of the ether in the hood (see Fig. 8.6). An aspirator tube also can be used for this purpose. Determine the weight of the crude product, and then recrystallize it from methanol–water if it is the low-melting compound. Reread Chapter 3 for detailed instructions on carrying out this process of crystallization from a mixed solvent. The product is dissolved in

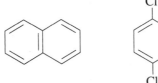

2-Chlorobenzoic acid
mp 141°C, pK_a 2.92

about 0.5 to 1 mL of methanol, and water is added until the solution gets cloudy, indicating the solution is saturated. This process is best carried out while heating the tube in a hot water bath at 50°C. Allow the tube to cool slowly to room temperature, and then cool it thoroughly in ice. If you have the high-melting compound, recrystallize it from ethanol (8 mL/g).

The products are best isolated by collection on the Hirsch funnel using an ice-cold alcohol–water mixture to transfer and wash the compounds. Determine the percent recovery and the melting point. Turn in the products in neatly labeled 1 ½-in. × 1 ½-in. (4 cm × 4 cm) ziplock plastic bags attached to the laboratory report. If the yield on crystallization is low, concentrate the filtrate (the mother liquor) and obtain a second crop of crystals.

☐ MICROSCALE

2. Separation of a Neutral and Basic Substance

      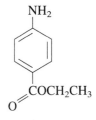

Naphthalene
mp 82°C

1,4-Dichlorobenzene
mp 56°C

4-Chloroaniline
mp 68–71°C, pK_b 4.15

Ethyl 4-aminobenzoate
mp 90°C, pK_b 4.92

A mixture of equal parts of a neutral substance, naphthalene or 1,4-dichlorobenzene, and a basic substance, 4-chloroaniline or ethyl 4-aminobenzoate, is to be separated by extraction from an ether solution. Naphthalene and 1,4-dichlorobenzene are completely insoluble in water. The bases will dissolve in hydrochloric acid, while the neutral compounds will remain in ether solution. The bases are insoluble in cold water but will dissolve to some extent in hot water and are soluble in ethanol. Naphthalene and 1,4-dichlorobenzene can be purified as described in Chapter 3. They sublime very easily also. Keep the samples covered.

Plan a procedure for separating 200 mg of the mixture into its components, and have the plan checked by the instructor before proceeding. A flow sheet is a convenient way to present the plan. Select the correct solvent or mixture of solvents for the recrystallization of the bases on the basis of solubility tests. Determine the weights and melting points of the isolated and purified products, and calculate the percent recovery of each. Turn in the products in neatly labeled vials or 1 ½-in. × 1 ½-in. ziplock plastic bags attached to the report.

FIG. 8.9 Correct positions for holding a separatory funnel when shaking. Point outlet away from yourself and your neighbors.

Cleaning Up   Combine all aqueous filtrates and solutions, neutralize them, and flush the resulting solution down the drain. Used ether should be placed in the organic solvents container, and the drying agent, once the solvent has evaporated from it, can be placed in the nonhazardous solid waste container. Any 4-chloroaniline or 1,4-dichlorobenzene should be placed in the halogenated waste container.

 **MACROSCALE**

Apparatus and Operations

In macroscale experiments, a frequently used method of working up a reaction mixture is to dilute the mixture with water and extract with ether in a separatory funnel (Fig. 8.9). When the stoppered funnel is shaken to distribute the components between the immiscible solvents *t*-butyl methyl ether and water, pressure always develops through volatilization of ether from the heat of the hands, and the liberation of a gas (CO_2) can increase the pressure. Consequently, the funnel is grasped so that the stopper is held in place by one hand and the stopcock by the other, as illustrated. After a brief shake or two, the funnel is held in the inverted position shown and the stopcock opened cautiously (with the funnel stem pointed away from nearby people) to release pressure. The mixture can then be shaken more vigorously and pressure released as necessary. When equilibration is judged to be complete, the slight, constant terminal pressure due to ether is released, the stopper is rinsed with a few drops of ether delivered by a Pasteur pipette, and the

Ether vapors are heavier than air and can travel along bench tops, run down drain troughs, and collect in sinks. Be extremely careful to avoid flames when working with volatile ethers.

2-Chlorobenzoic acid
mp 141°C, pK_a 2.92

1,4-Dichlorobenzene
mp 56°C

Biphenyl
mp 71°C

4-*t*-Butylphenol
mp 101°C

Foaming occurs when bicarbonate is added to acid; use care.

layers are allowed to separate. The organic reaction product is distributed wholly or largely into the upper ether layer, whereas inorganic salts, acids, and bases pass into the water layer, which can be drawn off and discarded. If the reaction was conducted in alcohol or some other water-soluble solvent, the bulk of the solvent is removed in the water layer and the rest can be eliminated in two or three washings with 1–2 volumes of water conducted with the techniques used in the first equilibration. The separatory funnel should be supported in a ring stand as shown in Fig. 8.10 on page 145.

If acetic acid were used as the reaction solvent it would also be distributed largely into the aqueous phase, but if the reaction product is a neutral substance the residual acetic acid in the ether can be removed by one washing with excess 5% sodium bicarbonate solution. If the reaction product is a higher molecular weight acid, for example benzoic acid (C_6H_5COOH), it will stay in the ether layer, while acetic acid is being removed by repeated washing with water; the benzoic acid can then be separated from neutral byproducts by extraction with sodium bicarbonate or sodium hydroxide solution and acidification of the extract. Acids of high molecular weight are extracted only slowly by sodium bicarbonate, so sodium carbonate is used in its place; however, carbonate is more prone than bicarbonate to produce emulsions. Some-

1,4-Dimethoxybenzene
(Hydroquinone dimehtyl ether)
mp 57°C

times an emulsion in the lower layer can be settled by twirling the separatory funnel by its stem. An emulsion in the upper layer can be broken by grasping the funnel by the neck and swirling it. Because the tendency to emulsify increases with removal of electrolytes and solvents, a little sodium chloride or hydrochloric acid solution is added with each portion of wash water. If the layers are largely clear but an emulsion persists at the interface, the clear part of the water layer can be drawn off and the emulsion run into a second funnel and shaken with fresh ether.

Before adding a liquid to the separatory funnel, check the stopcock. If it is glass, see that it is properly greased, bearing in mind that too much grease will clog the hole in the stopcock and also contaminate the extract. If the stopcock is Teflon, see that it is adjusted to a tight fit in the bore. Store the separatory funnel with the Teflon stopcock loosened to prevent sticking. Because Teflon has a much larger temperature coefficient of expansion than glass, a stuck stopcock can be loosened by cooling the stopcock in ice or dry ice. Do not store liquids in the separatory funnel; they often leak or cause the stopper or stopcock to freeze. To have sufficient room for mixing the layers, fill the separatory funnel no more than three-fourths full. Withdraw the lower layer from the separatory funnel through the stopcock, and pour the upper layer out through the neck.

All too often the inexperienced chemist discards the wrong layer when using a separatory funnel. Through incomplete neutralization, a desired component may still remain in the aqueous layer or the densities of the layers may change. Cautious workers save all layers until the desired product has been isolated. The organic layer is not always the top layer. If in doubt, test the layers by adding a few drops of each to water in a test tube.

 MACROSCALE

$pH = -log\ [H^+]$

$pK_a = acidity\ constant$

$pK_b = basicity\ constant$

3. Separation of Acidic and Neutral Substances

A mixture of equal proportions of benzoic acid, 2-naphthol, and 1,4-dimethoxybenzene is to be separated by extraction from *t*-butyl methyl ether. Note the detailed directions for extraction carefully. Prepare a flowsheet (see Fig. 8.8) for this sequence of operations. In the next experiment you will work out your own extraction procedure.

Procedure

Dissolve 3 g of the mixture in 30 mL of *t*-butyl methyl ether, and transfer the mixture to a 125-mL separatory funnel (Fig. 8.10) using a little t-butyl methyl ether to complete the transfer. Add 10 mL of water, and note which layer is organic and which is aqueous. Add 10 mL of a 3 *M* aqueous solution of sodium bicarbonate to the funnel. Stopper the funnel, and cautiously mix the contents. Vent the liberated carbon dioxide, and then shake the mixture thoroughly with frequent vent-

O   OH
 \\ /
  C

Benzoic acid
mp 123°C, pK$_a$ 4.17

OH

H$_3$C — C — CH$_3$
        |
       CH$_3$

4-*t*-Butylphenol
mp 101°C

OCH$_3$

OCH$_3$

1,4-Dimethoxybenzene
(Hydroquinone dimethyl ether)
mp 57°C

Extinguish all flames when working with t-butyl methyl ether! The best method for removing the ether is by simple distillation. Dispose of waste ether in container provided.

ing of the funnel. Allow the layers to separate completely, and then draw off the lower layer into a 50-mL Erlenmeyer flask (labeled Flask 1). What does this layer contain?

Add 10 mL of 1.5 *M* aqueous sodium hydroxide to the separatory funnel, shake the mixture thoroughly, allow the layers to separate, and draw off the lower layer into a 25-mL Erlenmeyer flask (labeled Flask 2). Add an additional 5 mL of water to the separatory funnel, shake the mixture as before, and add this to Flask 2. What does Flask 2 contain?

Add 15 mL of a saturated aqueous solution of sodium chloride to the separatory funnel, shake the mixture thoroughly, allow the layers to separate, and draw off the lower layer, which can be discarded. What is the purpose of adding saturated sodium chloride solution? Carefully pour the ether layer into a 50-mL Erlenmeyer flask (labeled Flask 3) from the top of the separatory funnel, taking great care not to allow any water droplets to be transferred. Add about 4 g of anhydrous calcium chloride pellets to the ether extract, and set it aside.

Acidify the contents of Flask 2 by dropwise addition of concentrated hydrochloric acid while testing with litmus paper. Cool the flask in an ice bath.

Cautiously add concentrated hydrochloric acid dropwise to Flask 1 until the contents are acidic to litmus, and then cool the flask in ice.

Decant (pour off) the ether from Flask 3 into a tared (previously weighed) flask, taking care to leave all of the drying agent behind. Wash the drying agent with additional ether to ensure complete transfer of the product. If decantation is difficult then remove the drying agent by gravity filtration (see Fig. 3.2). Put a boiling stick in the flask, and evaporate the ether in the hood. An aspirator tube can be used for this purpose (see Fig. 8.11). Determine the weight of the crude *p*-dimethoxybenzene, and then recrystallize it from methanol. See Chapter 3 for detailed instructions on how to carry out crystallization.

Isolate the *t*-butylphenol from Flask 2 employing vacuum filtration on a Hirsch funnel (see Fig. 3.2), and wash it on the filter with a small quantity of ice water. Determine the weight of the crude product, and then recrystallize it from ethanol. Similarly isolate, weigh, and recrystallize from boiling water the benzoic acid in Flask 1. The solubility of benzoic acid in water is 1.9 g/L at 0°C and 68 g/L at 95°C.

Dry the purified products, determine their melting points and weights, and calculate the percent recovery of each substance, bearing in mind that the original mixture contained 1 g of each compound. Hand in the three products in neatly labeled vials.

Cleaning Up   Combine all aqueous layers, washes, and filtrates. Dilute with water, neutralize using either sodium carbonate or dilute hydrochloric acid. Methanol filtrate and any ether go in the organic solvents container. Allow ether to evaporate from the calcium chloride in the hood. It can be placed in the non-hazardous solid waste container.

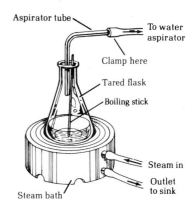

FIG. 8.11   Aspirator tube in use.

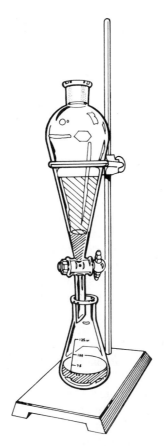

FIG. 8.10   *Separatory funnel with Teflon stopcock.*

4. Separation of a Neutral and Basic Substance

Naphthalene
mp 80°C

A mixture of equal parts of a neutral substance, naphthalene, and a basic substance, 4-chloroaniline, are to be separated by extraction from *t*-butyl methyl ether solution. The base will dissolve in hydrochloric acid while the neutral naphthalene will remain in the *t*-butyl methyl ether solution. 4-Chloroaniline is insoluble in cold water but will dissolve to some extent in hot water and is soluble in ethanol. Naphthalene can be purified as described in Chapter 3.

Plan a procedure for separating 2.0 g of the mixture into its components and have the plan checked by the instructor before proceeding. A flowsheet is a convenient way to present the plan. Using solubility tests, select the correct solvent or mixture of solvents to crystallize 4-chloroaniline. Determine the weights and melting points of the isolated and purified products, and calculate the percent recovery of each. Turn in the products in neatly labeled vials.

Handle aromatic amines with care. Most are toxic and some are carcinogenic. Avoid breathing the dust and vapor from the solid and keep the compounds off the skin, best done by wearing gloves.

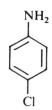

4-Chloroaniline
mp 68–71°C, pK_b 10.0

Cleaning Up   Combine all aqueous filtrates and solutions, neutralize them, and flush the resulting solution down the drain with a large excess of water. Used *t*-butyl methyl ether should be placed in the organic solvents container, and the calcium chloride, once the solvent has evaporated from it, can be placed in the non-hazardous solid waste container. Any 4-chloroaniline should be placed in the chlorinated organic compounds container.

5. Extraction of Caffeine from Tea

Tea and coffee have been popular beverages for centuries, primarily because they contain the stimulant caffeine. It stimulates respiration, the heart, and the central nervous system, and is a diuretic (promotes urination). It can cause nervousness and insomnia and, like many drugs, can be addictive, making it difficult to reduce the daily dose. A regular coffee drinker who consumes just four cups per day can experience headache, insomnia, and even nausea upon withdrawal from the drug. On the other hand, it helps people to pay attention and can sharpen moderately complex mental skills as well as prolong the ability to exercise.

Caffeine may be the most widely abused drug in the United States. During the course of a day an average person may unwittingly consume up to a gram of this substance. The caffeine content of some common foods and drugs is given in Table 8.1.

Caffeine belongs to a large class of compounds known as alkaloids. These are of plant origin, contain basic nitrogen, often have a bitter taste and complex structure, and usually have physiological activity. Their names usually end in "ine"; many are quite familiar by name if not chemical structure—nicotine, cocaine, morphine, strychnine.

TABLE 8.1   Caffeine Content of Common Foods and Drugs

Espresso	120 mg per 2 oz
Coffee, regular, brewed	103 mg per cup
Instant coffee	57 mg per cup
Coffee, decaffeinated	2 to 4 mg per cup
Tea	30 to 75 mg per cup
Cocoa	5 to 40 mg per cup
Milk chocolate	6 mg per oz
Baking chocolate	35 mg per oz
Coca-Cola, Classic	46 mg per 12 oz
Jolt Cola	72 mg per 12 oz
Anacin, Bromo-Seltzer, Midol	32 mg per pill
Excedrin, extra strength	65 mg per pill
Dexatrim, Dietac, Vivarin	200 mg per pill
Dristan	16 mg per pill
No-Doz	100 mg per pill

Tea leaves contain tannins, which are acidic, as well as a number of colored compounds and a small amount of undecomposed chlorophyll (soluble in dichloromethane). To ensure that the acidic substances remain water soluble and that the caffeine will be present as the free base, sodium carbonate is added to the extraction medium.

The solubility of caffeine in water is 2.2 mg/mL at 25°C, 180 mg/mL at 80°C, and 670 mg/mL at 100°C. It is quite soluble in dichloromethane, the solvent used in this experiment to extract the caffeine from water.

Caffeine can be extracted easily from tea bags. The procedure one would use to make a cup of tea—simply "steeping" the tea with very hot water for about 7 min—extracts most of the caffeine. There is no advantage to boiling the tea leaves with water for 20 min. Since caffeine is a white, slightly bitter, odorless, crystalline solid, it is obvious that water extracts more than just caffeine. When the brown aqueous solution is subsequently extracted with dichloromethane, primarily caffeine dissolves in the organic solvent. Evaporation of the solvent leaves crude caffeine, which on sublimation yields a relatively pure product. When the concentrated tea solution is extracted with dichloromethane, emulsions can form very easily. There are substances in tea that cause small droplets of the organic layer to remain suspended in the aqueous layer. This emulsion formation results from vigorous shaking. To avoid this problem, it might seem that one could boil the tea leaves with dichloromethane first and then extract the caffeine from the dichloromethane solution with water. In fact this does not work. Boiling 25 g of tea leaves with 50 mL of dichloromethane gives only 0.05 g of residue after evaporation of the solvent. Subsequent extractions give less material. Hot water causes the tea leaves to swell and is obviously a much more efficient extraction solvent. An attempt to sublime caffeine directly from tea leaves was also unsuccessful.

Microscale Procedure

In a 30-mL beaker place 15 mL of water, 2 g of sodium carbonate, and a wooden boiling stick. Bring the water to a boil on the sand bath, remove the boiling stick, and brew a very concentrated tea solution by immersing a tea bag (2.4 g tea) in the very hot water for 5 min. Squeeze as much water from the bag as possible after it cools enough to handle. Be careful not to break the bag. Again bring the water to a boil, and add a new tea bag to the hot solution. After 5 min, remove the tea bag, and squeeze out as much water as possible. This can be done easily on the Hirsch funnel. Rinse the bag with a few milliliters of very hot water, but be sure the total volume of aqueous extract does not exceed 12 mL. Pour the extract into a 15-mL centrifuge tube, and cool the solution in ice to below 40°C (the boiling point of dichloromethane).

CAUTION: Do not breathe the vapors of dichloromethane, and if possible, work with this solvent in the hood.

Balance the centrifuge tubes.

Using three 2-mL portions of dichloromethane, extract the caffeine from the tea. Cork the tube, and use a gentle rocking motion to carry out the extraction. Vigorous shaking will produce an intractable emulsion, while extremely gentle mixing will fail to extract the caffeine. If you have ready access to a centrifuge, the shaking can be very vigorous because any emulsions formed can be broken fairly well by centrifugation for about 90 sec. After each extraction, remove the lower organic layer into a reaction tube, leaving any emulsion layer behind. Dry the combined extracts over anhydrous calcium chloride pellets for 5 or 10 min in an Erlenmeyer flask. Add the drying agent in portions with shaking until it no longer clumps together. Transfer the dry solution to a tared 25-mL filter flask, wash the drying agent twice with 2-mL portions of dichloromethane, and evaporate it to dryness (see Fig. 8.7). The residue will be crude caffeine (determine its weight) that is to be purified by sublimation.

Fit the filter flask with a Pluro stopper or no. 2 neoprene adapter through which is thrust a 15-mL centrifuge tube. Put a pipette bulb on the side arm. Clamp the flask with a large three-prong clamp, fill the centrifuge tube with ice and water, and heat the flask on a hot sand bath (Fig. 8.12). Caffeine is reported to sublime at about 170°C. Tilt the filter flask, and rotate it in the hot sand bath to drive more caffeine onto the centrifuge tube. Use a heat gun to heat the upper walls of the filter flask. When sublimation ceases, remove the ice water, and allow the flask to cool somewhat before removing the centrifuge tube. Scrape the caffeine onto a tared weighing paper, weigh, and using the plastic funnel, transfer it to a small vial or a plastic bag. At the discretion of the instructor, determine the melting point using a sealed capillary. The melting point of caffeine is 238°C. Using the centrifugation technique to separate the extracts, about 30 mg of crude caffeine can be obtained. This will give you 10 to 15 mg of sublimed material, depending on the caffeine content of the particular tea being used. The isolated caffeine can be used to prepare caffeine salicylate (Experiment 7).

Cleaning Up   Discard the tea bags in the nonhazardous solid waste container. Allow the solvent to evaporate from the drying agent, and discard in the same

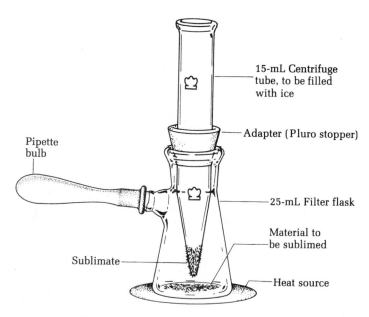

FIG. 8.12 Sublimation apparatus.

container. Place any unused and unrecovered dichloromethane in the chlorinated organic compounds container. The apparatus can be cleaned with soap and hot water. Caffeine can be flushed down the drain, since it is biodegradable.

 ## Macroscale Procedure

To an Erlenmeyer flask containing 25 g of tea leaves (or 10 tea bags) and 20 g of sodium carbonate, add 225 mL of vigorously boiling water. Allow the mixture to stand for 7 min, and then decant into another Erlenmeyer flask. To the hot tea leaves add another 50 mL of hot water, and then immediately decant and combine with the first extract. Very little, if any, additional caffeine is extracted by boiling the tea leaves for 20 min. Decantation works nearly as well as vacuum filtration and is much faster.

Caution: Carry out this work with dichloromethane in the hood.

Rock the separatory funnel very gently to avoid emulsions.

Cool the aqueous solution to near room temperature, and extract it twice with 30-mL portions of dichloromethane. Take great care not to shake the separatory funnel so vigorously as to cause emulsion formation, bearing in mind that if it is not shaken vigorously enough the caffeine will not be extracted into the organic layer. Use a gentle rocking motion of the separatory funnel. Drain off the dichloromethane layer on the first extraction; include the emulsion layer on the second extraction. Dry the combined dichloromethane solutions and any emulsion layer with anhydrous calcium chloride pellets. Add sufficient drying agent until it no longer clumps together on the bottom of the flask. Carefully decant or filter the dichloromethane solution into a tared (previously weighed) Erlenmeyer or distilling flask. Silicone-impregnated filter paper passes dichloromethane and retains water. Wash the drying agent with a further portion of solvent, and evaporate or distill the solvent. A wooden stick is better than a boiling chip to promote smooth boiling because it is easily removed once the solvent is gone. The residue of greenish-white crystalline caffeine should weigh about 0.25 g.

Dispose of used dichloromethane in the container provided.

Crystallization of Caffeine.   To recrystallize the caffeine, dissolve it in 5 mL of hot acetone, transfer it with a Pasteur pipette to a small Erlenmeyer flask, and, while it is hot, add ligroin to the solution until a faint cloudiness appears. Set the flask aside, and allow it to cool slowly to room temperature. This mixed solvent method of recrystallization depends on the fact that caffeine is much more soluble in acetone than ligroin, so a combination of the two solvents can be found where the solution is saturated in caffeine (the cloud point). Cool the solution containing the crystals, and remove them by vacuum filtration, employing the Hirsch funnel or a very small Büchner funnel. Use a few drops of ligroin to transfer the crystals and wash the crystals. If you wish to obtain a second crop of crystals, collect the filtrate in a test tube, concentrate it to the cloud point using the aspirator tube (Fig. 3.21), and repeat the crystallization process.

Cleaning Up   The filtrate can be diluted with water and washed down the drain. Any dichloromethane collected goes into the halogenated organic waste container. After the solvent is allowed to evaporate from the drying agent in the hood, it can be placed in the nonhazardous solid waste container; otherwise it goes in the hazardous waste container. The tea leaves go in the nonhazardous solid waste container.

MICROSCALE AND MACROSCALE

Caffeine
mp 238°C

Cocaine

CAUTION: Do not breathe the vapor of dichloromethane. Work with this solvent in the hood.

6. Extraction of Caffeine from Cola Syrup

Coca-Cola was originally flavored with extracts from the leaves of the coca plant and the kola nut. Coca is grown in northern South America; the Indians of Peru and Bolivia have for centuries chewed the leaves to relieve the pangs of hunger and high mountain cold. The cocaine from the leaves causes local anesthesia of the stomach. It has limited use as a local anesthetic for surgery on the eye, nose, and throat. Unfortunately it is now a widely abused illicit drug. Kola nuts contain about 3% caffeine as well as a number of other alkaloids. The kola tree is in the same family as the cacao tree from which cocoa and chocolate are obtained. Modern cola drinks do not contain cocaine; however, Coca-Cola contains 43 mg of caffeine per 12-oz serving. The acidic taste of many soft drinks comes from citric, tartaric, phosphoric, and benzoic acids.

Automatic soft drink dispensing machines mix a syrup with carbonated water. In the following experiment caffeine is extracted from concentrated cola syrup.

Microscale Procedure

Add 1 mL of concentrated ammonium hydroxide to a mixture of 5 mL commercial cola syrup and 5 mL of water in a 15-mL centrifuge tube. Add 1 mL dichloromethane, and tip the tube gently back and forth for 5 min. Do not shake the mixture as in a normal extraction, because an emulsion will form and the layers will not separate. After the layers have separated as much as possible, remove the clear lower layer, leaving the emulsion behind. Using 1.5 mL dichloromethane, repeat the extraction in the same way twice more. At the final separation, include the emulsion layer with the dichloromethane. If a centrifuge is available, the mixture can be shaken vigorously and the emulsion broken by centrifugation for 90 sec. Combine the extracts in a reaction tube, and dry the solution with anhydrous calcium chloride pellets. Add the drying agent with shaking until it no longer clumps together. After 5 to 10 min, remove the solution with a Pasteur pipette, and place it in a tared filter flask. Wash off the drying agent with more dichloromethane, and evaporate the mixture to dryness. Determine the crude weight of caffeine, and then sublime it as described in the preceding experiment.

Macroscale Procedure

Add 10 mL of concentrated ammonium hydroxide to a mixture of 50 mL of commercial cola syrup and 50 mL of water. Place the mixture in a separatory funnel, add 50 mL of dichloromethane, and swirl the mixture and tip the funnel back and forth for at least 5 min. Do not shake the solutions together as in a normal extraction, because an emulsion will form and the layers will not separate. An emulsion is made up of droplets of one phase suspended in the other (milk is an emulsion). Separate the layers. Repeat the extraction with a second 50-mL portion of dichloromethane. From your knowledge of the density of dichloromethane and water you should be able to predict which is the top layer and which is the bottom layer. If in doubt, add a few drops of each layer to water. The aqueous layer will be soluble, and the organic layer will not. Combine the dichloromethane extracts and any emulsion that has formed in a 125-mL Erlenmeyer flask, and add anhydrous calcium chloride pellets to remove water from the solution. Add the drying agent until it no longer clumps together at the bottom of the flask but swirls freely in solution. Swirl the flask with the drying agent from time to time over a 10-min period. Carefully decant (pour off) the dichloromethane or remove it by filtration through a fluted filter paper, add about 5 mL more solvent to the drying agent to wash it, and decant this also. Combine the dried dichloromethane solutions in a tared flask, and remove the dichloromethane by distillation or evaporation on the steam bath. Remember to add a wooden boiling stick to the solution to promote even boiling. Determine the weight of the crude product.

Chlorinated solvents are toxic, insoluble in water, expensive, and should never be poured down the drain.

Crystallization of Caffeine

To recrystallize the caffeine dissolve it in 5 mL of hot acetone, transfer it with a Pasteur pipette to a small Erlenmeyer flask, and, while it is hot, add ligroin to the solution until a faint cloudiness appears. Set the flask aside, and allow it to cool slowly to room temperature. This mixed solvent method of recrystallization depends on the fact that caffeine is much more soluble in acetone than ligroin, so a combination of the two solvents can be found where the solution is saturated in caffeine (the cloud point). Cool the solution containing the crystals, and remove them by vacuum filtration, employing the Hirsch funnel or a very small Büchner funnel. Use a few drops of ligroin to transfer the crystals and wash the crystals. If you wish to obtain a second crop of crystals, collect the filtrate in a test tube, concentrate it to the cloud point using the aspirator tube (Fig. 3.9), and repeat the crystallization process.

Cleaning Up   Combine all aqueous filtrates and solutions, neutralize them, and flush the resulting solution down the drain. Used dichloromethane should be placed in the halogenated waste container, and the drying agent, once the solvent has evaporated from it, can be placed in the nonhazardous solid waste container. The ligroin–acetone filtrates should be placed in the organic solvents container.

Sublimation of Caffeine

Sublimation is a fast and easy way to purify caffeine. Using the apparatus depicted in Fig. 8.12, sublime the crude caffeine at atmospheric pressure following the procedure in Part 2 of Chapter 7.

7. Isolation of Caffeine from Instant Coffee

Instant coffee, according to the manufacturer, contains between 55 and 62 mg of caffeine per 6-oz cup, and a cup is presumably made from a teaspoon of the powder, which weighs 1.3 g; so 2 g of the powder should contain 85 to 95 mg of caffeine. Unlike tea, however, coffee contains other compounds that are soluble in dichloromethane, so obtaining pure caffeine from coffee is not easy. The object of this experiment is to extract instant coffee with dichloromethane (the easy part) and then to try to devise a procedure for obtaining pure caffeine from the extract.

From the thin-layer chromatography you may deduce that certain impurities have a high R_f value in hydrocarbons (in which caffeine is insoluble). Consult reference books (see especially the *Merck Index*) to determine the solubility (and lack of solubility) of caffeine in various solvents. You might try trituration (grinding the crude solid with a solvent) to preferentially dissolve impurities. Column chromatography is another possible means of purifying the product. Or you might convert all of it to the salicylate and then regenerate the caffeine from the salicylate. Experiment! Or you can simply follow the following procedure.

Procedure

In a 10-mL Erlenmeyer flask, place 2 g of sodium carbonate and 2 g of instant coffee powder. Add to this 9 mL of boiling water, stir the mixture well, bring it to a boil again with stirring, cool it to room temperature, and then pour it into a 15-mL plastic centrifuge tube fitted with a screw cap. Add 2 mL of dichloromethane, cap the tube, shake it vigorously for 60 sec, and then centrifuge it at high speed for 90 sec. Remove the clear yellow dichloromethane layer, and place it in a 10-mL Erlenmeyer flask. Repeat this process twice more. To the combined extracts add anhydrous calcium chloride pellets until they no longer clump together, allow the solution to dry for a few minutes, and then transfer it to a tared 25-mL filter flask, and wash the drying agent with more solvent. Remove the solvent as was done in the tea extraction experiment, and determine the weight of the crude caffeine. You should obtain about 60 mg of crude product. Sublimation of this orange powder gives an impure orange sublimate that smells strongly of coffee, so sublimation is not a good way to purify this material.

Caffeine has no odor.

Dissolve a very small quantity of the product in a drop of dichloromethane, and analyze the crude material by thin-layer chromatography. Dissolve the remainder of the material in 1 mL of boiling 95% ethanol, and then dilute the mixture with 1 mL of *tert*-butyl methyl ether, heat to boiling, and allow to cool slowly to room temperature. Long, needlelike crystals should form in the orange solution. Alternatively, crystallize the product from a 1:1 mixture of ligroin [hexane(s)] and 2-propanol, using about 2 mL. Cool the mixture in ice for at least 10 min, and then collect the product on the Hirsch funnel. Complete the transfer with the filtrate, and then wash the crystals twice with cold 50/50 ethanol/*tert*-butyl methyl ether. The yield of white fluffy needles of caffeine should be more than 30 mg.

Cleaning Up Allow the solvent to evaporate from the drying agent, and discard it in the nonhazardous waste container. Place any unused and unrecovered dichloromethane in the chlorinated organic solvents container.

8. Caffeine Salicylate

Preparation of a derivative of caffeine.

One way to confirm the identity of an organic compound is to prepare a derivative of it. Caffeine melts and sublimes at 238°C. It is an organic base and can therefore accept a proton from an acid to form a salt. The salt formed when caffeine combines with hydrochloric acid, like many amine salts, does not have a sharp melting point; it simply decomposes when heated. But the salt formed from salicylic acid, even though ionic, has a sharp melting point and can thus be used to help characterize caffeine. See Fig. 8.14 for the ^{1}H NMR spectrum of caffeine.

Caffeine   **Salicylic acid**   **Caffeine salicylate**

Procedure

CAUTION: Petroleum ether is very flammable. Extinguish all flames.

Crystallization from mixed solvents

The quantities given can be multiplied by 5 or 10 if necessary. To 10 mg of sublimed caffeine in a tared reaction tube add 7.5 mg of salicylic acid and 0.5 mL of dichloromethane. Heat the mixture to boiling, and add petroleum ether (a poor solvent for the product) dropwise until the mixture just turns cloudy, indicating the solution is saturated. If too much petroleum ether is added, then clarify it by adding a very small quantity of dichloromethane. Insulate the tube in order to allow it to cool slowly to room temperature, and then cool it in ice. The needle-like crystals are isolated by removing the solvent with a Pasteur pipette while the reaction tube is in the ice bath. Evaporate the last traces of solvent under vacuum (Fig. 8.13), and determine the weight of the derivative and its melting point. Caffeine salicylate is reported to melt at 137°C.

Cleaning Up Place the filtrate in the halogenated organic solvents container.

Questions

1. Suppose a reaction mixture, when diluted with water, afforded 300 mL of an aqueous solution of 30 g of the reaction product malononitrile,

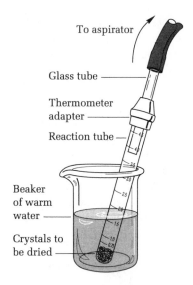

FIG. 8.13 Drying of crystals under vacuum in beaker of warm water.

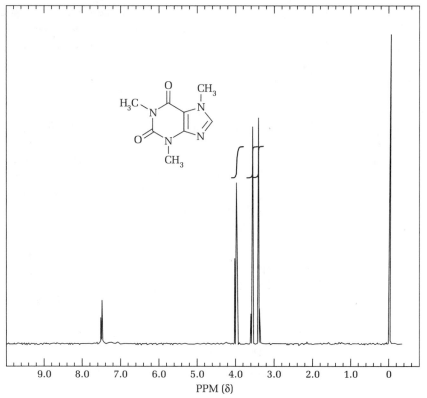

FIG. 8.14 ¹H NMR spectrum of caffeine (250 MHz).

$CH_2(CN)_2$, which is to be isolated by extraction with ether. The solubility of malononitrile in ether at room temperature is 20.0 g per 100 mL, and in water is 13.3 g per 100 mL. What weight of malononitrile would be recovered by extraction with (a) three 100-mL portions of ether; (b) one 300-mL portion of ether? *Suggestion:* For each extraction let *x* equal the weight extracted into the ether layer. In case (a) the concentration in the ether layer is $x/100$, and in the water layer is $(30 - x)/300$; the ratio of these quantities is equal to $k = 20/13.3$.

2. Why is it necessary to remove the stopper from a separatory funnel when liquid is being drained from it through the stopcock?

3. The pK_a of *p*-nitrophenol is 7.15. Would you expect this to dissolve in sodium bicarbonate solution? The pK_a of 2,5-dinitrophenol is 5.15. Will it dissolve in bicarbonate solution?

4. The distribution coefficient, k = (conc. in ligroin/conc. in water), between ligroin and water for solute A is 7.5. What weight of A would be removed from a solution of 10 g of A in 100 mL of water by a single extraction with 100 mL of ligroin? What weight of A would be removed by four successive

extractions with 25-mL portions of ligroin? How much ligroin would be required to remove 98.5% of A in a single extraction?

5. In Experiment 1, how many moles of benzoic acid are present? How many moles of sodium bicarbonate are contained in 1 mL of a 10% aqueous solution? (A 10% solution has 1 g of solute in 9 mL of solvent.) Is the amount of sodium bicarbonate sufficient to react with all of the benzoic acid?

6. To isolate the benzoic acid from the bicarbonate solution, it is acidified with concentrated hydrochloric acid in Experiment 1. What volume of acid is needed to neutralize the bicarbonate? The concentration of hydrochloric acid is expressed in various ways on the inside back cover of this laboratory manual.

7. How many moles of 2-naphthol are in the mixture to be separated in Experiment 1? How many moles of sodium hydroxide are contained in 1 mL of 5% sodium hydroxide solution? (Assume the density of the solution is 1.0.) What volume of concentrated hydrochloric acid is needed to neutralize this amount of sodium hydroxide solution?

8. Draw a flow diagram to show how you would separate the components of a mixture containing an acid substance, toluic acid, a basic substance, *p*-bromo-aniline, and a neutral substance, anthracene.

Surfing the Web

http://ull.chemistry.uakron.edu/organic_lab/distribution/

This University of Akron site with some 15 graphics shows the macroscale determination of the distribution coefficient (partition coefficient) of crotonic acid and benzoic acid in the water/dichloromethane system. The concentration of acid in the aqueous phase is determined by titration.

http://ull.chemistry.uakron.edu/organic_lab/cola/

The extraction of caffeine from 10 mL of cola syrup (Experiment 4) is very clearly demonstrated in 14 color photos. Preparation of caffeine salicylate (Experiment 5) is demonstrated with 8 close-up color photos.

For updated information visit:

www.mtholyoke.edu/courses/kwilliam/microscale.shtml

or

www.hmco.com/hmco/college/chemistry/Home.html

9

Thin-Layer Chromatography: Analysis of Analgesics and Isolation of Lycopene from Tomato Paste

Prelab Exercise: Compare thin-layer chromatography with column chromatography with regard to: (1) quantity of material that can be separated; (2) the speed; (3) the solvent systems; and (4) the ability to separate compounds.

Thin-layer chromatography (TLC) is a sensitive, fast, simple, and inexpensive analytical technique that will be used repeatedly in carrying out organic experiments. It is a micro technique; as little as 10^{-9} g of material can be detected, although the usual sample size is from 1 to 100×10^{-6} g.

TLC requires micrograms of material.

TLC involves spotting the sample to be analyzed near one end of a sheet of glass or plastic that is coated with a thin layer of an adsorbent. The sheet, which can be the size of a microscope slide, is placed on end in a covered jar containing a shallow layer of solvent. As the solvent rises by capillary action up through the adsorbent, differential partitioning occurs between the components of the mixture dissolved in the solvent and the stationary adsorbent phase. The more strongly a given component of the mixture is adsorbed onto the stationary phase, the less time it will spend in the mobile phase, and the more slowly it will migrate up the TLC plate.

Uses of Thin-Layer Chromatography

1. **To determine the number of components in a mixture.** TLC affords a quick and easy method for analyzing such things as a crude reaction mixture, an extract from some plant substance, or a painkiller. Knowing the number and relative amounts of the components aids in planning further analytical and separation steps.
2. **To determine the identity of two substances.** If two substances spotted on the same TLC plate give spots in identical locations, they *may* be identical. If the spot positions are not the same, the substances cannot be the same. It is possible for two closely related compounds that are not identical to have the same positions on a TLC plate.
3. **To monitor the progress of a reaction.** By sampling a reaction from time to time it is possible to watch the reactants disappear and the products appear using TLC. Thus, the optimum time to halt the reaction can be determined, and the effect of changing such variables as temperature, concentrations, and solvents can be followed without having to isolate the product.

4. **To determine the effectiveness of a purification.** The effectiveness of distillation, crystallization, extraction, and other separation and purification methods can be monitored using TLC, with the caveat that a single spot does not guarantee a single substance.
5. **To determine the appropriate conditions for a column chromatographic separation.** Thin-layer chromatography is generally unsatisfactory for purifying and isolating macroscopic quantities of material; however, the adsorbents most commonly used for TLC—silica gel and alumina—are used for column chromatography, discussed in the next chapter. Column chromatography is used to separate and purify up to about a gram of a solid mixture. The correct adsorbent and solvent used to carry out the chromatography can be determined rapidly by TLC.
6. **To monitor column chromatography.** As column chromatography is carried out, the solvent is collected in a number of small flasks. Unless the desired compound is colored, the various fractions must be analyzed in some way to determine which ones have the desired components of the mixture. TLC is a fast and effective method for doing this.

Adsorbents and Solvents

The two most common coatings for thin-layer chromatography plates are alumina, Al_2O_3, and silica gel, SiO_2. These are the same adsorbents most commonly used in column chromatography (Chapter 10) for the purification of macroscopic quantities of material. Of the two, alumina, when anhydrous, is the more active, i.e., it will adsorb substances more strongly. It is thus the adsorbent of choice when the separation involves relatively nonpolar substrates such as hydrocarbons, alkyl halides, ethers, aldehydes, and ketones. To separate the more polar substrates such as alcohols, carboxylic acids, and amines, the less active adsorbent, silica gel, is used. In an extreme situation very polar substances on alumina do not migrate very far from the starting point (give low R_f values), and nonpolar compounds travel with the solvent front (give high R_f values) if chromatographed on silica gel. These extremes of behavior are markedly affected, however, by the solvents used to carry out the chromatography. A polar solvent will carry along with it polar substrates, and nonpolar solvents will do the same with nonpolar compounds—another example of the generalization "like dissolves like."

R_f is the ratio of the distance the spot travels from the origin to the distance the solvent travels.

Table 9.1 lists common solvents used in chromatography, both thin-layer and column. Only the environmentally safe solvents are listed; the polarities of such solvents as benzene, carbon tetrachloride, or chloroform can be matched by other less toxic solvents. In general these solvents are characterized by having low boiling points and low viscosities that allow them to migrate rapidly. They are listed in order of increasing polarity. A solvent more polar than methanol is seldom needed. Often just two solvents are used in varying proportions; the polarity of the mixture is a weighted average of the two. Ligroin–ether mixtures are often employed in this way.

Avoid the use of benzene, carbon tetrachloride, and chloroform. Benzene is a carcinogen; the others are suspect carcinogens.

The order in which solutes migrate on thin-layer chromatography is the

TABLE 9.1 Chromatography Solvents

Solvent	bp (°C)
Petroleum ether (pentanes)	35–60
Ligroin (hexanes)	60–80
Dichloromethane	40
t-Butyl methyl ether	55
Ethyl acetate	77
Acetone	56
2-Propanol	82
Ethanol	78
Methanol	65
Water	100
Acetic acid	118

TABLE 9.2 Order of Solute Migration on Chromatography

Solute	Solute
Fastest	
Alkanes	Ketones
Alkyl halides	Aldehydes
Alkenes	Amines
Dienes	Alcohols
Aromatic hydrocarbons	Phenols
Aromatic halides	Carboxylic acids
Ethers	Sulfonic acids
Esters	*Slowest*

same as the order of solvent polarity. The largest R_f values are shown by the least polar solutes. In Table 9.2 the solutes are arranged in order of increasing polarity.

Apparatus and Procedure

A very dilute solution (1%) of the test substance is employed for TLC.

A 1% solution of the substance to be examined is spotted onto the plate about 1 cm from the bottom end, and the plate is inserted into a beaker or a 4-oz wide-mouth bottle containing 4 mL of an organic solvent. The bottle is lined with filter paper wet with solvent to saturate the atmosphere within the container. The top is put in place and the time noted. The solvent travels rapidly up in the thin layer by capillary action, and if the substance is a pure colored compound, one soon sees a spot traveling either along with the solvent front or, more usually, at some distance behind the solvent front. One can remove the slide, quickly mark the front before the solvent evaporates, and calculate the R_f value. The R_f value is the ratio of the distance the spot travels from the point of origin to the distance the solvent travels (Fig. 9.1). The best separations are achieved when the R_f value falls between 0.3 and 0.7.

Visualization of the Chromatogram

Colored compounds

And colorless ones

If the substances being chromatographed are colored, then it is possible to detect the compounds visually. Colorless substances can be detected when the solvent is allowed to evaporate and the plate allowed to stand in a stoppered 4-oz bottle containing a few crystals of iodine. Iodine vapor is adsorbed by the organic compound to form a brown spot. A spot should be outlined at once with a pencil because it will soon disappear as the iodine sublimes away; brief return to the iodine chamber will regenerate the spot. The order of elution and the elution power for solvents are the same as for column chromatography.

The use of commercial TLC sheets such as Whatman flexible plates for TLC, cat. no. 4410 222 (Fisher cat. no. 05-713-162), is strongly recommended. These poly(ethylene terephthalate) (Mylar) sheets are coated with silica gel using

FIG. 9.1   Thin-layer chromatography plate.

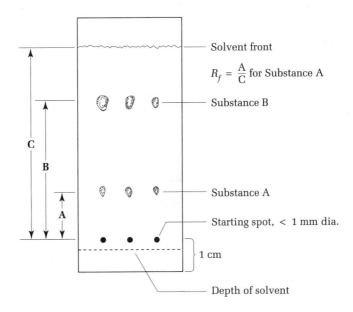

Solvent front

$R_f = \dfrac{A}{C}$ for Substance A

Substance B

C

B

Substance A

A

Starting spot, < 1 mm dia.

1 cm

Depth of solvent

TLC tests for

1. Completeness of reaction

2. Purity of product

3. Side reactions

polyacrylic acid as a binder. A fluorescent indicator has been added to the silica gel so that when the sheet is observed under 254-nm ultraviolet light, spots that either quench or enhance fluorescence can be seen. Iodine can also be used to visualize spots. The coating on these sheets is only 100 μm thick, so very small spots must be applied. Unlike student-prepared plates, these coated sheets (cut to 1- $\times$ 3-in. size with scissors) give very consistent results. A light pencil mark 1 cm from the end will guide spotting. A supply of these little precut sheets makes it a simple matter to examine most of the reactions in this book for completeness of reaction, purity of product, and side reactions.

A large number of specialized spray reagents have been developed that give specific colors for certain types of compounds, and there is a large amount of literature on the solvents and adsorbents to use for the separation of given types of material.[1]

Spotting Test Solutions

It is extremely important that the spots be as small as possible and that they be applied using a 1% (not 2% or more) solution of the compounds being separated. This is done with micropipettes made by drawing open-end mp capillaries in a burner flame (Fig. 9.2). The bore should be of such a size that, when the pipette is dipped deep into ligroin, the liquid flows in to form a tiny thread that, when the pipette is withdrawn, does not flow out to form a drop. To spot a test solution, let a 2–3 cm column of solution flow into the pipette, hold this vertically over a coated plate, aim it at a point on the right side of the plate and about 1 cm from the bottom, and lower the pipette until the tip just touches the adsorbent and liq-

1. Egon Stahl, *Thin-Layer Chromatography*, Springer Verlag, New York, 1969.

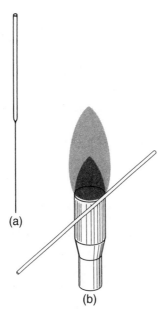

(a)

(b)

FIG. 9.2 (a) Micropipette. (b) Making a micropipette, which is pulled from a melting point capillary that is open on each end. Heat it at the base of the flame as shown.

uid flows onto the plate; withdraw when the spot is about 1 mm in diameter. Make a second 1-mm spot on the left side of the plate, let it dry, and make two more applications of the same size (1 mm) at the same place. Determine whether the large or the small spot gives the better results.

Experiments

MICROSCALE

1. Analgesics

Analgesics are substances that relieve pain. The most common of these is aspirin, a component of more than 100 nonprescription drugs. In Chapter 32, the history and background of this most popular drug is discussed. In the present experiment, analgesic tablets will be analyzed by thin-layer chromatography to determine which analgesics they contain and whether they contain caffeine, which is often added to counteract the sedative effects of the analgesic.

In addition to aspirin and caffeine, the most common components of analgesics are, at present, acetaminophen and ibuprofen (Motrin). In addition to one or more of these substances, each tablet contains a binder, often starch, microcrystalline cellulose, or silica gel. And to counteract the acidic properties of aspirin, an inorganic buffering agent is added to some analgesics. Inspection of labels will reveal that most cold remedies and decongestants contain both aspirin and caffeine in addition to the primary ingredient.

Because of the insoluble binder, not all the unknown will dissolve.

To identify an unknown by TLC, the usual strategy is to run chromatograms of known substances (the standards) and the unknown at the same time. If the unknown has one or more spots that correspond to spots with the same R_f values as the standards, then those substances are probably present.

Aspirin
Acetylsalicylic acid

Acetaminophen
4-Acetamidophenol

Ibuprofen
2-(4-Isobutylphenyl)propionic acid

Caffeine

Proprietary drugs that contain one or more of the common analgesics and sometimes caffeine are sold under the names of Bayer Aspirin, Anacin, Datril, Advil, Excedrin, Extra Strength Excedrin, Tylenol, and Vanquish. Note that ibuprofen has a chiral carbon atom. One enantiomer is more effective than the other.

Procedure

Following the procedure outlined earlier, draw a light pencil line about 1 cm from the end of a chromatographic plate, and on this line spot aspirin, acetaminophen, ibuprofen, and caffeine, which are available as reference standards. Use a separate capillary for each standard, or rinse the capillary carefully. Make each spot as small as possible, preferably less than 0.5 mm in diameter. Examine the plate under the ultraviolet (UV) light to see that enough of each compound has been applied; if not, add more. On a separate plate run the unknown and one or more of the standards.

The unknown sample is prepared by crushing a part of a tablet, adding this powder to a test tube or small vial along with an appropriate amount of ethanol, and then mixing the suspension. Not all of the tablet will dissolve, but enough

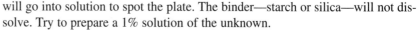

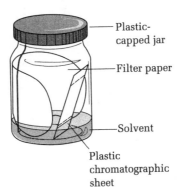

FIG. 9.3   A method for developing TLC plates.

FIG. 9.4   An alternative method for developing TLC plates.

will go into solution to spot the plate. The binder—starch or silica—will not dissolve. Try to prepare a 1% solution of the unknown.

Use as the solvent for the chromatogram a mixture of 95% ethyl acetate and 5% acetic acid (Fig. 9.3 or 9.4). After the solvent has risen to near the top of the plate, mark the solvent front with a pencil, remove the plate from the developing chamber, and allow the solvent to dry. Examine the plate under UV light to see the components as dark spots against a bright green-blue background. Outline the spots with a pencil. The spots can also be visualized by putting the plate in an iodine chamber made by placing a few crystals of iodine in the bottom of a capped 4-oz jar. Calculate the R_f values for the spots, and identify the components in the unknown.

Cleaning Up   Solvents should be placed in the organic solvents container, and dry, used chromatographic plates can be discarded in the nonhazardous solid waste container.

2. Plant Pigments

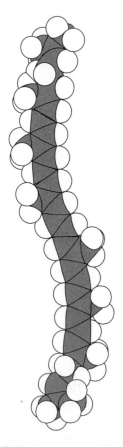

FIG. 9.5   An energy-minimized space-filling model of lycopene. The molecule is flat, but steric hindrance of the methyl groups causes the molecule to bend into the S shape.

The botanist Michael Tswett discovered the technique of chromatography and applied it, as the name implies, to colored plant pigments. The leaves of plants contain, in addition to chlorophyll-a and -b, other pigments that are revealed in the fall when the leaf dies and the chlorophyll rapidly decomposes. Among the most abundant of the other pigments are the carotenoids, which include the carotenes and their oxygenated homologs, the xanthophylls. The bright orange β-carotene is the most important of these, because it is transformed in the liver to vitamin A, which is required for night vision.

Cows eat fresh, green grass that contains carotene, but they do not metabolize the carotene entirely, and so it ends up in their milk. Butter made from this milk is therefore yellow. In the winter the silage cows eat does not contain carotene because it readily undergoes air oxidation, and the butter made at that time is white. For some time an azo dye called Butter Yellow was added to winter butter to give it the accustomed color, but the dye was found to be a carcinogen. Now winter butter is colored with synthetic carotene, as is all margarine.

Lycopene (Fig. 9.5), the red pigment of the tomato, is a C_{40}-carotenoid made up of eight isoprene units. β-Carotene, the yellow pigment of the carrot, is an isomer of lycopene in which the double bonds at C_1—C_2 and C'_1—C'_2 are replaced by bonds extending from C_1 to C_6 and from C'_1 to C'_6 to form rings. The chromophore in each case is a system of 11 all-*trans* conjugated double bonds; the closing of the two rings renders β-carotene less highly pigmented than lycopene.

Lycopene and β-carotene from tomato paste and strained carrots

Fresh tomato fruit is about 96% water, and R. Willstätter and H. R. Escher isolated from this source 20 mg of lycopene per kilogram of fruit. They then found a more convenient source in commercial tomato paste, from which seeds and skin have been eliminated and the water content reduced by evaporation in vacuum to a content of 26% solids. From this they isolated 150 mg of lycopene per kilogram of paste. The expected yield in the present experiment is 0.075 mg.

As an interesting variation, try extraction of lycopene from commercial catsup.

A jar of strained carrots sold as baby food serves as a convenient source of β-carotene. The German investigators isolated 1 g of β-carotene per kilogram of "dried" shredded carrots of unstated water content.

The following procedure calls for dehydration of tomato or carrot paste with ethanol and extraction with dichloromethane, an efficient solvent for lipids.

Experimental Considerations

Carotenoids are very sensitive to light-catalyzed air oxidation. Perform this experiment as rapidly as possible; keep solutions as cool and dark as possible. This extraction gives a mixture of products that can be analyzed by both TLC and column chromatography (next chapter). If enough material for TLC only is desired, use one-tenth the quantities of starting material and solvents employed in the following procedure. This extraction also can be carried out with hexane if the ventilation is not adequate to use dichloromethane. Hexane is more prone to form emulsions than the chlorinated solvent.

CAUTION: Do not breathe the vapors of dichloromethane. Carry out the extraction in the hood. Dichloromethane is a cancer-suspect agent.

**MICROSCALE
AND MACROSCALE**

Procedure

A 5-g sample of fresh tomato or carrot paste (baby food) is transferred to the bottom of a 25 × 150 mm test tube followed by 10 mL of acetone. The mixture is stirred and shaken before being filtered on the Hirsch funnel. Scrape as much of the material from the tube as possible, and press it as dry as possible on the funnel. Let the tube drain thoroughly. Place the filtrate in a 125-mL Erlenmeyer flask.

Return the solid residue to the test tube, shake it with a 10-mL portion of dichloromethane, and again filter the material on the Hirsch funnel. Add the filtrate to the 125-mL flask. Repeat this process twice more, and then pour the combined filtrates into a separatory funnel. Add water and sodium chloride solution (which aids in the breaking of emulsions), and shake the funnel gently. This aqueous extraction will remove the acetone and any water-soluble components from the mixture, leaving the hydrocarbon carotenoids in the dichloromethane. Dry the colored organic layer over anhydrous calcium chloride, and filter the

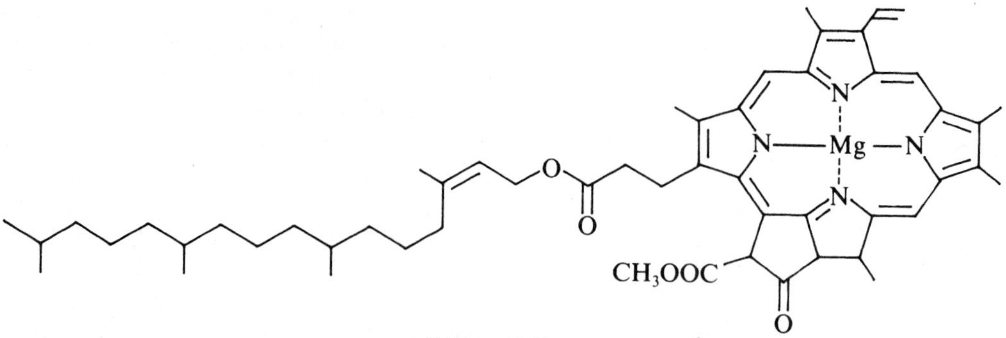

Chlorophyll-a

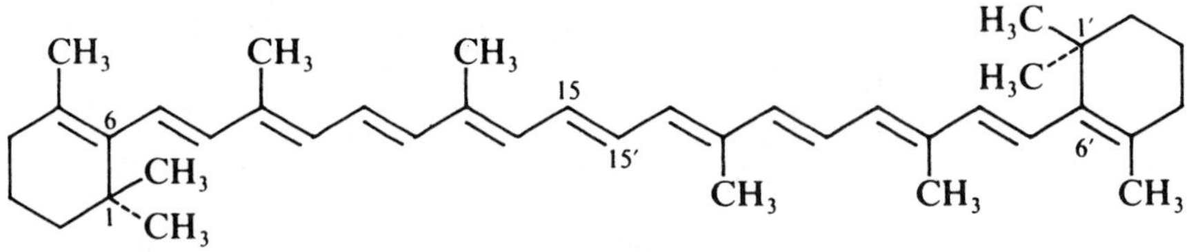

β-Carotene ($C_{40}H_{56}$)
mp 183°C, λ_{max}^{hexane} 451 nm

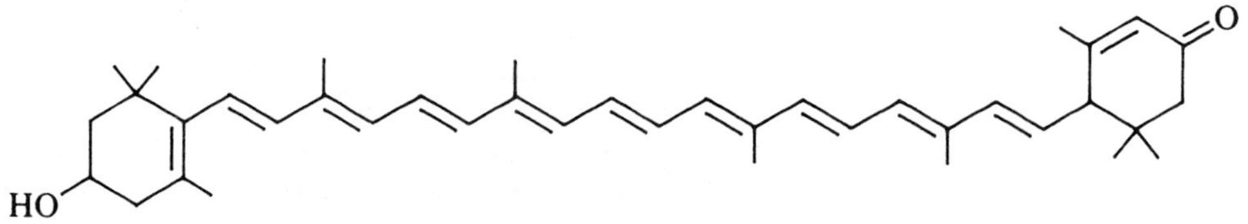

3′-Dehydrolutein (a xanthophyll)

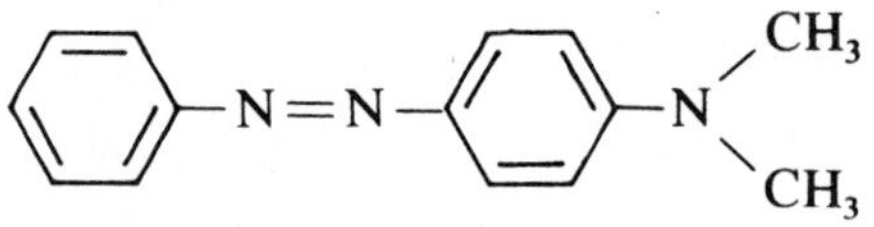

Butter Yellow

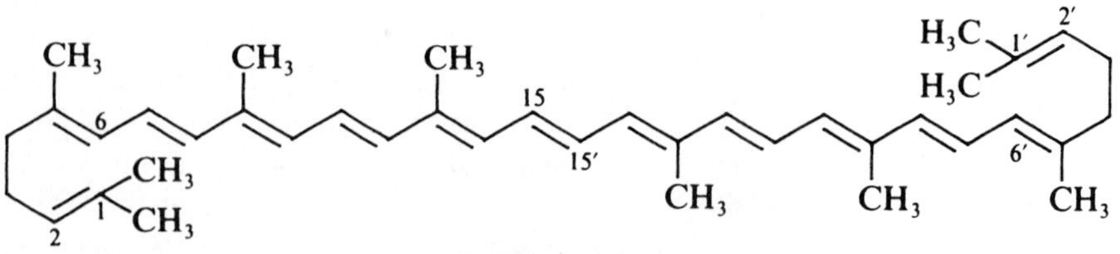

Lycopene ($C_{40}H_{56}$)
MW 536.85
mp 173°C, λ_{max}^{hexane} 475 nm

Air can be used for the evaporation, but nitrogen is better because these hydrocarbons air-oxidize with great rapidity.

solution into a dry flask. Remove about 0.5 mL of this solution and store it under nitrogen in the dark until it can be analyzed by thin-layer chromatography. Evaporate the remainder of the dichloromethane solution to dryness under a stream of nitrogen or under vacuum on a rotary evaporator. This material will be used for column chromatography (see next chapter). If it is to be stored, fill the flask with nitrogen and store it in a dark place.

Thin-Layer Chromatography

Spot the mixture on a TLC plate about 1 cm from the bottom and 8 mm from the edge. Make one spot concentrated by repeatedly touching the plate, but ensure that the spot is as small as possible, certainly less than 1 mm in diameter. The other spot can be of lower concentration. Develop the plate with 80 : 20 hexane : acetone. With other plates you could try cyclohexane and toluene as eluents and also hexane–ethanol mixtures of various compositions.

Many spots may be seen. There are two common carotene and chlorophyll isomers and four xanthophyll isomers.

The container in which the chromatography is carried out should be lined with filter paper that is wet with the solvent so that the atmosphere in the container will be saturated with solvent vapor. On completion of elution, mark the solvent front with a pencil, and outline the colored spots. Examine the plate under UV light. Also place the plate in an iodine chamber to visualize spots (see next experiment).

Cleaning Up   The aqueous saline filtrate containing acetone can be flushed down the drain. Recovered and unused dichloromethane should be placed in the halogenated organic waste container; the solvents used for TLC should be placed in the organic solvents container: and the drying agents, once free of solvents, can be placed in the nonhazardous solid waste container along with the used plant material and the TLC plates.

 **MICROSCALE AND MACROSCALE**

Procedure

In a small mortar grind 2 g of green or brightly colored fall leaves (don't use ivy or waxy leaves) with 10 mL of ethanol, pour off the ethanol, which serves to break up and dehydrate the plant cells, and grind the leaves successively with three 1-mL portions of dichloromethane that are decanted or withdrawn with a Pasteur pipette and placed in a test tube. The pigments of interest are extracted by the dichloromethane. Alternatively, place 0.5 g of carrot paste (baby food) or tomato paste in a test tube, stir and shake the paste with 3 mL of ethanol until the paste has a somewhat dry or fluffy appearance, remove the ethanol, and extract the dehydrated paste with three 1-mL portions of dichloromethane. Stir and shake the plant material with the solvent in order to extract as much of the pigments as possible.

Fill the tube containing the dichloromethane extract from leaves or vegetable paste with a saturated sodium chloride solution, and shake the mixture. Remove the aqueous layer and to the dichloromethane solution add anhydrous calcium chloride pellets until the drying agent no longer clumps together. Shake the mixture with the drying agent for about 5 min, and then withdraw the solvent with a Pasteur pipette and place it in a test tube. Add to the solvent a few pieces of Drierite to complete the drying process. Gently stir the mixture for about 5 min, transfer the solvent to a test tube, wash off the drying agent with more solvent, and then evaporate the combined dichloromethane solutions under a stream of nitrogen while warming the tube in the hand or in a beaker of warm water. Carry out this evaporation in the hood.

These hydrocarbons air-oxidize with great rapidity.

Immediately cork the tube filled with nitrogen, and then add a drop or two of dichloromethane to dissolve the pigments for TLC analysis. Carry out the analysis without delay by spotting the mixture on a TLC plate about 1 cm from the bottom and 8 mm from the edge. Make one spot concentrated by repeatedly touching the plate, but ensure that the spot is as small as possible—less than 1.0 mm in diameter. The other spot can be of lower concentration. Develop the plate with 70 : 30 hexane : acetone. With other plates try cyclohexane and toluene as eluents and also hexane–ethanol mixtures of various compositions. The container in which the chromatography is carried out should be lined with filter paper that is wet with the solvent so the atmosphere in the container will be saturated with solvent vapor. On completion of elution, mark the solvent front with a pencil, and outline the colored spots. Examine the plate under the UV light. Are any new spots seen? Report colors and R_f values for all of your spots, and identify each as lycopene, carotene, chlorophyll, or xanthophyll.

Cleaning Up   The ethanol used for dehydration of the plant material can be flushed down the drain along with the saturated sodium chloride solution. Recovered and unused dichloromethane should be placed in the halogenated organic waste container. The solvents used for TLC should be placed in the organic solvents container. The drying agents, once free of solvents, can be placed in the nonhazardous solid waste container along with the used plant material and TLC plates.

MICROSCALE AND MACROSCALE

3. Colorless Compounds

You are now to apply the thin-layer technique to a group of colorless compounds. The spots can be visualized under an ultraviolet light if the plates have been coated with a fluorescent indicator, or chromatograms can be developed in a 4-oz bottle containing crystals of iodine. During development, spots appear rapidly, but remember that they also disappear rapidly. Therefore, outline each spot with a pencil immediately on withdrawal of the plate from the iodine chamber. Solvents suggested are as follows:

Make your own selections.

Cyclohexane	Toluene (3 mL)–dichloromethane (1 mL)
Toluene	9 : 1 Toluene–methanol (use 4 mL)

Compounds for trial are to be selected from the following list (all 1% solutions in toluene):

1. Anthracene*
2. Cholesterol

3. 2,7-Dimethyl-3,5-octadiyne-2,7-diol
4. Diphenylacetylene
5. *trans,trans*-1,4-Diphenyl-1,3-butadiene*
6. *p*-Di-*t*-butylbenzene
7. 1,4-Di-*t*-butyl-2,5-dimethoxybenzene
8. *trans*-Stilbene
9. 1,2,3,4-Tetraphenylnaphthalene*
10. Tetraphenylthiophene
11. *p*-Terphenyl*
12. Triphenylmethanol
13. Triptycene

*Fluorescent under UV light.

It is up to you to make selections and to plan your own experiments. Do as many as time permits. One plan would be to select a pair of compounds estimated to be separable and that have R_f values determinable with the same solvent. One can assume that a hydroxyl compound will travel less rapidly with a hydrocarbon solvent than a hydroxyl-free compound, and so you will know what to expect if the solvent contains a hydroxylic component. An aliphatic solvent should carry along an aromatic compound with aliphatic substituents better than one without such groups. However, instead of relying on assumptions, you can do brief preliminary experiments on used plates on which previous spots are visible or outlined. If you spot a pair of compounds on such a plate and let the solvent rise about 3 cm from the starting line before development, you might be able to tell if a certain solvent is appropriate for a given sample. Alternatively, make some spots on a plate (new or used) and then touch each spot with a different solvent held in a capillary. In Figure 9.6(a), the mixture did not move away from the point of origin; in Figure 9.6(b), two concentric rings are seen between the origin and the solvent front. This is how a good solvent behaves. In Figure 9.6(c), the mixture of compounds traveled with the solvent front.

Preliminary trials on used plates

Once a solvent is chosen, run a complete chromatogram on the two compounds on a fresh plate. If separation of the two seems feasible, put two spots of one compound on a plate, let the solvent evaporate, and put spots of the second compound over the first ones. Run a chromatogram and see if you can detect two spots in either lane (with colorless compounds, it is advisable not to attempt

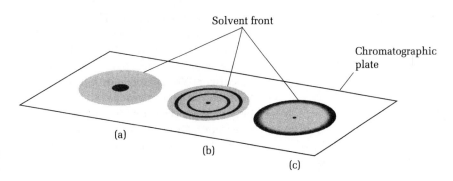

FIG. 9.6 Fast method for determining the correct solvent for TLC. See text for procedure.

a three-lane chromatogram until you have acquired considerable practice and skill).

Cleaning Up   Solvents should be placed in the organic solvents container, and dry, used chromatographic plates can be discarded in the nonhazardous solid waste container.

Discussion

If you have investigated hydroxylated compounds, you doubtless have found that it is reasonably easy to separate a hydroxylated from a nonhydroxylated compound, or a diol from a mono-ol. How, by a simple reaction followed by a thin-layer chromatogram, could you separate cholesterol from triphenylmethanol? Heating a sample of each with acetic anhydride-pyridine for 5 min on the steam bath, followed by chromatography, should do it. A first trial of a new reaction leaves questions about what has happened and how much, if any, starting material is present. A comparative chromatogram of reaction mixture with starting material may tell the story. How crude is a crude reaction product? How many components are present? The thin-layer technique may give the answers to these questions and suggest how best to process the product. A preparative column chromatogram may afford a large number of fractions of eluent (say, 1 to 30). Some fractions probably contain nothing and should be discarded, while others should be combined for evaporation and workup. How can you identify the good and the useless fractions? Take a few used plates and put numbered circles on clean places of each; spot samples of each of the fractions; and, without any chromatography, develop the plates with iodine. Negative fractions for discard will be obvious, and the pattern alone of positive fractions may allow you to infer which fractions can be combined. Thin-layer chromatograms of the first and last fractions of each suspected group would then show whether or not your inferences are correct.

Fluorescence

Do not look into a UV lamp.

Four of the compounds listed in Experiment 3 are fluorescent under UV light, and such compounds give colorless spots that can be picked up on a chromatogram by fluorescence (after removal from the UV-absorbing glass bottle). If a UV light source is available, spot the four compounds on a used plate and observe the fluorescence. Take this opportunity to examine a white shirt or handkerchief under UV light to see if it contains a brightener, that is, a fluorescent white dye or optical bleach. These substances are added to counteract the yellow color that repeated washing gives to cloth. Brighteners of the type of Calcofluor White MR, a sulfonated *trans*-stilbene derivative, are commonly used in detergent formulations for cotton; the substituted coumarin derivative formulated is typical of brighteners used for nylon, acetate, and wool. Detergents normally contain 0.1–0.2% of optical bleach. The amount of dye on a freshly laundered shirt is approximately 0.01% of the weight of the fabric.

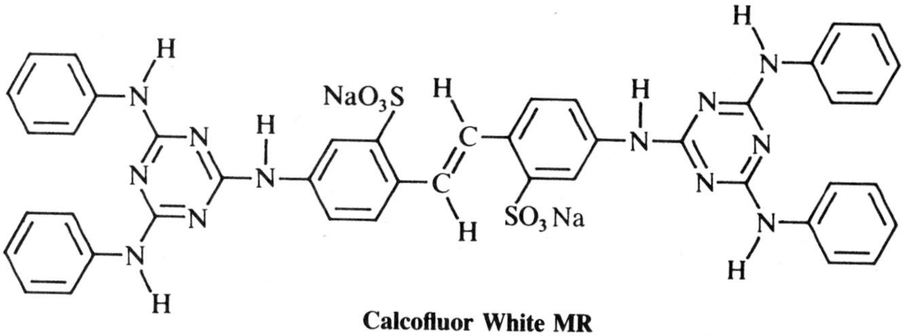

Calcofluor White MR

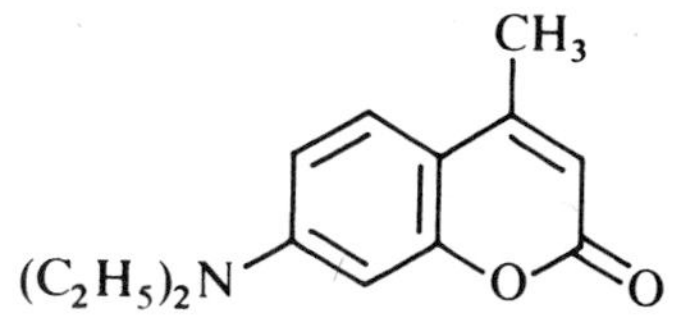

$(C_2H_5)_2N$

7-Diethylamino-4-methylcoumarin

Questions

1. Why might it be very difficult to visualize the separation of *cis-* and *trans-*2-butene by thin-layer chromatography?

2. What error is introduced into the determination of an R_f value if the top is left off of the developing chamber?

3. What problem will ensue if the level of the developing liquid is higher than the applied spot in a TLC analysis?

4. In what order (from top to bottom) would you expect to find naphthalene, butyric acid, and phenyl acetate on a silica gel TLC plate developed with dichloromethane?

5. In carrying out an analysis of a mixture, what do you expect to see when the TLC plate has been allowed to remain in the developing chamber too long, so that the solvent front has reached the top of the plate?

6. Arrange the following in order of increasing R_f on thin-layer chromatography: acetic acid, acetaldehyde, 2-octanone, decane, and 1-butanol.

7. Why must the spot applied to a TLC plate be above the level of the developing solvent?

8. What will be the result of applying too much compound to a TLC plate?

9. Why is it necessary to run TLC in a closed container and to have the interior vapor saturated with the solvent?

10. What will be the appearance of a TLC plate if a solvent of too low polarity is used for the development? too high polarity?

11. A TLC plate showed two spots of R_f 0.25 and 0.26. The plate was removed from the developing chamber, dried carefully, and returned to the developing chamber. What would you expect to see after the second development was complete?

12. One of the analgesics has a chiral center. Which compound is it? One of the two enantiomers is much more effective at reducing pain than the other.

13. Using a ruler to measure distances, calculate the R_f value for Substance B in Fig. 9.1.

10

Column Chromatography: Acetylferrocene, Cholesteryl Acetate, and Fluorenone

Column chromatography is one of the most useful methods for the separation and purification of both solids and liquids when carrying out small-scale experiments. It becomes expensive and time consuming, however, when more than about 10 g of material must be purified.

The application in the present experiment is typical: A reaction is carried out, it does not go to completion, and so column chromatography is used to separate the product from starting material, reagents, and byproducts.

The theory of column chromatography is analogous to that of thin-layer chromatography. The most common adsorbents—silica gel and alumina—are the same ones used in TLC. The sample is dissolved in a small quantity of solvent (the eluent) and applied to the top of the column. The eluent, instead of rising by capillary action up a thin layer, flows down through the column filled with the adsorbent. Just as in TLC, there is an equilibrium established between the solute adsorbed on the silica gel or alumina and the eluting solvent flowing down through the column. Under some conditions the solute may be partitioning between an adsorbed solvent and the elution solvent; the partition coefficient, just as in the extraction process, determines the efficiency of separation in chromatography. The partition coefficient is determined by the solubility of the solute in the two phases, as was discussed in the extraction experiment (Chapter 8).

Three mutual interactions must be considered in column chromatography: the polarity of the sample, the polarity of the eluting solvent, and the activity of the adsorbent.

Adsorbent

A large number of adsorbents have been used for column chromatography—cellulose, sugar, starch, inorganic carbonates—but most separations employ alumina (Al_2O_3) and silica gel (SiO_2). Alumina comes in three forms: acidic, neutral, and basic. The neutral form of Brockmann activity II or III, 150 mesh, is most commonly employed. The surface area of this alumina is about 150 m^2/g. Alumina as purchased will usually be activity I, meaning it will strongly adsorb solutes. It must be deactivated by adding water, shaking, and allowing the mixture to reach equilibrium over an hour or so. The amount of water needed to achieve certain activities is given in Table 10.1. The activity of the alumina on TLC plates is usually about III. Silica gel for column chromatography, 70–230 mesh, has a surface area of about 500 m^2/g and comes in only one activity.

TABLE 10.1   Alumina Activity

Brockmann activity	I	II	III	IV	V
Percent by weight of water	0	3	6	10	15

Solvents

The elutropic series for a number of solvents is given in Table 10.2. The solvents are arranged in increasing polarity, with *n*-pentane being the least polar. This is the order of ability of these solvents to dissolve polar organic compounds and to dislodge a polar substance adsorbed onto either silica gel or alumina, with *n*-pentane having the lowest solvent power.

Petroleum ether: mostly isometric pentanes; ligroin: mostly isomeric hexanes

As a practical matter, the following sequence of solvents is recommended in an investigation of unknown mixtures: elute first with petroleum ether; then ligroin, followed by ligroin containing 1%, 2%, 5%, 10%, 25%, and 50% *t*-butyl methyl ether; pure *t*-butyl methyl ether; *t*-butyl methyl ether and dichloromethane mixtures, followed by dichloromethane and methanol mixtures. A sudden change in solvent polarity will cause heat evolution as the alumina or silica gel adsorbs the new solvent. This will cause undesirable vapor pockets and cracks in the column.

TABLE 10.2   Elutropic Series for Solvents

n-Pentane (first)
Petroleum ether
Cyclohexane
Ligroin
Carbon disulfide
t-Butyl methyl ether
Dichloromethane
Tetrahydrofuran
Dioxane
Ethyl acetate
2-Propanol
Ethanol
Methanol
Acetic acid (last)

Solutes

The ease with which different classes of compounds elute from a column is indicated in Table 10.3. The order is similar to that of the eluting solvents—another application of "like dissolves like."

Sample and Column Size

In general the amount of alumina or silica gel used should weigh at least 30 times as much as the sample, and the column, when packed, should have a height at least 10 times the diameter. The density of silica gel is 0.4 g/mL, and the density of alumina is 0.9 g/mL, so the optimum size for any column can be calculated. A microscale column for the chromatography of about 50 mg of material is shown in Fig. 10.1.

TABLE 10.3   Elution Order for Solutes

Alkanes (first)
Alkenes
Dienes
Aromatic hydrocarbons
Ethers
Esters
Ketones
Aldehydes
Amines
Alcohols
Phenols
Acids (last)

Packing the Chromatography Column

Uniform packing of the chromatography column is critical to the success of this technique. The sample is applied as a pure liquid or, if it is a solid, as a very concentrated solution in the solvent that will dissolve it best, regardless of polarity. As elution takes place, this narrow band of sample will separate into several bands corresponding to the number of components in the mixture and their relative polarities and molecular weights. It is essential that the components move through the column as a narrow horizontal band in order to come off the column

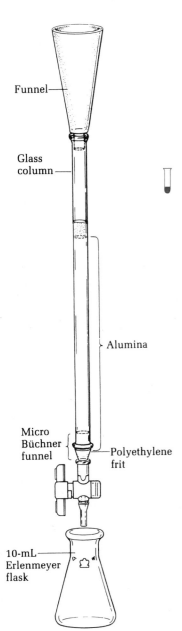

Funnel

Glass column

Alumina

Micro Büchner funnel

Polyethylene frit

10-mL Erlenmeyer flask

FIG. 10.1 Microscale chromatographic column.

Extinguish all flames; work in laboratory hood.

in the least volume of solvent and not overlap with other components of the mixture. Therefore, the column should be vertical, and the packing should be perfectly uniform, without voids caused by air bubbles.

The preferred method for packing silica gel and alumina columns is the slurry method, whereby a slurry of the adsorbent and the first eluting solvent is made and poured into the column. When nothing is known about the mixture being separated, the column is prepared in petroleum ether, the least polar of the eluting solvents.

Microscale Procedure

Packing the Column. Assemble the column as depicted in Figure 10.1. To measure the adsorbent, fill the column one-half to two-thirds full, and then pour the powder into a 10-mL Erlenmeyer flask. Clamp the column in a vertical position, and close the valve. Always grasp the valve with one hand while turning it with the other. Fill the column with ligroin or hexane to the top of the glass column. Add about 8 mL hexane to the adsorbent in the flask, stir the mixture to eliminate air bubbles, and then (this is the hard part) swirl the mixture to get the adsorbent suspended in the solvent and immediately pour the entire slurry into the funnel. Open the valve, drain some solvent into the flask that had the adsorbent in it, and finish transferring the slurry to the column. Place an empty flask under the column, and allow the solvent to drain to about 5 mm above the top surface of the adsorbent. *Never allow the column to dry out;* this creates channels that will result in uneven bands and poor separation.

Adding the Sample and Eluting the Column. Dissolve the sample completely in the very minimum volume of dichloromethane (just a few drops) in an Erlenmeyer flask. Add to this solution 300 mg of the adsorbent, stir, and evaporate the solvent completely. Heat the flask *very gently* with *constant* stirring to avoid having the material bump. Remember that dichloromethane boils at 55°C. Pour this dry powder into the funnel of the chromatography column, wash it down onto the column with a few drops of hexane, and then tap the column to remove air bubbles from this layer of adsorbent-solute mixture just added. Open the valve, and carefully add new solvent in such a manner that the top surface of the column is not disturbed. Run the solvent down near to the surface several times to apply the sample as a narrow band at the top of the column. Then fill the column with the solvent, and elute the sample from the column.

Macroscale Procedure

The column can be prepared using a 50-mL burette such as the one shown in Fig. 10.2 or using the less expensive and equally satisfactory chromatographic tube shown in Fig. 10.3, in which the flow of solvent is controlled by a screw pinchclamp. Weigh out the required amount of silica gel (12.5 g in the first experiment), close the pinchclamp on the tube, and fill about half full with 90 : 10

Dry packing

ligroin : ether. With a wooden dowel or glass rod push a small plug of glass wool through the liquid to the bottom of the tube, dust in through a funnel enough sand to form a 1-cm layer over the glass wool, and level the surface by tapping the tube. Unclamp the tube. With the right hand grasp both the top of the tube and the funnel so that the whole assembly can be shaken to dislodge silica gel that may stick to the walls, and with the left hand pour in the silica gel slowly (Fig. 10.4) while tapping the column with a rubber stopper fitted on the end of a pencil. If necessary, use a Pasteur pipette full of 90 : 10 ligroin : ether to wash down any silica gel that adheres to the walls of the column above the liquid. When the silica gel has settled, add a little sand to provide a protective layer at the top. Open the pinchclamp, let the solvent level fall until it is just a little above the upper layer of sand, and then stop the flow.

Slurry packing

Alternatively, the silica gel can be added to the column (half filled with ligroin) by slurrying the silica gel with 90 : 10 ligroin : ether in a beaker. The powder is stirred to suspend it in the solvent and immediately poured through a wide-mouth funnel into the chromatographic tube. Rap the column with a rubber stopper to cause the silica gel to settle and to remove bubbles. Add a protective layer of sand to the top. The column is now ready for use.

Prepare several Erlenmeyer flasks as receivers by taring (weighing) each one carefully and marking them with numbers on the etched circle.

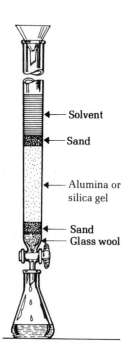

FIG. 10.2 Macroscale chromatographic column.

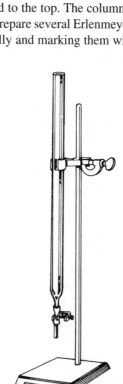

FIG. 10.3 Chromatographic tube on ring stand.

FIG. 10.4 A useful technique for filling a chromatographic tube with silica gel.

Cleaning Up   After use, the tube is conveniently emptied by pointing the open end into a beaker, opening the pinchclamp, and applying gentle air pressure to the tip. If the plug of glass wool remains in the tube after the alumina leaves, wet it with acetone and reapply air pressure. Allow the adsorbent to dry in the hood, and then dispose of it in the nonhazardous waste container.

Experiments

MICROSCALE

Ferrocene
MW 186.04
mp 172–174°C

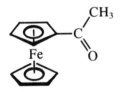

Acetylferrocene
MW 228.08, mp 85–86°C

Caution: Toxic.

1. Chromatography of a Mixture of Ferrocene and Acetylferrocene

Both these compounds are colored (see Chapter 44 for their preparation), so it is easy to follow the progress of the chromatographic separation.

Prepare the microscale alumina column exactly as described above. Then add a dry slurry of 90 mg of a 50 : 50 mixture of acetylferrocene (*Caution!* toxic) and ferrocene that has been adsorbed onto 300 mg of alumina following the above procedure for preparing and adding the sample.

Carefully add hexane to the column, open the valve (use both hands), and elute the two compounds. The first to be eluted, ferrocene, will be seen as a yellow band. Collect this in a 10-mL flask. Any crystalline material seen at the tip of the valve should be washed into the flask with a drop or two of ether. Without allowing the column to run dry, add a 50 : 50 mixture of hexane and *t*-butyl methyl ether, and elute the acetylferrocene, which will be seen as an orange band. Collect it in a 10-mL flask. Spot a thin-layer silica gel chromatography plate with these two solutions. Evaporate the solvents from the two flasks, and determine the weights of the residues. An easy way to evaporate the solvent is to place it in a tared 25-mL filter flask and heat the flask in the hand under vacuum while swirling the contents (Fig. 10.5).

Recrystallize the products from the minimum quantities of hot hexane or ligroin. Isolate the crystals, dry them, and determine their weights and melting points. Calculate the percent recovery of the crude and recrystallized products based on the 45 mg of each in the original mixture.

The thin-layer chromatography plate is eluted with 30 : 1 toluene : absolute ethanol. Do you detect any contamination of one compound by the other?

Cleaning Up   Empty the chromatography column onto a piece of aluminum foil in the hood. After the solvent has evaporated, place the alumina and sand in the nonhazardous waste container. Evaporate the crystallization mother liquor to dryness, and place the residue in the hazardous waste container.

MICROSCALE AND MACROSCALE

2. Acetylation of Cholesterol

Cholesterol is a solid alcohol; the average human body contains about 200 g distributed in brain, spinal cord, and nerve tissue and occasionally clogging the arteries and the gall bladder.

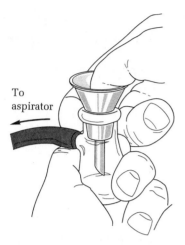

FIG. 10.5 Evaporation of a low-boiling liquid under vacuum. Heat is supplied by the hand, the contents of the flask are swirled, and the vacuum is controlled with the thumb.

In the present experiment, cholesterol is dissolved in acetic acid and allowed to react with acetic anhydride to form the ester, cholesteryl acetate. The reaction does not take place rapidly and consequently does not go to completion under the conditions of this experiment. Thus, when the reaction is over, both unreacted cholesterol and the product, cholesteryl acetate, are present. Separating these by fractional crystallization would be extremely difficult; but because they differ in polarity (the hydroxyl group of the cholesterol is the more strongly adsorbed on alumina), they are easily separated by column chromatography. Both molecules are colorless and hence cannot be detected visually. Each fraction should be sampled for thin-layer chromatography. In that way not only the presence but also the purity of each fraction can be assessed. It is also possible to put a drop of each fraction on a watch glass and evaporate it to see if the fraction contains product. Solid will also appear on the tip of the column while a compound is being eluted.

$$\text{Cholesterol} + CH_3\overset{O}{\underset{||}{C}}O\overset{O}{\underset{||}{C}}CH_3 \longrightarrow$$

Acetic anhydride

Cholesterol

$$\longrightarrow \text{Cholesteryl acetate} + CH_3COOH$$

Cholesteryl acetate

Microscale Procedure

In a reaction tube, add 0.5 mL of acetic acid to 50 mg of cholesterol, which can be material isolated from human gallstones. The initial thin slurry may set into a stiff paste of the molecular complex consisting of one molecule of cholesterol and one of acetic acid. Add 0.10 mL of acetic anhydride and a boiling chip, and gently reflux the reaction mixture on a hot sand bath for no more than 30 min.

While the reaction is taking place, prepare the microscale chromatography column as described above, using silica gel as the adsorbent. Cool the mixture, add 2 mL of water, and extract the product with three 2-mL portions of *tert*-butyl methyl ether that are placed in the 15-mL centrifuge tube. Wash the ether extracts in the tube with two 2-mL portions of water and one 2.5-mL portion of 3 M sodium hydroxide (these three washes remove the acetic acid), and dry the ether by shaking it with 2.5 mL of saturated sodium chloride solution. Then complete the drying by adding enough anhydrous calcium chloride pellets to the solution so that it does not clump together.

Shake the ether solution with the drying agent for 10 min, and then transfer it in portions to a tared reaction tube and evaporate to dryness. Use a drop of this ether solution to spot a TLC plate for later analysis. If the crude material weighs more than the theoretical weight, you will know it is not dry or it contains acetic acid, which can be detected by its odor. Dissolve this crude cholesteryl acetate in the minimum quantity of *tert*-butyl methyl ether, and apply it to the top of the chromatography column.

To prevent the solution from dribbling from the pipette, use a pipette pump to make the transfer. It also could be applied as a dry powder adsorbed on silica gel as in Experiment 1. Elute the column with ligroin or hexane, and collect two 5-mL fractions in tared 10-mL Erlenmeyer flasks or other suitable containers. Add a boiling stick to each flask, and evaporate the solvent under an aspirator tube on a steam bath or sand bath. If the flask appears empty, it can be used to collect later fractions. Lower the solvent layer to the top of the sand and elute with 25 mL of 70 : 30 ligroin : *t*-butyl methyl ether, collecting the five 5-mL fractions. Evaporate the ligroin under an aspirator tube (Fig. 10.6). The last traces of ligroin can be removed using reduced pressure as shown in Fig. 10.7. Follow the 70 : 30 mixture with 20 mL of 50 : 50 ligroin : *t*-butyl methyl ether, collecting four 5-mL fractions. Save any flask that has any visible residue. Analyze the original mixture and each fraction by thin-layer chromatography on silica gel plates using 1:1 ether : ligroin to develop the plates and either ultraviolet light or iodine vapor to visualize the spots.

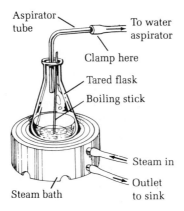

FIG. 10.6 Aspirator tube in use. A boiling stick may be necessary to promote even boiling.

FIG. 10.7 Drying a solid by reduced air pressure.

Cholesteryl acetate (mp 115°C) and cholesterol (mp 149°C) should appear, respectively, in early and late fractions with a few empty fractions (no residue) in between. If so, combine consecutive fractions of early and late material, and determine the weights and melting points. Calculate the percentage of the acetylated material compared with the total recovered, and calculate the percentage yield from cholesterol.

Cleaning Up   Acetic acid, aqueous layers, and saturated sodium chloride layers from the extraction, after neutralization, can be flushed down the drain with water. Ether, ligroin, and TLC solvents should be placed in the organic solvents container and the drying agent, and chromatography adsorbent, once free of solvent, can be placed in the nonhazardous solid water container.

Macroscale Procedure

Carry out procedure in laboratory hood.

Cover 0.5 g of cholesterol with 5 mL of acetic acid in a small Erlenmeyer flask; swirl, and note that the initially thin slurry soon sets to a stiff paste of the molecular compound $C_{27}H_{45}OH \cdot CH_3CO_2H$. Add 1 mL of acetic anhydride, and heat the mixture on the steam bath for any convenient period of time from 15 min to 1 h; record the actual heating period. While the reaction takes place, prepare the chromatographic column. Cool the reaction mixture, add 20 mL of water, and extract with two 25-mL portions of *tert*-butyl methyl ether. Wash the combined ethereal extracts twice with 15-mL portions of water and once with 25 mL of 3 M sodium hydroxide, dry by shaking the ether extracts with 25 mL saturated sodium chloride solution; then dry the ether over anhydrous calcium chloride pellets for 10 min in an Erlenmeyer flask, filter, and evaporate the ether. Save a few crystals of this material for TLC (thin-layer chromatography) analysis. Dissolve the residue in 3 to 4 mL of ether, transfer the solution with a Pasteur pipette onto a column of 12.5 g of silica gel, and rinse the flask with another small portion of *tert*-butyl methyl ether.[1]

In order to apply the ether solution to the top of the sand and avoid having it coat the interior of the column, pipette the solution down a 6-mm-diameter glass tube that is resting on the top of the sand. Label a series of 50-mL Erlenmeyer flasks as fractions 1 to 10. Open the pinchclamp, run the eluant solution into a 50-mL Erlenmeyer flask, and as soon as the solvent in the column has fallen to the level of the upper layer of sand, fill the column with a part of a measured 125 mL of 70 : 30 ligroin : *t*-butyl methyl ether. When about 25 mL of eluant has collected in the flask (fraction 1), change to a fresh flask; add a boiling stone to the first flask, and evaporate the solution to dryness on the steam bath under an aspirator tube (Fig. 10.6). Evacuation using the aspirator helps to remove last traces of ligroin (Fig. 10.7). If this fraction 1 is negative (no residue),

---

1. Ideally, the material to be adsorbed is dissolved in ligroin, the solvent of least elutant power. The present mixture is not soluble enough in ligroin and so ether is used, but the volume is kept to a minimum.

use the flask for collecting further fractions. Continue adding the ligroin–
t-butyl methyl ether mixture until the 125-mL portion is exhausted, and then
use 100 mL of a 1:1 ligroin : *t*-butyl methyl ether mixture. A convenient bubbler
(Fig. 10.8) made from a 125-mL Erlenmeyer flask, a short piece of 10-mm-
diameter glass tubing, and a cork will automatically add solvent. A separatory
funnel with stopper and partially open stopcock serves the same purpose.
Collect and evaporate successive 25-mL fractions of eluant. Save any flask
that has any visible solid residue. The ideal method for removal of solvents
involves the use of a rotary evaporator (Fig. 10.9). Analyze the original mixture and each fraction by TLC on silica gel plates using 1 : 1 ether : ligroin to
develop the plates and either ultraviolet light or iodine vapor to visualize the
spots.

Cholesteryl acetate (mp 115°C) and cholesterol (mp 149°C) should appear,
respectively, in early and late fractions with a few empty fractions (no residue) in
between. If so, combine consecutive fractions of early and of late material, and
determine the weights and melting points. Calculate the percentage of the acetylated material compared with the total recovered, and compare your result with
those of others in your class employing different reaction periods.

FIG. 10.8   Bubbler for adding
solvent automatically.

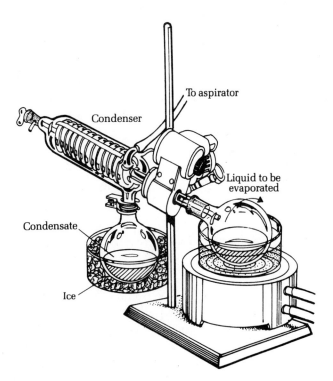

FIG. 10.9   Rotary evaporator. The rate of evaporation with this apparatus is very
fast due to the thin film of liquid spread over the entire inner surface of the
rotating flask, which is heated under a vacuum. Foaming and bumping are also
greatly reduced.

Cleaning Up   Acetic acid, aqueous layers, and saturated sodium chloride layers from the extraction, after neutralization, can be flushed down the drain with water. Ether, ligroin, and TLC solvents should be placed in the organic solvents container, and the drying agent, once free of solvent, can be placed in the nonhazardous solid waste container. Ligroin and ether from the chromatography go into the organic solvents container. If possible, spread out the silica gel in the hood to dry. It can then be placed in the nonhazardous solid waste container. If it is wet with organic solvents, it is a hazardous solid waste and must be disposed of, at great expense, in a secure landfill.

MICROSCALE AND MACROSCALE

3. Fluorene and Fluorenone

The 9-position of fluorene is unusually reactive for a hydrocarbon. The protons on this carbon atom are acidic by virtue of being doubly benzylic, and, consequently, this carbon can be oxidized by several reagents, including elemental oxygen. In the present experiment, the very powerful and versatile oxidizing agent Cr(VI), in the form of chromium trioxide, is used to carry out this oxidation. Cr(VI) in a variety of other forms is used to carry out about a dozen oxidation reactions in this text. The *dust* of Cr(VI) salts is reported to be a carcinogen, so avoid breathing it.

$$\xrightarrow[\text{CH}_3\text{COOH}]{\text{Na}_2\text{Cr}_2\text{O}_7}$$

Fluorene
mp 114°C
MW 166.22

Fluorenone
mp 83°C
MW 180.21

Microscale Procedure

In a reaction tube dissolve 50 mg of fluorene in a 0.25 mL of acetic acid by heating, and add this hot solution to a solution of 0.15 g of sodium dichromate dihydrate in 0.5 mL of acetic acid. Heat the reaction mixture to 80°C for 15 min in a hot water bath; then cool it, and add 1.5 mL of water. Stir the mixture for 2 min, and then filter it on the Hirsch funnel. Wash the product well with water, and press out as much water as possible. Return the product to the reaction tube, add 2 mL of *tert*-butyl methyl ether, and add anhydrous calcium chloride pellets until it no longer clumps together. Cork and shake the tube, and allow the product to dry for 5 or 10 min before evaporating the ether in another tared reaction tube. Use ether to wash off the drying agent and to complete the transfer of product. Use this ether solution to spot a TLC plate. This crude mixture of fluorene and fluorenone will be separated by column chromatography.

Column Chromatography of the Fluorene-Fluorenone Mixture.

The sample can also be applied to the column using the technique described on p. 173.

Prepare a microscale chromatographic column exactly as described above. Dissolve the crude mixture of fluorene and fluorenone in 0.2 mL of warm toluene, and add this to the surface of the alumina. Be sure to add the sample as a solution; should any sample crystallize, add a drop more toluene. Run the ligroin down to the surface of the alumina, add a few drops more ligroin, and repeat the process until the sample is seen as a narrow band at the top of the column.

Ligroin = hexane = "hexanes."

Carefully add a 3-mm layer of sand, then fill the column with ligroin, and collect 5-mL fractions in tared 10-mL Erlenmeyer flasks. Sample each flask for thin-layer chromatography (Fig. 10.10), and evaporate each to dryness. Final drying can be done under vacuum using the technique shown in Fig. 10.7. You are to decide when all the product has been eluted from the column. The thin-layer plates can be developed using 20% dichloromethane in ligroin. Combine fractions that are identical, and determine the melting points of the two substances.

$$\xrightarrow[\text{CH}_3\text{COOH}]{\text{Na}_2\text{Cr}_2\text{O}_7}$$

Fluorene
mp 114°C
MW 166.22

Fluorenone
mp 83°C
MW 180.21

 Macroscale Procedure

CAUTION: Sodium dichromate is toxic. The dust is corrosive to nasal passages and skin and is a cancer-suspect agent. Hot acetic acid is very corrosive to skin; handle with care.

In a 250-mL Erlenmeyer flask dissolve 5.0 g of practical grade fluorene in 25 mL of acetic acid by heating on the steam bath with occasional swirling. In a 125-mL Erlenmeyer flask dissolve 15 g of sodium dichromate dihydrate in 50 mL of acetic acid by swirling and heating on a hot plate. Adjust the temperature of the dichromate solution to 80°C, transfer the thermometer, and adjust the fluorene–acetic acid solution to 80°C, and then, **in the hood,** pour in the dichromate solution. Note the time and the temperature of the solution, and heat on the steam bath for 30 min. Observe the maximum and final temperature, and then cool the solution and add 150 mL of water. Swirl the mixture for a full 2 min to coagulate the product and so promote rapid filtration, and collect the yellow solid in an 8.5-cm Büchner funnel (in case filtration is slow, empty the funnel and flask into a beaker and stir vigorously for a few minutes). Wash the filter cake well with water and then suck the filter cake as dry as possible. Either let the product dry overnight, or dry it quickly as follows: Put the moist solid into a 50-mL Erlenmeyer flask, add ether (20 mL) and swirl to dissolve, and add anhydrous calcium chloride (10 g) to scavenge the water. Decant the ethereal solution through a cone of anhydrous calcium chloride in a funnel into a 125-mL Erlenmeyer flask, and rinse the flask and funnel with *t*-butyl methyl ether. Evaporate on the steam bath under an aspirator, heat until the ether is all removed, and pour the hot oil into a 50-ml beaker to cool and solidify. Scrape out the yellow solid. Yield: 4.0 g.

One-half hour unattended heating

Handle dichromate and acetic acid in laboratory hood; wear gloves.

FIG. 10.10 Spot each fraction on a chromatography plate. Examine under UV light to see which fractions contain compound.

Cleaning Up   The filtrate probably contains unreacted dichromate. To destroy it, add 3 M sulfuric acid until the pH is 1, and then complete the reduction by adding solid sodium thiosulfate until the solution becomes cloudy and blue-colored. Neutralize with sodium carbonate, and filter the flocculent precipitate of $Cr(OH)_3$ through Celite in a Büchner funnel. The filtrate can be diluted with water and flushed down the drain, while the precipitate and Celite should be placed in the heavy metal hazardous waste container.

4. Separation of Fluorene and Fluorenone

Prepare a column of 12.5 g of alumina, run out excess solvent, and pour onto the column a solution of 0.5 g of fluorene–fluorenone mixture. Elute at first with ligroin, and use tared 50-mL flasks as receivers. The yellow color of fluorenone provides one index of the course of the fractionation, and the appearance of solid around the delivery tip provides another. Wash the solid on the tip frequently into the receiver with ether. When you think that one component has been eluted completely, change to another receiver until you judge that the second component is beginning to appear. Then, when you are sure the second component is being eluted, change to a 1 : 1 ligroin : *t*-butyl methyl ether mixture, and continue until the column is exhausted. It is possible to collect practically all the two components in the two receiving flasks, with only a negligible intermediate fraction. After evaporation of solvent, evacuate each flask under vacuum (Fig. 10.7) and determine the weight and melting point of the products. A convenient method for evaporating fractions is to use a rotary evaporator (Fig. 10.9).

Cleaning Up   All organic material from this experiment can go in the organic solvents container. The alumina absorbent, if free of organic solvents, can go in the nonhazardous solid waste container. If it is wet with organic solvents, it is a hazardous solid waste. Spread it in the hood to dry.

Questions

1. Predict the order of elution of a mixture of triphenylmethanol, biphenyl, benzoic acid, and methyl benzoate from an alumina column.

2. What would be the effect of collecting larger fractions when carrying out either of the experiments described?

3. What would have been the result if a large quantity of petroleum ether alone were used as the eluent in either of the experiments described?

4. Once the chromatographic column has been prepared, why is it important to allow the level of the liquid in the column to drop to the level of the alumina before applying the solution of the compound to be separated?

5. A chemist started to carry out column chromatography on a Friday afternoon, got to the point at which the two compounds being separated were about three-fourths of the way down the column, and then returned on Monday to find that the compounds came off the column as a mixture. Speculate on the reason for this. The column had not run dry over the weekend.

12

Infrared Spectroscopy

Prelab Exercise: When an infrared spectrum is run, there is a possibility that the chart paper is not properly placed or that the spectrometer is not mechanically adjusted. Describe how you could calibrate an infrared spectrum.

The presence and also the environment of functional groups in organic molecules can be identified by infrared spectroscopy. Like nuclear magnetic resonance (NMR) and ultraviolet spectroscopy, infrared spectroscopy is nondestructive. Moreover, the small quantity of sample needed, the speed with which a spectrum can be obtained, the relatively small cost of the spectrometer, and the wide applicability of the method combine to make infrared spectroscopy one of the most useful tools available to the organic chemist.

Infrared radiation, which is electromagnetic radiation of longer wavelength than visible light, is detected not with the eyes but by a feeling of warmth on the skin. When absorbed by molecules, radiation of this wavelength (typically 2.5 to 25 μm) increases the amplitude of vibrations of the chemical bonds joining atoms.

2.5 to 25 μm equals 4000 to 400 cm^{-1}.
Wavenumbers, cm^{-1}, are proportional to frequency:

$$\bar{v}(\text{cm}^{-1}) = \frac{v}{c}$$

Infrared spectra are measured in units of frequency or wavelength. The wavelength is measured in micrometers or microns, μm (1 μm = 1 × 10^{-4} cm). The positions of absorption bands are measured in frequency units by wavenumbers $\bar{v}$, which are expressed in reciprocal centimeters, cm^{-1}, corresponding to the number of cycles of the wave in each centimeter.

$$\text{cm}^{-1} = \frac{10,000}{\mu\text{m}}$$

Examine the scale carefully.

IR spectroscopy easily detects
Hydroxyl groups —OH

Amines —NH$_2$

Nitriles —C≡N

Nitro groups —NO$_2$

Unlike ultraviolet and NMR spectra, infrared spectra are inverted and are not always presented on the same scale. Some spectrometers record the spectra on an ordinate linear in microns, but this compresses the low-wavelength region. Other spectrometers present the spectra on a scale linear in reciprocal centimeters, but linear on two different scales, one between 4000 and 2000 cm^{-1}, which spreads out the low-wavelength region, and the other a smaller one between 2000 and 667 cm^{-2}. Consequently, spectra of the same compound run on two different spectrometers will not always look the same.

To picture the molecular vibrations that interact with infrared light, imagine a molecule as being made up of balls (atoms) connected by springs (bonds). The vibration can be described by Hooke's law from classical mechanics, which says that the frequency of a stretching vibration is directly proportional to the strength of the spring (bond) and inversely proportional to the masses connected by the spring. Thus we find C—H, N—H, and O—H bond-stretching vibrations are high

IR spectroscopy is especially useful for detecting and distinguishing among all carbonyl-containing compounds:

$$\text{Acids} \quad \overset{\overset{\displaystyle O}{\|}}{-C}-OH$$

$$\text{Amides} \quad \overset{\overset{\displaystyle O}{\|}}{-C}-NH_2$$

$$\text{Anhydrides} \quad \overset{\overset{\displaystyle O}{\|}}{-C}-O-\overset{\overset{\displaystyle O}{\|}}{C}-$$

$$\text{Aldehydes} \quad \overset{\overset{\displaystyle O}{\|}}{-C}-H$$

$$\text{Ketones} \quad \overset{\overset{\displaystyle O}{\|}}{-C}-$$

$$\text{Esters} \quad \overset{\overset{\displaystyle O}{\|}}{-C}-O-$$

$$\text{Lactones} \quad \overset{\overset{\displaystyle O}{\|}}{-C}-O-$$

frequency (short wavelength) compared with those of C—C and C—O because of the low mass of hydrogen compared with that of carbon or oxygen. The bonds connecting carbon to bromine and iodine, atoms of large mass, vibrate so slowly that they are beyond the range of most common infrared spectrometers. A double bond can be regarded as a stiffer, stronger spring, so we find C=C and C=O vibrations at higher frequency than C—C and C—O stretching vibrations. And C≡C and C≡N stretch at even higher frequencies than C=C and C=O (but at lower frequencies than C—H, N—H, and O—H). These frequencies are in keeping with the bond strengths of single (~100 kcal/mol), double (~160 kcal/mol), and triple bonds (~220 kcal/mol).

The stretching vibrations noted above are intense and particularly easy to analyze. A nonlinear molecule of n atoms can undergo $3n - 6$ possible modes of vibration, which means cyclohexane with 18 atoms can undergo 48 possible modes of vibration. A single CH_2 group can vibrate in six different ways. Each vibrational mode produces a peak in the spectrum because it corresponds to the absorption of energy at a discrete frequency. These many modes of vibration create a complex spectrum that defies simple analysis, but even in very complex molecules, certain functional groups have characteristic frequencies that can easily be recognized. Within these functional groups are the above-mentioned atoms and bonds, C—H, N—H, O—H, C=C, C=O, C≡C, and C≡N. Their absorption frequencies are given in Table 12.1.

When the frequency of infrared light is the same as the natural vibrational frequency of an interatomic bond, light will be absorbed by the molecule, and the amplitude of the bond vibration will increase. The intensity of infrared absorption bands is proportional to the change in dipole moment that a bond undergoes when it stretches. Thus the most intense bands (peaks) in an infrared spectrum are often from C=O and C—O stretching vibrations, while the C≡C stretching band for a symmetrical acetylene is almost nonexistent because the molecule undergoes no net change of dipole moment when it stretches:

$$\overset{+}{\underset{/}{\overset{\backslash}{C}}}=O \;\longleftrightarrow\; \overset{+}{\underset{/}{\overset{\backslash}{C}}}=O \qquad H_3C-C\equiv C-CH_3 \;\longleftrightarrow\; H_2C-C\equiv C-CH_3$$

Change in dipole moment   No change in dipole moment

Intensity of absorption is proportional to change in dipole moment.

Unlike proton NMR spectroscopy, where the area of the peaks is strictly proportional to the number of hydrogen atoms causing the peaks, the intensities of infrared peaks are not proportional to the numbers of atoms causing them. Given the chemical shifts and coupling constants, it is possible to calculate a theoretical NMR spectrum that is an exact match to the experimental one. It is not possible, except for very simple molecules, to do this for infrared spectra. Every peak or group of peaks in an NMR spectrum can be assigned to specific hydrogens in a molecule, but the assignment of the majority of peaks in an infrared spectrum is usually not possible. Peaks to the right (longer wavelength) of 1250 cm^{-1} are the result of combinations of vibrations that are characteristic not of individual functional groups but of the molecule as a whole. This part of the spectrum is often

TABLE 12.1 Characteristic Infrared Absorption Wavenumbers

Functional Group	Wavenumber (cm^{-1})
O—H	3600–3400
N—H	3400–3200
C—H	3080–2760
C≡N	2260–2215
C≡C	2150–2100
C=O	1815–1650
C=C	1660–1600
C—O	1200–1050

referred to as the *fingerprint region*, because it is uniquely characteristic of each molecule. While two organic compounds can have the same melting points or boiling points and can have identical ultraviolet and NMR spectra, they cannot have identical infrared spectra (except, as usual, for enantiomers). Infrared spectroscopy is thus the final arbiter in deciding whether two compounds are identical.

Analysis of Infrared Spectra

Very few simple equations or rules govern infrared spectroscopy. Since it is not practical to calculate theoretical spectra, the analysis is done almost entirely by correlation with other spectra. In printed form, these comparisons take the form of lengthy discussions, so detailed analysis of a spectrum is best done with a good reference book at hand.

In a modern analytical or research laboratory, a collection of many thousands of spectra is maintained on a computer. When the spectrum of an unknown compound is run, the analyst picks out five or six of the strongest peaks and asks the computer to list all compounds that have peaks within a few reciprocal centimeters of the listed peaks. From the printout of a dozen or so compounds, it is often possible to pinpoint all the functional groups in the molecule being analyzed. There may be a perfect match of all peaks, in which case the unknown will have been identified.

For relatively simple molecules, a computer search is hardly necessary. Much information can be gained about the functional groups in a molecule from relatively few correlations.

To carry out an analysis, (1) pay most attention to the strongest absorptions, (2) pay more attention to peaks to the left (shorter wavelength) of 1250 cm^{-1}, and (3) pay as much attention to the absence of certain peaks as to the presence of others. The absence of characteristic peaks will definitely exclude certain functional groups. Be wary of weak O—H peaks because water is a common contaminant of many samples. Because potassium bromide is hygroscopic, it is often found in the spectra of KBr pellets.

Step-by-Step Analysis of Infrared Spectra

1. Is there a peak between 1820 to 1625 cm^{-1}? If not, go to Step 2.
   (a) Is there also a strong, wide O—H peak between 3200 and 2500 cm^{-1}? If so, the compound is a carboxylic acid (see Fig. 12.1, oleic acid). If not:
   (b) Is there a medium-to-weak N—H band between 3520 and 3070 cm^{-1}? If there are two peaks in this region, then it is a primary amide; if not, it is a secondary amide. If there is no peak in this region:
   (c) Are there two strong peaks, one in the region 1870 to 1800 cm^{-1} and the other in the region 1800 to 1740 cm^{-1}? If so, an acid anhydride is present. If not:
   (d) Is there a peak in the region of 2720 cm^{-1}? If so, is the carbonyl peak in the region 1715 to 1680 cm^{-1}? If so, it is a conjugated aldehyde; if not, it is an isolated aldehyde (see Fig. 12.2, benzaldehyde). However, if there is no peak near 2720 cm^{-1}:
   (e) Does the strong carbonyl peak fall in the range 1815 to 1770 cm^{-1} and the molecule give a positive Beilstein test? If so, it is an acid halide. If not:
   (f) Does the strong carbonyl peak fall in the range 1690 to 1675 cm^{-1}? If so, it is a conjugated ketone. If not:
   (g) Does the strong carbonyl peak fall in the range 1670 to 1630 cm^{-1}? If so, it is a tertiary amide. If not:
   (h) Does the molecule have a strong, wide peak in the range 1310 to 1100 cm^{-1}? If so, does the carbonyl peak fall in the range 1730 to 1715 cm^{-1}? If so, it is a conjugated ester; if not, the ester is not conjugated

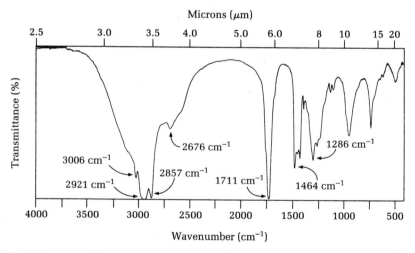

FIG. 12.1 Infrared spectrum of oleic acid (thin film).

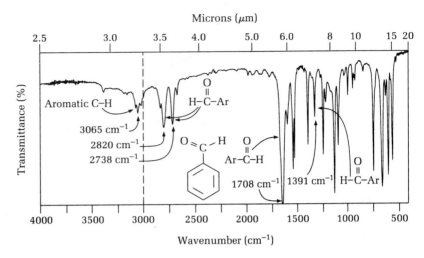

FIG. 12.2   Infrared spectrum of benzaldehyde (thin film).

(see Fig. 12.3, *n*-butyl acetate). If there is no strong, wide peak in the range 1310 to 1100 cm^{-1}, then:

(i)   The molecule is an ordinary nonconjugated ketone.

2.   If the molecule lacks a carbonyl peak in the range 1820 to 1625 cm^{-1}, does it have a broad band in the region 3650 to 3200 cm^{-1}? If so, does it also have a peak at about 1200 cm^{-1}, a C—H stretching peak to the left of 3000 cm^{-1}, and a peak in the region 1600 to 1470 cm^{-1}? If so, it is a phenol. If it does not meet these latter three criteria, it is an alcohol (see Fig. 12.4, cyclohexanol). However, if there is no broad band in the region 3650 to 3200 cm^{-1}, then:

(a)   Is there a broad band in the region 3500 to 3300 cm^{-1}, does the mole-

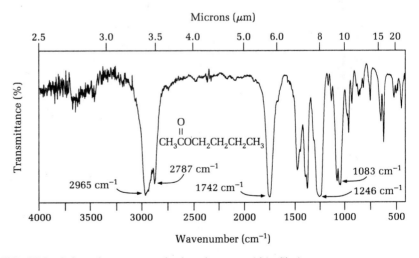

FIG. 12.3   Infrared spectrum of *n*-butyl acetate (thin film).

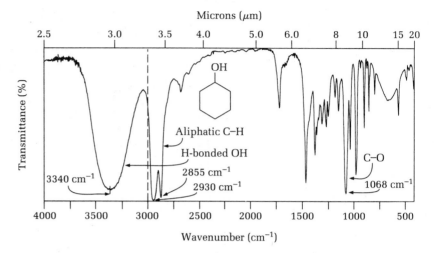

The effect of ring size on the carbonyl frequencies of lactones and esters

1727 cm⁻¹

1745 cm⁻¹

1740 cm⁻¹

1775 cm⁻¹

1832 cm⁻¹

FIG. 12.4 Infrared spectrum of cyclohexanol (thin film).

cule smell like an amine, or does it contain nitrogen? If so, are there two peaks in this region? If so, it is a primary amine; if not, it is a secondary amine. However, if there is no broad band in the region 3500 to 3300 cm⁻¹, then:

(b) Is there a sharp peak of medium-to-weak intensity at 2260 to 2100 cm⁻¹? If so, is there also a peak at 3320 to 3310 cm⁻¹? If so, the molecule is a terminal acetylene. If not, then the molecule is most likely a nitrile (see Fig. 12.5, benzonitrile), although it might be an asymmetrically substituted acetylene. If there is no sharp peak of medium-to-weak intensity at 2260 to 2100 cm⁻¹, then:

(c) Are there strong peaks in the region 1600 to 1540 cm⁻¹ and 1380 to 1300 cm⁻¹? If so, the molecule contains a nitro group. If not:

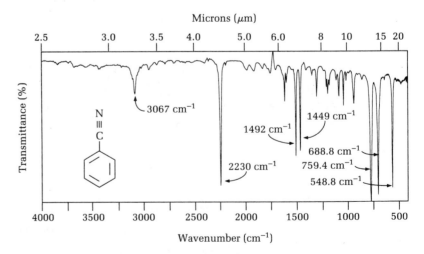

FIG. 12.5 Infrared spectrum of benzonitrile (thin film).

The effect of ring size on the carbonyl frequency

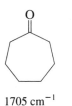

1705 cm⁻¹

1715 cm⁻¹

1715 cm⁻¹

1745 cm⁻¹

1780 cm⁻¹

1815 cm⁻¹

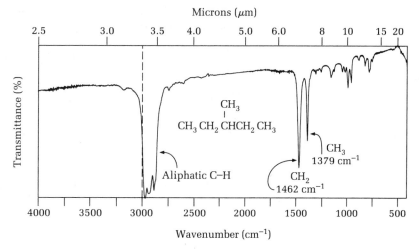

FIG. 12.6   Infrared spectrum of 3-methylpentane (thin film).

(d) Is there a strong peak in the region 1270 to 1060 cm⁻¹? If so, the molecule is an ether. If not:

(e) The molecule is either a tertiary amine (odor?), a halogenated hydrocarbon (Beilstein test?), or just an ordinary hydrocarbon (see Fig. 12.6, 3-methylpentane, and Fig. 12.7, *tert*-butylbenzene).

Many comments can be added to this bare outline. For example, dilute solutions of alcohols will show a sharp peak at about 3600 cm⁻¹ for a nonhydrogen-bonded O—H in addition to the usual broad hydrogen-bonded O—H peak.

Aromatic hydrogens give peaks just to the left of 3000 cm⁻¹, while aliphatic hydrogens appear just to the right of 3000 cm⁻¹. However, NMR spectroscopy is the best method for identifying aromatic hydrogens.

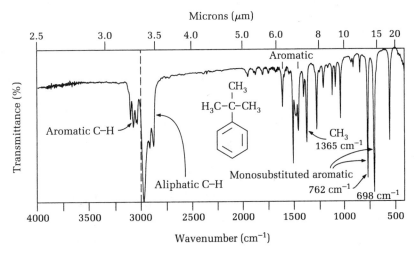

FIG. 12.7   Infrared spectrum of *tert*-butylbenzene (thin film).

TABLE 12.2   Characteristic Infrared Carbonyl Stretching Peaks (Chloroform Solutions)

	Carbonyl-Containing Compounds	Wavenumber (cm^{-1})
$\overset{\displaystyle O}{\overset{\displaystyle \|}{RCR}}$	Aliphatic ketones	1725–1705
$\overset{\displaystyle O}{\overset{\displaystyle \|}{RCCl}}$	Acid chlorides	1815–1785
$R-\overset{\displaystyle \|}{C}=\overset{\displaystyle \|}{C}-\overset{\overset{\displaystyle O}{\displaystyle \|}}{C}-R$	α,β-Unsaturated ketones	1685–1666
$Ar\overset{\displaystyle O}{\overset{\displaystyle \|}{C}}R$	Aryl ketones	1700–1680
⬡=O	Cyclohexanones	1725–1705
$\overset{\displaystyle O}{\overset{\displaystyle \|}{-C}}-CH_2-\overset{\displaystyle O}{\overset{\displaystyle \|}{C}}-$	β-Diketones	1640–1540
$\overset{\displaystyle O}{\overset{\displaystyle \|}{RCH}}$	Aliphatic aldehydes	1740–1720
$R-\overset{\displaystyle \|}{C}=\overset{\displaystyle \|}{C}-\overset{\overset{\displaystyle O}{\displaystyle \|}}{C}H$	α,β-Unsaturated aldehydes	1705–1685
$Ar\overset{\displaystyle O}{\overset{\displaystyle \|}{C}}H$	Aryl aldehydes	1715–1695
RCOOH	Aliphatic acids	1725–1700
$R-\overset{\displaystyle \|}{C}=\overset{\displaystyle \|}{C}-COOH$	α,β-Unsaturated acids	1700–1680
ArCOOH	Aryl acids	1700–1680
$\overset{\displaystyle O}{\overset{\displaystyle \|}{RCOR'}}$	Aliphatic esters	1740
$R-\overset{\displaystyle \|}{C}=\overset{\displaystyle \|}{C}-\overset{\overset{\displaystyle O}{\displaystyle \|}}{C}OR'$	α,β-Unsaturated esters	1730–1715
$Ar\overset{\displaystyle O}{\overset{\displaystyle \|}{C}}OR$	Aryl esters	1730–1715

TABLE 12.2   Characteristic Infrared Carbonyl Stretching Peaks (Chloroform Solutions) *continued*

	Carbonyl-Containing Compounds	Wavenumber (cm^{-1})
$\overset{\displaystyle O}{\overset{\displaystyle \|}{HCOR}}$	Formate esters	1730–1715
$CH_2{=}CHOCCH_3$ $\overset{O}{\|}$ $C_6H_5OCCH_3$	Vinyl and phenyl acetate	1776
$R{-}\overset{O}{\overset{\|}{C}}{\diagdown}_O$ $R{-}\underset{\|}{\underset{O}{C}}{\diagup}$	Acyclic anhydrides (two peaks)	1840–1800 1780–1740
$\overset{O}{\overset{\|}{RCNH_2}}$	Primary amides	1694–1650
$\overset{O}{\overset{\|}{RCNHR'}}$	Secondary amides	1700–1670
$\overset{O}{\overset{\|}{RCNR'_2}}$	Tertiary amides	1670–1630

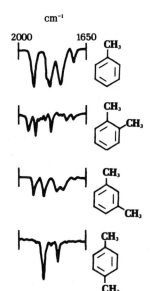

FIG. 12.8 Band patterns of toluene and *o-*, *m-*, and *p*-xylene. These peaks are *very weak*. They are characteristic of aromatic substitution patterns in general, not just for these four molecules. Try to find these patterns in other spectra throughout this text.

The carbonyl frequencies listed earlier refer to the open chain or unstrained functional group in a nonconjugated system. If the carbonyl group is conjugated with a double bond or an aromatic ring, the peak will be displaced to the right by 30 cm^{-1} (see the margin notes). When the carbonyl group is in a ring smaller than six members or if there is oxygen substitution on the carbon adjacent to an aldehyde or ketone carbonyl, the peak will be moved to the left (see the margin notes and Table 12.2).

Methyl groups often give a peak near 1375 cm^{-1}, but NMR is a better method for detecting this group.

The pattern of substitution on an aromatic ring (mono-, *ortho-*, *meta-*, and *para*, di-, tri-, tetra-, and penta-) can be determined from C—H out-of-plane bending vibrations in the region 670–900 cm^{-1}. Much weaker peaks between 1650 and 2000 cm^{-1} are illustrated in Fig. 12.8.

Extensive correlation tables and discussions of characteristic group frequencies can be found in the specialized references listed at the end of this chapter.

The Fourier Transform Infrared (FTIR) Spectrometer

The double-beam infrared spectrometer is rapidly being supplanted by Fourier transform instruments. Like their NMR counterparts, they are computer based, can sum a number of scans to increase the signal-to-noise ratio, and being digitally oriented, allow enormous flexibility in the ways spectra can be analyzed and displayed. In addition, they are faster and more accurate than double-beam spectrometers.

A schematic diagram of a single-beam FTIR spectrometer is given in Fig. 12.9. Infrared radiation goes to a Michelson interferometer in which half the light beam passes through a partially coated mirror to a fixed mirror and half goes to a moving mirror. The combined beams pass through the sample and are then focused on the detector. The motion of the mirror gives a signal that varies sinusoidally. Depending on the mirror position, the different frequencies of light either reinforce or cancel each other, resulting in an interferogram. The mirror, the only moving part of the spectrometer, thus gives rise to a signal that encodes the very high optical frequencies as a low-frequency signal that changes as the mirror moves back and forth. The Fourier transform converts the digitized signal into a signal that is a function of frequency, that is, a spectrum.

Like Fourier transform NMR spectroscopy, all infrared frequencies are sampled at once instead of being scanned successively, so a spectrum is obtained in seconds. Because there is no slit to sort out the wavelengths, high resolution is possible without losing signal strength. Extremely small samples or very dilute solutions can be examined because it is easy to sum hundreds of scans in the computer. It is even possible to take a spectrum of an object seen under a microscope. The spectrum of one compound can be subtracted from, say, a binary mixture spectrum to reveal the nature of the other component. Data can be smoothed, added, resized, and so on because of the digital nature of the output from the spectrometer.

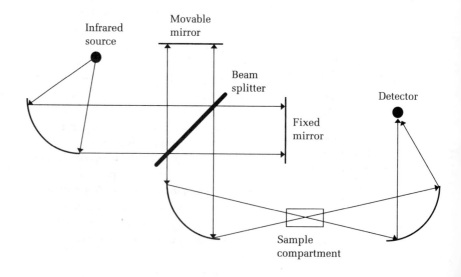

FIG. 12.9 Optical path diagram of an FTIR spectrometer.

Experimental Aspects

*Sample, solvents, and equipment **must be dry.***

Infrared spectra can be determined on neat (undiluted) liquids, on solutions with an appropriate solvent, and on solids as mulls and KBr pellets. Glass is opaque to infrared radiation; therefore, the sample and reference cells used in infrared spectroscopy are sodium chloride plates. The sodium chloride plates are fragile and can be attacked by moisture. *Handle only by the edges.*

Spectra of Neat Liquids

To run a spectrum of a neat (free of water!) liquid, remove a demountable cell (Fig. 12.10) from the desiccator, place a drop of the liquid between the salt plates, press the plates together to remove any air bubbles, and add the top rubber gasket and metal top plate. Next, put on all four of the nuts and *gently* tighten them to apply an even pressure to the top plate. Place the cell in the sample compartment (nearest the front of the spectrometer), and run the spectrum.

Although running a spectrum on a neat liquid is convenient and results in no extraneous bands to interpret, it is not possible to control the path length of the light through the liquid in a demountable cell. A low-viscosity liquid when squeezed between the salt plates may be so thin that the short path length gives peaks that are too weak. A viscous liquid, on the other hand, may give peaks that are too intense. A properly run spectrum will have the most intense peak with an absorbance of about 1.0.

Another demountable cell is pictured in Fig. 12.11. The plates are thin wafers of silver chloride, which is transparent to infrared radiation. This cell has advantages over the salt cell in that the silver chloride disks are more resistant to

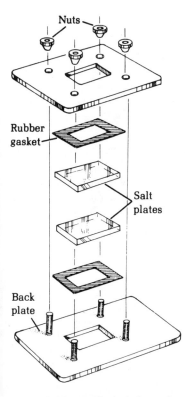

FIG. 12.10 Exploded view of a demountable salt cell for analyzing the infrared spectra of neat liquids. Salt plates are fragile and expensive. Do not touch front surfaces. Use only dry solvents and samples.

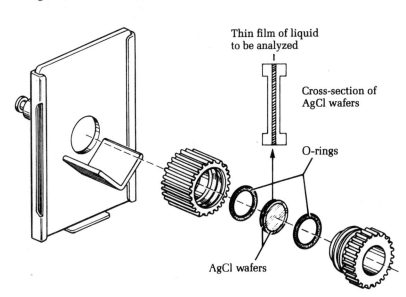

FIG. 12.11 Demountable silver chloride cell.

A fast, simple alternative: Place a drop of the compound on a round salt plate, add a top plate, and mount the two on the holder pictured in Fig. 12.11.

breakage than NaCl plates, less expensive, and not affected by water. Because silver chloride is photosensitive, the wafers must be stored in the dark to prevent them from turning black. Because one side of each wafer is recessed, the thickness of the sample can be varied according to the manner in which the cell is assembled. In general, spectra of pure liquids are run as the thinnest possible films. Most of the spectra in this chapter have been obtained in this way. The disks are cleaned by rinsing them with an organic solvent such as acetone or ethanol and wiping dry with an absorbent paper towel.

A very simple "cell" consists of two circular sodium chloride disks (1" dia. × $\frac{3}{16}$" thick, 25 mm × 4 mm). The sample, one drop of a pure liquid or solution, is applied to the center of a disk with a polyethylene pipette (to avoid scratching the sodium chloride). The other disk is added, the sample squeezed to a thin film, and the two disks placed on the V-shaped holder seen in Fig. 12.11.

Spectra of Solutions

Solvents: $CHCl_3$, CS_2, CCl_4

CAUTION: Chloroform, carbon tetrachloride, and carbon disulfide are toxic. The first two are carcinogens. Use laboratory hood. Avoid the use of these solvents if possible.

The most widely applicable method of running spectra of solutions involves dissolving an amount of the liquid or solid sample in an appropriate solvent to give a 10% solution. Just as in NMR spectroscopy, the best solvents to use are carbon disulfide and carbon tetrachloride, but because these compounds are not polar enough to dissolve many substances, chloroform is used as a compromise. Unlike NMR solvents, no solvent suitable in infrared spectroscopy is entirely free of absorption bands in the frequency range of interest (Figs. 12.12, 12.13, and 12.14). In chloroform, for instance, no light passes through the cell between 650 and 800 cm^{-1}. As can be seen from the figures, spectra obtained using carbon disulfide and chloroform cover the entire infrared frequency range. Carbon tetrachloride would appear to be a good choice because it has few interfering peaks, but it is a poor solvent for polar compounds. In practice, a base line is run with

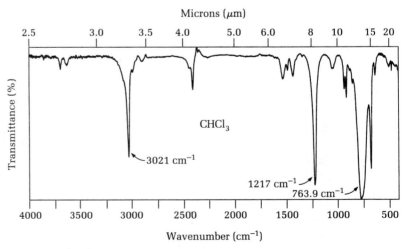

FIG. 12.12 Infrared spectrum of chloroform (thin film).

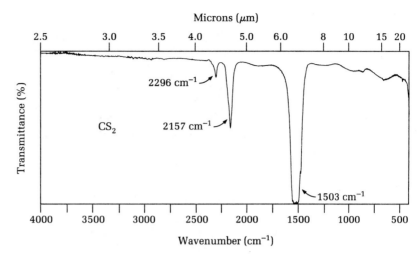

FIG. 12.13   Infrared spectrum of carbon disulfide (thin film).

the same solvent in both cells to ascertain if the cells are clean and matched. Often it is necessary to obtain only one spectrum employing one solvent, depending on which region of the spectrum you need to use.

Three drops are needed to fill the cell.

Three large drops of solution will fill the usual sealed infrared cell (Fig. 12.15). A 10% solution of a liquid sample can be approximated by dilution of one drop of the liquid sample with nine drops of the solvent. Since weights are more difficult to estimate, solid samples should be weighed to obtain a 10% solution.

Solvent and sample must be dry. Do not touch or breathe on NaCl plates. Cells are very expensive.

The infrared cell is filled by inclining it slightly and placing about three drops of the solution in the lower hypodermic port with a capillary dropper. The cell must be completely dry because the new sample will not enter if the cell contains solvent. The liquid can be seen rising between the salt plates through the window.

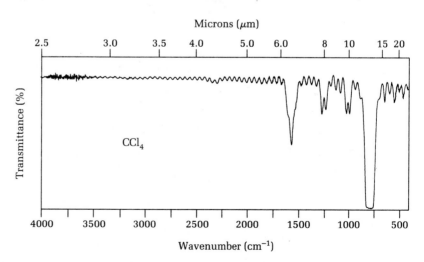

FIG. 12.14   Infrared spectrum of carbon tetrachloride (thin film).

FIG. 12.15 Sealed infrared sample cell.

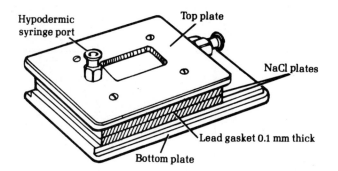

Hypodermic syringe port
Top plate
NaCl plates
Lead gasket 0.1 mm thick
Bottom plate

In the most common sealed cell, the salt plates are spaced 0.1 mm apart. Make sure that the cell is filled past the window and that no air bubbles are present. Then place the Teflon stopper lightly but firmly in the hypodermic port. Be particularly careful not to spill any of the sample on the outside of the cell windows.

Fill the reference cell from a clean hypodermic syringe in the same manner as the sample cell, and place both cells in the spectrometer, with the sample cell toward the front of the instrument. After running the spectrum, force clean solvent through the sample cell using a syringe attached to the top port of the cell (Fig. 12.16). Finally, with the syringe, pull the last bit of solvent from both cells or suck clean dry air through the cells to dry them, and store them in a desiccator.

Dispose of waste solvents in the container provided.

Cleaning Up   Discard halogenated liquids in the halogenated organic waste container. Other solutions should be placed in the organic solvents container.

Mulls

Solids insoluble in the usual solvents can be run as mulls. In preparing a mull, the sample is ground to a particle size less than that of the wavelength of light going

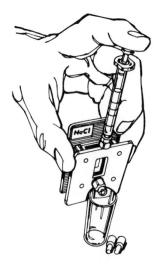

FIG. 12.16 Flushing the infrared sample cell. The solvent used to dissolve the sample is used in this process.

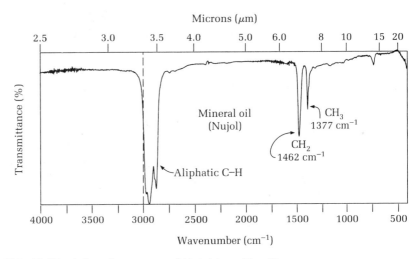

FIG. 12.17   Infrared spectrum of Nujol (paraffin oil).

Sample must be finely ground.

A fast, simple alternative: Grind a few milligrams of the solid with a drop of tetrachloro-ethylene between two round salt plates. Mount on the holder shown in Fig. 12.11.

through the sample (2.5 μm) in order to avoid scattering the light. About 15 to 20 mg of the sample is ground for 3 to 10 min in an agate mortar until it is spread over the entire inner surface of the mortar and has a caked and glassy appearance. Then, to make a mull, 1 or 2 drops of paraffin oil (Nujol) (Fig. 12.17) are added, and the sample ground 2 to 5 more minutes. The mull, which should have the consistency of thin margarine, is transferred to the bottom salt plate of a demountable cell (Fig. 12.10) using a rubber policeman, the top plate is added and twisted to distribute the sample evenly and to eliminate all air pockets, and the spectrum is run. Since the bands from Nujol obscure certain frequency regions, running another mull using Fluorolube as the mulling agent will allow the entire infrared spectral region to be covered. If the sample has not been ground sufficiently fine, there will be marked loss of transmittance at the short-wavelength end of the spectrum. After running the spectrum, the salt plates are wiped clean with a cloth saturated with an appropriate solvent.

Potassium Bromide Disk

The spectrum of a solid sample also can be run by incorporating the sample in a potassium bromide (KBr) disk. This procedure needs only one disk to cover the entire spectral range, since KBr is completely transparent to infrared radiation. Although very little sample is required, making the disk calls for special equipment and time to prepare it. Since KBr is hygroscopic, water is a problem.

Into a stainless steel capsule containing a ball bearing are weighed 1.5 to 2 mg of the compound and 200 mg of spectroscopic-grade potassium bromide (previously dried and stored in a desiccator). The capsule is shaken for 2 min on a Wig-L-Bug (the device used by dentists to mix silver amalgam). The sample is evenly distributed over the face of a 13-mm die and subjected to 14,000 to 16,000 lb/in.^{2} pressure for 3 to 6 min while under vacuum in a hydraulic press. A transparent disk is produced, which is removed from the die with tweezers and placed in a holder like that shown in Fig. 12.11 prior to running the spectrum.

Gas Phase Infrared Spectroscopy: The Williamson Gas Phase IR Cell®

In the past it has been difficult to obtain the infrared spectra of gases. A commercial gas cell costs hundreds of dollars and the cell must be evacuated and the dry gas carefully introduced—not a routine process. But we have found that a uniquely simple gas phase IR cell can be assembled at virtually no cost from the 105° adapter in your microscale kit.

To make the Williamson gas phase IR cell, attach a thin piece of polyethylene film from, for example, a sandwich bag to each end of the adapter with a small rubber band, fine wire, or thread. Place a loose wad of cotton in the side arm, and mount the IR cell in the beam of the spectrometer. (Figs. 12.18 and 12.19).

The adapter can be supported on a V-block as shown in Fig. 12.19 or, temporarily, on a block of modeling clay. Be sure the beam, usually indicated by a red laser, strikes both ends of the cell. Run a background spectrum on the cell. The spectrum of polyethylene (Fig. 12.20) is very simple, so interfering bands will be few. This spectrum is automatically subtracted when you put a sample in the cell and run a spectrum.

A more permanent cell can be constructed by attaching two thin plates of silver chloride to ends of the adapter with epoxy glue. These silver chloride plates can be made in the press used for making potassium bromide discs or they can be purchased (Fisher 14-385-860). See the *Instructor's Guide.*

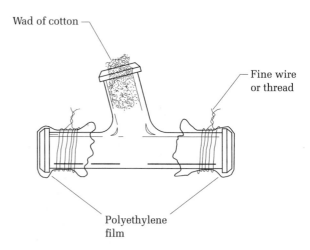

Wad of cotton

Fine wire or thread

Polyethylene film

FIG. 12.18 The Williamson Gas Phase IR Cell® utilizing the 105° adapter from the microscale kit.

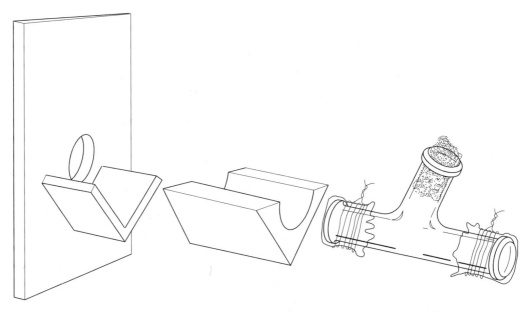

FIG. 12.19   The Williamson Gas Phase IR Cell® mounted in a cell holder.

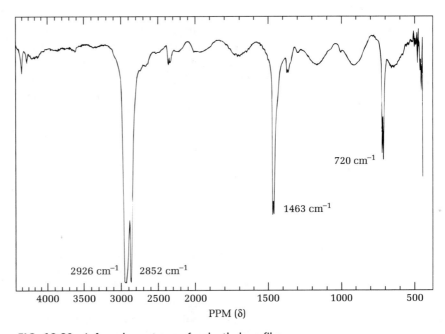

FIG. 12.20   Infrared spectrum of polyethylene film.

Obtaining a Spectrum

To run a gas phase spectrum, remove the cell from the spectrometer and spray onto the cotton a very short burst of a gas from an aerosol can. The nonvolatile components of the spray will stick on the cotton, and the propellant gas will diffuse into the cell. Run the spectrum in the usual way. The concentration of the gas is about the same as a thin film of liquid run between salt plates. If the concentration of the gas is too high, remove the cell from the spectrometer, remove the cotton, and "pour out" half the invisible gas by holding the cell in a vertical position.

You may be fortunate in having in your institution's library a copy of *The Aldrich Library of FT-IR Spectra: Vapor Phase,* Volume 3 ($500). Most libraries do not have it. This 2000-page book has more than 6500 gas phase spectra that will help you analyze the IR spectra of propellants in aerosol cans and any other gases you may encounter. Otherwise you may need to compare your spectra with the few in this text and in the *Instructor's Guide* and begin to assemble your own library of gas phase spectra. It is possible to make approximate calculations of IR spectra (vibrational spectra) using computational chemistry at the AM1 level, for example with the program Spartan.

For Further Investigation

The Gas Phase IR Spectra of Aerosol Propellants

Acquire gas phase spectra from a number of aerosol cans. Some cans will be labeled with the name of the propellant gas, others will not. Analyze the spectra, bearing in mind that the gas will be a small molecule such as carbon dioxide (Fig. 12.21), methane (Fig. 12.22), nitrous oxide (Fig. 12.23), propane, butane, isobutane, or a fluorocarbon such as 1,1,1,2-tetrafluoroethane. A very old aerosol can may contain an illegal chlorofluorocarbon, now outlawed because they destroy the ozone layer. Some possibilities: hair sprays, lubricants (WD-40, Teflon), Freeze-It, inhalants for asthma, cigarette lighters, butane torches, natural gas from the lab.

Other Gas Phase Spectral Research

You can deliberately generate hydrogen chloride (or deuterium chloride) and sulfur dioxide and then analyze the gas that is evolved from a thionyl chloride reaction. Can you detect carbon monoxide in automobile exhaust? How about "marsh gas" that you see bubbling out of ponds? With perhaps dozens of scans, can you record the spectra of vanillin over vanilla beans, of eugenol vapor over cloves, of anisaldehyde over anise seeds? What is the nature of the volatile components of chili peppers, orange peel, nail polish, and nail polish remover? Send me your results (kwilliam@mtholyoke.edu), and I will post them on my Web page (www.mtholyoke.edu/courses/kwilliam/microscale.shtml).

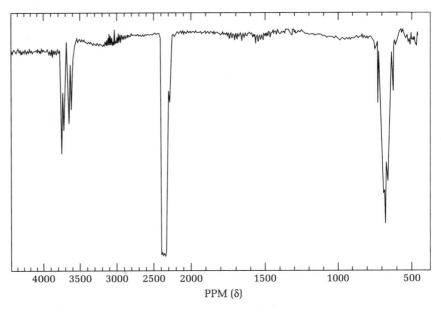

FIG. 12.21   Infrared spectrum of carbon dioxide, gas phase.

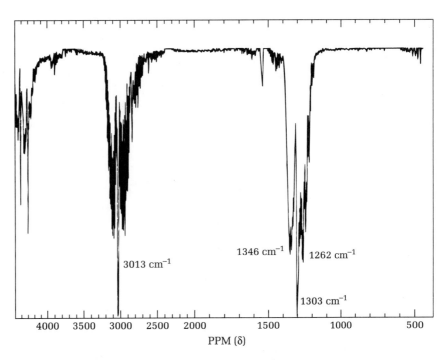

FIG. 12.22   Infrared spectrum of methane, gas phase.

FIG. 12.23 Infrared spectrum of nitrous oxide, gas phase.

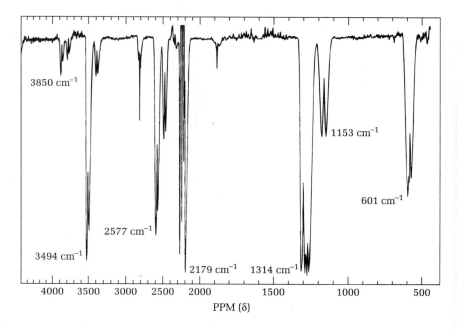

Running the Spectrum

Satisfactory spectra are easily obtained with the lower-cost analog spectrometers, even those that have only a few controls and require few adjustments. To run a spectrum on these instruments, the paper must be positioned accurately, the pen

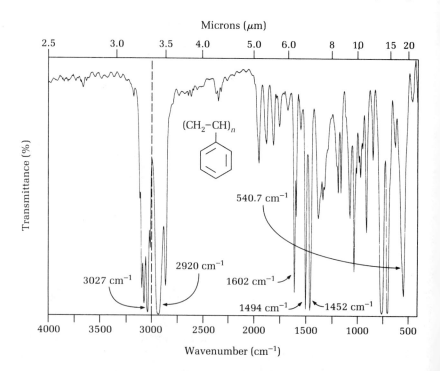

FIG. 12.24 Infrared spectrum of polystyrene film calibration standard.

Calibration with polystyrene

set between 90 and 100% transmittance with the 100% control (0.0 and 0.05 absorbance), and the speed control set for a fast scan (usually one of about 3 min). The calibration of a given spectrum can be checked by backing up the pen and superimposing a spectrum of a thin polystyrene film. This film, mounted in a cardboard holder, will be found near most spectrometers. The film is held in the sample beam, and parts of the spectrum to be calibrated are rerun. See Fig. 12.24 for the spectrum of polystyrene. The spectrometer gain (amplification) should be checked frequently and adjusted when necessary. To check the gain, put the pen on the 90% transmittance line with the 100% control. Place your finger in the sample beam so that the pen goes down to 70% *T*. Then quickly remove your finger. The pen should overshoot the 90% *T* line by 2%.

Fourier transform spectrometers are faster, more sensitive, and can print out peak locations to at least four significant figures. They do not usually require routine calibration or gain adjustments, and the size of the most intense peak can be adjusted. A background spectrum (the empty cell, of whatever nature, or the cell plus a pure solvent) is run first and automatically stored in digital form in the spectrometer. The sample is introduced (a thin film, a solution, a mull, or a gas) and the background spectrum automatically subtracted, leaving only the spectrum of the sample.

Throughout the remainder of this book, representative infrared spectra of starting materials and products are presented and the important bands in each spectrum identified.

Experiment

Unknown Carbonyl Compound

Sample, solvents, and apparatus must be dry.

Run the infrared spectrum of an unknown carbonyl compound obtained from the laboratory instructor. Be particularly careful that all apparatus and solvents are completely free of water, which will damage the sodium chloride cell plates. The spectrum can be calibrated by positioning the spectrometer pen at a wavelength of about 1610 cm^{-1} without disturbing the paper and rerunning the spectrum in the region from 1610 to 1575 cm^{-1} while holding the polystyrene calibration film in the sample beam (see Fig. 12.24). This will superimpose a sharp calibration peak at 1601 cm^{-1} and a less intense peak at 1583 cm^{-1} on the spectrum. Fourier transform spectrometers do not need frequent calibrating. Determine the frequency of the carbonyl peak in the unknown, and list the possible types of compounds that could correspond to this frequency (Table 12.2).

Surfing the Web

http://www.cc.columbia.edu/cu/chemistry/irtutor/Edison.html

An excellent demo of an infrared spectroscopy tutorial is available from this Columbia University site. The infrared spectrum of 1-hexene can, for example, be expanded and each of the 11 major peaks can be selected, giving animations of the molecular motions responsible for each peak.

For updated information visit:

www.mtholyoke.edu.courses.kwilliam.microscale.shtml

or

www.hmco.com/hmco/college/chemistry/Home.html

References

1. Noel P. G. Roeges, *A Guide to the Complete Interpretation of Infrared Spectra of Organic Structures,* John Wiley, New York, 1994.

2. Norman B. Colthup, Lawrence H. Daly, and Stephen E. Wiberley, *Introduction to Infrared and Raman Spectroscopy,* 3rd ed., Academic Press, Boston, 1990.

3. *The Handbook of Infrared and Raman Characteristic Frequencies of Organic Molecules,* Academic Press, Boston, 1991.

4. *Infrared and Raman Spectroscopy: Methods and Applications,* VCH, New York, 1995.

5. Charles J. Pouchert, *The Aldrich Library of FT-IR Spectra,* 1st ed., Aldrich Chemical Co., Milwaukee, WI, 1985.

6. J. W. Cooper, *Spectroscopic Techniques for Organic Chemists,* John Wiley, New York, 1980.

CHAPTER

13

Nuclear Magnetic Resonance Spectroscopy

Prelab Exercise: Outline the preliminary solubility experiments you would carry out on an unknown using inexpensive solvents, before preparing a solution of a compound for nuclear magnetic resonance spectroscopy.

Proton NMR Spectroscopy

NMR: Determination of the number, kind, and relative locations of hydrogen atoms (protons) in a molecule

Chemical shift, δ

Integration: The area under a peak or group of peaks

Nuclear magnetic resonance (NMR) spectroscopy is a means of determining the number, kind, and relative locations of certain atoms, principally hydrogen, in molecules. The number of peaks or groups of coupled peaks indicate the number of chemically and magnetically distinct hydrogen atoms in a molecule. The *integral* indicates the relative number of protons within a peak or group of peaks. The separation between the lines within a group of peaks, called the *coupling constant, J,* can give information about the locations of the protons relative to other nearby protons and, thus, the geometry of the molecule. And the location of a peak in the spectrum, called the *chemical shift, δ,* indicates what kind of proton gave rise to the peak, be it a methyl group, an alkene, or an aromatic ring.

In the process of analyzing a sample, it is possible to expand portions of the spectrum so that patterns of peaks become clear, to *integrate* all peaks, which is the process of determining the relative areas of the peaks numerically or graphically and printing out the frequency of every peak. The integral indicates how many of each type of proton are present. If one or more sets of peaks are well resolved, then the coupling pattern can be analyzed to determine how many protons are adjacent to the proton or protons giving rise to that peak. And measurement of the magnitude of the coupling constant can give information about the geometry of the molecule.

Spectral Analysis: Proton Chemical Shifts

The first place to turn in analyzing a spectrum is a table of chemical shifts. Table 13.1 in this text and in similar general organic chemistry texts is just barely adequate for the task. In books devoted to NMR spectroscopy, such as the one by Friebolin (see the references at the end of this chapter), dozens of detailed tables are supplied for all types of functional groups. Many of the tables contain additivity parameters that allow the approximate calculation of chemical shifts for, say, the protons in a 1,4-disubstituted aromatic ring containing a bromine atom and a methyl group.

TABLE 13.1 Proton Chemical Shifts

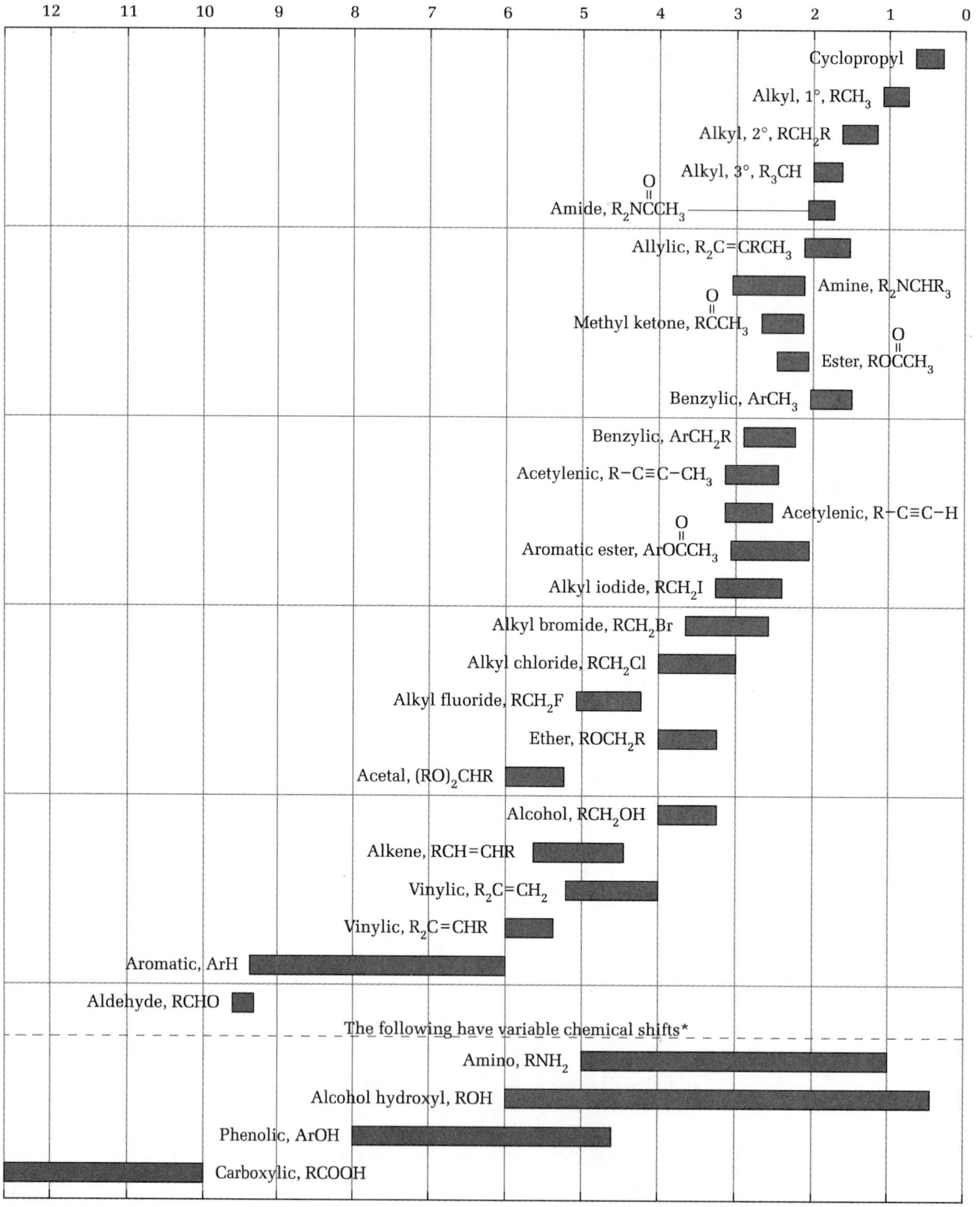

Chemical shift (ppm)	12	11	10	9	8	7	6	5	4	3	2	1	0

Cyclopropyl

Alkyl, 1°, RCH_3

Alkyl, 2°, RCH_2R

Alkyl, 3°, R_3CH

Amide, R_2NCCH_3 (with $\overset{O}{\overset{\|}{}}$)

Allylic, $R_2C=CRCH_3$

Amine, R_2NCHR_3

Methyl ketone, $RCCH_3$ (with $\overset{O}{\overset{\|}{}}$)

Ester, $ROCCH_3$ (with $\overset{O}{\overset{\|}{}}$)

Benzylic, $ArCH_3$

Benzylic, $ArCH_2R$

Acetylenic, $R-C≡C-CH_3$

Acetylenic, $R-C≡C-H$

Aromatic ester, $ArOCCH_3$ (with $\overset{O}{\overset{\|}{}}$)

Alkyl iodide, RCH_2I

Alkyl bromide, RCH_2Br

Alkyl chloride, RCH_2Cl

Alkyl fluoride, RCH_2F

Ether, $ROCH_2R$

Acetal, $(RO)_2CHR$

Alcohol, RCH_2OH

Alkene, $RCH=CHR$

Vinylic, $R_2C=CH_2$

Vinylic, $R_2C=CHR$

Aromatic, ArH

Aldehyde, $RCHO$

The following have variable chemical shifts*

Amino, RNH_2

Alcohol hydroxyl, ROH

Phenolic, $ArOH$

Carboxylic, $RCOOH$

*Shifts depend on concentration, temperature, and solvent.

FIG. 13.1 Proton NMR spectrum of ethyl iodide. The staircaselike line is the integral. In the integral mode of operation, the recorder pen moves from left to right and moves vertically a distance proportional to the areas of the peaks over which it passes. Hence the relative area of the quartet of peaks at 3.20 ppm to the triplet of peaks at 1.83 ppm is given by the relative heights of the integral (4 cm is to 6 cm as 2 is to 3). The relative numbers of hydrogen atoms are proportional to the peak areas (2H and 3H) (60-MHz spectrum).

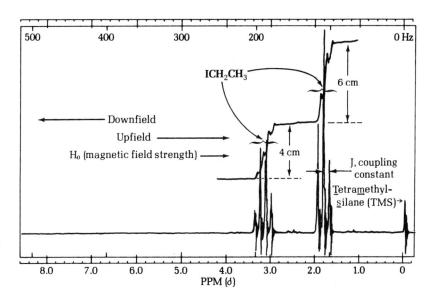

A spectrum of ethyl iodide, typical of those obtained in an older low-field spectrometer operating at 60 MHz, is seen in Fig. 13.1. Figure 13.2 shows a spectrum for the same compound obtained at 250 MHz. The information contained in these two spectra is identical. The chemical shifts reported in parts per million (δ) are identical, and expansion of the pattern of lines in Fig. 13.2 shows that the coupling is exactly the same.

Every proton and carbon spectrum contains tetramethylsilane (TMS), which serves as the zero reference point. Chemical shifts are measured in dimensionless

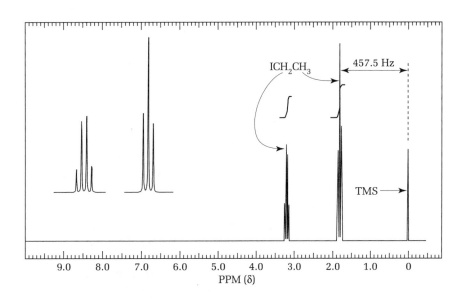

FIG. 13.2 Proton NMR spectrum of ethyl iodide (250 MHz). Compare this spectrum with Fig. 13.1, run at 60 MHz.

parts per million (ppm) downfield from the reference TMS according to the equation

$$\delta(\text{ppm}) = \frac{\text{Shift of peak downfield from TMS (measured in Hz)}}{\text{Spectrometer frequency (measured in MHz)}}$$

An NMR spectrum is characterized completely by the chemical shifts and coupling constants of the nuclei; this is the only information reported in research reports. Using just this information, one can calculate NMR spectra using programs such as gNMR (see the "Surfing the Web" section at the end of this chapter).

The Coupling Constant, J

Coupling Constants.   In an open-chain molecule with free rotation about the bonds and no chiral centers, protons couple with each other over three chemical bonds to give characteristic patterns of lines. If one or more equivalent protons couple to one adjacent proton, then the coupling hydrogen(s) appears as a doublet of equal intensity lines separated by the coupling constant, *J,* measured in hertz. If the coupling proton or protons couple equally to two protons three chemical bonds away, they appear as a triplet of lines with relative intensities of 1 : 2 : 1, again separated by the coupling constant, *J.* In general, chemically equivalent protons give a pattern of lines containing one more line than the number of protons being coupled to, and the intensities of the peaks follow the binomial expansion, conveniently represented by Pascal's triangle. Thus an ethyl group, as in ethyl iodide (Figs. 13.1 and 13.2), appears as a quartet of lines at 3.20 ppm with relative intensities of 1 : 3 : 3 : 1 because the two methylene protons have coupled to the three equivalent methyl protons. The methyl peak is split into a 1 : 2 : 1 triplet centered at 1.83 ppm because the methyl protons have coupled to the two adjacent methylene protons.

Pascal's triangle

			1				*singlet, s*
		1		1			*doublet, d*
	1		2		1		*triplet, t*
1		3		3		1	*quartet, q*
1	4		6		4	1	*pentet*
1	5	10		10	5	1	*sextet*

Other characteristic proton coupling constants are given in Table 13.2. In alkenes *trans* coupling is larger than *cis* coupling, and both are much larger than geminal coupling. *Ortho, meta,* and *para* couplings in aromatic rings range from 9 to 0 Hz. The couplings in a rigid system of saturated bonds are strongly dependent on the dihedral angle between the coupling protons as seen in cyclohexane.

The Integral.   The relative numbers of hydrogen atoms (protons) in the molecule of ethyl iodide are determined from the *integral,* the stair-step line over the peaks. The height of the step is proportional to the area under the NMR peak or group of peaks. In NMR spectroscopy (contrasted with infrared spectroscopy, for instance) the area of each group of peaks is directly proportional to the number of hydrogen atoms causing the peaks. Integrators are part of all NMR spectrometers, and running the integral takes little more time than running the spectrum. Most spectrometers print out a numerical value for the integral (with many more significant figures than are justified!).

TABLE 13.2   Spin–Spin Coupling Constants for Various Geometries

Fragment	J (Hz)	Fragment	J (Hz)
H,H / C=C \ (cis)	7–12	geminal CH$_2$	12–15
H \ C=C / H (trans)	13–18	H–C–C–H	0–10
\ C=C / with H,H	0.5–3	(aromatic ortho)	6–9
		(aromatic meta)	1–3
H \ C=C / C—H	0.5–2.5	(aromatic para)	0–1
H,H C=C—C=C \ /	9–13	H \ C=C / with C—H	0
—C–C(H)(=O)	1–3	CH$_3$—CH$_2$—	6.5–7.5
\ C=C / C—H	4–10	CH$_3$, CH$_3$ CH—	5.5–7
		(chair, axial–axial)	5–9
		(chair, axial–equatorial)	2–4

A more complex spectrum   Some NMR spectra are not as easily analyzed as the spectrum for ethyl iodide. Consider the spectra shown in Fig. 13.3. The proton spectrum of this unsaturated chloroester has been run at 500 MHz. Each chemically and magnetically nonequivalent proton is well resolved so that all of the couplings can be seen. Only the quartet of peaks at 4.1 ppm (area 2) and the triplet at 1.2 ppm (area 3) follow the simple first-order coupling rules outlined above. This quartet/triplet pattern is very characteristic of the commonly encountered ethyl group.

Because of the chiral carbon (marked with an asterisk), the protons on carbons D and E are diastereotopic, have different chemical shifts, and couple with each other and with adjacent protons to give the patterns seen in the spectrum.

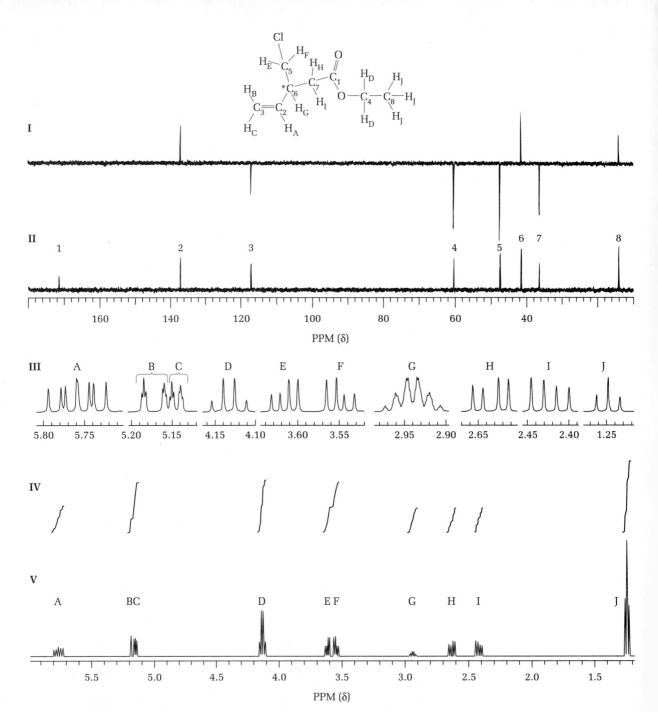

FIG. 13.3 The 500-MHz ^1H and 75-MHz ^{13}C NMR spectra of ethyl (3-chloromethyl)-4-pentenoate.* *I. ^{13}C DEPT spectrum.* The CH_3 and CH peaks are upright and the CH_2 peaks inverted. The quaternary carbon (the carbonyl carbon) does not appear. *II. The normal 75-MHz noise-decoupled ^{13}C spectrum.* Note the small size of the carbonyl peak. *III. Expansions of each group of proton NMR peaks.* Protons E and F as well as protons H and I are not equivalent to each other. These pairs of protons are diastereotopic because they are on a carbon adjacent to a chiral carbon atom. The frequencies of all peaks are found in the *Instructor's Guide. IV. The integral.* The height of the integral is proportional to the number of protons under it. *V. The 500-MHz ^1H spectrum.*

*Spectra courtesy of Professor Scott Virgil.

Many of the peaks can be assigned to specific hydrogens based simply on their chemical shifts. The coupling patterns then confirm these assignments.

Carbon-13 Spectroscopy

The element carbon consists of 98.9% carbon with mass 12 and spin 0 (NMR inactive) and only 1.1% ^{13}C with spin 1/2 (NMR active). Carbon, with such a low concentration of spin 1/2 nuclei, gives a very small signal when run under the same conditions as a proton spectrum. Carbon resonates at 75 MHz in a spectrometer where protons resonate at 300 MHz. Because only 1 in 100 carbon atoms has mass 13, the chances of a molecule having two ^{13}C atoms adjacent to one another are small. Consequently, coupling of one carbon with another is not observed.

^{13}C spectra: Broadband noise decoupling gives a single line for each carbon.

Each ^{13}C atom couples to hydrogen atoms over one, two, and three bonds. The coupling constants are large, so there is much overlap of peaks. To simplify the spectra as well as to increase the signal-to-noise ratio, a special technique is routinely used in obtaining ^{13}C spectra: *broadband noise decoupling*. Decoupling has the effect of collapsing all multiplets (quartets, triplets, etc.) into a single peak. Furthermore, the energy put into decoupling the protons can be looked on as appearing in the carbon spectrum in the form of an enhanced peak. This nuclear Overhauser enhancement (NOE) effect makes the peak appear three times larger than it would otherwise be. The result of decoupling is that every chemically and magnetically distinct carbon atom will appear as a single sharp line in the spectrum. Because the NOE effect is somewhat variable and does not affect carbons bearing no protons, one cannot obtain reliable information about peak areas by integration of the carbon spectrum.

Carbon Chemical Shifts

The range of carbon chemical shifts is 200 ppm compared with the 10-ppm range for protons. It is not common to have accidental overlap of carbon peaks. In the unsaturated chloroester seen in Fig. 13.3 there are eight sharp peaks corresponding to the eight carbon atoms in the molecule.

The generalities governing carbon chemical shifts are very similar to those governing proton shifts, as seen by comparing Table 13.1 with Table 13.3. Most of the downfield peaks are due to those carbon atoms near electron-withdrawing groups. In Fig. 13.3 the most downfield peak is that from the carbonyl carbon of the ester. The attached electronegative oxygen makes the peak appear at about 172 ppm. The peak is smaller than any other in the spectrum because it does not have an attached proton and thus does not benefit from a full NOE effect.

The ^{13}C spectrum of sucrose seen in Fig. 13.4 displays a single line for each carbon atom, and in Fig. 20.3 a single line is seen for each of the 27 carbon atoms in cholesterol.

TABLE 13.3 Carbon Chemical Shifts

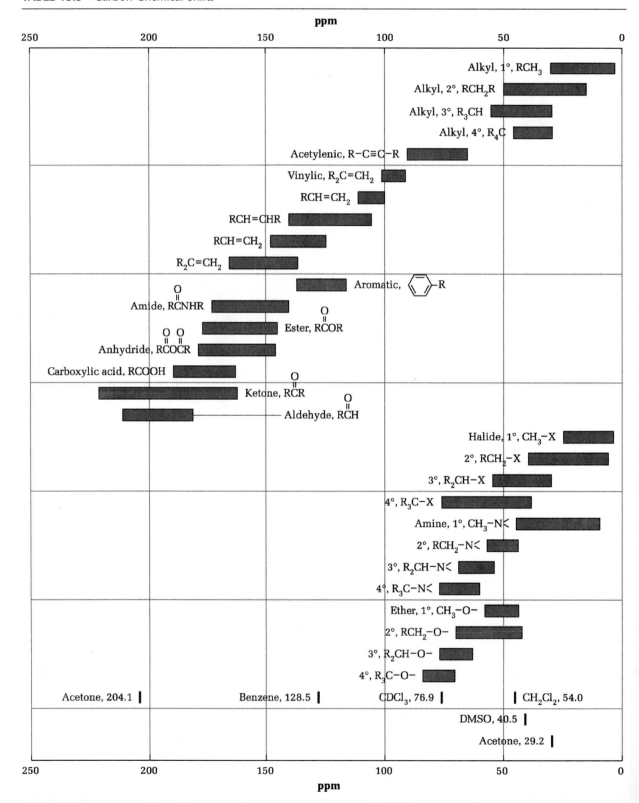

FIG. 13.4 ^{13}C NMR spectrum of sucrose (22.6 MHz). Not all lines have been assigned to individual carbon atoms.

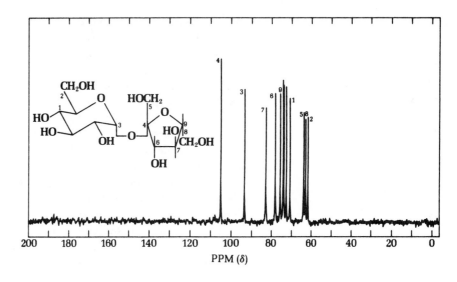

Fourier Transform Spectroscopy

The Fourier transform spectrometer

Even with broadband decoupling, the signal from ^{13}C spectra can get lost in the random noise produced by the spectrometer. Similarly, dilute solutions of samples give very noisy proton spectra. To increase the signal-to-noise ratio, the data for a number of spectra are averaged in the spectrometer computer. Because noise is random and the signal coherent, the signal will increase in size and the noise decrease as many spectra are averaged together. The improvement in the signal-to-noise ratio is proportional to the square root of the number of scans.

Spectra are accumulated rapidly by applying a very short pulse of radio-frequency energy to the sample and then storing the resulting free induction decay (FID) signal in digital form in the computer. The FID signal, which takes seconds to acquire, contains frequency information about all the signals in the spectrum. In a few minutes several hundred FID signals can be obtained and averaged in the computer. The FID signal is converted to a spectrum of conventional appearance by carrying out a Fourier transform computation on the signal using the spectrometer's computer.

Because the spectral information is in digital form, a large number of operations can be performed on it. The spectrum can be smoothed, at the expense of resolution, or the resolution can be enhanced, at the expense of noise. As indicated earlier, the spectrum can be numerically integrated and the position of each peak, in hertz or parts per million, printed above the peak. The spectra can be expanded both vertically and horizontally to clarify complex couplings, and all the parameters used to acquire the spectrum can be printed as well.

Protons with Variable Chemical Shifts

Protons attached to oxygen and nitrogen form hydrogen bonds to each other and with protonic solvents. As a result the chemical shifts of these protons depend on

Labile Protons	δ *(ppm)*
ROH	*0.5–6*
ArOH	*4.5–8*
RCOOH	*10–12*
Enols	*10–17*
RNH$_2$	*1–5*
Amides	*5–6.5*

solvent, temperature, and concentration and can appear almost anywhere in a spectrum. They will exchange with each other, a process catalyzed by small concentrations of acid or base. If this exchange is rapid (a common occurrence in alcohols, for example), only a single sharp line for the hydroxyl proton will be seen. At intermediate rates of exchange the line becomes broad, and at slow rates of exchange it couples to other protons within three chemical bonds.

Protons bound to nitrogen often give a broad line because of the nonuniform distribution of charge on the nucleus of ^{14}N. Obviously NMR spectroscopy is a poor means for detecting hydroxylic, amine, and amide protons; infrared spectroscopy on the other hand is an excellent means.

Deuterium exchange

Because labile protons can undergo rapid exchange with each other they can also exchange with deuterium. If a drop of D_2O is added to a $CDCl_3$ solution of an NMR sample of a compound that contains such protons and gently mixed, the protons will exchange for deuterium atoms. The water will, of course, float on top of the denser chloroform. The peak for the labile proton will disappear, thus simplifying the spectrum and allowing for assignment of the peak.

Shift Reagents

Some spectra can be simplified by addition of shift reagents to the sample. The resulting spectrum is similar to that one might obtain in a high-field spectrometer.

Addition of a few milligrams of a hexacoordinate complex of europium {tris(dipivaloylmethanato)europium(III), [Eu(dpm)$_3$]} to an NMR sample that contains a Lewis base center (an amine or basic oxygen, such as a hydroxyl group) has a dramatic effect on the spectrum. This lanthanide (soluble in $CDCl_3$) causes large shifts in the positions of peaks arising from the protons near the metal atom in this molecule and is therefore referred to as a *shift reagent*. It produces the shifts by complexing with the unshared electrons of the hydroxyl oxygen, the amine nitrogen, or other Lewis base center.

With no shift reagent present, the NMR spectrum of 2-methyl-3-pentanol [Fig. 13.5(a)] is not readily analyzed. Addition of 10-mg portions of the shift reagent to the sample causes very large downfield shifts of peaks owing to protons near the coordination site [Figs. 13.5(b)–(g)].[1] The two protons on C-4 and the two methyls on C-2 are diastereotopic and thus magnetically nonequivalent because they are adjacent to a chiral center C-3; each gives a separate set of peaks. When enough shift reagent is added, this spectrum can be analyzed by inspection. (See Fig. 13.6.)

Quantitative information about molecular geometry can be obtained from shifted spectra. The shift induced by the shift reagent is related to the distance and the angle that the proton bears to the europium atom.

Chiral shift reagents

Chiral shift reagents (derivatives of camphor) will cause differential shifts of the protons or carbon atoms in enantiomers. The separated peaks can be

FIG. 13.5 The 60-MHz ¹H NMR spectrum of 2-methyl-3-pentanol (0.4 *M* in CS₂) with various amounts of shift reagent present. (A) No shift reagent present. All methyl peaks are superimposed. The peak for the proton adjacent to the hydroxyl group is downfield from the others because it is adjacent to the electronegative oxygen atom. (B) 2-Methyl-3-pentanol + Eu(dpm)₃. Mole ratio of Eu(dpm)₃ to alcohol = 0.05. The hydroxyl proton peak at 1.6 ppm in spectrum A appears at 6.2 ppm in spectrum B because it is closest to the Eu in the complex formed between Eu(dpm)₃ and the alcohol. The next closest proton, the one on the hydroxyl-bearing carbon atom, gives a peak at 4.4 ppm. Peaks due to the three different methyl groups at 1.1 to 1.5 ppm begin to differentiate. (C) Mole ratio of Eu(dpm)₃ to alcohol = 0.1. The hydroxyl proton does not appear in this spectrum because its chemical shift is greater than 8.6 ppm with this much shift reagent present. (D) Mole ratio of Eu(dpm)₃ to alcohol = 0.25. Further differentiation of methyl peaks (2.3 to 3.0 ppm) is evident. (E) Mole ratio of Eu(dpm)₃ to alcohol = 0.5. Separate groups of peaks begin to appear in the region 4.2 to 6.2 ppm. (F) Mole ratio of Eu(dpm)₃ to alcohol = 0.7. Three groups of peaks (at 6.8, 7.7, and 8.1 ppm) due to the protons on C-2 and C-4 are evident, and three different methyls are now apparent. (G) Mole ratio of Eu(dpm)₃ to alcohol = 0.9. Only the methyl peaks appear on the spectrum. The two doublets come from the methyls attached to C-2, and the triplet comes from the terminal methyl at C-5.

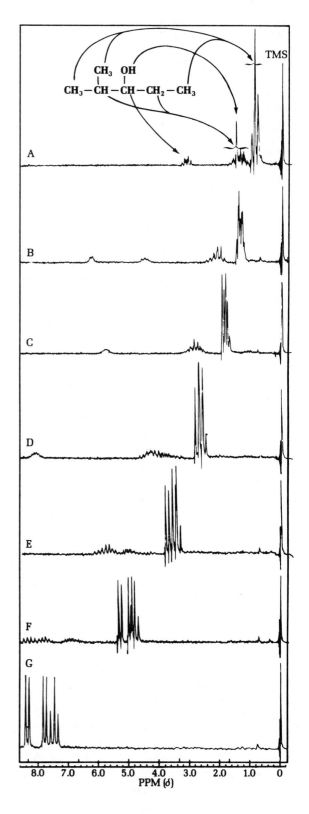

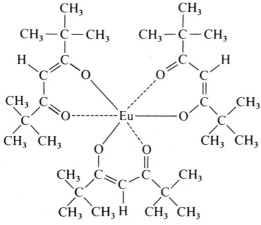

Tris(dipivaloylmethanato)europium(III), Eu(dpm)₃
MW 701.78, mp 188–189°C

FIG. 13.6 Proton NMR spectrum of 2-methyl-3-pentanol containing Eu(dpm)$_3$ (60 MHz). Mole ratio of Eu(dpm)$_3$ to alcohol = 1.0. Compare this spectrum with those shown in Fig. 13.5. Protons nearest the hydroxyl group are shifted most. Methyl groups are recorded at reduced spectrum amplitude. Note the large chemical shift difference between the two diastereotopic protons on C-4.

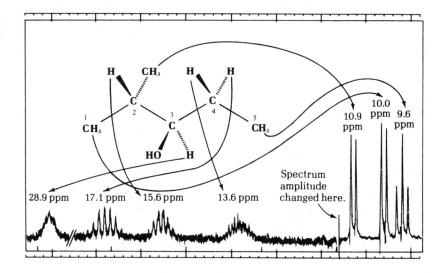

integrated to determine enantiomeric purity. A chiral shift reagent is used in Chapter 66 to determine the enantiomeric purity of a chiral alcohol made by enzymatic reduction of a ketone.

Experiments

1. Running an NMR Spectrum

Sample Preparation

A typical ^{1}H NMR sample consists of about 10–50 mg of sample dissolved in about 0.9 mL of deuterochloroform, CDCl$_3$, that contains a very small percentage of TMS, the reference compound. Because the tiniest particles of dust, especially metal particles, can adversely affect resolution, it is best to filter every sample routinely through a wad of cotton or glass wool in a Pasteur pipette (Fig. 13.7).

If very high resolution spectra (all lines very sharp) are desired, oxygen, a paramagnetic impurity, must be removed by bubbling a fine stream of pure nitrogen through the sample for 60 sec. Routine samples do not require this treatment.

It is most convenient if all tubes in a laboratory are filled to exactly the same height with the CDCl$_3$ solution; this will greatly facilitate tuning of the spectrometer. High-quality NMR tubes give the best spectra, free of spinning side bands. A good tube should roll at a slow, even rate down a very slightly inclined piece of plate glass.

Chemical shifts of protons and carbon are measured relative to the sharp peak in the TMS (taken as 0.0 ppm). Because the deuterochloroform is not 100% pure there will always be a very small peak at 7.27 ppm in the proton spectrum that arises from the tiny amount of residual ordinary chloroform, CHCl$_3$, in the

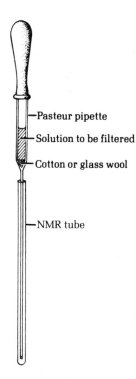

FIG. 13.7 Microfilter for NMR samples. Solution to be filtered is placed in the top of the Pasteur pipette, the rubber bulb is put in place, and pressure is applied to force the sample through the cotton or glass wool into an NMR sample tube.

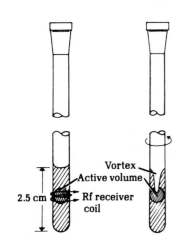

2.5 cm

Vortex
Active volume
Rf receiver
coil

FIG. 13.8 Effect of too rapid spinning or insufficient sample. The active volume is the only part of the sample detected by the spectrometer.

sample. In the carbon spectrum three lines of equal intensity appear at 77 ppm due to coupling of the deuterium atom with the carbon in $CDCl_3$.

If the sample does not dissolve in deuterochloroform, a number of other deuterated solvents are available including deuteroacetone (CD_3COCD_3), deuterodimethylsulfoxide (DMSO-d_6), and deuterobenzene (C_6D_6). All of these solvents are expensive, so the solubility of the sample should be checked in non-deuterated solvents first. For highly polar samples, a mixture of the more expensive deuterodimethylsulfoxide with the less expensive deuterochloroform is often satisfactory. If it is necessary to use D_2O as the solvent, then a special water-soluble reference, sodium 2,2-dimethyl-2-silapentane-5-sulfonate [$(CH_3)_3$$Si(CH_2)_3SO_3^-Na^+$ (DSS)], must be used. The protons on the three methyl groups bound to the silicon in this salt absorb at 0.0 ppm.

The usual NMR sample has a volume of about 0.9 mL, even though the volume sensed by the spectrometer receiver coils (referred to as the *active volume*) is much smaller. To average the magnetic fields produced by the spectrometer within the sample, the tube is spun by an air turbine at about 30 revolutions per second while taking the spectrum. Too rapid spinning or an insufficient amount of solution will cause the vortex produced by the spinning to penetrate the active volume, giving erratic nonreproducible spectra (Fig. 13.8).

Cleaning Up   Place halogenated solvents and compounds in the halogenated organic waste container. All others go into the organic solvents container.

Adjusting the Spectrometer

To be certain the spectrometer is correctly adjusted and working properly, record the spectrum of the standard sample of chloroform and TMS usually found with the instrument.

Small peaks symmetrically placed on each side of a principal peak are artifacts called *spinning side bands*. They are recognized as such by changing the spin speed, which causes the spinning side bands to change positions. They can be minimized by proper adjustment of the homogeneity controls.

Since Fourier transform (FT) spectrometers lock on the resonance of deuterium to achieve field/frequency stabilization, all samples must be dissolved in a solvent containing deuterium. The fact that lock is obtained is registered on a meter or oscilloscope. The Z and Z^2 controls are used to maximize the field homogeneity and achieve the highest resolution. This adjustment is needed for virtually every sample, but, as noted earlier, if all sample tubes in a laboratory are filled to exactly the same height, these adjustments will be minimized.

Two-Dimensional NMR Spectroscopy

The fast computers associated with FT spectrometers allow for a series of precisely timed pulses and data accumulations to give a large data matrix that can be subjected to Fourier transformation in two dimensions to produce a two-dimensional (2D) NMR spectrum.

One of the most common and useful of these is the COSY (<u>co</u>rrelated <u>s</u>pectrosco<u>py</u>) spectrum (Fig. 13.9). In this spectrum, two ordinary one-dimensional (1D) spectra are correlated with each other through spin–spin coupling. The 2D spectrum is a topographic representation, where spots represent peaks. The 1D spectra at the top and side are projections of these peaks. Along the diagonal of the 2D spectrum is a spot for each group of peaks in the molecule.

Figure 13.9 shows the 2D spectrum of citronellol. (See Fig. 13.10 for the 1D spectrum of this compound.) Consider spot A (Fig. 13.9) on the diagonal of the 2D spectrum. From a table of chemical shifts we know that this is a vinyl proton, the single proton on the double bond. From the structure of citronellol, we can expect this proton to have a small coupling, over four bonds, to the methyl groups and a stronger coupling to the protons on carbon-6. In the absence of a 2D spectrum, it is not obvious which group of peaks belongs to C-6, but the spot at B correlates with spot C on the diagonal, which is directly below the peak labeled 6 on the spectrum.

The diagonal spot C, which we have just assigned to C-6, correlates through the off-diagonal spot D with the diagonal spot E, which lies just below the group of peaks labeled 5. Spot A on the diagonal also correlates through spots F and G

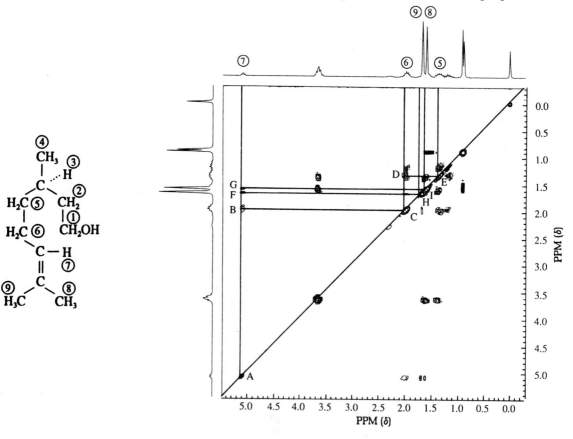

FIG. 13.9 The 2D COSY NMR spectrum of citronellol.

FIG. 13.10 ¹H NMR spectrum of citronellol (250 MHz).

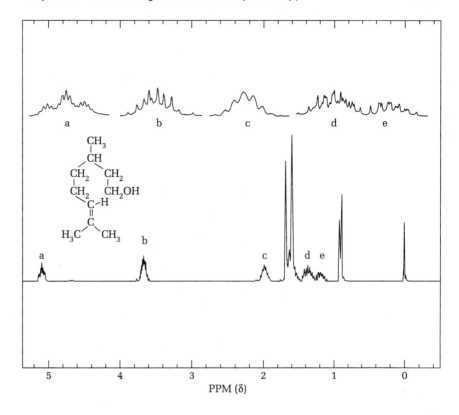

with spots H and I on the diagonal, which lie directly below methyl peaks 8 and 9. In this way we can determine the complete connectivity pattern of the molecule, seeing which protons are coupled to other protons.

Other 2D experiments allow proton spectra on one axis to be correlated with carbon spectra on the other axis. NOESY (<u>n</u>uclear <u>O</u>verhauser <u>e</u>ffect <u>s</u>pectroscopy) experiments give cross-peaks for protons that are near to each other in space but not spin coupled to each other.

2. Identification of Unknown Alcohol or Amine by ¹H NMR

Prepare a solution of the unknown in deuterochloroform, and run a spectrum in the normal way. To the unknown solution add about 5 mg of Eu(dpm)₃ (the shift reagent), shake thoroughly to dissolve, and run another spectrum. Continue adding Eu(dpm)₃ in 5- to 10-mg portions until the spectrum is shifted enough for easy analysis. Integrate peaks and groups of peaks if in doubt about their relative areas. To protect the Eu(dpm)₃ from moisture, store it in a desiccator.

Shift reagents are expensive.

Cleaning Up   All samples containing shift reagents go into a hazardous waste container for heavy metals.

Questions

1. Propose a structure or structures consistent with the proton NMR spectrum of Fig. 13.11. Numbers adjacent to groups of peaks refer to relative peak areas. Account for missing lines.

2. Propose a structure or structures consistent with the proton NMR spectrum of Fig. 13.12. Numbers adjacent to groups of peaks refer to relative peak areas.

3. Propose a structure or structures consistent with the proton NMR spectrum of Fig. 13.13.

4. Propose structures for (a), (b), and (c) consistent with the ^{13}C NMR spectra of Figs. 13.14, 13.15, and 13.16. These are isomeric alcohols with the empirical formula $C_4H_{10}O$.

Surfing the Web

The digital nature of modern NMR spectroscopy naturally lends itself to the graphical and computer-intensive material available on the Internet. The demonstration programs available for prospective buyers (which can be downloaded from the Internet) are often very useful, the complete program even more so. From this wealth of material the following sites have been chosen:

http://www.cherwell.com/ProdHome/gnmrhome.html

gNMR is a demonstration program that allows you to calculate spectra given the chemical shifts and coupling constants for the molecule (for PCs and Macs). You cannot save files, and the word DEMO will be superimposed on any printout, but otherwise it is very worthwhile. Ten nonequivalent nuclei can be handled if your computer's memory is large enough.

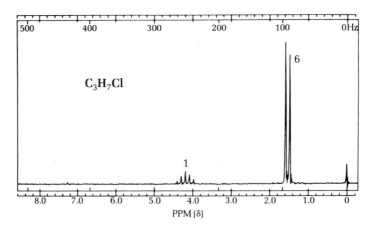

FIG. 13.11 Proton NMR spectrum (60 MHz), Question 1.

FIG. 13.12 Proton NMR spectrum (60 MHz), Question 2.

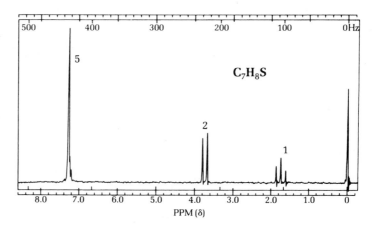

FIG. 13.13 Proton NMR spectrum (60 MHz), Question 3.

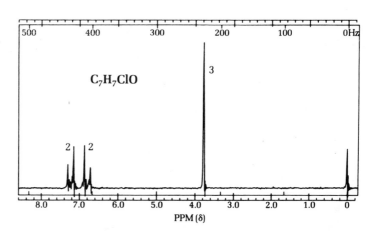

FIG. 13.14 ^{1}H NMR spectrum $C_4H_{10}O$ (90 MHz), Question 4(a).

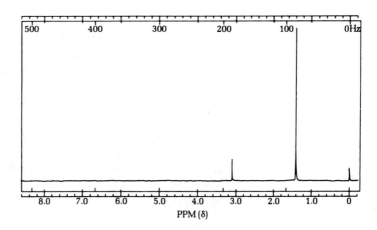

FIG. 13.15 ^{13}C NMR spectrum $C_4H_{10}O$ (22.6 MHz), Question 4(b).

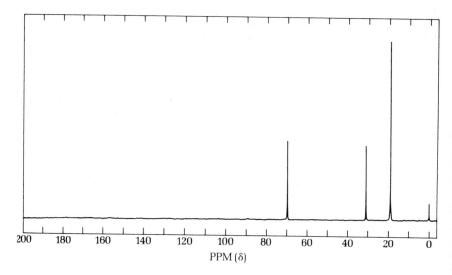

FIG. 13.16 ^{13}C NMR spectrum $C_4H_{10}O$ (22.6 MHz), Question 4(c).

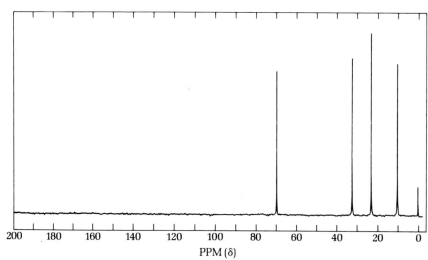

http://www.chem.vt.edu/simulation/VTNMR.html

An excellent program (for PCs only) by Harold Bell from Virginia Polytechnic Institute and State University. Allows for spectral simulation as well as spectrometer simulation, with processing of FIDs, data enhancement, phasing, etc. Just like having your own spectrometer.

http://www.chem.uni-potsdam.de/calcnmr.html

Calculations of the carbon chemical shifts of the aromatic carbons in benzenes, pyridines, pyridizines, biphenyls, and naphthalenes with 32 different substituents can be carried out by simply entering the substituents in the table provided at this University of Potsdam Web site.

http://www.chem.uni-potsdam.de/cgi-bin/perl_prog/lineform.pg

Dynamic NMR line shape simulator. This program allows for the very easy simulation of spectra resulting from exchange in a two-spin system.

http://bmrl.med.uiuc.edu:8080/EduNMRSoft13.2.html

This site contains a complete compilation of software programs dealing with all aspects of NMR spectroscopy. It lists the above sites as well as 100 others, including shareware, commercial programs, demos, and freeware. A commercial program, for instance, will list the carbon chemical shifts for molecules whose structures are entered into the program.

For updated informatin visit:
www.mtholyoke.edu/courses/kwilliam/microscale.shtml
or
www.hmco.com/hmco/college/chemistry/Home.html

References

1. R. J. Abraham, J. Fisher, and P. Loftus, *Introduction to NMR Spectroscopy,* John Wiley & Sons, Chichester, 1988.

2. J. Hore, *Nuclear Magnetic Resonance,* Oxford University Press, Oxford, 1995.

3. J. K. M. Sanders and B. K. Hunter, *Modern NMR Spectroscopy,* 2nd ed., Oxford University Press, Oxford, 1993.

4. H. Friebolin, *Basic One- and Two-Dimensional NMR Spectroscopy,* 2nd ed., VCH, New York, 1993.

5. A. E. Derome, *Modern NMR Techniques for Chemistry Research,* Pergamon Press, Oxford, 1987.

6. D. Canet, *Nuclear Magnetic Resonance. Concepts and Methods,* John Wiley and Sons, West Sussex, 1996.

7. D. G. Gadian, *NMR and Its Applications to Living Systems,* Oxford University Press, Oxford, 1996.

8. D. M. Grant and R. K. Harris (eds.), *Encyclopedia of NMR,* 8-vol. set, John Wiley and Sons, New York, 1996.

9. W. R. Croasmun and R. M. K. Carlson, *Two-Dimensional NMR Spectroscopy. Applications for Chemists and Biochemists,* 2nd ed., VCH Publishers, New York, 1994.

10. J. W. Akitt, *NMR and Chemistry,* 2nd ed., Chapman and Hall, London, 1983.

11. Charles J. Pouchert, *The Aldrich Library of C and H FT NMR Spectra,* 3 vols., Aldrich Chemical Co., Milwaukee, WI, 1993.

12. E. L. Eliel and S. H. Wilen, *Stereochemistry of Organic Compounds,* John Wiley and Sons, New York, 1994.

Ultraviolet Spectroscopy

Prelab Exercise: Predict the appearance of the ultraviolet spectrum of 1-butyl-amine in acid, of methoxybenzene in acid and base, and of benzoic acid in acid and base.

UV: Electronic transitions within molecules

Ultraviolet (UV) spectroscopy gives information about electronic transitions within molecules. Whereas absorption of low-energy infrared radiation causes bonds in a molecule to stretch and bend, the absorption of short-wavelength, high-energy ultraviolet radiation causes electrons to move from one energy level to another with energies that are often capable of breaking chemical bonds.

We shall be most concerned with transitions of π-electrons in conjugated and aromatic ring systems. These transitions occur in the wavelength region of 200 to 800 nm (nanometers, 10^{-9} meters, formerly known as mμ, millimicrons). Most common ultraviolet spectrometers cover the region of 200 to 400 nm as well as the visible spectral region of 400 to 800 nm. Below 200 nm air (oxygen) absorbs UV radiation; spectra in that region must therefore be obtained in a vacuum or in an atmosphere of pure nitrogen.

Consider ethylene, even though it absorbs UV radiation in the normally inaccessible region at 163 nm. The double bond in ethylene has two *s* electrons in a σ-molecular orbital and two, less tightly held, *p* electrons in a π-molecular orbital. Two unoccupied, high-energy-level, antibonding orbitals are associated with these orbitals. When ethylene absorbs UV radiation, one electron moves up from the bonding π-molecular orbital to the antibonding π^*-molecular orbital (Fig. 14.1). As the diagram indicates, this change requires less energy than the excitation of an electron from the σ to the σ^* orbital.

By comparison with infrared spectra and NMR spectra, UV spectra are fairly featureless (Fig. 14.2). This condition results as molecules in a number of different vibrational states undergo the same electronic transition, to produce a band spectrum instead of a line spectrum.

Band spectra

Unlike IR spectroscopy, ultraviolet spectroscopy lends itself to precise quantitative analysis of substances. The intensity of an absorption band is usually given by the molar extinction coefficient, ε, which, according to the Beer–Lambert law, is equal to the absorbance, A, divided by the product of the molar concentration, c, and the path length, l, in centimeters.

Beer–Lambert law

$$\varepsilon = \frac{A}{cl}$$

FIG. 14.1 Electronic energy
levels of ethylene.

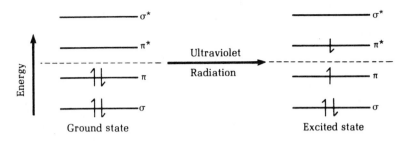

*λ_{max}, wavelength of maximum
absorption*

The wavelength of maximum absorption (the tip of the peak) is given by λ_{max}. Because UV spectra are so featureless, it is common practice to describe a spectrum like that of cholesta-3,5-diene (Fig. 14.2) as λ_{max} 234 nm (ε = 20,000) and not bother to reproduce the actual spectrum.

The extinction coefficients of conjugated dienes and enones are in the range of 10,000–20,000, so only very dilute solutions are needed for spectra. In the example of Fig. 14.2 the absorbance at the tip of the peak, *A*, is 1.2, and the path length is the usual 1 cm; so the molar concentration needed for this spectrum is 6×10^{-5} mole per liter,

ε, extinction coefficient

$$c = \frac{A}{l\varepsilon} = \frac{1.2}{20,000} = 6 \times 10^{-5} \text{ mole per liter}$$

which is 0.221 mg per 10 mL of solvent.

Spectro grade solvents

The usual solvents for UV spectroscopy are 95% ethanol, methanol, water, and saturated hydrocarbons such as hexane, trimethylpentane, and isooctane; the three hydrocarbons are often specially purified to remove impurities that absorb in the UV region. Any transparent solvent can be used for spectra in the visible region.

Sample cells for spectra in the visible region are made of glass, but UV cells must be of the more expensive fused quartz, since glass absorbs UV radiation.

*UV cells are expensive; handle
with care.*

The cells and solvents must be clean and pure, since very little of a substance produces a UV spectrum. A single fingerprint will give a spectrum!

Ethylene has λ_{max} 163 nm (ε = 15,000), and butadiene has λ_{max} 217 nm (ε = 20,900). As the conjugated system is extended, the wavelength of maximum

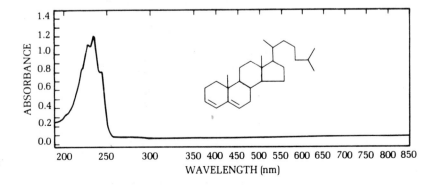

FIG. 14.2 The ultraviolet
spectrum of cholesta-3,5-diene
in ethanol.

FIG. 14.3 The ultraviolet–visible spectrum of lycopene in isooctane.

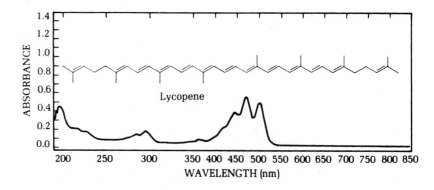

absorption moves to longer wavelengths (toward the visible region). For example, lycopene with 11 conjugated double bonds has λ_{max} 470 nm ($\varepsilon = 185,000$; Fig. 14.3). Because lycopene absorbs blue visible light at 470 nm, the substance appears bright red. It is responsible for the color of tomatoes; its isolation is described in Chapter 9.

Woodward and Fieser rules for dienes and dienones

The wavelengths of maximum absorption of conjugated dienes and polyenes and conjugated enones and dienones are given by the Woodward and Fieser rules, Tables 14.1 and 14.2. The application of the rules in these tables is demonstrated by the spectra of pulegone (1) and carvone (2) in Fig. 14.4. The solvent correction is given in Table 14.3. The calculations are given in Tables 14.4 and 14.5.

These rules will be applied in a later experiment in which cholesterol is converted into an α,β-unsaturated ketone.

No simple rules exist for calculation of aromatic ring spectra, but several generalizations can be made. From Fig. 14.5 it is obvious that as polynuclear aromatic rings are extended linearly, λ_{max} shifts to longer wavelengths.

As alkyl groups are added to benzene, λ_{max} shifts from 255 nm for benzene to 261 nm for toluene to 272 nm for hexamethylbenzene. Substituents bearing nonbonding electrons also cause shifts of λ_{max} to longer wavelengths, e.g., from 255 nm for benzene to 257 nm for chlorobenzene, 270 nm for phenol, and 280

TABLE 14.1 Rules for the Prediction of λ_{max} for Conjugated Dienes and Polyenes

	Increment (nm)
Parent acyclic diene (butadiene)	217
Parent heteroannular diene	214
Double bond extending the conjugation	30
Alkyl substituent or ring residue	5
Exocyclic location of double bond to any ring	5
Groups: OAc, OR	0
	0
Solvent correction, see Table 14.3 ( )	
λ_{max}^{EtOH} = Total	

TABLE 14.2   Rules for the Prediction of λ_{max} for Conjugated Enones and Dienones

$$\overset{\beta}{\underset{|}{\beta}}\overset{\alpha}{\underset{|}{}}\overset{R}{\underset{|}{}} \qquad \overset{\delta}{\underset{|}{\delta}}\overset{\gamma}{\underset{|}{}}\overset{\beta}{\underset{|}{}}\overset{\alpha}{\underset{|}{}}\overset{R}{\underset{|}{}}$$
$$\beta-C{=}C-C{=}O \quad \text{and} \quad \delta-C{=}C-C{=}C-C{=}O \qquad \text{Increment (nm)}$$

	Increment (nm)
Parent α,β-unsaturated system	215
Double bond extending the conjugation	30
R (alkyl or ring residue), OR, OCOCH$_3$ α	10
β	12
λ, δ, and higher	18
α-Hydroxyl, enolic	35
α-Cl	15
α-Br	23
exo-Location of double bond to any ring	5
Homoannular diene component	39

Solvent correction, see Table 14.3 ( )

$\lambda_{max}^{EtOH} = $ Total

TABLE 14.3   Solvent Correction

Solvent	Factor for Correction to Ethanol
Hexane	+11
Ether	+7
Dioxane	+5
Chloroform	+1
Methanol	0
Ethanol	0
Water	−8

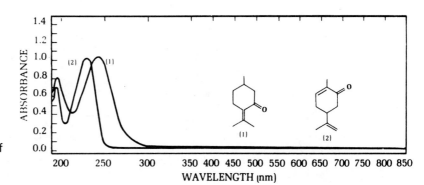

FIG. 14.4   Ultraviolet spectra of (1) pulegone and (2) carvone in hexane.

TABLE 14.4 Calculation of λ_{max} for Pulegone (See Fig. 14.4)

Parent α,β-unsaturated system	215 nm
α-Ring residue, R	10
β-Alkyl group (two methyls)	24
Exocyclic double bond	5
Solvent correction (hexane)	−11

Calcd λ_{max} 245 nm; found 244 nm

TABLE 14.5 Calculation of λ_{max} for Carvone (See Fig. 14.4)

Parent α,β-unsaturated system	215 nm
α-Alkyl group (methyl)	10
β-Ring residue	12
Solvent correction (hexane)	−11

Calcd λ_{max} 226 nm; found 229 nm

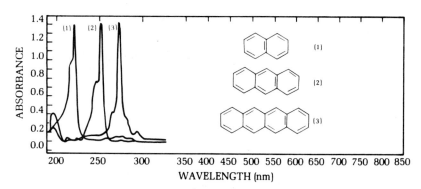

FIG. 14.5 The ultraviolet spectra of (1) naphthalene, (2) anthracene, and (3) tetracene.

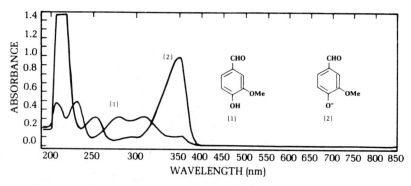

FIG. 14.6 Ultraviolet spectra of (1) neutral vanillin and (2) the anion of vanillin.

FIG. 14.7 Ultraviolet spectra of (1) aniline and (2) aniline hydrochloride.

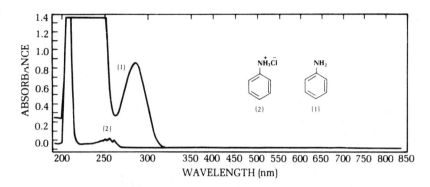

Effect of acid and base on λ_{max}

nm for aniline (ε = 6200–8600). That these effects are the result of interaction of the π-electron system with the nonbonded electrons is seen dramatically in the spectra of vanillin and the derived anion (Fig. 14.6). Addition of two more nonbonding electrons in the anion causes λ_{max} to shift from 279 to 351 nm and ε to increase. Removing the electrons from the nitrogen of aniline by making the anilinium cation causes λ_{max} to decrease from 280 to 254 nm (Fig. 14.7). These changes of λ_{max} as a function of pH have obvious analytical applications.

Intense bands result from π–π conjugation of double bonds and carbonyl groups with the aromatic ring. Styrene, for example, has λ_{max} 244 nm (ε = 12,000) and benzaldehyde λ_{max} 244 nm (ε = 15,000).

Experiment

Ultraviolet Spectrum of Unknown Acid, Base, or Neutral Compound

Determine whether an unknown compound obtained from the instructor is acidic, basic, or neutral from the ultraviolet spectra in the presence of acid and base as well as in neutral media.

Cleaning Up   Because UV samples are extremely dilute solutions in ethanol, they can normally be flushed down the drain.

Questions

1. Calculate the ultraviolet absorption maximum for 2-cyclohexene-1-one.

2. Calculate the ultraviolet absorption maximum for 3,4,4-trimethyl-2-cyclo-hexene-1-one.

3. Calculate the ultraviolet absorption maximum for 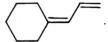 .

4. What concentration, in g/mL, of a substance with MW 200 should be prepared in order to give an absorbance value A equal to 0.8 if the substance has $\varepsilon = 16{,}000$ and a cell with a path length of 1 cm is employed?

References

1. A. E. Gillam and E. S. Stern, *An Introduction to Electronic Absorption Spectroscopy in Organic Chemistry,* Edward Arnold, London, 1967.

2. C. N. R. Rao, *Ultraviolet and Visible Spectroscopy,* 2nd ed., Butterworths, London, 1967.

3. H. H. Jaffe and M. Orchin, *Theory and Application of Ultraviolet Spectroscopy,* John Wiley, New York, 1962.

4. R. M. Silverstein, C. G. Bassler, and T. C. Morrill, *Spectrometric Identification of Organic Compounds,* 4th ed., John Wiley, New York, 1981. (Includes IR, UV, and NMR.)

Grignard Synthesis of Triphenylmethanol and Benzoic Acid

Prelab Exercise: Prepare a flow sheet for the preparation of triphenylmethanol. Through a knowledge of the physical properties of the solvents, reactants, and products, show how the products are purified. Indicate which layer in separations should contain the product.

In 1912 Victor Grignard received the Nobel prize in chemistry for his work on the reaction that bears his name, a carbon–carbon bond-forming reaction by which almost any alcohol may be formed from appropriate alkyl halides and carbonyl compounds. The Grignard reagent is easily formed by reaction of an alkyl halide, in particular a bromide, with magnesium metal in anhydrous diethyl ether. Although the reaction can be written and thought of as simply

$$R—Br + Mg \longrightarrow R—Mg—Br$$

it appears that the structure of the material in solution is rather more complex. There is evidence that dialkylmagnesium is present

$$2\ R—Mg—Br \rightleftharpoons R—Mg—R + MgBr_2$$

Structure of the Grignard reagent

and that the magnesium atoms, which have the capacity to accept two electron pairs from donor molecules to achieve a four-coordinated state, are solvated by the unshared pairs of electrons on diethyl ether:

$$
\begin{array}{c}
\text{Et} \diagdown \quad \diagup \text{Et} \\
\ddot{\text{O}} \\
R — \overset{\cdot\cdot}{\text{Mg}} — Br \\
\ddot{\text{O}} \\
\text{Et} \diagup \quad \diagdown \text{Et}
\end{array}
$$

A strong base and strong nucleophile

The Grignard reagent is a strong base and a strong nucleophile. As a base it will react with all protons that are more acidic than those found on alkenes and alkanes. Thus, Grignard reagents react readily with water, alcohols, amines, thiols, etc., to regenerate the alkane:

$$R—Mg—Br + H_2O \longrightarrow R—H + MgBrOH$$

$$R—Mg—Br + R'OH \longrightarrow R—H + MgBrOR'$$

$$R—Mg—Br + R'NH_2 \longrightarrow R—H + MgBrNHR'$$

$$R—Mg—Br + R'C \equiv C—H \longrightarrow R—H + R'C \equiv CMgBr$$

(an acetylenic Grignard reagent)

The starting material for preparing the Grignard reagent can contain no acidic protons. The reactants and apparatus must all be completely dry; otherwise the reaction will not start. If proper precautions are taken, however, the reaction proceeds smoothly.

The magnesium metal, in the form of a coarse powder, has a coat of oxide on the outside. A fresh surface can be exposed by crushing the powder under the absolutely dry ether in the presence of the organic halide. Reaction will begin at exposed surfaces, as evidenced by a slight turbidity in the solution and evolution of bubbles. Once the exothermic reaction starts it proceeds easily, the magnesium dissolves, and a solution of the Grignard reagent is formed. The solution is often turbid and gray due to impurities in the magnesium. The reagent is not isolated but reacted immediately with, most often, an appropriate carbonyl compound

$$R — Mg — Br + R' — \overset{\overset{\ddot{O}:}{\|}}{C} — R'' \longrightarrow R' — \overset{:\ddot{O}:^- MgBr^+}{\underset{R}{C}} — R''$$

to give, in another exothermic reaction, the magnesium alkoxide, a salt insoluble in ether. In a simple acid–base reaction this alkoxide is reacted with acidified ice water to give the covalent, ether-soluble alcohol and the ionic water-soluble magnesium salt:

$$R' — \overset{:\ddot{O}:^- MgBr^+}{\underset{R}{C}} — R'' \ + H^+Cl^- \longrightarrow R' — \overset{:\ddot{O} — H}{\underset{R}{C}} — R'' \ + Mg^{2+}Br^-Cl^-$$

The great versatility of this reaction lies in the wide range of reactants that undergo the reaction. Thirteen representative reactions are shown on the following page.

A versatile reagent

In every case except reaction 1 the intermediate alkoxide must be hydrolyzed to give the product. The reaction with oxygen (reaction 2) is usually not a problem because the ether vapor over the reagent protects it from attack by oxygen, but this reaction is one reason why the reagent cannot usually be stored without special precautions. Reactions 6 and 7 with ketones and aldehydes giving, respectively, tertiary and secondary alcohols are among the most common. Reactions 8–13 are not nearly so common.

In the present experiment we shall carry out another common type of Grignard reaction, the formation of a tertiary alcohol from 2 mol of the reagent and one of an ester. The ester employed is the methyl benzoate synthesized in Chapter 40. The initially formed product is unstable and decomposes to a ketone, which, being more reactive than an ester, immediately reacts with more Grignard reagent:

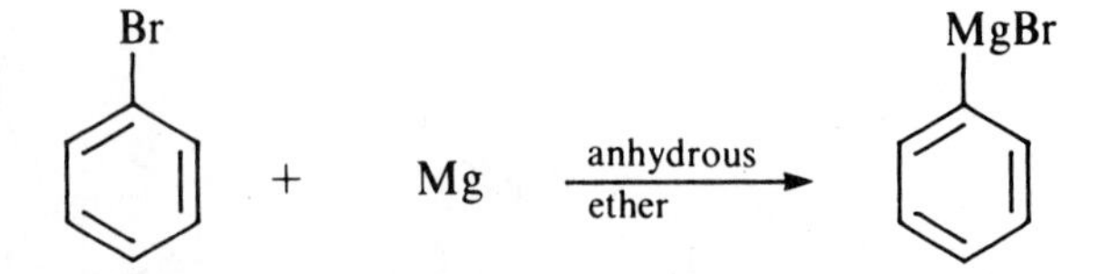

Bromobenzene[1]
MW 157.02
bp 156.4°C
den. 1.491

Magnesium
At. Wt. 24.1

**Phenylmagnesium
bromide**

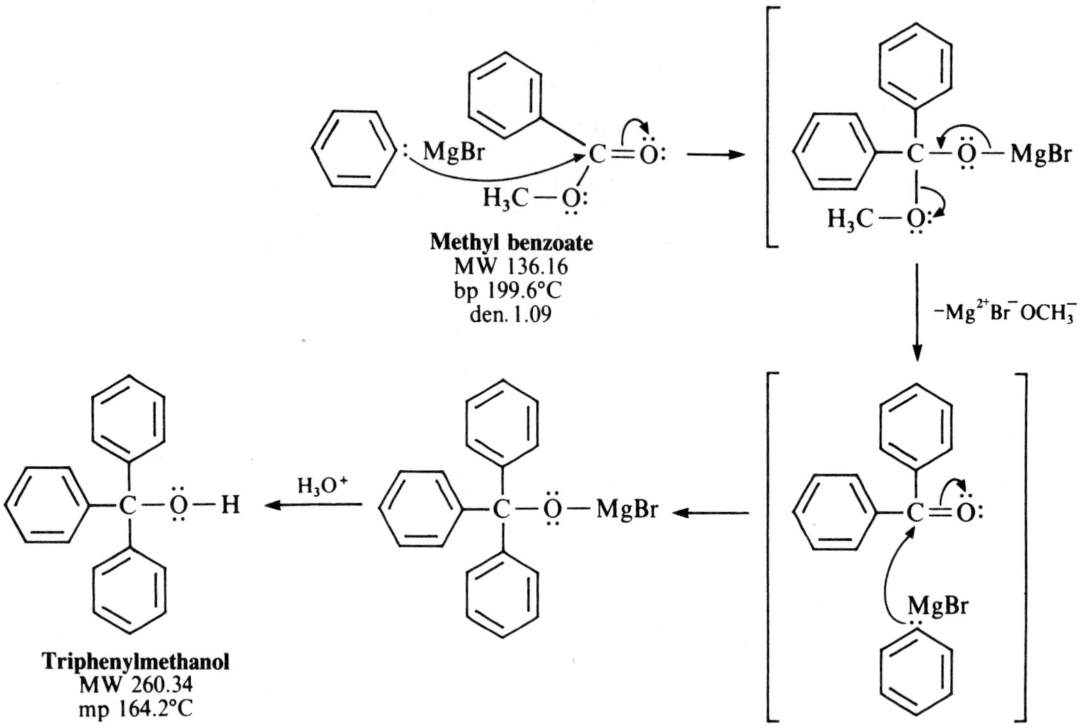

Methyl benzoate
MW 136.16
bp 199.6°C
den. 1.09

Triphenylmethanol
MW 260.34
mp 164.2°C

Biphenyl has a characteristic odor. Triphenylmethanol is odorless.

The primary impurity in the present experiment is biphenyl, formed by the reaction of phenylmagnesium bromide with unreacted bromobenzene. The most effective way to lessen this side reaction is to add the bromobenzene slowly to the reaction mixture so it will react with the magnesium and not be present in high concentration to react with previously formed Grignard reagent. The impurity is easily eliminated because it is much more soluble in hydrocarbon solvents than triphenylmethanol.

---

1. See Fig. 38.7 at the end of the chapter for the ^{13}C NMR spectrum.

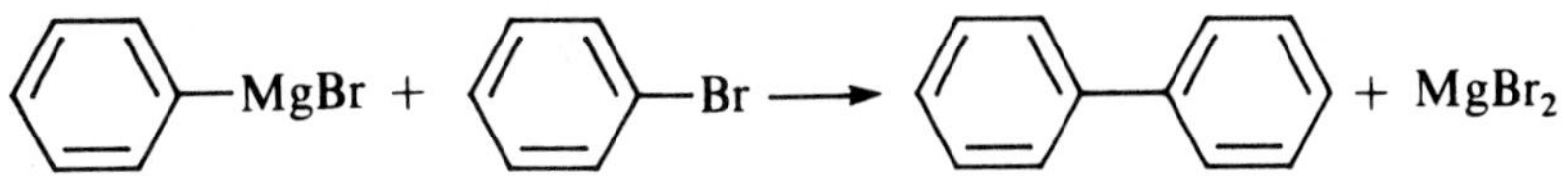

Biphenyl
mp 72°C

Triphenylmethanol can also be prepared from benzophenone.

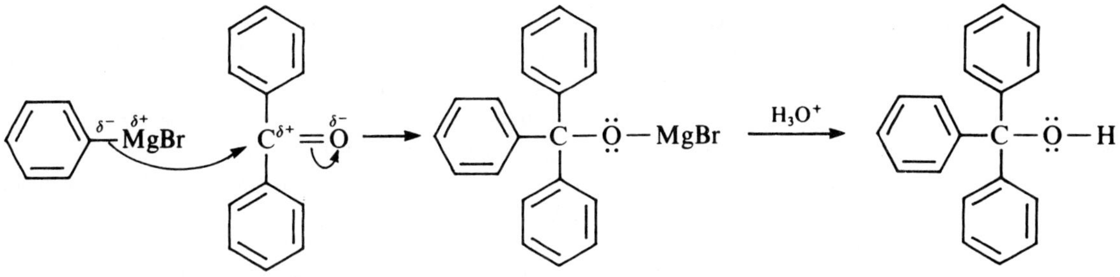

Phenylmagnesium
bromide

Benzophenone
MW 182.22
mp 48°C

Triphenylmethanol
MW 260.34
mp 164.2°C

Experiments

MICROSCALE

1. Phenylmagnesium Bromide (Phenyl Grignard Reagent)

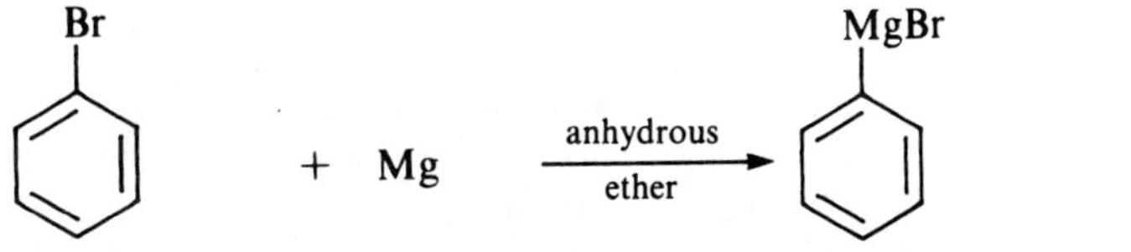

Bromobenzene
MW 157.02
bp 156°C
den. 1.491

Magnesium
At. Wt. 24.31

Phenylmagnesium bromide
not isolated, used *in situ*

Advance Preparation

It is imperative that all equipment and reagents be absolutely dry. The glassware to be used—two reaction tubes, two 1-dram vials, and a stirring rod—can be dried in a 110°C oven for at least 30 min, along with the magnesium. Alternatively, if the glassware, syringe, septa, and magnesium appear to be perfectly dry, they can be used without special drying. The plastic and rubber ware should be rinsed with acetone if it appears to be either dirty or wet with water and then placed in a desiccator for at least 12 h. Do not place plastic ware in the oven. New, sealed packages of syringes can be used without prior drying. The ether used throughout this reaction must be absolutely dry (absolute ether). To prepare the Grignard reagent, absolute diethyl ether must be used; elsewhere, *tert*-butyl methyl ether can be used. Ether extractions of aqueous solutions do not need to be carried out with dry ether.

A very convenient container for absolute diethyl ether is a 50-mL septum-capped bottle. This method of dispensing the solvent has three advantages: The ether is kept anhydrous, the exposure to oxygen is minimized, and there is little possibility of its catching fire. Ether is extremely flammable; do not work with this solvent near flames.

To remove ether from a septum-capped bottle, inject a volume of air into the bottle equal to the amount of ether being removed. Pull more ether than needed into the syringe, and then push the excess back into the bottle before removing the syringe. In this way there will be no air bubbles in the syringe, and it will not dribble (Fig. 38.1).

Procedure

Remove a reaction tube from the oven, and immediately cap it with a septum. In the operations that follow, keep the tube capped except when it is necessary to open it. After it cools to room temperature, add about 2 mmol (about 50 mg) of magnesium powder. Record the weight of magnesium used to the nearest milligram. We will make it the limiting reagent by using a 5% molar excess of bromobenzene (about 2.1 mmol). (See below).

Diethyl ether can be made and kept anhydrous by storing over Linde 5A molecular sieves. Discard diethyl ether within 90 days because of peroxide formation. tert-*Butyl methyl ether does not have this problem.*

Using a dry syringe, add to the magnesium by injection through the septum 0.5 mL of anhydrous diethyl ether. Your laboratory instructor will demonstrate transfer from the storage container used in your laboratory.

Into an oven-dried vial weigh about 2.1 mmol (about 330 mg) of dry (stored over molecular sieves) bromobenzene. Using a syringe, add to this vial 0.7 mL anhydrous diethyl ether, and *immediately,* with the same syringe, remove all the solution from the vial. This can be done virtually quantitatively so you do not need to rinse the vial. Immediately cap the empty vial to keep it dry for later use. Inject about 0.1 mL of the bromobenzene–ether mixture into the reaction tube, and mix the contents by flicking the tube. Pierce the septum with another syringe needle for pressure relief (Fig. 38.2).

It takes much force to crush the magnesium. Place the tube on a hard surface and bear down with the stirring rod while twisting the reaction tube. Do not pound the magnesium.

The reaction will not ordinarily start at this point, so remove the septum, syringe, and empty syringe needle and crush the magnesium with a dry stirring rod. You can do this easily in the confines of the 10-mm-diameter reaction tube while it is placed on a hard surface. There is little danger of poking the stirring rod through the bottom of the tube (Fig. 38.3). Immediately replace the septum, syringe, and empty syringe needle (for pressure relief). The reaction should start within seconds. The formerly clear solution becomes cloudy and soon begins to boil as the magnesium metal reacts with the bromobenzene to form the Grignard reagent, phenylmagnesium bromide.

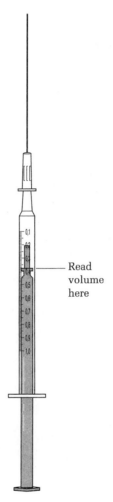

Read
volume
here

FIG. 38.1   Polypropylene syringe (1 mL, with 0.01-mL graduations). The needle is blunt. When there are no air bubbles in the syringe, it will not dribble ether.

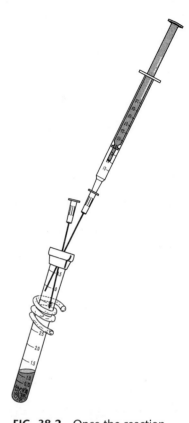

FIG. 38.2   Once the reaction has started, bromobenzene in ether is added slowly from the syringe. The empty needle is for pressure relief, but if condensation is complete (aided by the damp pipe cleaner), it will not be needed. Once the reaction slows down, stir it with the magnetic stirring bar.

If the reaction does not start within 1 min, begin again with completely different, dry equipment (syringe, syringe needle, reaction tube, etc.). Once the Grignard reaction starts, it will continue. To prevent the ether from boiling away, wrap a pipe cleaner around the top part of the reaction tube. Dampen this with water or, if the room temperature is very hot, with alcohol.

To the refluxing mixture add slowly and dropwise over a period of several

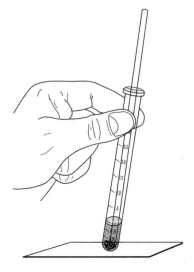

FIG. 38.3   To start the Grignard reaction, remove the septum and apply pressure to the stirring rod while rotating the reaction tube on a hard surface that will not scratch the tube, such as a book.

minutes the remainder of the solution of bromobenzene in ether at such a rate that the reaction remains under control at all times. After all the bromobenzene solution is added, spontaneous boiling of the diluted mixture may be slow or become slow. At this point, add a magnetic stirring bar to the reaction tube and stir the reaction mixture with a magnetic stirrer. If the rate of reaction is too fast, slow down the stirrer. The reaction is complete when none or a very small quantity of the metal remains. Check to see that the volume of ether has not decreased. If it has, add more anhydrous diethyl ether. Since the solution of the Grignard reagent deteriorates on standing, the next step should be started at once. The phenylmagnesium bromide can be converted to triphenylmethanol or to benzoic acid.

MICROSCALE

2. Triphenylmethanol

| Phenylmagnesium bromide | Benzophenone MW 182.22 mp 48°C | | Triphenylmethanol MW 260.34 mp 164.2°C |

Make t-butyl methyl ether anhydrous by storing it over molecular sieves.

In an oven-dried vial dissolve 2.0 mmol (0.364 g) of benzophenone in 1.0 mL of anhydrous *tert*-butyl methyl ether by capping the vial and mixing the contents thoroughly. With a dry syringe, remove all the solution from the vial and add it dropwise with *thorough* shaking after each drop to the solution of the Grignard reagent. Add the benzophenone at such a rate as to maintain the ether at a gentle reflux. Rinse the vial with a few drops of anhydrous ether after all the first solution has been added, and add this rinse to the reaction tube.

Mixing the reaction mixture is very important.

After all the benzophenone has been added, the mixture should be homogeneous. If not, mix it thoroughly, using a stirring rod if necessary. The syringe can be removed, but leave the pressure-relief needle in place. Allow the reaction mixture to stand at room temperature. The reaction apparently is complete when the red color disappears.

At the end of the reaction period, cool the tube in ice, and add to it dropwise with stirring (use a glass rod or a spatula) 2 mL of 3 N hydrochloric acid. A creamy-white precipitate of triphenylmethanol will separate between the layers. Add more ether (it need not be anhydrous) to the reaction tube, and shake the contents to dissolve all the triphenylmethanol. The result should be two perfectly clear layers. Remove a drop of the ether layer for TLC analysis. Any bubbling seen at the interface or in the lower layer is leftover magnesium reacting with the hydrochloric acid. Remove the aqueous layer, and shake the ether layer with an equal volume of saturated aqueous sodium chloride solution in order to remove water and any remaining acid. Carefully remove all the aqueous layer, and then dry the ether layer by adding anhydrous calcium chloride pellets to the reaction tube until the drying agent no longer clumps together. Cork the tube, and shake it from time to time over a 5- or 10-min period to complete the drying.

Using a Pasteur pipette, remove the ether from the drying agent and place it in another tared, dry reaction tube or the centrifuge tube. Use more ether to wash off the drying agent, and combine these ether extracts. Evaporate the ether in a hood by blowing nitrogen or air onto the surface of the solution while warming the tube in a beaker of water or in the hand.

After all the solvent has been removed, determine the weight of the crude product. Note the odor of biphenyl, the product of the side reaction that takes place between bromobenzene and phenylmagnesium bromide during the first reaction.

Trituration (grinding) of the crude product with petroleum ether will remove the biphenyl. Stir the crystals with 0.5 mL of petroleum ether in the ice bath, remove the solvent as thoroughly as possible, add a boiling stick, and recrystallize the residue from boiling 2-propanol (no more than 2 mL). Allow the solution to cool slowly to room temperature, and then cool it thoroughly in ice. Triphenylmethanol crystallizes slowly, so allow the mixture to remain in the ice as long as possible. Stir the ice-cold mixture well, and collect the product by vacuum filtration on the Hirsch funnel. Save the filtrate. Concentration may give a second crop of crystals.

An alternative method for purification of the triphenylmethanol utilizes a mixed solvent. Dissolve the crystals in the smallest possible quantity of warm ether, and add to the solution 1.5 mL of ligroin. Add a boiling stick to the solution, and boil off some of the ether until the solution becomes slightly cloudy, indicating it is saturated. Allow the solution to cool slowly to room temperature. Triphenylmethanol is deposited slowly as large, thick prisms. Cool the solution in ice, and after allowing time for complete crystallization to occur, remove the ether with a Pasteur pipette and wash the crystals once with a few drops of a cold 1:4 ether–ligroin mixture. Dry the crystals in the tube under vacuum (Fig. 38.4).

Determine the weight, melting point, and percentage yield of the triphenylmethanol. Analyze the crude and recrystallized product by TLC on silica gel (see Chapter 10), developing the plate with dichloromethane–petroleum ether, 1:5. An IR spectrum can be determined in chloroform solution or by preparing a mull or KBr disk (see Chapter 13). Compare the apparatus used in this experiment to the research-type apparatus shown in Fig. 38.5.

FIG. 38.4 Apparatus for drying crystals in reaction tube under vacuum.

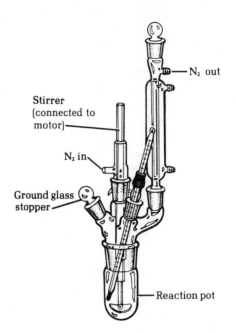

FIG. 38.5 Semimicroscale, research-type apparatus for Grignard reaction, with provision for a motor-driven stirrer and an inlet and outlet for dry nitrogen.

Cleaning Up The acidic aqueous layer and the saturated sodium chloride layer are combined, diluted with water, neutralized with sodium carbonate, and flushed down the drain. Ether is allowed to evaporate from the drying agent in the hood, and then it is discarded in the nonhazardous solid waste container. The petroleum ether and 2-propanol or ether–ligroin mother liquor are placed in the organic solvents container.

MICROSCALE

3. Benzoic Acid

Phenylmagnesium bromide

$+$ **Carbon dioxide** CO_2 $\longrightarrow$ benzoate $MgBr^+$ salt $\xrightarrow{HCl}$ **Benzoic acid** $+$ $MgBrCl$

Phenylmagnesium bromide

Carbon dioxide
MW 44.01
mp $-78.5°C$ (sublimes)

Benzoic acid
MW 122.12
mp 123°C

Prepare 2 mmol of phenylmagnesium bromide exactly as described in Part 1 of this experiment. Wipe off the surface of a small piece of dry ice (solid carbon dioxide) with a dry towel to remove frost, and place it in a dry 30-mL beaker. Remove the pressure-relief needle from the reaction tube, and then insert a syringe through the septum, turn the tube upside down, and draw into the syringe as much of the reagent solution as possible. Squirt this solution onto the piece of dry ice, and then, using a clean needle, rinse out the reaction tube with a milliliter of anhydrous diethyl ether and squirt this onto the dry ice. Allow excess dry ice to

CAUTION: Handle dry ice with a towel or gloves. Contact with the skin can cause frostbite, because dry ice sublimes at $-78.5°C$.

sublime, and then hydrolyze the salt by the addition of 2 mL of 3 M hydrochloric acid.

Transfer the mixture from the beaker to a reaction tube, and shake it thoroughly. Two homogeneous layers should result. Add 1 to 2 mL of acid or of ordinary (not anhydrous) *tert*-butyl methyl ether if necessary. Remove the aqueous layer, and shake the ether layer with 1 mL of water, which is removed and discarded. Then extract the benzoic acid by adding to the ether layer 0.7 mL of 3 M sodium hydroxide solution, shaking the mixture thoroughly, and withdrawing the aqueous layer, which is placed in a very small beaker or vial. The extraction is repeated with another 0.5-mL portion of base and finally 0.5 mL of water. Now that the extraction is complete, the ether, which can be discarded, contains primarily biphenyl, the byproduct formed during the preparation of the phenylmagnesium bromide.

The combined aqueous extracts are heated briefly to about 50°C to drive off dissolved ether from the aqueous solution and then made acidic by the addition of concentrated hydrochloric acid (test with indicator paper). Cool the mixture thoroughly in an ice bath. Collect the benzoic acid on the Hirsch funnel, and wash it with about 1 mL of ice water while on the funnel. A few crystals of this crude material are saved for a melting-point determination, and the remainder of the product is recrystallized from boiling water.

The solubility of benzoic acid in water is 68 g/L at 95°C and 1.7 g/L at 0°C. Dissolve the acid in very hot water. Let the solution cool slowly to room temperature; then cool it in ice for several minutes before collecting the product by vacuum filtration on the Hirsch funnel. Use the ice-cold filtrate in the filter flask to complete the transfer of benzoic acid from the reaction tube. Turn the product out onto a piece of filter paper, squeeze out excess water, and allow it to dry thoroughly. Once dry, weigh it, calculate the percentage yield, and determine the melting point along with the melting point of the crude material. The infrared spectrum may be determined as a solution in chloroform (1 g of benzoic acid dissolves in 4.5 mL of chloroform) or as a mull or KBr disk (see Chapter 13).

Cleaning Up   Combine all aqueous layers, dilute with a large quantity of water, and flush the slightly acidic solution down the drain.

 **MACROSCALE**

4. Phenylmagnesium Bromide (Phenyl Grignard Reagent)

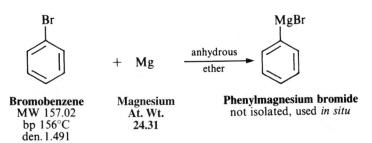

Bromobenzene	**Magnesium**	**Phenylmagnesium bromide**
MW 157.02	At. Wt.	not isolated, used *in situ*
bp 156°C	24.31	
den. 1.491		

All equipment and reagents must be absolutely dry. The Grignard reagent is prepared in a dry 100-mL round-bottomed flask fitted with a long reflux condenser. A calcium chloride drying tube inserted in a cork that will fit either the flask or the top of the condenser is also made ready [Fig. 38.6(a)]. (See also Fig. 38.5.) The flask, condenser, and magnesium (2 g = 0.082 mol of magnesium turnings) should be as dry as possible to begin with, and then should be dried in a 110°C oven for at least 35 min. Alternatively, the magnesium is placed in the flask, the calcium chloride tube is attached directly, and the flask is heated gently but thoroughly with a cool luminous flame. Do not overheat the magnesium. It will become deactivated through oxidation or, if strongly overheated, can burn. The flask on cooling pulls dry air through the calcium chloride. Cool to room

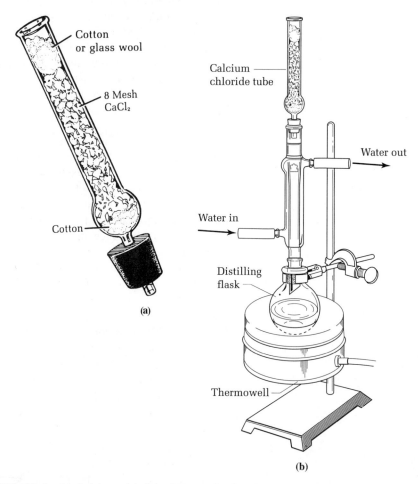

(a)

(b)

FIG. 38.6 (a) Calcium chloride drying tube fitted with a rubber stopper. Store for future use with cork in top, pipette bulb on bottom. (b) Apparatus for refluxing Grignard reaction.

temperature before proceeding! **Extinguish all flames!** Ether vapor is denser than air and can travel along bench tops and into sinks. Use care.

CAUTION: *Ether is extremely flammable. Extinguish all flames before using ether.*

Specially dried ether is required.

Make an ice bath ready in case control of the reaction becomes necessary, although this is usually not the case. Remove the drying tube, and fit it to the top of the condenser. Then pour into the flask through the condenser 15 mL of *absolute* ether (absolutely dry, anhydrous) and 9 mL (13.5 g = 0.086 mol) of bromobenzene. Be sure the graduated cylinders used to measure the ether and bromobenzene are absolutely dry. (More ether is to be added as soon as the reaction starts, but at the outset the concentration of bromobenzene is kept high to promote easy starting.) If there is no immediate sign of reaction, insert a *dry* stirring rod with a flattened end and crush a piece of magnesium firmly against the bottom of the flask under the surface of the liquid, giving a twisting motion to the rod. When this is done properly the liquid becomes slightly cloudy, and ebullition commences at the surface of the compressed metal. Be careful not to punch a hole in the bottom of the flask. Attach the condenser at once, swirl the flask to provide fresh surfaces for contact, and, as soon as you are sure that the reaction has started, add 25 mL more absolute ether through the top of the condenser before spontaneous boiling becomes too vigorous (replace the drying tube). Note the volume of ether in the flask. Cool in ice if necessary to slow the reaction, but do not overcool the mixture; the reaction can be stopped by too much cooling. Any difficulty in initiating the reaction can be dealt with by trying the following expedients in succession.

Starting the Grignard reaction

1. Warm the flask with your hands or a beaker of warm water. Then see if boiling continues when the flask (condenser attached) is removed from the warmth.
2. Try further mashing of the metal with a stirring rod.
3. Add a tiny crystal of iodine as a starter (in this case the ethereal solution of the final reaction product should be washed with sodium bisulfite solution to remove the yellow color).
4. Add a few drops of a solution of phenylmagnesium bromide or of methylmagnesium iodide (which can be made in a test tube).
5. Start afresh, taking greater care with the dryness of apparatus, measuring tools, and reagents, and sublime a crystal or two of iodine on the surface of the magnesium to generate Gattermann's "activated magnesium" before beginning the reaction again.

Diethyl ether can be kept anhydrous by storing over Linde 5A molecular sieves. Discard the ether after 90 days because of peroxide formation.

Use minimum steam to avoid condensation on outside of the condenser.

Once the reaction begins, spontaneous boiling in the diluted mixture may be slow or become slow. If so, mount the flask and condenser on the steam bath (one clamp supporting the condenser suffices), and reflux gently until the magnesium has disintegrated and the solution has acquired a cloudy or brownish appearance [Fig. 38.6(b)]. The reaction is complete when only a few small remnants of metal (or metal contaminants) remain. Check to see that the volume of ether has not decreased. If it has, add more anhydrous ether. Since the solution of Grignard reagent deteriorates on standing, the next step should be started at once.

 **MACROSCALE**

5. Triphenylmethanol from Methyl Benzoate

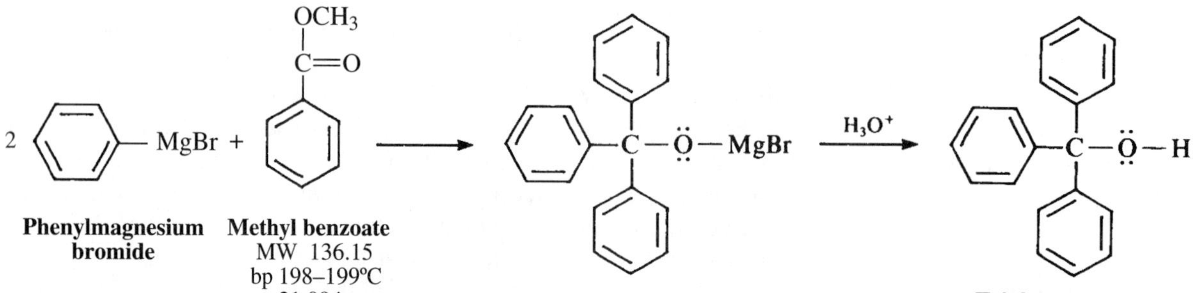

$$2 \quad \text{(C}_6\text{H}_5\text{)—MgBr} + \text{Methyl benzoate} \longrightarrow \text{(C}_6\text{H}_5)_3\text{C—}\overset{..}{\text{O}}\text{—MgBr} \xrightarrow{\text{H}_3\text{O}^+} \text{(C}_6\text{H}_5)_3\text{C—}\overset{..}{\text{O}}\text{—H}$$

Phenylmagnesium bromide

Methyl benzoate
MW 136.15
bp 198–199°C
21.094

Triphenylmethanol
MW 260.34
mp 164.2°C

Mix 5 g (0.037 mol) of methyl benzoate and 15 mL of absolute ether in a separatory funnel, cool the flask containing phenylmagnesium bromide solution briefly in an ice bath, remove the drying tube, and insert the stem of the separatory funnel into the top of the condenser. Run in the methyl benzoate solution *slowly* with only such cooling as is required to control the mildly exothermic reaction, which affords an intermediate salt that separates as a white solid. Replace the calcium chloride tube; swirl the flask until it is at room temperature and the reaction has subsided.

MACROSCALE

6. Triphenylmethanol from Benzophenone

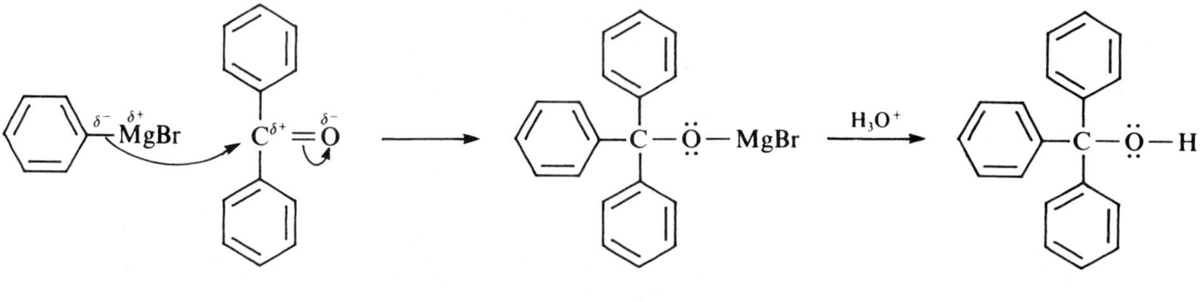

Phenylmagnesium bromide

Benzophenone
MW 182.22
mp 48°C

Triphenylmethanol
MW 260.34
mp 164.2°C

Dissolve 6.75 g (0.037 mol) of benzophenone in 25 mL of absolute ether in a separatory funnel, and cool the flask containing *half* the phenylmagnesium bromide solution (0.041 mol) briefly in an ice bath. (The other half can be used to make benzoic acid.) Remove the drying tube, and insert the stem of the separatory funnel into the top of the condenser. Add the benzophenone solution *slowly* with swirling and only such cooling as is required to control the mildly exothermic reaction, which gives a bright-red solution and then precipitates a white salt. Replace the calcium chloride tube; swirl the flask until it is at room temperature and the reaction has subsided. Go to Part 7.

7. Completion of Grignard Reaction

This is a suitable stopping point.

The reaction is then completed by either refluxing the mixture for one-half hour, or stoppering the flask with the calcium chloride tube and letting the mixture stand overnight (subsequent refluxing is then unnecessary).[2]

Pour the reaction mixture into a 250-mL Erlenmeyer flask containing 50 mL of 10% sulfuric acid and about 25 g of ice, and use both ordinary ether and 10% sulfuric acid to rinse the flask. Swirl well to promote hydrolysis of the addition compound; basic magnesium salts are converted into water-soluble neutral salts, and triphenylmethanol is distributed into the ether layer. An additional amount of ether (ordinary) may be required. Pour the mixture into a separatory funnel (rinse the flask with ether), shake, and draw off the aqueous layer. Shake the ether solution with 10% sulfuric acid to further remove magnesium salts, and wash with saturated sodium chloride solution to remove water that has dissolved in the ether. The amounts of liquid used in these washing operations are not critical. In general, an amount of wash liquid equal to one-third of the ether volume is adequate.

In this part of the experiment, ordinary (not anhydrous) diethyl ether or t-*butyl methyl ether may be used.*

Saturated aqueous sodium chloride solution removes water from ether.

To effect final drying of the ether solution, pour the ether layer out of the neck of the separatory funnel into an Erlenmeyer flask, add about 5 g of calcium chloride pellets, swirl the flask from time to time, and after 5 min remove the drying agent by gravity filtration through a filter paper held in a funnel into a tared Erlenmeyer flask. Rinse the drying agent with a small amount of ether. Add 25 mL of 66–77°C ligroin, and concentrate the ether-ligroin solutions (steam bath) in an Erlenmeyer flask under an aspirator tube (see Fig. 8.5). Evaporate slowly until crystals of triphenylcarbinol just begin to separate, and then let crystallization proceed, first at room temperature and then at 0°C. The product should be colorless and should melt not lower than 160°C. Concentration of the mother liquor may yield a second crop of crystals. A typical student yield is 5.0 g. Evaporate the mother liquors to dryness, and save the residue for later isolation of the components by chromatography.

Analyze the first crop of triphenylmethanol and the residue from the evaporation of the mother liquors by thin-layer chromatography. Dissolve equal quantities of the two solids (a few crystals) and also biphenyl in equal quantities of dichloromethane (1 or 2 drops). Using a microcapillary, spot equal quantities of material on silica gel TLC plates, and develop the plates in an appropriate solvent system. Try 1 : 3 dichloromethane–petroleum ether first, and adjust the relative quantities of solvent as needed. The spots can be seen by examining the TLC plate under a fluorescent lamp or by treating the TLC plate with iodine vapor. From this analysis decide how pure each of the solids is and whether it would be worthwhile to attempt to isolate more triphenylmethanol from the mother liquors.

Dispose of recovered and waste solvents in the appropriate containers.

Turn in the product in a vial labeled with your name, the name of the compound, its melting point, and the overall percent yield from benzoic acid.

---

2. A rule of thumb for organic reactions: A 10°C rise in temperature will double the rate of the reaction.

 MACROSCALE

8. Benzoic Acid

Wipe the frost from a piece of dry ice, transfer the ice to a cloth towel, and crush it with a hammer. Without delay (so moisture will not condense on the cold solid) transfer about 10 g of dry ice to a 250-mL beaker. Cautiously pour one-half of the solution of phenylmagnesium bromide prepared in Part 1 of this experiment onto the dry ice. A vigorous reaction will ensue. Allow the mixture to warm up; stir it until the dry ice has evaporated. To the beaker add 20 mL of 3 *M* hydrochloric acid, and then heat the mixture over a steam bath in the hood to boil off the ether. Cool the beaker thoroughly in an ice bath, and collect the solid product by vacuum filtration on a Büchner funnel.

Transfer the solid back to the beaker, and dissolve it in the minimum quantity of saturated sodium bicarbonate solution (2.8 *M*). Note that a small quantity of a byproduct remains suspended and floating on the surface of the solution. Note the odor of the mixture. Transfer it to a separatory funnel, and shake it briefly with about 15 mL of *t*-butyl methyl ether. Discard the ether layer, place the clear aqueous layer in the beaker, and heat it briefly to drive off dissolved ether. Carefully add 3 *M* hydrochloric acid to the mixture until the solution tests acid to pH paper. Cool the mixture in ice, and collect the product on a Büchner funnel. Recrystallize it from the minimum quantity of hot water, and isolate it in the usual manner. Determine the melting point and the weight of the benzoic acid, and calculate its yield based on the weight of magnesium used to prepare the Grignard reagent.

Cleaning Up   Combine all aqueous layers, dilute with a large quantity of water, and flush the slightly acidic solution down the drain. The ether–ligroin mother liquor from the crystallization goes in the organic solvents container. The thin-layer chromatography developer, which contains dichloromethane, is placed in the halogenated organic waste container. Calcium chloride from the drying tube should be dissolved in water and flushed down the drain.

Questions _____

1. Triphenylmethanol also can be prepared from the reaction of ethyl benzoate with phenylmagnesium bromide and by the reaction of diethylcarbonate

with phenylmagnesium bromide. Write stepwise reaction mechanisms for these two reactions.

2. If the ethyl benzoate used to prepare triphenylmethanol is wet, what byproduct is formed?

3. Exactly what weight of dry ice is needed to react with 2 mmol of phenylmagnesium bromide?

4. In the synthesis of benzoic acid, benzene is often detected as an impurity. How does this come about?

5. The benzoic acid could have been extracted from the ether layer using

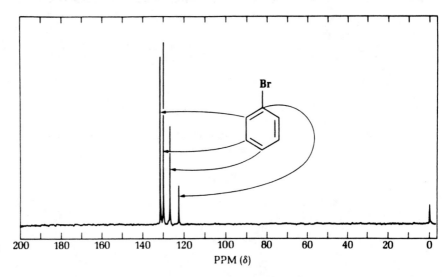

FIG. 38.7 ¹³C NMR spectrum of bromobenzene (22.6 MHz).

sodium bicarbonate solution. Give equations showing how this might be done and how the benzoic acid would be regenerated. What practical reason makes this extraction less desirable than sodium hydroxide extraction?

6. What is the weight of frost (ice) on the dry ice that will react with all of Grignard reagent used in Experiment 8?

7. How many moles of carbon dioxide are contained in 10 g of dry ice?

8. Just after the dry ice has evaporated from the beaker, what is the white solid remaining?

9. Write an equation for the reaction of the white solid with 3 *M* hydrochloric acid.

10. Write an equation for the reaction of the product with sodium bicarbonate.

11. Would you expect sodium benzoate to have an odor?

12. What is the odor you detect after the product has dissolved in sodium bicarbonate solution?

13. What is the purpose of the *t*-butyl methyl ether extraction?

14. What is meant by the sentence "Isolate the product in the usual way"?

Surfing the Web

http://odin.chemistry.uakron.edu/organic_lab/grignard/

The synthesis of phenylmagnesium bromide (Experiment 1) is shown in 10 good close-up color photos at this University of Akron site. A further 15 photos show the synthesis of triphenylmethanol from benzophenone. The synthesis of benzoic acid, with three photos, is left, as it is here, as an open-ended experiment.

For updated information visit:
www.mtholyoke.edu/courses/kwilliam/microscale.shtml
or
www.hmco.com/hmco/college/chemistry/Home.html

Diels-Alder Reaction

Prelab Exercise: Describe in detail the laboratory operations, reagents, and solvents you would employ to prepare

Otto Diels and his pupil Kurt Alder received the Nobel Prize in 1950 for their discovery and work on the reaction that bears their names. Its great usefulness lies in its high yield and high stereospecificity. A cycloaddition reaction, it involves the 1,4-addition of a conjugated diene in the s-*cis* conformation to an alkene in which two new σ (sigma) bonds are formed from two π (pi) bonds.

s-*trans*   s-*cis*

The adduct is a six-membered ring alkene. The diene can have the two conjugated bonds contained within a ring system, as with cyclopentadiene or cyclohexadiene, or the molecule can be an acyclic diene that must be in the *cis* conformation about the single bond before reaction can occur.

The reaction works best when there is a marked difference between the electron densities in the diene and the alkene with which it reacts, the dienophile. Usually the dienophile has electron-attracting groups attached to it, while the diene is electron rich, for example, as in the reaction of methyl vinyl ketone with 1,3-butadiene.

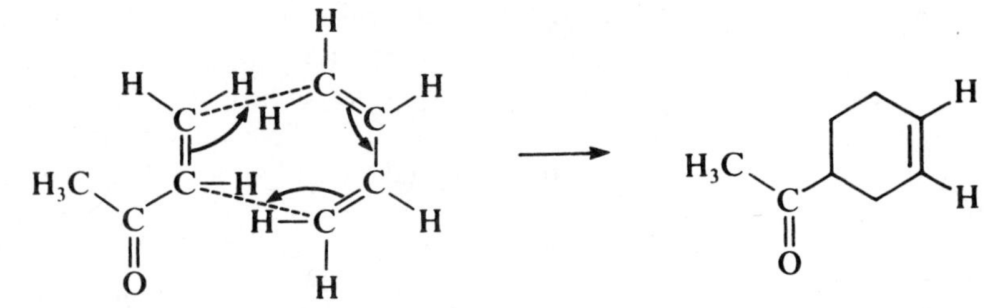

Methyl vinyl ketone   1,3-Butadiene

Retention of the configurations of the reactants in the products implies that both new σ bonds are formed almost simultaneously. If not, then the intermediate with a single new bond could rotate about that bond before the second σ bond is formed, thus destroying the stereospecificity of the reaction.

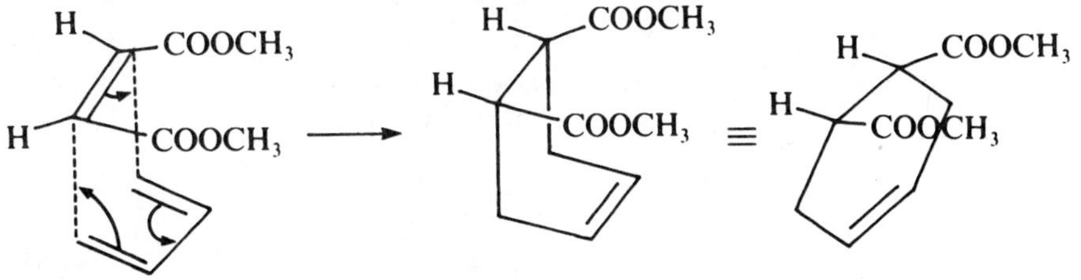

Dimethyl maleate
+
1,3-butadiene

cis **Isomer**

This does not happen:

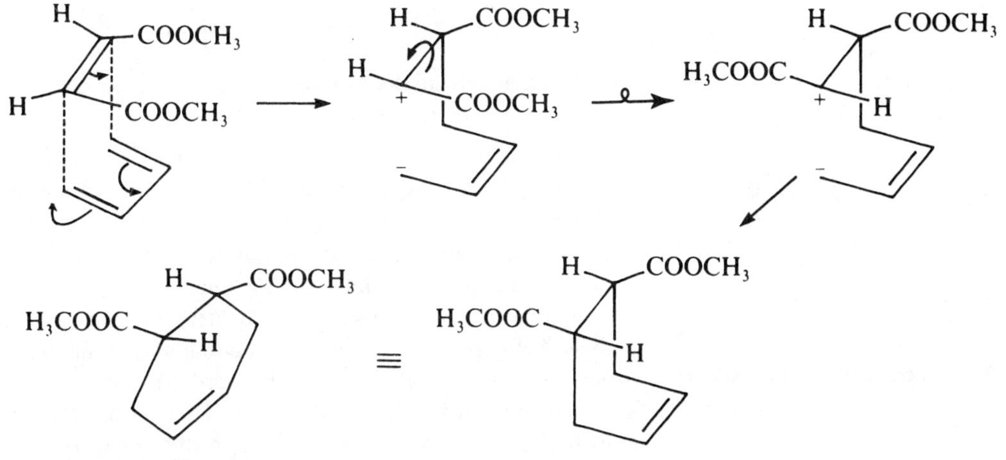

trans **Isomer**

This reaction is not polar in that no charged intermediates are formed. Neither is it a radical reaction, because no unpaired electrons are involved. It is instead known as a *concerted reaction,* or one in which several bonds in the transition state are simultaneously made and broken. When a cyclic diene and a cyclic dienophile react with each other as in the present reaction, more than one stereoisomer may be formed. The isomer that predominates is the one that involves maximum overlap of π electrons in the transition state. The transition state for the formation of the *endo* isomer in the present reaction involves a sandwich with the diene directly above the dienophile. To form the *exo* isomer, the diene and dienophile would need to be arranged in a stair-step fashion.

**Maximum overlap
of π electrons**

***endo* Isomer
predominant product**

π Electron overlap not so large

***exo* Isomer**

Woodward's Diels-Alder adduct

The Diels-Alder reaction has been used extensively in the synthesis of complex natural products because it is possible to exploit the formation of a number of chiral centers in one reaction and also the regioselectivity of the reaction. For example, the first step in R. B. Woodward's synthesis of cortisone was the formation of a Diels-Alder adduct.

But the reaction is also subject to steric hindrance, especially when the difference between the electron-withdrawing and -donating characters of the two reactants is not great. When Woodward tried to synthesize cantharidin, the active ingredient in Spanish fly, by the Diels-Alder condensation of furan with dimethylmaleic anhydride, the reaction did not work. The reaction possesses

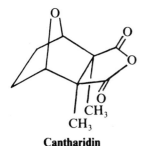

Cantharidin

$-\Delta V^*$ (it proceeds with a net decrease in volume). High pressure should overcome this problem, but this reaction will not proceed even at 600,000 lb/in.[2] (4.1 × 10[10] dynes/cm[2]). A closely related reaction will proceed at 300,000 lb/in.[2] and has been used to synthesize this molecule.[1] Cantharidin is a powerful vesicant (blister-former).

R. B. Woodward and Roald Hoffmann formulated the theoretical rules involving the correlation of orbital symmetry, which govern the Diels-Alder and other electrocyclic reactions.

Cyclopentadiene is obtained from the light oil from coal tar distillation but exists as the stable dimer, dicyclopentadiene, which is the Diels-Alder adduct from two molecules of the diene. Thus generation of cyclopentadiene by pyrolysis of the dimer represents a reverse Diels-Alder reaction. See Figs. 49.5 and 49.6 at the end of the chapter for NMR and IR spectra, respectively, of dicyclopentadiene.

In the Diels-Alder addition of cyclopentadiene and maleic anhydride, the two molecules approach each other in the orientation shown in the top drawing on the previous page, because this orientation provides maximal overlap of π bonds of the two reactants and favors formation of an initial π complex and then the final *endo* product. Dicyclopentadiene also has the *endo* configuration.

The infrared spectrum of dicyclopentadiene appears in Fig. 49.6 and the ^{13}C NMR spectrum in Fig. 49.7 at the end of the chapter.

Experiments

1. Microscale Cracking of Dicyclopentadiene

$$\underset{\substack{\text{room} \\ \text{temperature}}}{\overset{\sim 160°C}{\rightleftharpoons}}$$

Dicyclopentadiene
den 0.98
MW 132.20
bp 170°C
n_D^{20} 1.5100

Cyclopentadiene
bp 41°C, den 0.80
MW 66.10

Half fill with mineral oil the short-necked 5-mL round-bottomed flask equipped with an addition port bearing a septum on the sidearm and topped with a distillation head and thermometer (Fig. 49.1). Heat the flask on a sand bath. Start the heating with the thermometer down in the oil. Heat it to about 250°C, and then raise the thermometer to the position shown in Fig. 49.1. Lubricate the thermometer with a drop of oil to make it slide easily.

1. W. G. Dauben, C. R. Kessel, and K. H. Takemura, *J. Am. Chem. Soc.*, **102**, 6893 (1980).

FIG. 49.1 Apparatus for microscale cracking of dicyclopentadiene. Add dicyclopentadiene dropwise via syringe so that distillate temperature does not exceed 45°C.

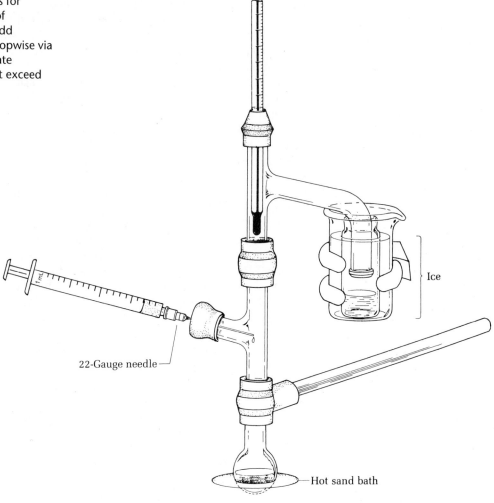

Ice

22-Gauge needle

Hot sand bath

Set controller on the flask heater at half maximum. Temperature can be controlled by piling up or scraping away sand from the flask. Turn down heat after finishing reaction.

Place a small tared collection vial in an ice-filled 30-mL beaker at the end of the distilling head, taking care to keep water out of the vial. Using a syringe, draw 0.6 mL of dicyclopentadiene (Fig. 49.2) from the septum-capped storage container after first injecting 0.6 mL of air into the container to overcome the vacuum. Stick the needle of the filled syringe into a rubber stopper or cork to avoid loss of the contents until they are used.

When the mineral oil is hot (250°C), inject the dicyclopentadiene through the septum on the addition port. Add it dropwise at such a rate that the temperature of the thermometer never exceeds 45°C. The boiling point of cyclopentadiene is 41°C. Add the dimer over a 10-min period. If the dimer is added too slowly, the yield will be lower. Once the dicyclopentadiene has all been added, remove

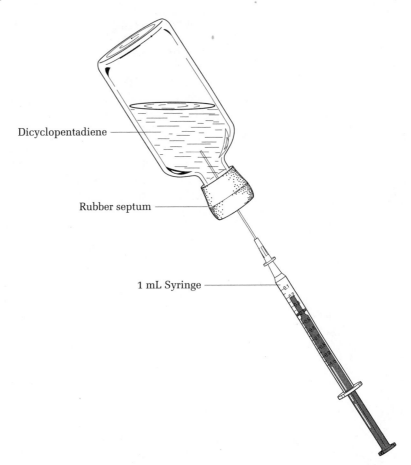

FIG. 49.2   Dicyclopentadiene has a very bad odor and so is dispensed from a closed container. Remove 0.6 mL from the septum-capped bottle after injecting 0.6 mL of air.

Don't disassemble the apparatus until you are sure you have 0.3 mL of product.

the syringe, and weigh the product after closing the vial. Rinse the syringe with acetone in the hood. Calculate the percentage yield of cyclopentadiene. If the product is cloudy, add a small quantity of anhydrous calcium chloride pellets to dry it if the maleic anhydride experiment is being done next. It need not be dry to make ferrocene. Keep this cyclopentadiene on ice, and use it the same day it is prepared.

Cleaning Up   Place the mineral oil from the reaction flask and any unused dicyclopentadiene in the organic solvents container. If calcium chloride was used, it should be freed of cyclopentadiene by evaporation in the hood and then placed in the nonhazardous solid waste container.

2. Macroscale Cracking of Dicyclopentadiene

The infrared spectrum of dicyclopentadiene appears in Fig. 49.6 at the end of the chapter.

Measure 20 mL of dicyclopentadiene into a 100-mL flask, and arrange for fractional distillation into an ice-cooled receiver (Fig. 19.2). Heat the dimer with an electric flask heater until it refluxes briskly and at such a rate that the monomeric diene begins to distill in about 5 min and soon reaches a steady boiling point in the range 40–42°C. Apply heat continuously to promote rapid distillation without exceeding the boiling point of 42°C. Distillation for 45 min should provide the 12 mL of cyclopentadiene required for two preparations of the adduct; continued distillation for another half hour gives a total of about 20 mL of monomer.

Reverse Diels-Alder

Check old dicyclopentadiene for peroxides.

Cleaning Up   Pour the pot residue of dicyclopentadiene and unused cyclopentadiene into the recovered dicyclopentadiene container. This recovered material can, despite its appearance, be cracked in the future to give cyclopentadiene. If the pot residue is not to be recycled, place it in the organic solvents container.

2. *cis*-Norbornene-5,6-*endo*-dicarboxylic Anhydride

Maleic anhydride
mp 53°C, MW 98.06

cis-**Norbornene-5,6-*endo*-dicarboxylic anhydride**
mp 165°C, MW 164.16

Microscale Procedure

Ligroin = hexane(s)

Mixing of the reactants is very important. Pull the reaction mixture into a pipette, and then expel it into the reaction tube or blow air from a pipette through the reaction mixture.

Dissolve 0.20 g of powdered maleic anhydride in 1 mL of ethyl acetate in a tared 10 × 100 mm reaction tube, and then add 1 mL bp 60–80°C ligroin. This combination of solvents is used because the product is too soluble in pure ethyl acetate and not soluble enough in pure ligroin. To the solution of maleic anhydride add 0.20 mL (0.160 g) of dry cyclopentadiene, mix the reactants, and observe the reaction. Allow the tube to cool to room temperature, during which time crystallization of the product should occur. If crystallization does not occur, scratch the inside of the test tube with a stirring rod at the liquid–air interface. The scratch marks on the inside of the tube often form the nuclei on which crystallization starts. Should crystallization occur very rapidly at room temperature, the crystals will be very small. If so, save a seed crystal, heat the mixture until the product dissolves, seed it, and allow it to cool slowly to room temperature. You will be rewarded with large platelike crystals. Remove the solvent from the crystals with a Pasteur pipette that is forced to the bottom of the tube, wash the crystals with one portion of cold ligroin, and remove the solvent (see Fig. 3.13). Scrape the product onto a piece of filter paper, allow the crystals to dry in air, determine their weight, and calculate the yield of the product. Determine the melting point of the product, and turn in any material not used in the next experiment. Thin-layer chromatography of the product is hardly necessary; it is quite pure. The IR spectrum of the anhydrite appears in Fig. 49.8, the ^{1}H NMR spectrum in Fig. 49.9, and the ^{13}C NMR spectrum in Fig. 49.10.

Cleaning Up   Place the crystallization solvent mixture in the organic solvents container. It contains a very small quantity of the product.

 ### Macroscale Procedure

Place 6 g of maleic anhydride in a 125-mL Erlenmeyer flask, and dissolve the anhydride in 16 mL of ethyl acetate by heating on a hot plate or steam bath. Add 16 mL of ligroin (bp 60–90°C) or hexane, cool the solution thoroughly in an ice-water bath, and leave it in the bath (some anhydride may crystallize).

Cyclopentadiene is flammable.

The distilled cyclopentadiene may be slightly cloudy because of the condensation of moisture in the cooled receiver and water in the starting material. Add about 1 g of calcium chloride pellets to remove the moisture. It will redimerize in a few hours; use it immediately. Measure 6 mL of dry cyclopentadiene, and add it to the ice-cold solution of maleic anhydride. Swirl the

Rapid addition at 0°C

solution in the ice bath for a few minutes until the exothermic reaction is over and the adduct separates as a white solid. Then heat the mixture on a hot plate or steam bath until the solid is all dissolved.[2] If you let the solution stand undisturbed, you will be rewarded with a beautiful display of crystal formation. The anhydride crystallizes in long spars (mp 164–165°C); a typical yield is 8.2 g.[3] The IR spectrum of the anhydride appears in Fig. 49.8, the ^{1}H NMR spectrum in Fig. 49.9, and the ^{13}C NMR spectrum in Fig. 49.10 at the end of the chapter.

---

2. In case moisture has gotten into the system, a little of the corresponding diacid may remain undissolved at this point and should be removed by filtration of the hot solution.

3. The student need not work up the mother liquor but may be interested in learning the result. Concentration of the solution to a small volume is not satisfactory because of the presence of dicyclopentadiene, formed by dimerization of excess monomer; the dimer has high solvent power. Hence the bulk of the solvent is evaporated on the steam bath, and the flask is connected to the water pump with a rubber stopper and glass tube and heated under vacuum on the steam bath until dicyclopentadiene is removed and the residue solidifies. Crystallization from 1:1 ethyl acetate–ligroin affords 1.3 g adduct (mp 156–158°C); total yield is 95%.

Cleaning Up   Place the crystallization solvent mixture in the organic solvents container. It contains a very small quantity of the product. Allow the organic material to evaporate from the drying agent (in the hood), and then place it in the nonhazardous solid waste container.

3. *cis*-Norbornene-5-6,-*endo*-dicarboxylic Acid

$$H_2O \; + \qquad \longrightarrow$$

endo,cis-Diacid

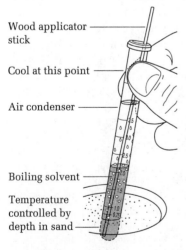

Microscale Procedure

To 0.2 g (200 mg) of the anhydride from the preceding experiment, add 2.5 mL of water and a boiling stick in a 10 × 100 mm reaction tube. Heat the mixture to boiling by immersing the tube in a hot sand bath (Fig. 49.3). The anhydride may appear to melt and form globules on the bottom of the tube. As the reaction proceeds, the anhydride will react with the water, and the diacid, which is soluble in boiling water, will be formed. Continue to heat for about 2 min after the last globule disappears. Remove the boiling stick from the hot solution, and allow the mixture to cool to room temperature.

    If crystallization of the diacid does not occur, follow exactly the same procedure used for the anhydride. On slow cooling with simultaneous crystal growth the solution will deposit long needlelike crystals. Again, cool the mixture in ice, allow sufficient time for crystal growth to occur, and then collect the product by filtration on the Hirsch funnel. Use the filtrate (ice cold) to complete the transfer. Wash the crystals once with a small quantity of ice water, and place the product on a piece of filter paper to dry. Do not discard the filtrate until you have weighed the product. More material can be recovered by concentration of the filtrate and allowing it to cool to give a second crop of crystals. This is a general strategy. Weigh the diacid, and determine the melting point and percentage yield. The melting point depends on the rate of heating as the anhydride reforms and water splits out. IR and ¹H NMR spectra are in Figs. 49.11 and 49.12 at the end of the chapter.[4]

Wood applicator stick

Cool at this point

Air condenser

Boiling solvent

Temperature controlled by depth in sand

FIG. 49.3 Hydrolysis of the anhydride to the *endo,cis*-diacid.

Cleaning Up   The aqueous filtrate from the crystallization contains a very small quantity of the diacid. It can be flushed down the drain.

Macroscale Procedure

$$H_2O +$$

endo,cis-**Diacid**

For preparation of the *endo,cis*-diacid, place 4.0 g of the anhydride from Experiment 2 and 50 mL of distilled water in a 125-mL Erlenmeyer flask, grasp this with a clamp, swirl the flask over a hot plate, and bring the contents to the boiling point, at which point the solid partly dissolves and partly melts. Continue to heat until the oil is all dissolved, and then let the solution stand undisturbed. Because the diacid has a strong tendency to remain in supersaturated solution, allow half an hour or more for the solution to cool to room temperature, and then drop in a boiling stone or touch the surface of the liquid once or twice with a stirring rod. Observe the stone and its surroundings carefully, waiting several minutes before applying the more effective method of making one scratch with a stirring rod on the inner wall of the flask at the air–liquid interface. Let crystallization proceed spontaneously to give large needles; then cool the solution in ice and collect the product. The melting point depends on the rate of heating as the anhydride reforms and water splits out. IR and ^{1}H NMR spectra of the diacid are found in Figs. 49.11 and 49.12 at the end of the chapter.[4]

The temperature of decomposition is variable.

Cleaning Up   The aqueous filtrate from the crystallization contains a very small quantity of the diacid. It can be flushed down the drain.

4. Synthesis of Compound X[5]

To a tared 10 × 100 mm reaction tube add 0.15 g of the *endo,cis*-diacid from the preceding experiment, followed by 0.25 mL of concentrated sulfuric acid. Warm the mixture on the steam bath or in a beaker of boiling water for about

---

4. The *endo,cis*-diacid is stable to alkali but can be isomerized to the *trans*-diacid (mp 192°C) by conversion to the dimethyl ester (3 g acid, 10 mL methanol, 0.5 mL concentrated H_2SO_4; reflux 1 h). This ester is equilibrated with sodium ethoxide in refluxing ethanol for 3 days and saponified. For an account of a related epimerization and discussion of the mechanism, see J. Meinwald and P. G. Gassman, *J. Am. Chem. Soc.,* **82,** 5445, 1960. See also K. L. Williamson, Y.-F. Li, R. Lacko, and C. H. Youn, *J. Am. Chem. Soc.,* **91,** 6129, 1969; and K. L. Williamson and Y.-F. Li, *J. Am. Chem. Soc.,* **92,** 7654, 1970.

5. Introduced by James A. Deyrup.

If you do not have the necessary quantity of diacid, scale down the amounts of reactants and solvents to match the quantity of starting material. This is a general rule.

Do not put a wood boiling stick into this solution. The sulfuric acid will attack the wood.

2 min to allow the anhydride to dissolve/react, cool, and then *cautiously* add 0.70 mL of water to the test tube. This should be done dropwise with vigorous mixing of the contents after the addition of each drop. The product will crystallize as a fine powder, often gray in color.

Save a seed crystal, and heat the tube on a hot sand bath until the crystals redissolve. Seed the solution, and allow it to cool slowly to room temperature. Compound X will crystallize in platelike crystals. The crystallization process for this compound is fairly slow; allow at least 10 min for the solution to come to room temperature and a further 10 min in the ice bath before collecting the crystals on the Hirsch funnel or with the Wilfilter (Fig. 49.4). The longer you wait to collect the product the higher your yield will be. Wash the crystals with one small portion of ice water, and scrape the product onto a piece of filter paper. Squeeze the crystals between sheets of filter paper to complete the drying process, and then determine the weight, yield, and melting point of the product.

Cleaning Up   Dilute the aqueous filtrate with water, neutralize it with sodium carbonate, and flush the resulting solution down the drain. It contains an extremely small quantity of compound X.

 ### Macroscale Procedure

For preparation of compound X, place 1 g of the *endo,cis*-diacid and 5 mL of concentrated sulfuric acid in a 50-mL Erlenmeyer flask, and heat gently on the hot plate for a minute or two until the crystals are all dissolved. Then cool in an ice bath, add a small piece of ice, swirl to dissolve, and add further ice until the volume is about 20 mL. Heat to the boiling point, and let the solution simmer on the hot plate for 5 min. Cool well in ice, scratch the flask (see Chapter 3) to induce crystallization, and allow for some delay in complete separation. The crystals will often be gray in color. Collect, wash with water, and crystallize from water. Compound X (about 0.7 g) forms large prisms (mp 203°C). To run an NMR spectrum of compound X, the compound must be dissolved in deutero-dimethyl sulfoxide (DMSO d_6).

Cleaning Up   Dilute the aqueous filtrate with water, neutralize it with sodium carbonate, and flush the resulting solution down the drain. It contains a small quantity of compound X.

 **MICROSCALE AND MACROSCALE**

7. Structure Determination of Compound X

To determine the formula for compound X, which is an isomer of the diacid, try to answer the following questions: What intermediate is formed when the diacid dissolves in concentrated sulfuric acid? Why is the ^{1}H NMR spectrum of X (Fig. 49.13) so much more complex than the anhydride and diacid spectra (Figs. 49.9 and 49.12)? What functional group is missing from X that is seen in Figs. 49.9 and 49.12? Write formulas for possible structures of X, and devise tests to distinguish among them. What functional group is present in X that is not found in the diacid as determined by an analysis of the infrared spectrum of X (Fig. 49.14)?

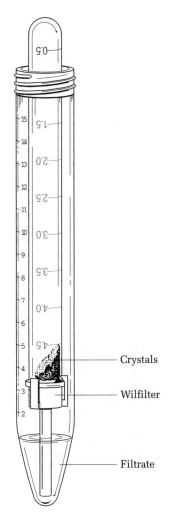

FIG. 49.4 The Wilfilter filtration apparatus.

Computational Chemistry

Would you predict that compound X is more or less stable than the isomeric diacid from which it is formed? Test your prediction by carrying out a heat of formation calculation on each of the isomers. To do this, first find the conformation of each isomer with the minimum steric energy using a molecular mechanics program. Then submit each of these to a heat of formation calculation at the AM1 or higher level of calculation.

Questions

1. In the cracking of dicyclopentadiene, why is it necessary to distill the product very slowly?

2. Draw the products of the following reactions:

(a)

(b)

(c)

3. What starting material would be necessary to prepare the following compound by the Diels-Alder reaction?

4. If the Diels-Alder reaction between dimethylmaleic anhydride and furan had worked, would cantharidin have been formed?

5. Determine the heats of formation or the steric energies of the *exo*- and

endo-anhydride adducts using a molecular mechanics program. What do these energies tell you about the mechanism of the reaction?

6. Which molecule, norbornene dicarboxylic acid or compound X, would you predict to be the more stable? Why?

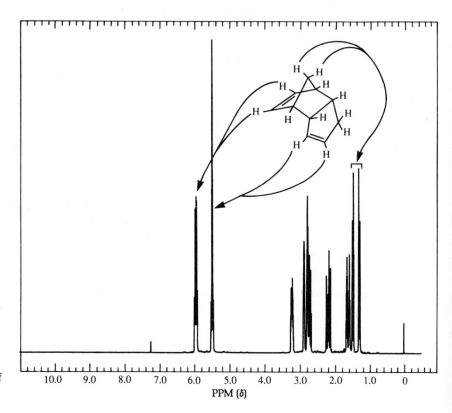

FIG. 49.5 ¹H NMR spectrum of dicyclopentadiene (250 MHz).

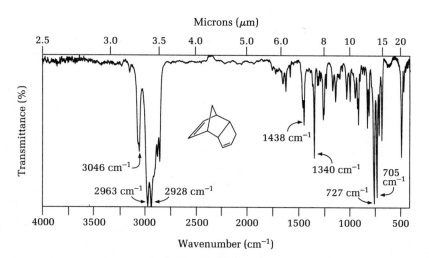

FIG. 49.6 IR spectrum of dicyclopentadiene (thin film).

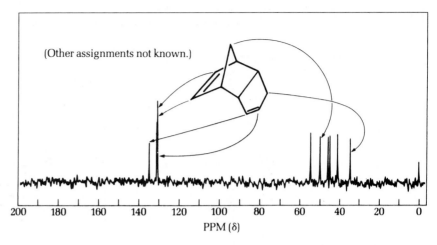

FIG. 49.7 ^{13}C NMR spectrum of dicyclopentadiene.

(Other assignments not known.)

200 180 160 140 120 100 80 60 40 20 0

PPM (δ)

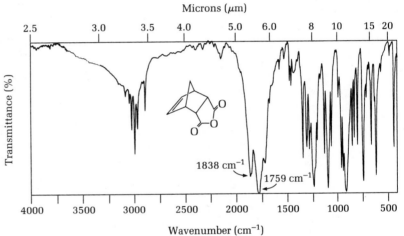

FIG. 49.8 Infrared spectrum of *cis*-norbornene-5,6-*endo*-dicarboxylic anhydride.

Microns (μm)

2.5   3.0   3.5   4.0   5.0   6.0   8   10   15 20

Transmittance (%)

1838 cm^{-1}

1759 cm^{-1}

4000   3500   3000   2500   2000   1500   1000   500

Wavenumber (cm^{-1})

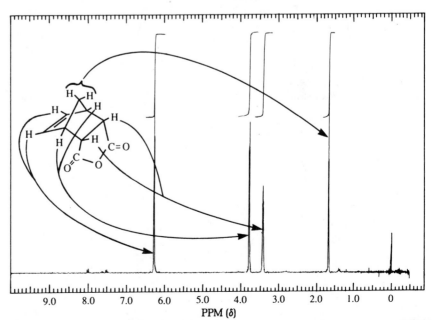

FIG. 49.9 ^{1}H NMR spectrum of *cis*-norbornene-5,6-*endo*-dicarboxylic anhydride. (250 MHz).

9.0   8.0   7.0   6.0   5.0   4.0   3.0   2.0   1.0   0

PPM (δ)

585

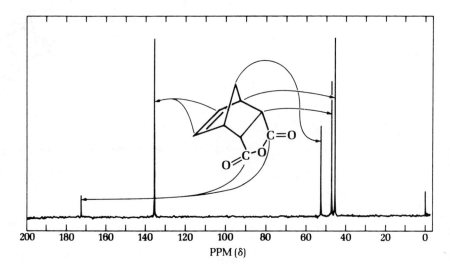

FIG. 49.10 ^{13}C NMR spectrum of *cis*-norbornene-5,6-*endo*-dicarboxylic anhydride (22.6 MHz).

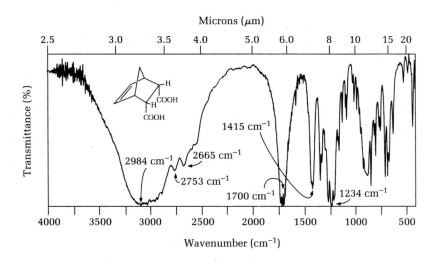

FIG. 49.11 Infrared spectrum of *cis*-5,6-*endo*-norbornene dicarboxylic acid (KBr disk).

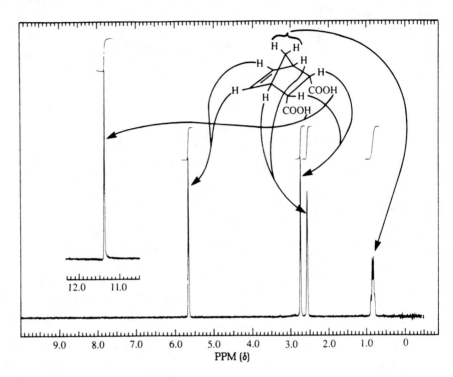

FIG. 49.12 ^{1}H NMR spectrum of *cis*-norbornene-5,6-*endo*-dicarboxylic acid (250 MHz).

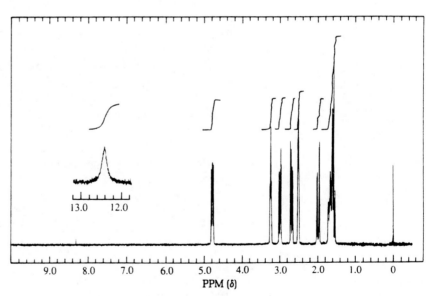

FIG. 49.13 ^{1}H NMR spectrum of compound X (250 MHz), dissolved in DMSO d_6.

70

Qualitative Organic Analysis

Prelab Exercise: In the identification of an unknown organic compound, certain procedures are more valuable than others. For example, much more information is obtained from an infrared spectrum than from a refractive index measurement. Outline, in order of priority, the steps you will employ in identifying your unknown.

Identification and characterization of the structures of unknown substances are an important part of organic chemistry. It is often, of necessity, a micro process, e.g., in drug analyses. It is sometimes possible to establish the structure of a compound on the basis of spectra alone (IR, UV, and NMR), but these spectra must usually be supplemented with other information about the unknown: physical state, elementary analysis, solubility, and confirmatory tests for functional groups. Conversion of the unknown to a solid derivative of known melting point will often provide final confirmation of structure.

However, before spectra are run, other information about the sample must be obtained. Is it homogeneous (test by thin-layer, gas, or liquid chromatography)? What are its physical properties (melting point, boiling point, color, solubility in various solvents)? Is it soluble in a common NMR solvent? It also might be necessary to determine what elements are present in the sample and its percentage composition (mass spectroscopy).

Nevertheless, an organic chemist can often identify a sample in a very short time by performing solubility tests and some simple tests for functional groups, coupled with spectra that have not been compared with a database. Conversion of the unknown to a solid derivative of known melting point will often provide final confirmation of structure. This chapter provides the information needed to carry out this type of qualitative analysis of an organic compound.

Procedures

All experiments in this chapter can, if necessary, be run on two to three times the indicated quantities of material.

Physical State

Check for Sample Purity

Distill or recrystallize as necessary. Constant boiling point and sharp melting point are indicators, but beware of azeotropes and eutectics. Check homogeneity by TLC, gas, HPLC, or paper chromatography.

Note the Color

Common colored compounds include nitro and nitroso compounds (yellow), α-diketones (yellow), quinones (yellow to red), azo compounds (yellow to red), and polyconjugated olefins and ketones (yellow to red). Phenols and amines are often brown to dark-purple because of traces of air oxidation products.

Note the Odor

Some liquid and solid amines are recognizable by their fishy odors; esters are often pleasantly fragrant. Alcohols, ketones, aromatic hydrocarbons, and aliphatic olefins have characteristic odors. On the unpleasant side are thiols, isonitriles, and low molecular weight carboxylic acids.

Make an Ignition Test

Heat a small sample on a spatula; first hold the sample near the side of a microburner to see if it melts normally and then burns. Heat it in the flame. If a large ashy residue is left after ignition, the unknown is probably a metal salt. Aromatic compounds often burn with a smoky flame.

Spectra

Obtain infrared and nuclear magnetic resonance spectra following the procedures of Chapters 12 and 13. If these spectra indicate the presence of conjugated double bonds, aromatic rings, or conjugated carbonyl compounds, obtain the ultraviolet spectrum following the procedures of Chapter 14. Interpret the spectra as fully as possible by reference to the sources cited at the end of the various spectroscopy chapters.

Explanation

Elementary Analysis, Sodium Fusion

This method for detection of nitrogen, sulfur, and halogen in organic compounds depends on the fact that fusion of substances containing these elements with sodium yields NaCN, Na_2S, and NaX (X = Cl, Br, I). These products can, in turn, be readily identified. The method has the advantage that the most usual elements other than C, H, and O present in organic compounds can all be detected following a single fusion, although the presence of sulfur sometimes interferes with the test for nitrogen. Unfortunately, even in the absence of sulfur, the test for nitrogen is sometimes unsatisfactory (nitro compounds in particular). Practicing organic chemists rarely perform this test. Either they know what elements their unknowns contain, or they have access to a mass spectrometer or atomic absorption instrument.

Rarely performed by professional chemists

Place a 3-mm cube of sodium[1] (30 mg, no more)[2] in a 10 × 75-mm Pyrex

Notes for the instructor

---

1. Sodium spheres $\frac{1}{16}$" to $\frac{1}{4}$" are convenient.

2. A dummy 3-mm cube of rubber can be attached to the sodium bottle to indicate the correct amount.

FIG. 70.1   Sodium fusion, just prior to addition of sample.

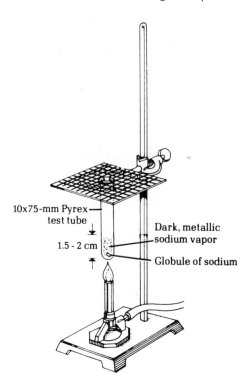

10x75-mm Pyrex test tube

1.5 - 2 cm

Dark, metallic sodium vapor

Globule of sodium

CAUTION: Manipulate sodium with a knife and forceps; never touch it with the fingers. Wipe it free of kerosene with a dry towel or filter paper; return scraps to the bottle or destroy scraps with methyl or ethyl alcohol, never with water. Safety glasses! Hood!

Do not use CHCl₃ or CCl₄ as samples in sodium fusion. They react extremely violently.

test tube, and support the tube in a vertical position (Fig. 70.1). Have a microburner with small flame ready to move under the tube, place an estimated 20 mg of solid on a spatula or knife blade, put the burner in place, and heat until the sodium first melts and then vapor rises 1.5–2.0 cm in the tube. Remove the burner, and at once drop the sample onto the hot sodium. If the substance is a liquid add 2 drops of it. If there is a flash or small explosion the fusion is complete; if not, heat briefly to produce a flash or a charring. Then let the tube cool to room temperature, be sure it is cold, add a drop of methanol, and let it react. Repeat until 10 drops have been added. With a stirring rod break up the char to uncover sodium. When you are sure that all sodium has reacted, empty the tube into a 13 × 100-mm test tube, hold the small tube pointing away from you or a neighbor, and pipette into it 1 mL of water. Boil and stir the mixture, and pour the water into the larger tube; repeat with 1 mL more water. Then transfer the solution with a Pasteur pipette to a 2.5-cm funnel (fitted with a fluted filter paper) resting in a second 13 × 100-mm test tube. Portions of the alkaline filtrate are used for the tests that follow.

(a) Nitrogen

Run each test on a known and an unknown.

The test is done by boiling a portion of the alkaline solution from the solution fusion with iron(II) sulfate and then acidifying. Sodium cyanide reacts with iron(II) sulfate to produce ferrocyanide, which combines with iron(III) salts, inevitably formed by air oxidation in the alkaline solution, to give insoluble Prussian Blue, $NaFe[Fe(CN)_6]$. Iron(II) and iron(III) hydroxide precipitate along with the blue pigment but dissolve on acidification.

Place 50 mg of powdered iron(II) sulfate (this is a large excess) in a 10 × 75-mm test tube, add 0.5 mL of the alkaline solution from the fusion, heat the mixture gently with shaking to the boiling point, and then—without cooling—acidify with dilute sulfuric acid (hydrochloric acid is unsatisfactory). A deep-blue precipitate indicates the presence of nitrogen. If the coloration is dubious, filter through a 2.5-cm funnel and see if the paper shows blue pigment.

Cleaning Up   The test solution should be diluted with water and flushed down the drain.

(b) Sulfur

$Na_2(NO)Fe(CN)_6 \cdot 2H_2O$

Sodium nitroprusside

1. Dilute one drop of the alkaline solution with 1 mL of water, and add a drop of sodium nitroprusside; a purple coloration indicates the presence of sulfur.
2. Prepare a fresh solution of sodium plumbite by adding 10% sodium hydroxide solution to 0.2 mL of 0.1 M lead acetate solution until the precipitate just dissolves, and add 0.5 mL of the alkaline test solution. A black precipitate or a colloidal brown suspension indicates the presence of sulfur.

Cleaning Up   The test solution should be diluted with water and flushed down the drain.

(c) Halogen

Differentiation of the halogens

Do not waste silver nitrate.

Acidify 0.5 mL of the alkaline solution from the fusion with dilute nitric acid (indicator paper) and, if nitrogen or sulfur has been found present, boil the solution (hood) to expel HCN or H_2S. On addition of a few drops of silver nitrate solution, halide ion is precipitated as silver halide. Filter with minimum exposure to light on a 2.5-cm funnel, wash with water, and then with 1 mL of concentrated ammonia solution. If the precipitate is white and readily soluble in ammonium hydroxide solution it is AgCl; if it is pale yellow and not readily soluble it is AgBr; if it is yellow and insoluble it is AgI. Fluorine is not detected in this test since silver fluoride is soluble in water.

Cleaning Up   The test solution should be diluted with water and flushed down the drain.

> Run tests on knowns in parallel with unknowns for all qualitative organic reactions. In this way, interpretations of positive reactions are clarified and defective test reagents can be identified and replaced.

Beilstein Test for Halogens

A fast, easy, reliable test

Heat the tip of a copper wire in a burner flame until no further coloration of the flame is noticed. Allow the wire to cool slightly, then dip it into the unknown (solid or liquid), and again heat it in the flame. A green flash is indicative of chlorine, blue-green of bromine, and blue of iodine; fluorine is not detected because copper fluoride is not volatile. The Beilstein test is very sensitive; halogen-containing impurities may give misleading results. Run the test on a compound known to contain halogen for comparison with your unknown.[3]

Solubility Tests

Weigh and measure carefully.

Like dissolves like; a substance is most soluble in that solvent to which it is most closely related in structure. This statement serves as a useful classification scheme for all organic molecules. The solubility measurements are done at room temperature with 1 drop of a liquid, or 5 mg of a solid (finely crushed), and 0.2 mL of solvent. The mixture should be rubbed with a rounded stirring rod and shaken vigorously. Lower members of a homologous series are easily classified; higher members become more like the hydrocarbons from which they are derived.

If a very small amount of the sample fails to dissolve when added to some of the solvent, it can be considered insoluble; and, conversely, if several portions dissolve readily in a small amount of the solvent, the substance is obviously soluble.

If an unknown seems to be more soluble in dilute acid or base than in water, the observation can be confirmed by neutralization of the solution; the original material will precipitate if it is less soluble in a neutral medium.

If both acidic and basic groups are present, the substance may be amphoteric and therefore soluble in both acid and base. Aromatic aminocarboxylic acids are amphoteric, like aliphatic ones, but they do not exist as zwitterions. They are soluble in both dilute hydrochloric acid and sodium hydroxide, but not in bicarbonate solution. Aminosulfonic acids exist as zwitterions; they are soluble in alkali but not in acid.

The solubility tests are not infallible and many borderline cases are known. Carry out the tests according to the scheme of Fig. 70.2 and the following "Notes to Solubility Tests," and tentatively assign the unknown to one of the groups I–X.

Cleaning Up Because the quantities of material used in these tests are extremely small, and because no hazardous substances are handed out as unknowns, it is possible to dilute the material with a large quantity of water and flush it down the drain.

---

3. http://odin.chemistry.uakron.edu/organic_lab/beil/
With seven very good color photos from the University of Akron, the Beilstein test is clearly demonstrated on this Web site. The dramatic differences among chlorine (green), bromine (blue-green), and iodine (blue) are quite clearly seen.

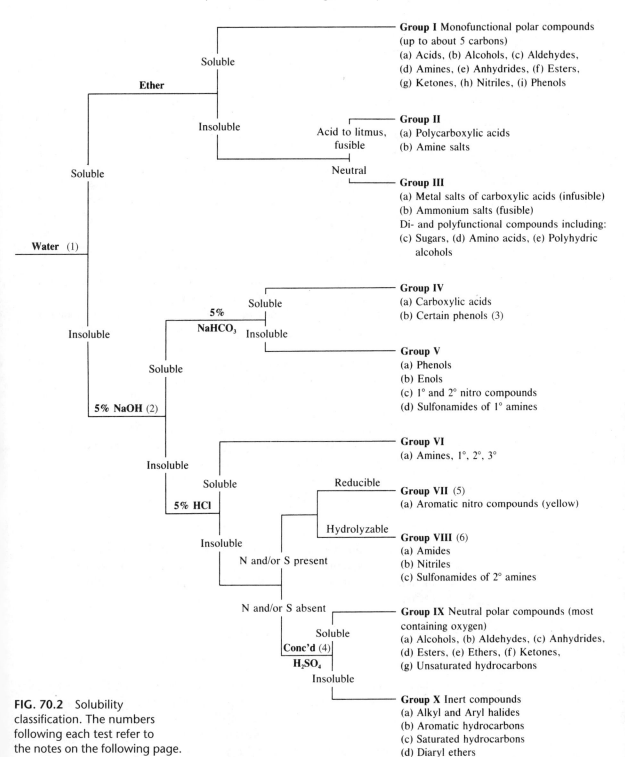

FIG. 70.2 Solubility classification. The numbers following each test refer to the notes on the following page.

Notes to Solubility Tests

See Fig. 70.2.

1. Groups I, II, III (soluble in water). Test the solution with pH paper. If the compound is not easily soluble in cold water, treat it as water insoluble but test with indicator paper.

2. If the substance is insoluble in water but dissolves partially in 5% sodium hydroxide, add more water; the sodium salts of some phenols are less soluble in alkali than in water. If the unknown is colored, be careful to distinguish between the *dissolving* and the *reacting* of the sample. Some quinones (colored) *react* with alkali and give highly colored solutions. Some phenols (colorless) *dissolve and then* become oxidized to give colored solutions. Some compounds (e.g., benzamide) are hydrolyzed with such ease that careful observation is required to distinguish them from acidic substances.

3. Nitrophenols (yellow), aldehydophenols, and polyhalophenols are sufficiently strongly acidic to react with sodium bicarbonate.

4. Oxygen- and nitrogen-containing compounds form oxonium and ammonium ions in concentrated sulfuric acid and dissolve.

5. On reduction in the presence of hydrochloric acid, these compounds form water-soluble amine hydrochlorides. Dissolve 250 mg of tin(II) chloride in 0.5 mL of concentrated hydrochloric acid, add 50 mg of the unknown, and warm. The material should dissolve with the disappearance of the color and give a clear solution when diluted with water.

6. Most amides can be hydrolyzed by short boiling with 10% sodium hydroxide solution; the acid dissolves with evolution of ammonia. Reflux 100 mg of the sample and 10% sodium hydroxide solution for 15–20 min. Test for the evolution of ammonia, which confirms the elementary analysis for nitrogen and establishes the presence of a nitrile or amide.

Classification Tests

After the unknown is assigned to one of the solubility groups (Fig. 70.2) on the basis of solubility tests, the possible type should be further narrowed by application of classification tests, e.g., for alcohols, or methyl ketones, or esters.

Complete Identification—Preparation of Derivatives

Once the unknown has been classified by functional group, the physical properties should be compared with those of representative members of the group (see tables at the end of this chapter). Usually, several possibilities present themselves, and the choice can be narrowed by preparation of derivatives. Select derivatives that distinguish most clearly among the possibilities.

Classification Tests

Group I. Monofunctional Polar Compounds (up to ca. 5 carbons)

(a) Acids

(Table 70.1; Derivatives, page 764)
No classification test is necessary. Carboxylic and sulfonic acids are detected by testing aqueous solutions with litmus. Acyl halides may hydrolyze during the solubility test.

(b) Alcohols

(Table 70.2; Derivatives, page 766)

Caution: Cr^{+6} dust is toxic.

Jones' Oxidation. Dissolve 5 mg of the unknown in 0.5 mL of pure acetone in a test tube, and add to this solution 1 small drop of Jones' reagent (chromic acid in sulfuric acid). A positive test is formation of a green color within 5 sec upon addition of the orange-yellow reagent to a primary or secondary alcohol. Aldehydes also give a positive test, but tertiary alcohols do not.
    Reagent: Dissolve/suspend 13.4 g of chromium trioxide in 11.5 mL of concentrated sulfuric acid, and add this carefully with stirring to enough water to bring the volume to 50 mL.

Cleaning Up   Place the test solution in the hazardous waste container.

Handle dioxane with care. It is a cancer-suspect agent.

Cerium(IV) Nitrate Test [Ammonium Hexanitratocerium(IV) Test]. Dissolve 15 mg of the unknown in a few drops of water or dioxane in a reaction tube. Add to this solution 0.25 mL of the reagent, and mix thoroughly. Alcohols cause the reagent to change from yellow to red.
    Reagent: Dissolve 22.5 g of ammonium hexanitratocerium(IV), $Ce(NH_4)_2(NO_3)_6$, in 56 mL of 2 N nitric acid.

Cleaning Up   The solution should be diluted with water and flushed down the drain.

(c) Aldehydes

(Table 70.3; Derivatives, page 767; Ch. 36)

2,4-Dinitrophenylhydrazones. All aldehydes and ketones readily form bright-yellow to dark-red 2,4-dinitrophenylhydrazones. Yellow derivatives are formed from isolated carbonyl groups and orange-red to red derivatives from aldehydes or ketones conjugated with double bonds or aromatic rings.

Dissolve 10 mg of the unknown in 0.5 mL of ethanol, and then add 0.75 mL of 2,4-dinitrophenylhydrazine reagent. Mix thoroughly and let sit for a few minutes. A yellow to red precipitate is a positive test.

Reagent: Dissolve 1.5 g of 2,4-dinitrophenylhydrazine in 7.5 mL of concentrated sulfuric acid. Add this solution, with stirring, to a mixture of 10 mL of water and 35 mL of ethanol.

Cleaning Up   Place the test solution in the hazardous waste container.

Schiff Test. Add 1 drop (30 mg) of the unknown to 1 mL of Schiff's reagent. A magenta color will appear within 10 min with aldehydes. Compare the color of your unknown with that of a known aldehyde.

Reagent: Prepare 50 mL of a 0.1% aqueous solution of *p*-rosaniline hydrochloride (fuchsin). Add 2 mL of a saturated aqueous solution of sodium bisulfite. After 1 h add 1 mL of concentrated hydrochloric acid.

Bisulfite Test. Follow the procedure in Chapter 36. Nearly all aldehydes and most methyl ketones form solid, water-soluble bisulfite addition products.

Destroy used Tollens' reagent promptly with nitric acid. It can form explosive fulminates.

Tollens' Test. Follow the procedure in Chapter 36. A positive test, deposition of a silver mirror, is given by most aldehydes, but not by ketones.

(d) Amides and Amines

(Tables 70.4, 70.5, and 70.6; Derivatives of amines, pages 769–771)

Hinsberg Test. Follow the procedure in Chapter 43, using benzenesulfonyl chloride to distinguish between primary, secondary, and tertiary amines.

(e) Anhydrides and Acid Halides

(Table 70.7; Derivatives, page 771) Anhydrides and acid halides will react with water to give acidic solutions, detectable with litmus paper. They easily form benzamides and acetamides.

Acidic Iron(III) Hydroxamate Test. With iron(III) chloride alone a number of substances give a color that can interfere with this test. Dissolve 2 drops (or about 30 mg) of the unknown in 1 mL of ethanol, and add 1 mL of 1 *N* hydrochloric acid followed by 1 drop of 10% aqueous iron(III) chloride solution. If any color except yellow appears you will find it difficult to interpret the results from the following test.

Add 2 drops (or about 30 mg) of the unknown to 0.5 mL of a 1 *N* solution of hydroxylamine hydrochloride in alcohol. Add 2 drops of 6 *M* hydrochloric acid to the mixture, warm it slightly for 2 min, and boil it for a few seconds. Cool the solution, and add 1 drop of 10% ferric chloride solution. A red-blue color is a positive test.

Cleaning Up   Neutralize the reaction mixture with sodium carbonate, dilute with water, and flush down the drain.

(f) Esters

(Table 70.8, page 772. Derivatives are prepared from component acid and alcohol obtained on hydrolysis.)

Esters, unlike anhydrides and acid halides, do not react with water to give acidic solutions and do not react with acidic hydroxylamine hydrochloride. They do, however, react with alkaline hydroxylamine.

Alkaline Iron(III) Hydroxamate Test. First test the unknown with iron(III) chloride alone. [See under Group I(e), Acidic Iron(III) Hydroxamate Test.]

To a solution of 1 drop (30 mg) of the unknown in 0.5 mL of 0.5 N hydroxylamine hydrochloride in ethanol, add 2 drops of 20% sodium hydroxide solution. Heat the solution to boiling, cool slightly, and add 1 mL of 1 N hydrochloric acid. If cloudiness develops add up to 1 mL of ethanol. Add 10% iron(III) chloride solution dropwise with thorough mixing. A red-blue color is a positive test. Compare your unknown with a known ester.

Cleaning Up   Neutralize the solutions with sodium carbonate, dilute with water, and flush down the drain.

(g) Ketones

(Table 70.14; Derivatives, page 776)

2,4-Dinitrophenylhydrazone. See under Group I(c), Aldehydes. All ketones react with 2,4-dinitrophenylhydrazine reagent.

Iodoform Test for Methyl Ketones. Follow the procedure in Chapter 36.

A positive iodoform test is given by substances containing the $CH_3\overset{\overset{\displaystyle O}{\displaystyle \|}}{C}-$ group or by compounds easily oxidized to this group, e.g., CH_3COR, CH_3CHOHR, CH_3CH_2OH, CH_3CHO, $RCOCH_2COR$. The test is negative for compounds of the structure CH_3COOR, CH_3CONHR, and other compounds of similar structure that give acetic acid on hydrolysis. It is also negative for $CH_3COCH_2CO_2R$, CH_3COCH_2CN, $CH_3COCH_2NO_2$.

Bisulfite Test. Follow the procedure in Chapter 36. Aliphatic methyl ketones and unhindered cyclic ketones form bisulfite addition products. Methyl aryl ketones, such as acetophenone, $C_6H_5COCH_3$, fail to react.

(h) Nitriles

(Table 70.15, page 777. Derivatives prepared from the carboxylic acid obtained by hydrolysis.)

At high temperature nitriles (and amides) are converted to hydroxamic acids by hydroxylamine:

$$RCN + 2\,H_2NOH \longrightarrow RCONHOH + NH_3$$

The hydroxamic acid forms a red-blue complex with iron(III) ion. The unknown must first give a negative test with hydroxylamine at lower temperature [Group I(f), Alkaline Iron(III) Hydroxamate Test] before trying this test.

Hydroxamic Acid Test for Nitriles (and Amides). To 1 mL of a 1 *M* hydroxylamine hydrochloride solution in propylene glycol add 15 mg of the unknown dissolved in the minimum amount of propylene glycol. Then add 0.5 mL of 1 *N* potassium hydroxide in propylene glycol, and boil the mixture for 2 min. Cool the mixture, and add 0.1 to 0.25 mL of 10% iron(III) chloride solution. A red-blue color is a positive test for almost all nitrile and amide groups, although benzanilide fails to give a positive test.

Cleaning Up   Since the quantity of material is extremely small, the test solution can be diluted with water and flushed down the drain.

(i) Phenols

(Table 70.17, page 778)

Iron(III) Chloride Test. Dissolve 15 mg of the unknown compound in 0.5 mL of water or water-alcohol mixture, and add 1 or 2 drops of 1% iron(III) chloride solution. A red, blue, green, or purple color is a positive test.

Cleaning Up   Since the quantity of material is extremely small, the test solution can be diluted with water and flushed down the drain.

A more sensitive test for phenols consists of dissolving or suspending 15 mg of the unknown in 0.5 mL of chloroform and adding 1 drop of a solution made by dissolving 0.1 g of iron(III) chloride in 10 mL of chloroform. (*Caution!* CHCl$_3$ is a carcinogen.) Addition of a drop of pyridine, with stirring, will produce a color if phenols or enols are present.

Group II. Water-Soluble Acidic Salts, Insoluble in Ether
Amine Salts

[Table 70.5 (1° and 2° amines), page 779; Table 70.6 (3° amines), page 771] The free amine can be liberated by addition of base and extraction into ether. Following evaporation of the ether, the Hinsberg test, Group I(d), can be applied to determine if the compound is a primary, secondary, or tertiary amine.

The acid iron(III) hydroxamate test, Group I(d), can be applied directly to the amine salt.

Group III. Water-Soluble Neutral Compounds, Insoluble in Ether

(a) Metal Salts of Carboxylic Acids

(Table 70.1, carboxylic acids; Derivatives, page 764)

The free acid can be liberated by addition of acid and extraction into an appropriate solvent, after which the carboxylic acid can be characterized by mp or bp before proceeding to prepare a derivative.

(b) Ammonium Salts

(Table 70.1, carboxylic acids; Derivatives, page 764)

Ammonium salts on treatment with alkali liberate ammonia, which can be detected by its odor and the fact that it will turn red litmus to blue. A more sensitive test utilizes the copper(II) ion, which is blue in the presence of ammonia [see Group VIII a(i)]. Ammonium salts will not give a positive hydroxamic acid test (Ih) as given by amides.

(c) Sugars

See Chapter 36 for Tollens' test and Chapter 63 for phenylosazone formation.

(d) Amino Acids

Add 2 mg of the suspected amino acid to 1 mL of ninhydrin reagent, boil for 20 sec, and note the color. A blue color is a positive test.

Reagent: Dissolve 0.2 g of ninhydrin in 50 mL of water.

Cleaning Up   Since the quantity of material is extremely small, the test solution can be diluted with water and flushed down the drain.

(e) Polyhydric Alcohols

(Table 70.2; Derivatives, page 766)

Periodic Acid Test for vic-Glycols.[4] Vicinal glycols (hydroxyl groups on adjacent carbon atoms) can be detected by reaction with periodic acid. In addition to 1,2-glycols, a positive test is given by α-hydroxy aldehydes, α-hydroxy ketones, α-hydroxy acids, and α-amino alcohols, as well as 1,2-diketones.

To 2 mL of periodic acid reagent add 1 drop (no more) of concentrated nitric acid and shake. Then add 1 drop or a small crystal of the unknown. Shake for 15 sec, and add 1 or 2 drops of 5% aqueous silver nitrate solution. Instantaneous formation of a white precipitate is a positive test.

---

4. R. L. Shriner, R. C. Fuson, D. Y. Curtin, and T. C. Morill. *The Systematic Identification of Organic Compounds,* 6th ed., John Wiley & Sons, Inc., New York, 1980.

Reagent: Dissolve 0.25 g of paraperiodic acid (H_5IO_6) in 50 mL of water.

Cleaning Up   Since the quantity of material is extremely small, the test solution can be diluted with water and flushed down the drain.

Group IV. Certain Carboxylic Acids, Certain Phenols, and Sulfonamides of 1° Amines

(a) Carboxylic Acids

Solubility in both 5% sodium hydroxide and sodium bicarbonate is usually sufficient to characterize this class of compounds. Addition of mineral acid should regenerate the carboxylic acid. The neutralization equivalent can be obtained by titrating a known quantity of the acid (ca. 50 mg) dissolved in water-ethanol with 0.1 *N* sodium hydroxide to a phenolphthalein end point.

(b) Phenols

Negatively substituted phenols such as nitrophenols, aldehydrophenols, and polyhalophenols are sufficiently acidic to dissolve in 5% sodium bicarbonate. See Group I(i) for the iron(III) chloride test for phenols; however, this test is not completely reliable for these acidic phenols.

Group V. Acidic Compounds, Insoluble in Bicarbonate

(a) Phenols

See Group I(i).

(b) Enols

See Group I(i).

(c) 1° and 2° Nitro Compounds

(Table 70.16; Derivatives, page 717)

Iron(II) Hydroxide Test. To a small vial (capacity (1–2 mL) add 5 mg of the unknown to 0.5 mL of freshly prepared ferrous sulfate solution. Add 0.4 mL of a 2 *N* solution of potassium hydroxide in methanol, cap the vial, and shake it. The appearance of a red-brown precipitate of iron(III) hydroxide within 1 min is a positive test. Almost all nitro compounds give a positive test within 30 sec.

Reagents: Dissolve 2.5 g of ferrous ammonium sulfate in 50 mL of deoxygenated (by boiling) water. Add 0.2 mL of concentrated sulfuric acid and a piece of iron to prevent oxidation of the ferrous ion. Keep the bottle tightly stoppered. The potassium hydroxide solution is prepared by dissolving 5.6 g of potassium hydroxide in 50 mL of methanol.

Cleaning Up   Since the quantity of material is extremely small, the test solution can be diluted with water and flushed down the drain after neutralization with dilute hydrochloric acid.

(d) Sulfonamides of 1° Amines

An extremely sensitive test for sulfonamides (Feigl, *Spot Tests in Organic Analysis*) consists of placing a drop of a suspension or solution of the unknown on sulfonamide test paper followed by a drop of 0.5% hydrochloric acid. A red color is a positive test for sulfonamides.

   The test paper is prepared by dipping filter paper into a mixture of equal volumes of a 1% aqueous solution of sodium nitrite and a 1% methanolic solution of *N,N*-dimethyl-1-naphthylamine. Allow the filter paper to dry in the dark.

Cleaning Up   Place the test paper in the solid hazardous waste container.

CAUTION: *Handle N,N-dimethyl-1-naphthylamine with care. As a class, aromatic amines are quite toxic and many are carcinogenic. Handle them all with care—in a hood if possible.*

Group VI. Basic Compounds, Insoluble in Water, Soluble in Acid

Amines

See Group I(d).

Group VII. Reducible, Neutral *N*- and *S*-Containing Compounds

Aromatic Nitro Compounds

See Group V(c).

Group VIII. Hydrolyzable, Neutral *N*- and *S*-Containing Compounds (identified through the acid and amine obtained on hydrolysis)

(a) Amides

Unsubstituted amides are detected by the hydroxamic acid test, Group I(h).

(1) Unsubstituted Amides. Upon hydrolysis, unsubstituted amides liberate ammonia, which can be detected by reaction with cupric ion [Group III(b)].

   To 1 mL of 20% sodium hydroxide solution, add 25 mg of the unknown. Cover the mouth of the reaction tube with a piece of filter paper moistened with a few drops of 10% copper(II) sulfate solution. Boil for 1 min. A blue color on the filter paper is a positive test for ammonia.

Cleaning Up Neutralize the test solution with 10% hydrochloric acid, dilute with water, and flush down the drain.

(2) Substituted Amides. The identification of substituted amides is not easy. There are no completely general tests for the substituted amide groups and hydrolysis is often difficult.

Hot sodium hydroxide solution is corrosive; use care.

Hydrolyze the amide by refluxing 250 mg with 2.5 mL of 20% sodium hydroxide for 20 min. Isolate the primary or secondary amine produced, by extraction into ether, and identify as described under Group I(d). Liberate the acid by acidification of the residue, isolate by filtration or extraction, and characterize by bp or mp and the mp of an appropriate derivative.

Cleaning Up The test solution can be diluted with water and flushed down the drain.

Use care in shaking concentrated sulfuric acid.

(3) Anilides. Add 50 mg of the unknown to 1.5 mL of concentrated sulfuric acid. Carefully stopper the reaction tube with a rubber stopper, and shake vigorously. (*Caution!*) Add 25 mg of finely powdered potassium dichromate. A blue-pink color is a positive test for an anilide that does not have substituents on the ring (e.g., acetanilide).

Dichromate dust is carcinogenic, when inhaled. Cr^{+6} is not a carcinogen when applied to the skin or ingested.

Cleaning Up Carefully add the solution to water, neutralize with sodium carbonate, and flush down the drain.

(b) Nitriles

See Group I(h).

(c) Sulfonamides

See Group V(d).

Group IX. Neutral Polar Compounds, Insoluble in Dilute Hydrochloric Acid, Soluble in Concentrated Sulfuric Acid (most compounds containing oxygen)

(a) Alcohols

See Group I(b).

(b) Aldehydes

See Group I(c).

(c) Anhydrides

See Group I(e).

(d) Esters

See Group I(f).

(e) Ethers

(See Table 70.9, page 773)
Ethers are very unreactive. Care must be used to distinguish ethers from those hydrocarbons that are soluble in concentrated sulfuric acid.

Fe[Fe(SCN)$_6$]

**Iron(III) hexathiocyanato-
ferrate(III)**

Ferrox Test. In a dry test tube grind together, with a stirring rod, a crystal of iron(III) ammonium sulfate (or iron(III) chloride) and a crystal of potassium thiocyanate. Iron(III) hexathiocyanatoferrate(III) will adhere to the stirring rod. In a clean tube place 3 drops of a liquid unknown or a saturated toluene solution of a solid unknown, and stir with the rod. The salt will dissolve if the unknown contains oxygen to give a red-purple color, but it will not dissolve in hydrocarbons or halocarbons. Diphenyl ether does not give a positive test.

Alkyl ethers are generally soluble in concentrated sulfuric acid; alkyl aryl and diaryl ethers are not soluble.

Cleaning Up   Place the mixture in the hazardous waste container.

(f) Ketones

(See page 776).

(g) Unsaturated Hydrocarbons

(Table 70.12, page 774)

Use care in working with the bromine solution

Bromine in Carbon Tetrachloride. Dissolve 1 drop (20 mg) of the unknown in 0.5 mL of carbon tetrachloride. Add a 2% solution of bromine in carbon tetrachloride dropwise with shaking. If more than 2 drops of bromine solution are required to give a permanent red color, unsaturation is indicated. The bromine solution must be fresh.

Cleaning Up   Place the mixture in the halogenated solvents container.

Potassium Permanganate Solution. Dissolve 1 drop (20 mg) of the unknown in reagent grade acetone and add a 1% aqueous solution of potassium permanganate dropwise with shaking. If more than one drop of reagent is required to give a purple color to the solution, unsaturation or an easily oxidized functional group is present. Run parallel tests on pure acetone and, as usual, a compound known to be an alkene.

Cleaning Up   The solution should be diluted with water and flushed down the drain.

Group X. Inert Compounds. Insoluble in Concentrated Sulfuric Acid

(a) Alkyl and Aryl Halides

(Table 70.10; Derivatives, page 773)

Do not waste silver nitrate.

Alcoholic Silver Nitrate. Add 1 drop of the unknown (or saturated solution of 10 mg of unknown in ethanol) to 0.2 mL of a saturated solution of silver nitrate. A precipitate that forms within 2 min is a positive test for an alkyl bromide, or iodide, or a tertiary alkyl chloride, as well as allyl halides.

If no precipitate forms within 2 min, heat the solution to boiling. A precipitate of silver chloride will form from primary and secondary alkyl chlorides. Aryl halides and vinyl halides will not react.

Cleaning Up   The quantity of material is extremely small. It can be diluted with water and flushed down the drain.

(b) Aromatic Hydrocarbons

(Table 70.13; Derivatives, page 775)
Aromatic hydrocarbons are best identified and characterized by UV and NMR spectroscopy, but the Friedel-Crafts reaction produces a characteristic color with certain aromatic hydrocarbons.

Keep moisture away from aluminum chloride.
Caution: Chloroform is carcinogenic. Carry out this test in a hood.

Friedel-Crafts Test. Heat a test tube containing about 50 mg of anhydrous aluminum chloride in a hot flame to sublime the salt up onto the sides of the tube. Add a solution of about 10 mg of the unknown dissolved in a drop of chloroform to the cool tube in such a way that it comes into contact with the sublimed aluminum chloride. Note the color that appears.

Nonaromatic compounds fail to give a color with aluminum chloride, benzene and its derivatives give orange or red colors, naphthalenes a blue or purple color, biphenyls a purple color, phenanthrene a purple color, and anthracene a green color.

Cleaning Up   Place the test mixture in the halogenated organic solvents container.

(c) Saturated Hydrocarbons

Saturated hydrocarbons are best characterized by NMR and IR spectroscopy, but they can be distinguished from aromatic hydrocarbons by the Friedel-Crafts test [Group X(b)].

(d) Diaryl Ethers

Because they are so inert, diaryl ethers are difficult to detect and may be mistaken for aromatic hydrocarbons. They do not give a positive Ferrox test (see

p. 757) for ethers and do not dissolve in concentrated sulfuric acid. Their infrared spectra, however, are characterized by an intense C—O single-bond, stretching vibration in the region 1270–1230 cm^{-1}.

Derivatives

1. Acids

(Table 70.1)

CAUTION: p-Toluidine is a highly toxic irritant.

***p*-Toluidides and Anilides.** Reflux a mixture of the acid (100 mg) and thionyl chloride (0.5 mL) in a reaction tube for 0.5 h. Cool the reaction mixture, and add 0.25 g of aniline or *p*-toluidine in 3 mL of toluene. Warm the mixture on the steam bath for 2 min, and then wash with 1-mL portions of water, 5% hydrochloric acid, 5% sodium hydroxide, and water. The toluene is dried briefly over anhydrous calcium chloride pellets and evaporated in the hood; the derivative is recrystallized from water or ethanol-water.

Cleaning Up   The combined aqueous layers can be diluted with water and flushed down the drain. The drying agent should be placed in the hazardous waste container.

Thionyl chloride is an irritant. Use it in a hood.

Amides. Reflux a mixture of the acid (100 mg) and thionyl chloride (0.5 mL) for 0.5 h. Transfer the cool reaction mixture into 1.4 mL of ice-cold concentrated ammonia. Stir until reaction is complete, collect the product by filtration, and recrystallize it from water or water-ethanol.

Cleaning Up   Neutralize the aqueous filtrate with 10% hydrochloric acid, dilute with water, and flush down the drain.

2. Alcohols

(Table 70.2)

Note to instructor: Check to ascertain that the 3,5-dinitrobenzoyl chloride has not hydrolyzed. The mp should be >65°C. Reported mp is 68–69°C.

3,5-Dinitrobenzoates. Gently boil 100 mg of 3,5-dinitrobenzoyl chloride and 25 mg of the alcohol for 5 min. Cool the mixture, pulverize any solid that forms, and add 2 mL of 2% sodium carbonate solution. Continue to grind and stir the solid with the sodium carbonate solution (to remove 3,5-dinitrobenzoic acid) for about a minute, filter, and wash the crystals with water. Dissolve the product in about 2.5–3 mL of hot ethanol, add water to the cloud point, and allow crystallization to proceed. Wash the 3,5-dinitrobenzoate with water-alcohol and dry.

Cleaning Up   The aqueous filtrate should be diluted with water and flushed down the drain.

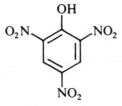

Phenyl isocyanate

CAUTION: *Lachrymator*

Phenylurethanes. Mix 100 mg of anhydrous alcohol (or phenol) and 100 mg of phenyl isocyanate (or α-naphthylurethane), and heat on the steam bath for 5 min. (If the unknown is a phenol add a drop of pyridine to the reaction mixture.) Cool, add about 1 mL of ligroin, heat to dissolve the product, filter hot to remove a small amount of diphenylurea which usually forms, and cool the filtrate in ice, with scratching, to induce crystallization.

Cleaning Up   The ligroin filtrate should be placed in the organic solvents container.

3. Aldehydes

(Table 70.3)

Semicarbazones. See Chapter 36. Use 0.5 mL of the stock solution and an estimated 1 mmol of the unknown aldehyde (or ketone).

2,4-Dinitrophenylhydrazones. See Chapter 36. Use 1 mL of the stock solution of 0.1 *M* 2,4-dinitrophenylhydrazine and an estimated 0.1 mmol of the unknown aldehyde (or ketone).

4. Primary and Secondary Amines

(Table 70.5)

Benzamides. Add about 0.25 g of benzoyl chloride in small portions with vigorous shaking and cooling to a suspension of 0.5 mmol of the unknown amine in 0.5 mL of 10% aqueous sodium hydroxide solution. After about 10 min of shaking the mixture is made pH 8 (pH paper) with dilute hydrochloric acid. The lumpy product is removed by filtration, washed thoroughly with water, and recrystallized from ethanol-water.

Cleaning Up   The filtrate should be diluted with water and flushed down the drain.

Picric acid
(2,4,6-Trinitrophenol)

Handle pure acid with care (explosive). It is sold as a moist solid. Do not allow to dry out.

Picrates. Add a solution of 30 mg of the unknown in 1 mL of ethanol (or 1 mL of a saturated solution of the unknown) to 1 mL of a saturated solution of picric acid (2,4,6-trinitrophenol, a strong acid) in ethanol, and heat the solution to boiling. Cool slowly, remove the picrate by filtration, and wash with a small amount of ethanol. Recrystallization is not usually necessary; in the case of hydrocarbon picrates the product is often too unstable to be recrystallized.

Cleaning Up   See page 508 for the treatment of solutions containing picric acid.

Acetamides. Reflux about 0.5 mmol of the unknown with 0.2 mL of acetic anhydride for 5 min, cool, and dilute the reaction mixture with 2.5 mL of water.

Initiate crystallization by scratching, if necessary. Remove the crystals by filtration, and wash thoroughly with dilute hydrochloric acid to remove unreacted amine. Recrystallize the derivative from alcohol-water. Amines of low basicity, e.g., p-nitroaniline, should be refluxed for 30–60 min with 1 mL of pyridine as a solvent. The pyridine is removed by shaking the reaction mixture with 5 mL of 2% sulfuric acid solution; the product is isolated by filtration and recrystallized.

Acetic anhydride is corrosive. Work with this in a hood.

Cleaning Up   The filtrate from the usual reaction should be neutralized with sodium carbonate. It can then be diluted with water and flushed down the drain. If pyridine is used as the solvent, the filtrate should be neutralized with sodium carbonate and extracted with ligroin. The ligroin/pyridine goes in the organic solvents container while the aqueous layer can be diluted with water and flushed down the drain.

5. Tertiary Amines
(Table 70.6)

Picrates. See under Primary and Secondary Amines.

$$R_3N + CH_3I$$
$$\downarrow$$
$$R_3\overset{+}{N}CH_3I^-$$

Methiodides. Reflux 100 mg of the amine and 100 mg of methyl iodide for 5 min on the steam bath. Cool, scratch to induce crystallization, and recrystallize the product from ethyl alcohol or ethyl acetate.

Methyl iodide is a cancer-suspect agent.

Cleaning Up   Since the filtrate may contain some methyl iodide, it should be placed in the halogenated solvents container.

6. Anhydrides and Acid Chlorides
(Table 70.7)

Acids. Reflux 40 mg of the acid chloride or anhydride with 1 mL of 5% sodium carbonate solution for 20 min or less. Extract unreacted starting material with 1 mL of ether, if necessary, and acidify the reaction mixture with dilute sulfuric acid to liberate the carboxylic acid.

Cleaning Up   Ether goes in the organic solvents container, and the aqueous layer should be diluted with water and flushed down the drain.

Amides. Since the acid chloride (or anhydride) is already present, simply mix the unknown (50 mg) and 0.7 mL of ice-cold concentrated ammonia until reaction is complete, collect the product by filtration, and recrystallize it from water or ethanol-water.

Cleaning Up   Neutralize the filtrate with dilute hydrochloric acid, and flush it down the drain.

Anilides. Reflux 40 mg of the acid halide or anhydride with 100 mg of aniline in 2 mL of toluene for 10 min. Wash the toluene solution with 5-mL portions each of water, 5% hydrochloric acid, 5% sodium hydroxide, and again with water. The toluene solution is dried over anhydrous calcium chloride and evaporated; the anilide is recrystallized from water or ethanol-water.

Cleaning Up   The combined aqueous layers are diluted with water and flushed down the drain. The sodium sulfate should be placed in the aromatic amines hazardous waste container.

7. Aryl Halides

(Table 70.11)

Nitration. Add 0.4 mL of concentrated sulfuric acid to 100 mg of the aryl halide (or aromatic compound) and stir. Add 0.4 mL of concentrated nitric acid dropwise with stirring and shaking while cooling the reaction mixture in water. Then heat and shake the reaction mixture in a water bath at about 50°C for 15 min, pour into 2 mL of cold water, and collect the product by filtration. Recrystallize from methanol to constant melting point.

To nitrate unreactive compounds, use fuming nitric acid in place of concentrated nitric acid.

Use great care when working with fuming nitric acid.

Cleaning Up   Dilute the filtrate with water, neutralize with sodium carbonate, and flush the solution down the drain.

Sidechain Oxidation Products. Dissolve 0.2 g of sodium dichromate in 0.6 mL of water, and add 0.4 mL of concentrated sulfuric acid. Add 50 mg of the unknown and boil for 30 min. Cool, add 0.4–0.6 mL of water, and then remove the carboxylic acid by filtration. Wash the crystals with water and recrystallize from methanol-water.

Cleaning Up   Place the filtrate from the reaction, after neutralization with sodium carbonate, in the hazardous waste container.

8. Hydrocarbons: Aromatic

(Table 70.13)

Nitration. See preceding, under Aryl Halides.

Picrates. See preceding, under Primary and Secondary Amines.

9. Ketones

(Table 70.14)

Semicarbazones and 2,4-dinitrophenylhydrazones. See preceding directions under Aldehydes.

10. Nitro Compounds

(Table 70.16)

Reduction to Amines. Place 100 mg of the unknown in a reaction tube, add 0.2 g of tin, and then—in portions—2 mL of 10% hydrochloric acid. Reflux for 30 min, add 1 mL of water, then add slowly, with good cooling, sufficient 40% sodium hydroxide solution to dissolve the tin hydroxide. Extract the reaction mixture with three 1-mL portions of *t*-butyl methyl ether, dry the ether extract over anhydrous calcium chloride pellets, wash the drying agent with ether, and evaporate the ether to leave the amine. Determine the boiling point or melting point of the amine and then convert it into a benzamide or acetamide as described under the section on Primary and Secondary Amines.

Cleaning Up   Neutralize the aqueous layer with 10% hydrochloric acid, remove the tin hydroxide by filtration, and discard it in the nonhazardous solid waste container. The filtrate should be diluted with water and flushed down the drain. Calcium chloride, after the ether evaporates from it, can be placed in the nonhazardous waste container.

11. Phenols

(Table 70.17)

α-Naphthylurethane. Follow the procedure for preparation of a phenylurethane under the Alcohols section.

Use great care when working with bromine. Should any touch the skin wash it off with copious quantities of water. Work in a hood and wear disposable gloves.

Bromo Derivative. In a reaction tube dissolve 160 mg of potassium bromide in 1 mL of water. *Carefully* add 100 mg of bromine. In a separate flask dissolve 20 mg of the phenol in 0.2 mL of methanol, and add 0.2 mL of water. Add about 0.3 mL of the bromine solution with swirling (hood); continue the addition of bromine until the yellow color of unreacted bromine persists. Add 0.6–0.8 mL of water to the reaction mixture, and shake vigorously. Remove the product by filtration, and wash well with water. Recrystallize from methanol-water.

Cleaning Up   Any unreacted bromine should be destroyed by adding sodium bisulfite solution dropwise until the color dissipates. The solution is then diluted with water and flushed down the drain.

TABLE 70.1   Acids

			Derivatives		
			p-Toluidide[a]	*Anilide*[b]	*Amide*[c]
bp	*mp*	*Compound*	*mp*	*mp*	*mp*
101		Formic acid	53	47	43
118		Acetic acid	126	106	79
139		Acrylic acid	141	104	85
141		Propionic acid	124	103	81
162		*n*-Butyric acid	72	95	115
163		Methacrylic acid		87	102
165		Pyruvic acid	109	104	124
185		Valeric acid	70	63	106
186		2-Methylvaleric acid	80	95	79
194		Dichloroacetic acid	153	118	98
202–203		Hexanoic acid	75	95	101
237		Octanoic acid	70	57	107
254		Nonanoic acid	84	57	99
	31–32	Decanoic acid	78	70	108
	43–45	Lauric acid	87	78	100
	47–49	Bromoacetic acid		131	91
	47–49	Hydrocinnamic acid	135	92	105
	54–55	Myristic acid	93	84	103
	54–58	Trichloroacetic acid	113	97	141
	61–62	Chloroacetic acid	162	137	121
	61–62.5	Palmitic acid	98	90	106
	67–69	Stearic acid	102	95	109
	68–69	3,3-Dimethylacrylic acid		126	107
	71–73	Crotonic acid	132	118	158
	77–78.5	Phenylacetic acid	136	118	156
	101–102	Oxalic acid dihydrate		257	400 (dec)
	98–102	Azelaic acid (nonanedioic)	164 (di)	107 (mono)	93 (mono)
				186 (di)	175 (di)
	103–105	*o*-Toluic acid	144	125	142
	108–110	*m*-Toluic acid	118	126	94
	119–121	DL-Mandelic acid	172	151	133
	122–123	Benzoic acid	158	163	130
	127–128	2-Benzoylbenzoic acid		195	165
	129–130	2-Furoic acid	107	123	143
	131–133	DL-Malic acid	178 (mono)	155 (mono)	
			207 (di)	198 (di)	163 (di)
	131–134	Sebacic acid	201	122 (mono)	170 (mono)
				200 (di)	210 (di)
					(*continued*)

a. For preparation, see page 759.
b. For preparation, see page 759.
c. For preparation, see page 759.

TABLE 70.1 *continued*

			Derivatives		
			p-Toluidide[a]	Anilide[b]	Amide[c]
bp	mp	Compound	mp	mp	mp
	134–135	*E*-Cinnamic acid	168	153	147
	134–136	Maleic acid	142 (di)	198 (mono)	260 (di)
				187 (di)	
	135–137	Malonic acid	86 (mono)	132 (mono)	
			253 (di)	230 (di)	
	138–140	2-Chlorobenzoic acid	131	118	139
	140–142	3-Nitrobenzoic acid	162	155	143
	144–148	Anthranilic acid	151	131	109
	147–149	Diphenylacetic acid	172	180	167
	152–153	Adipic acid	239	151 (mono)	125 (mono)
				241 (di)	220 (di)
	153–154	Citric acid	189 (tri)	199 (tri)	210 (tri)
	157–159	4-Chlorophenoxyacetic acid		125	133
	158–160	Salicylic acid	156	136	142
	163–164	Trimethylacetic acid		127	178
	164–166	5-Bromosalicylic acid		222	232
	166–167	Itaconic acid		190	191 (di)
	171–174	D-Tartaric acid		180 (mono)	171 (mono)
				264 (di)	196 (di)
	179–182	3,4-Dimethoxybenzoic acid		154	164
	180–182	4-Toluic acid	160	145	160
	182–185	4-Anisic acid	186	169	167
	187–190	Succinic acid	180 (mono)	143 (mono)	157 (mono)
			255 (di)	230 (di)	260 (di)
	201–203	3-Hydroxybenzoic acid	163	157	170
	203–206	3,5-Dinitrobenzoic acid		234	183
	210–211	Phthalic acid	150 (mono)	169 (mono)	149 (mono)
			201 (di)	253 (di)	220 (di)
	214–215	4-Hydroxybenzoic acid	204	197	162
	225–227	2,4-Dihydroxybenzoic acid		126	228
	236–239	Nicotinic acid	150	132	128
	239–241	4-Nitrobenzoic acid	204	211	201
	299–300	Fumaric acid		233 (mono)	270 (mono)
				314 (di)	266 (di)
	>300	Terephthalic acid		334	

a. For preparation, see page 759.
b. For preparation, see page 759.
c. For preparation, see page 759.

TABLE 70.2   Alcohols

| | | | Derivatives | |
| | | | 3,5-Dinitrobenzoate[a] | Phenylurethane[b] |
bp	mp	Compound	mp	mp
65		Methanol	108	47
78		Ethanol	93	52
82		2-Propanol	123	88
83		*t*-Butyl alcohol	142	136
96–98		Allyl alcohol	49	70
97		1-Propanol	74	57
98		2-Butanol	76	65
102		2-Methyl-2-butanol	116	42
104		2-Methyl-3-butyn-2-ol	112	
108		2-Methyl-1-propanol	87	86
114–115		Propargyl alcohol		63
114–115		3-Pentanol	101	48
118		1-Butanol	64	61
118–119		2-Pentanol	62	oil
123		3-Methyl-3-pentanol	96(62)	43
129		2-Chloroethanol	95	51
130		2-Methyl-1-butanol	70	31
132		4-Methyl-2-pentanol	65	143
136–138		1-Pentanol	46	46
139–140		Cyclopentanol	115	132
140		2,4-Dimethyl-3-pentanol	75	95
146		2-Ethyl-1-butanol	51	
151		2,2,2-Trichloroethanol	142	87
157		1-Hexanol	58	42
160–161		Cyclohexanol	113	82
170		Furfuryl alcohol	80	45
176		1-Heptanol	47	60(68)
178		2-Octanol	32	oil
178		Tetrahydrofurfuryl alcohol	83	61
183–184		2,3-Butanediol		201 (di)
183–186		2-Ethyl-1-hexanol		34
187		1,2-Propanediol		153 (di)
194–197		Linaloöl		66
195		1-Octanol	61	74
196–198		Ethylene glycol	169	157 (di)
204		1,3-Butanediol		122
203–205		Benzyl alcohol	113	77
204		1-Phenylethanol	95	92
219–221		2-Phenylethanol	108	78
230		1,4-Butanediol		183 (mono)
231		1-Decanol	57	59

(*continued*)

a. For preparation, see page 759.
b. For preparation, see page 759.

TABLE 70.2   *continued*

			Derivatives	
			3,5-Dinitrobenzoate[a]	*Phenylurethane*[b]
bp	*mp*	*Compound*	*mp*	*mp*
259		4-Methoxybenzyl alcohol		92
	33–35	Cinnamyl alcohol	121	90
	38–40	1-Tetradecanol	67	74
	48–50	1-Hexadecanol	66	73
	58–60	1-Octadecanol	77(66)	79
	66–67	Benzhydrol	141	139
	147	Cholesterol	195	168

a. For preparation, see page 759.
b. For preparation, see page 759.

TABLE 70.3   Aldehydes

			Derivatives	
			Semicarbazone[a]	*2,4-Dinitrophenylhydrazone*[b]
bp	*mp*	*Compound*	*mp*	*mp*
21		Acetaldehyde	162	168
46–50		Propionaldehyde	89(154)	148
63		Isobutyraldehyde	125(119)	187(183)
75		Butyraldehyde	95(106)	123
90–92		3-Methylbutanal	107	123
98		Chloral	90	131
104		Crotonaldehyde	199	190
117		2-Ethylbutanal	99	95(130)
153		Heptaldehyde	109	108
162		2-Furaldehyde	202	212(230)
163		2-Ethylhexanal	254	114(120)
179		Benzaldehyde	222	237
195		Phenylacetaldehyde	153	121(110)
197		Salicylaldehyde	231	248
204–205		4-Tolualdehyde	234(215)	232
209–215		2-Chlorobenzaldehyde	146(229)	213
247		2-Ethoxybenzaldehyde	219	
248		4-Anisaldehyde	210	253

(continued)

a. For preparation, see page 431.
b. For preparation, see page 429.

TABLE 70.3   *continued*

			Derivatives	
			Semicarbazone[a]	*2,4-Dinitrophenylhydrazone*[b]
bp	*mp*	*Compound*	*mp*	*mp*
250–252		*E*-Cinnamaldehyde	215	255
	33–34	1-Naphthaldehyde	221	254
	37–39	2-Anisaldehyde	215	254
	42–45	3,4-Dimethoxybenzaldehyde	177	261
	44–47	4-Chlorobenzaldehyde	230	254
	57–59	3-Nitrobenzaldehyde	246	293
	81–83	Vanillin	230	271

a. For preparation, see page 431.
b. For preparation, see page 429.

TABLE 70.4   Amides

bp	mp	Name of Compound	mp	Name of Compound
153		*N,N*-Dimethylformamide	127–129	Isobutyramide
164–166		*N,N*-Dimethylacetamide	128–129	Benzamide
210		Formamide	130–133	Nicotinamide
243–244		*N*-Methylformanilide	177–179	4-Chloroacetanilide
	26–28	*N*-Methylacetamide		
	79–81	Acetamide		
	109–111	Methacrylamide		
	113–115	Acetanilide		
	116–118	2-Chloroacetamide		

TABLE 70.5   Primary and Secondary Amines

			Derivatives		
			Benzamide[a]	Picrate[b]	Acetamide[c]
bp	mp	Compound	mp	mp	mp
33–34		Isopropylamine	71	165	
46		t-Butylamine	134	198	
48		n-Propylamine	84	135	
53		Allylamine		140	
55		Diethylamine	42	155	
63		s-Butylamine	76	139	
64–71		Isobutylamine	57	150	
78		n-Butylamine	42	151	
84		Diisopropylamine		140	
87–88		Pyrrolidine	oil	112	
106		Piperidine	48	152	
111		Di-n-propylamine	oil	75	
118		Ethylenediamine	244 (di)	233	172 (di)
129		Morpholine	75	146	
137–139		Diisobutylamine		121	86
145–146		Furfurylamine		150	
149		N-Methylcyclohexylamine	85	170	
159		Di-n-butylamine	oil	59	
182–185		Benzylamine	105	199	60
184		Aniline	163	198	114
196		N-Methylaniline	63	145	102
199–200		2-Toluidine	144	213	110
203–204		3-Toluidine	125	200	65
205		N-Ethylaniline	60	138(132)	54
208–210		2-Chloroaniline	99	134	87
210		2-Ethylaniline	147	194	111
216		2,6-Dimethylaniline	168	180	177
218		2,4-Dimethylaniline	192	209	133
218		2,5-Dimethylaniline	140	171	139
221		N-Ethyl-m-toluidine	72		
225		2-Anisidine	60(84)	200	85
230		3-Chloroaniline	120	177	72(78)
231–233		2-Phenetidine	104		79
241		4-Chloro-2-methylaniline	142		140
242		3-Chloro-4-methylaniline	122		105
250		4-Phenetidine	173	69	137
256		Dicyclohexylamine	153(57)	173	103

(*continued*)

a. For preparation, see page 760.
b. For preparation, see page 760.
c. For preparation, see page 760.

TABLE 70.5   *continued*

			Derivatives		
			Benzamide[a]	*Picrate*[b]	*Acetamide*[c]
bp	*mp*	*Compound*	*mp*	*mp*	*mp*
	35–38	*N*-Phenylbenzylamine	107	48	58
	41–44	4-Toluidine	158	182	147
	49–51	2,5-Dichloroaniline	120	86	132
	52–54	Diphenylamine	180	182	101
	57–60	4-Anisidine	154	170	130
	57–60	2-Aminopyridine	165 (di)	216(223)	
	60–62	*N*-Phenyl-1-naphthylamine	152		115
	62–65	2,4,5-Trimethylaniline	167		162
	64–66	1,3-Phenylenediamine	125 (mono) 240 (di)	184	87 (mono) 191 (di)
	66	4-Bromoaniline	204	180	168
	68–71	4-Chloroaniline	192	178	179(172)
	71–73	2-Nitroaniline	110(98)	73	92
	97–99	2,4-Diaminotoluene	224 (di)		224 (di)
	100–102	1,2-Phenylenediamine	301	208	185
	104–107	2-Methyl-5-nitroaniline	186		151
	107–109	2-Chloro-4-nitroaniline	161		139
	112–114	3-Nitroaniline	157(150)	143	155(76)
	115–116	4-Methyl-2-nitroaniline	148		99
	117–119	4-Chloro-2-nitroaniline			104
	120–122	2,4,6-Tribromoaniline	198(204)		232
	131–133	2-Methyl-4-nitroaniline			202
	138–140	2-Methoxy-4-nitroaniline	149		
	138–142	1,4-Phenylenediamine	128 (mono) 300 (di)		162 (mono) 304 (di)
	148–149	4-Nitroaniline	199	100	215
	162–164	4-Aminoacetanilide			304
	176–178	2,4-Dinitroaniline	202(220)		120

a. For preparation, see page 760.
b. For preparation, see page 760.
c. For preparation, see page 760.

TABLE 70.6   Tertiary Amines

| | | Derivatives | |
| | | Picrate[a] | Methiodide[b] |
bp	Compound	mp	mp
85–91	Triethylamine	173	280
115	Pyridine	167	117
128–129	2-Picoline	169	230
143–145	2,6-Lutidine	168(161)	233
144	3-Picoline	150	92(36)
145	4-Picoline	167	149
155–158	Tri-n-propylamine	116	207
159	2,4-Lutidine	180	113
183–184	N,N-Dimethylbenzylamine	93	179
216	Tri-n-butylamine	105	186
217	N,N-Diethylaniline	142	102
237	Quinoline	203	133(72)

a. For preparation, see page 760.
b. For preparation, see page 760.

TABLE 70.7   Anhydrides and Acid Chlorides

| | | | Derivatives | | | |
| | | | Acid[a] | | Amide[b] | Anilide[c] |
bp	mp	Compound	bp	mp	mp	mp
52		Acetyl chloride	118		82	114
77–79		Propionyl chloride	141		81	106
102		Butyryl chloride	162		115	96
138–140		Acetic anhydride	118		82	114
167		Propionic anhydride	141		81	106
198–199		Butyric anhydride	162		115	96
198		Benzoyl chloride		122	130	163
225		3-Chlorobenzoyl chloride		158	134	122
238		2-Chlorobenzoyl chloride		142	142	118
	32–34	cis-1,2-Cyclohexanedicarboxylic anhydride		192		
	35–37	Cinnamoyl chloride		133	147	151
	39–40	Benzoic anhydride		122	130	163
	54–56	Maleic anhydride		130	181 (mono)	173 (mono)
					266 (di)	187

(continued)

a. For preparation, see page 761.
b. For preparation, see page 761.
c. For preparation, see page 762.

TABLE 70.7   *continued*

			Derivatives			
			Acid[a]		*Amide*[b]	*Anilide*[c]
bp	*mp*	*Compound*	*bp*	*mp*	*mp*	*mp*
	72–74	4-Nitrobenzoyl chloride	241		201	211
	119–120	Succinic anhydride	186		157 (mono)	148 (mono)
					260 (di)	230 (di)
	131–133	Phthalic anhydride	206		149 (mono)	170 (mono)
					220 (di)	253 (di)
	254–258	Tetrachlorophthalic anhydride	250			
	267–269	1,8-Naphthalic anhydride	274			250–282 (di)

a. For preparation, see page 761.
b. For preparation, see page 761.
c. For preparation, see page 762.

TABLE 70.8   Esters

bp	mp	Compound	bp	mp	Compound
34		Methyl formate	169–170		Methyl acetoacetate
52–54		Ethyl formate	180–181		Dimethyl malonate
72–73		Vinyl acetate	181		Ethyl acetoacetate
77		Ethyl acetate	185		Diethyl oxalate
79		Methyl propionate	198–199		Methyl benzoate
80		Methyl acrylate	206–208		Ethyl caprylate
85		Isopropyl acetate	208–210		Ethyl cyanoacetate
93		Ethyl chloroformate	212		Ethyl benzoate
94		Isopropenyl acetate	217		Diethyl succinate
98		Isobutyl formate	218		Methyl phenylacetate
98		*t*-Butyl acetate	218–219		Diethyl fumarate
99		Ethyl propionate	222		Methyl salicylate
99		Ethyl acrylate	225		Dimethyl maleate
100		Methyl methacrylate	229		Ethyl phenylacetate
101		Methyl trimethylacetate	234		Ethyl salicylate
102		*n*-Propyl acetate	268		Diethyl suberate
106–113		*s*-Butyl acetate	271		Ethyl cinnamate
120		Ethyl butyrate	282		Dimethyl phthalate
127		*n*-Butyl acetate	298–299		Diethyl phthalate
128		Methyl valerate	298–299		Phenyl benzoate
130		Methyl chloroacetate	340		Dibutyl phthalate
131–133		Ethyl isovalerate		56–58	Ethyl *p*-nitrobenzoate
142		*n*-Amyl acetate		88–90	Ethyl *p*-aminobenzoate
142		Isoamyl acetate		94–96	Methyl *p*-nitrobenzoate
143		Ethyl chloroacetate		95–98	*n*-Propyl *p*-hydroxybenzoate
154		Ethyl lactate		116–118	Ethyl *p*-hydroxybenzoate
168		Ethyl caproate (ethyl hexanoate)		126–128	Methyl *p*-hydroxybenzoate

TABLE 70.9   Ethers

bp	mp	Compound	bp	mp	Compound
32		Furan	215		4-Bromoanisole
33		Ethyl vinyl ether	234–237		Anethole
65–67		Tetrahydrofuran	259		Diphenyl ether
94		*n*-Butyl vinyl ether	273		2-Nitroanisole
154		Anisole	298		Dibenzyl ether
174		4-Methylanisole		50–52	4-Nitroanisole
175–176		3-Methylanisole		56–60	1,4-Dimethoxybenzene
198–203		4-Chloroanisole		73–75	2-Methoxynaphthalene
206–207		1,2-Dimethoxybenzene			

TABLE 70.10   Halides

bp	Compound	bp	Compound
34–36	2-Chloropropane	100–105	1-Bromobutane
40–41	Dichloromethane	105	Bromotrichloromethane
44–46	Allyl chloride	110–115	1,1,2-Trichloroethane
57	1,1-Dichloroethane	120–121	1-Bromo-3-methylbutane
59	2-Bromopropane	121	Tetrachloroethylene
68	Bromochloromethane	123	3,4-Dichloro-1-butene
68–70	2-Chlorobutane	125	1,3-Dichloro-2-butene
69–73	Iodoethane	131–132	1,2-Dibromoethane
70–71	Allyl bromide	140–142	1,2-Dibromopropane
71	1-Bromopropane	142–145	1-Bromo-3-chloropropane
72–74	2-Bromo-2-methylpropane	146–150	Bromoform
74–76	1,1,1-Trichloroethane	147	1,1,2,2-Tetrachloroethane
81–85	1,2-Dichloroethane	156	1,2,3-Trichloropropane
87	Trichloroethylene	161–163	1,4-Dichlorobutane
88–90	2-Iodopropane	167	1,3-Dibromopropane
90–92	1-Bromo-2-methylpropane	177–181	Benzyl chloride
91	2-Bromobutane	197	(2-Chloroethyl)benzene
94	2,3-Dichloro-1-propene	219–223	Benzotrichloride
95–96	1,2-Dichloropropane	238	1-Bromodecane
96–98	Dibromomethane		

TABLE 70.11   Aryl Halides

			Derivatives			
			Nitration Product[a]		*Oxidation Product*[b]	
bp	*mp*	*Compound*	*Position*	*mp*	*Name*	*mp*
132		Chlorobenzene	2, 4	52		
156		Bromobenzene	2, 4	70		
157–159		2-Chlorotoluene	3, 5	63	2-Chlorobenzoic acid	141
162		4-Chlorotoluene	2	38	4-Chlorobenzoic acid	240
172–173		1,3-Dichlorobenzene	4, 6	103		
178		1,2-Dichlorobenzene	4, 5	110		
196–203		2,4-Dichlorotoluene	3, 5	104	2,4-Dichlorobenzoic acid	164
201		3,4-Dichlorotoluene	6	63	3,4-Dichlorobenzoic acid	206
214		1,2,4-Trichlorobenzene	5	56		
279–281		1-Bromonaphthalene	4	85		
	51–53	1,2,3-Trichlorobenzene	4	56		
	54–56	1,4-Dichlorobenzene	2	54		
	66–68	1,4-Bromochlorobenzene	2	72		
	87–89	1,4-Dibromobenzene	2, 5	84		
	138–140	1,2,4,5-Tetrachlorobenzene	3	99		
			3, 6	227		

a. For preparation, see page 762.
b. For preparation, see page 762.

TABLE 70.12   Hydrocarbons: Alkenes

bp	Compound	bp	Compound
34	Isoprene	149–150	1,5-Cyclooctadiene
83	Cyclohexene	152	DL-α-Pinene
116	5-Methyl-2-norbornene	160	Bicyclo[4.3.0]nona-3,7-diene
122–123	1-Octene	165–167	(−)-β-Pinene
126–127	4-Vinyl-1-cyclohexene	165–169	α-Methylstyrene
132–134	2,5-Dimethyl-2,4-hexadiene	181	1-Decene
141	5-Vinyl-2-norbornene	181	Indene
143	1,3-Cyclooctadiene	251	1-Tetradecene
145	4-Butylstyrene	274	1-Hexadecene
145–146	Cyclooctene	349	1-Octadecene
145–146	Styrene		

TABLE 70.13   Hydrocarbons: Aromatic

| | | | Melting Point of Derivatives | | |
| | | | Nitro[a] | | Picrate[b] |
bp	mp	Compound	Position	mp	mp
80		Benzene	1, 3	89	84
111		Toluene	2, 4	70	88
136		Ethylbenzene	2, 4, 6	37	96
138		p-Xylene	2, 3, 5	139	90
138–139		m-Xylene	2, 4, 6	183	91
143–145		o-Xylene	4, 5	118	88
145		4-t-Butylstyrene	2, 4	62	
145–146		Styrene			
152–154		Cumene	2, 4, 6	109	
163–166		Mesitylene	2, 4	86	97
			2, 4, 6	235	
165–169		α-Methylstyrene			
168		1,2,4-Trimethylbenzene	3, 5, 6	185	97
176–178		p-Cymene	2, 6	54	
189–192		4-t-Butyltoluene			
197–199		1,2,3,5-Tetramethylbenzene	4, 6	181(157)	
203		p-Diisopropylbenzene			
204–205		1,2,3,4-Tetramethylbenzene	5, 6	176	92
207		1,2,3,4-Tetrahydronaphthalene	5, 7	95	
240–243		1-Methylnaphthalene	4	71	142
	34–36	2-Methylnaphthalene	1	81	116
	50–51	Pentamethylbenzene	6	154	131
	69–72	Biphenyl	4, 4'	237(229)	
	80–82	1,2,4,5-Tetramethylbenzene	3, 6	205	
	80–82	Naphthalene	1	61(57)	149
	90–95	Acenaphthene	5	101	161
	99–101	Phenanthrene			144(133)
	112–115	Fluorene	2	156	87(77)
			2, 7	199	
	214–217	Anthracene			138

a. For preparation, see page 762.
b. For preparation, see page 760.

TABLE 70.14 Ketones

bp	mp	Compound	Semicarbazone[a] mp	2,4-Dinitrophenylhydrazone[b] mp
56		Acetone	187	126
80		2-Butanone	136, 186	117
88		2,3-Butanedione	278	315
100–101		2-Pentanone	112	143
102		3-Pentanone	138	156
106		Pinacolone	157	125
114–116		4-Methyl-2-pentanone	132	95
124		2,4-Dimethyl-3-pentanone	160	88, 95
128–129		5-Hexen-2-one	102	108
129		4-Methyl-3-penten-2-one	164	205
130–131		Cyclopentanone	210	146
133–135		2,3-Pentanedione	122 (mono) 209 (di)	209
145		4-Heptanone	132	75
145		5-Methyl-2-hexanone	147	95
145–147		2-Heptanone	123	89
146–149		3-Heptanone	101	81
156		Cyclohexanone	166	162
162–163		2-Methylcyclohexanone	195	137
169		2,6-Dimethyl-4-heptanone	122	66, 92
169–170		3-Methylcyclohexanone	180	155
173		2-Octanone	122	58
191		Acetonylacetone	185 (mono) 224 (di)	257 (di)
202		Acetophenone	198	238
216		Phenylacetone	198	156
217		Isobutyrophenone	181	163
218		Propiophenone	182	191
226		4-Methylacetophenone	205	258
231–232		2-Undecanone	122	63
232		n-Butyrophenone	188	191
232		4-Chloroacetophenone	204	236
235		Benzylacetone	142	127
	35–37	4-Chloropropiophenone	176	223
	35–39	4-Phenyl-3-buten-2-one	187	227
	36–38	4-Methoxyacetophenone	198	228
	48–49	Benzophenone	167	238
	53–55	2-Acetonaphthone	235	262
	60	Desoxybenzoin	148	204
	76–78	3-Nitroacetophenone	257	228
	78–80	4-Nitroacetophenone		257
	82–85	9-Fluorenone	234	283
	134–136	Benzoin	206	245
	147–148	4-Hydroxypropiophenone		240

a. For preparation, see page 431.
b. For preparation, see page 429.

TABLE 70.15   Nitriles

bp	mp	Compound	bp	mp	Compound
77		Acrylonitrile	212		3-Tolunitrile
83–84		Trichloroacetonitrile	217		4-Tolunitrile
97		Propionitrile	233–234		Benzyl cyanide
107–108		Isobutyronitrile	295		Adiponitrile
115–117		n-Butyronitrile		30.5	4-Chlorobenzyl cyanide
174–176		3-Chloropropionitrile		32–34	Malononitrile
191		Benzonitrile		38–40	Stearonitrile
205		2-Tolunitrile		46–48	Succinonitrile
				71–73	Diphenylacetonitrile

TABLE 70.16   Nitro Compounds

					Amine Obtained by Reduction of Nitro Groups	
					Acetamide[a]	*Benzamide*[b]
bp	*mp*	*Compound*	*bp*	*mp*	*mp*	*mp*
210–211		Nitrobenzene	184		114	160
225		2-Nitrotoluene	200		110	146
225		2-Nitro-m-xylene	215		177	168
230–231		3-Nitrotoluene	203		65	125
245		3-Nitro-o-xylene	221		135	189
245–246		4-Ethylnitrobenzene	216		94	151
	34–36	2-Chloro-6-nitrotoluene	245		157(136)	173
	36–38	4-Chloro-2-nitrotoluene		21	139(131)	
	40–42	3,4-Dichloronitrobenzene		72	121	
	43–50	1-Chloro-2,4-dinitrobenzene		91	242 (di)	178 (di)
	52–54	4-Nitrotoluene		45	147	158
	55–56	1-Nitronaphthalene		50	159	160
	83–84	1-Chloro-4-nitrobenzene		72	179	192
	88–90	m-Dinitrobenzene		63	87 (mono)	125 (mono)
					191 (di)	240 (di)

a. For preparation, see page 760.
b. For preparation, see page 760.

TABLE 70.17   Phenols

| | | | Derivatives | |
| | | | α-Naphthylurethane[a] | Bromo[b] |
bp	mp	Compound	mp	mp
175–176		2-Chlorophenol	120	48 (mono)
				76 (di)
181	42	Phenol	133	95 (tri)
202	32–34	p-Cresol	146	49 (di)
				108 (tetra)
203		m-Cresol	128	84 (tri)
228–229		3,4-Dimethylphenol	141	171 (tri)
	32–33	o-Cresol	142	56 (di)
	42–43	2,4-Dichlorophenol		68
	42–45	4-Ethylphenol	128	
	43–45	4-Chlorophenol	166	90 (di)
	44–46	2,6-Dimethylphenol	176	79
	44–46	2-Nitrophenol	113	117 (di)
	49–51	Thymol	160	55
	62–64	3,5-Dimethylphenol		166 (tri)
	64–68	4-Bromophenol	169	95 (tri)
	74	2,5-Dimethylphenol	173	178 (tri)
	92–95	2,3,5-Trimethylphenol	174	
	95–96	1-Naphthol	152	105 (di)
	98–101	4-t-Butylphenol	110	50 (mono)
				67 (di)
	104–105	Catechol	175	192 (tetra)
	109–110	Resorcinol	275	112 (tri)
	112–114	4-Nitrophenol	150	142 (di)
	121–124	2-Naphthol	157	84
	133–134	Pyrogallol	173	158 (di)

a. For preparation, see page 760.
b. For preparation, see page 763.

Index

MULTIPLES OF ELEMENTS' WEIGHTS

C	12.0112	C_{41}	492.457	H_{31}	31.2471	O_6	95.9964
C_2	24.0223	C_{42}	504.468	H_{32}	32.2550	O_7	111.996
C_3	36.0335	C_{43}	516.479	H_{33}	33.2630	O_8	127.995
C_4	48.0446	C_{44}	528.491	H_{34}	34.2710	O_9	143.995
C_5	60.0557	C_{45}	540.502	H_{35}	35.2790	O_{10}	159.994
C_6	72.0669	C_{46}	552.513	H_{36}	36.2869		
C_7	84.0780	C_{47}	564.524	H_{37}	37.2949	N	14.0067
C_8	96.0892	C_{48}	576.535	H_{38}	38.3029	N_2	28.0134
C_9	108.100	C_{49}	588.546	H_{39}	39.3108	N_3	42.0201
C_{10}	120.111	C_{50}	600.558	H_{40}	40.3188	N_4	56.0268
						N_5	70.0335
C_{11}	132.123	H	1.00797	H_{41}	41.3268	N_6	84.0402
C_{12}	144.134	H_2	2.01594	H_{42}	42.3347		
C_{13}	156.145	H_3	3.02391	H_{43}	43.3427	S	32.064
C_{14}	168.156	H_4	4.03188	H_{44}	44.3507	S_2	64.128
C_{15}	180.167	H_5	5.03985	H_{45}	45.3587	S_3	96.192
C_{16}	192.178	H_6	6.04782	H_{46}	46.3666	S_4	128.256
C_{17}	204.190	H_7	7.05579	H_{47}	47.3746	S_5	160.320
C_{18}	216.201	H_8	8.06376	H_{48}	48.3826	S_6	192.384
C_{19}	228.212	H_9	9.07173	H_{49}	49.3905		
C_{20}	240.223	H_{10}	10.0797	H_{50}	50.3985	F	18.9984
						F_2	37.9968
C_{21}	252.234	H_{11}	11.0877	H_{51}	51.4065	F_3	56.9952
C_{22}	264.245	H_{12}	12.0956	H_{52}	52.4144	F_4	75.9936
C_{23}	276.256	H_{13}	13.1036	H_{53}	53.4224	F_5	94.992
C_{24}	288.268	H_{14}	14.1116	H_{54}	54.4304	F_6	113.99
C_{25}	300.279	H_{15}	15.1196	H_{55}	55.4384	F_7	132.989
C_{26}	312.290	H_{16}	16.1275	H_{56}	56.4463	F_8	151.987
C_{27}	324.301	H_{17}	17.1355	H_{57}	57.4543	F_9	170.986
C_{28}	336.312	H_{18}	18.1435	H_{58}	58.4623	F_{10}	189.984
C_{29}	348.323	H_{19}	19.1514	H_{59}	59.4702		
C_{30}	360.334	H_{20}	20.1594	H_{60}	60.4782		
				H_{61}	61.4862	Cl	35.453
C_{31}	372.346	H_{21}	21.1674	H_{62}	62.4941	Cl_2	70.906
C_{32}	384.357	H_{22}	22.1753	H_{63}	63.5021	Cl_3	106.359
C_{33}	396.368	H_{23}	23.1833	H_{64}	64.5101	Cl_4	141.812
C_{34}	408.379	H_{24}	24.1913	H_{65}	65.5181	Cl_5	177.265
C_{35}	420.390	H_{25}	25.1993				
C_{36}	432.401	H_{26}	26.2072	O	15.9994	Br	79.904
C_{37}	444.413	H_{27}	27.2152	O_2	31.9988	Br_2	159.808
C_{38}	456.424	H_{28}	28.2232	O_3	47.9982	Br_3	239.712
C_{39}	468.435	H_{29}	29.2311	O_4	63.9976	Br_4	319.616
C_{40}	480.446	H_{30}	30.2391	O_5	79.9970	Br_5	399.52

I	126.904	P	30.9738
I_2	253.809	P_2	61.9476
I_3	380.713	P_3	92.9214
		P_4	123.895
OCH_3	31.0345	P_5	154.869
$(OCH_3)_2$	62.0689	P_6	185.843
$(OCH_3)_3$	93.1034		
$(OCH_3)_4$	124.138	Na	22.9898
$(OCH_3)_5$	155.172	Na_2	45.9796
$(OCH_3)_6$	186.207	Na_3	68.9694
$(OCH_3)_7$	217.241		
$(OCH_3)_8$	248.276	K	39.102
$(OCH_3)_9$	279.31	K_2	78.204
$(OCH_3)_{10}$	310.345	K_3	117.306
OC_2H_5	45.0616	Ag	107.868
$(OC_2H_5)_2$	90.1231	Ag_2	215.736
$(OC_2H_5)_3$	135.185		
$(OC_2H_5)_4$	180.246	Cu	63.546
$(OC_2H_5)_5$	225.308	Cu_2	127.092
$(OC_2H_5)_6$	270.369	Cr	51.996
$(OC_2H_5)_7$	315.431	Hg	200.59
$(OC_2H_5)_8$	360.492	Pb	207.19
		Pt	195.09
$OCOCH_3$	59.045	Pt_2	390.18
$(OCOCH_3)_2$	118.090	Se	78.96
$(OCOCH_3)_3$	177.135	Th	204.37
$(OCOCH_3)_4$	236.180		
$(OCOCH_3)_5$	295.225		
$(OCOCH_3)_6$	354.270		
$(OCOCH_3)_7$	413.315		
$(OCOCH_3)_8$	472.360		
$(OCOCH_3)_9$	531.405		
$(OCOCH_3)_{10}$	590.450		
$(H_2O)_{1/2}$	9.00767		
H_2O	18.0153		
$(H_2O)_{1\,1/2}$	27.0230		
$(H_2O)_2$	36.0307		
$(H_2O)_3$	54.0460		
$(H_2O)_4$	72.0614		
$(H_2O)_5$	90.0767		
$(H_2O)_6$	108.092		

BUFFER SOLUTIONS (0.2 M, except as indicated)

pH	Components	pH	Components
0.1	1 M Hydrochloric acid	8.0	11.8 g Boric acid + 9.1 g Borax
1.1	0.1 M Hydrochloric acid		($Na_2B_4O_7 \cdot 10H_2O$) per L
2.2	15.0 g D-Tartaric acid per L (0.1 M solution)	9.0	6.2 g Boric acid + 38.1 g Borax per L
3.9	40.8 g Potassium acid phthalate per L	10.0	6.5 g $NaHCO_3$ + 13.2 g Na_2CO_3 per L
5.0	14.0 g KH-Phthalate + 2.7 g $NaHCO_3$ per L	11.0	11.4 g Na_2HPO_4 + 19.7 g Na_3PO_4 per L
	(heat to expel carbon dioxide, then cool)	12.0	24.6 g Na_3PO_4 per L (0.15 M solution)
6.0	23.2 g KH_2PO_4 + 4.3 g Na_2HPO_4 (anhyd., Merck) per L	13.0	4.1 g Sodium hydroxide pellets per L (0.1 M)
7.0	9.1 g KH_2PO_4 + 18.9 g Na_2HPO_4 per L	14.0	41.3 g Sodium hydroxide pellets per L (1 M)

ATOMIC WEIGHTS

Aluminum	Al	26.9815	Molybdenum	Mo	95.94
Antimony	Sb	121.75	Nickel	Ni	58.71
Arsenic	As	74.9216	Nitrogen	N	14.0067
Barium	Ba	137.34	Osmium	Os	190.2
Beryllium	Be	9.0122	Oxygen	O	15.9994
Bismuth	Bi	208.980	Palladium	Pd	106.4
Boron	B	10.811	Phosphorus	P	30.9738
Bromine	Br	79.904	Platinum	Pt	195.09
Cadmium	Cd	112.40	Potassium	K	39.102
Calcium	Ca	40.08	Praseodymium	Pr	140.907
Carbon	C	12.01115	Rhodium	Rh	102.9055
Cerium	Ce	140.12	Ruthenium	Ru	101.07
Cesium	Cs	132.905	Selenium	Se	78.96
Chlorine	Cl	35.453	Silicon	Si	28.086
Chromium	Cr	51.996	Silver	Ag	107.868
Cobalt	Co	58.9332	Sodium	Na	22.9898
Copper	Cu	63.546	Strontium	Sr	87.62
Europium	Eu	151.96	Sulfur	S	32.064
Fluorine	F	18.9984	Tantalum	Ta	180.948
Gold	Au	196.967	Tellurium	Te	127.60
Hydrogen	H	1.00797	Thallium	Tl	204.37
Iodine	I	126.9044	Thorium	Th	232.038
Iridium	Ir	192.22	Tin	Sn	118.69
Iron	Fe	55.847	Titanium	Ti	47.90
Lead	Pb	207.19	Tungsten	W	183.85
Lithium	Li	6.939	Vanadium	V	50.942
Magnesium	Mg	24.312	Ytterbium	Yb	173.04
Manganese	Mn	54.9380	Zinc	Zn	65.37
Mercury	Hg	200.59	Zirconium	Zr	91.22

ACIDS AND BASES

	Sp. Gr.	% by Wt	Moles per L	Grams per 100 mL
Hydrochloric acid, concd.	1.19	37	12.0	44.0
3 M (124.3 mL concd. acid diluted to 500 mL)	1.05	10.8	3.0	10.9
Constant boiling (252 mL concd. acid + 200 mL water, bp 110°)	1.10	22.2	6.1	22.2
10% (100 mL concd. acid + 321 mL water)	1.05	10	2.9	10.5
5% (50 mL concd. acid + 380.5 mL water)	1.03	5	1.4	5.2
1 M (41.5 mL concd. acid diluted to 500 mL)	1.02	3.6	1	3.6
Hydrobromic acid, constant-boiling (bp 126°)	1.49	47.5	8.8	70.7
Hydriodic acid, constant-boiling (bp 126°)	1.7	57	7.6	97
Sulfuric acid, concd.	1.84	96	18	177
1.5 M (41.7 mL concd. acid diluted to 500 mL)	1.09	14.1	1.5	14.7
10% (25 mL concd. acid + 398 mL water)	1.07	10	1.1	10.7
0.5 M (13.9 mL concd. acid diluted to 500 mL)	1.03	4.7	0.5	4.9
Nitric acid, concd.	1.42	71	16	101
Sodium hydroxide, 3 M solution	1.12	11	3.0	12.0
10% solution	1.11	10	2.8	11.1
Ammonia solution, concd.	0.90	28.4	15	25.6
Acetic acid, glacial	1.05	100.0	17.5	105
Sodium bicarbonate	1.03	4	0.5	4.2
Saturated solution	1.05	8	1	8.3
Sodium chloride, saturated solution	1.20	26	5.3	31.1

Grams of sodium carbonate required to neutralize 1 mL of concd. acid:

0.636 g	1 mL HCl
0.848 g	1 mL HNO_3
1.91 g	1 mL H_2SO_4
0.928 g	1 mL CH_3COOH

CENTIMETER RULER